The Munros

A WALKHIGHLANDS GUIDE

The authors and publisher have made every effort to ensure that the information in this publication is accurate, and accept no responsibility whatsoever for any loss, injury or inconvenience experienced by any person or persons whilst using this book.

published by
pocket mountains ltd
The Old Church, Annanside, Moffat
Dumfries and Galloway
DG10 9HB

ISBN: 978-1-9070252-7-3

Printed in Poland

Introduction

Look beneath the waterproofs of any keen hillwalker in Scotland and, once past the midge bites, it's likely you will find a Munro-bagger. Even those who protest and mumble about it being 'trainspotting for outdoor types' often secretly know their Munro tally and are working towards the triumphant moment when they top out on that final summit.

This guide is for anyone who wants to climb the Munros. It aims to provide reliable routes and tips for ascending all of these magical 282 peaks. The other half of the deal is that you have to provide the energy and enthusiasm to make it as enjoyable and safe as possible.

Setting out to climb all the Munros is to embark on a huge adventure. No two mountains are the same; weather conditions, companions – and the state of your squashed sandwiches and frozen Mars bars – make every outing different. The Munros will ensure you reach parts of Scotland you might otherwise have overlooked, spend evenings in pubs, bothies and wild camps all with their own delights, and have encounters with other walkers, locals and wildlife that will enhance the adventure.

Ordnance Survey mapping and downloadable routes for GPS devices are available for all of the Munros online at *walkhighlands.co.uk*. If you register free on the website you also get your own online Munro-bagging progress map where you can keep track of your ascents, and you can also keep a detailed walking blog and photos of all your trips to share with others.

What are the Munros?

Scottish mountains over 3000 feet high are collectively called the Munros after Sir Hugh Munro, the man who first catalogued them. A founder member of the Scottish Mountaineering Club (SMC), Munro was landed gentry, with an estate near Kirriemuir. His first list was published in 1891, the result of meticulous study of the Ordnance Survey one-inch- and six-inch-to-the-mile maps together with knowledge and notes gleaned from his numerous mountaineering expeditions. Other SMC members assisted and Munro spent the next two and a half decades painstakingly, and some would say, pedantically, refining the list – a habit the SMC has continued to the present day. Munro divided the summits into Mountains and Tops, the former being for the main peaks – now referred to as Munros – whilst the Tops are the lesser, subsidiary summits. Munro died in 1919 with only three Munros on his current list remaining unclimbed; the Inaccessible Pinnacle on Skye, Carn an Fhidhleir in the Cairngorms, and Carn Cloich-mhuilinn which was later demoted to a Top.

Credit is given to the Rev A E Robertson as the first person to climb all the Munros in 1901. A small trickle followed in his footsteps, but it wasn't until after the Second World War that Munro-bagging started to take off. People who complete (or compleat as the SMC retains the Victorian spelling) can notify the Clerk of the List; their names are recorded in the book, Munro's Tables. More excitingly, being a compleator also qualifies you to purchase a commemorative tie or brooch for the ladies! Traditionally a bastion of the male climbing world, the SMC list refers to the early female compleators as Miss or Mrs although it dropped this by the 1990s. The first continuous round was undertaken by Hamish Brown and it was his classic book *Hamish's Mountain Walk* that spurred increasing interest, as well as being the forerunner of ever harder or more obscure challenges, such as rounds undertaken entirely in winter or running.

Since then people have tackled the Munros in increasingly diverse ways, from Paul Tattersall who was the first (and only!) person to take a mountain bike up all the Munros – yes, it was mainly in bits in a rucksack for the Skye Cuillin – to Stephen Pyke who set a new record in 2010 for a continuous round involving running, cycling and kayaking between all the then 283 peaks in 40 days. It's only when you are part way round your Munros that you realise what amazing achievements these are. More and more people are attempting second, third and fourth rounds. Hillrunner Steven Fallon holds the current record for the most rounds, having completed 15 circuits. None of this excess of testosterone (or chutzpah) should diminish the achievement of your first Munro, your first winter ascent, your first solo Munro, or the ascent of the trickiest peaks – and ultimately, your final Munro.

What you need to know
So what do you need to climb the Munros? Well, you'll need a good range of layered clothing to keep warm, waterproofs and suitable footwear – boots provide the most support, but dedicated hillrunning shoes are also becoming popular. More important still is navigation – a map, compass (a GPS is also useful) and the knowledge of how to use them. Navigational errors are a factor in a huge proportion of accidents as walkers lose their route and wander onto difficult terrain.

If you are planning on climbing many Munros, you'll be getting yourself a good range of walking clothes and gear. Hugh Munro, Robertson and the early Scottish hillwalking and climbing pioneers often set out in not much more than tweed jackets, woollen breeches and hob-nailed boots, with the trusty A-frame haversack on their back. In Munro's case he often went about at night using a candle lantern to avoid encounters with unfriendly landowners and gamekeepers – this was, after all, long before the Access legislation. Whilst the lack of decent breathable waterproofs must have made things hard going, they were also venturing out in the era before Mountain Rescue, mobile phones and GPS and would have had to rely on their common sense, mountain experience and navigation skills. These remain the most important items to carry with you at all times.

In terms of gear; for summer walking, a decent set of waterproofs and boots, hat, gloves, map, compass, torch and first aid kit are the must haves to begin with. Good quality gear will last for years. Remember that weather varies greatly with altitude and whilst it might seem a lovely day in the car park – up there it could be blowing a hoolie or feel like an ice-storm.

In winter the hills become much more serious – under snow, climbing Munros is nothing short of mountaineering, and an ice-axe, crampons and the knowledge of how to use them, plus some awareness of the risk of avalanches, becomes essential.

If you aren't so sure on your navigation, or need to learn those winter skills, you really have a couple of options. There are a range of mountaineering and hillwalking clubs across all parts of Scotland – a great way to meet experienced friends and to learn from them. Scotland also has an increasing number of instructors and companies offering guiding and skills courses. The Scottish National Outdoor Training Centre at Glenmore Lodge offers a huge range of superb courses for beginners and can help you take your hillwalking into the realms of scrambling, rock or ice-climbing if you become tempted to take things further.

Opinions vary widely on what food to take up the hills and it really is a matter of personal preference. The only givens should be to include some quick release, high-energy food, and to have something that is kept for emergencies – and no, having eaten all the sandwiches by 9am does not constitute an emergency. Most walkers will also carry all the water they need for the day. If you need to replenish, try to find a fast and clear running stream near its source and away from obvious livestock and deer gathering points as the animals cause contamination. Most walkers will use some kind of steriliser – and never drink water where animals are using the water supply higher up, from standing water, or where people have been camping. Although sterilising tablets can make the water taste slightly funny you'll feel better about it if you pass the carcass of a decomposing sheep in a burn higher up. Filters and boiling water can also be used to improve safety. Even if the weather is not hot, keeping hydrated is important.

In an Emergency

If one of your party has an accident and cannot be moved phone or text 999 or 112 and ask for Police and then Mountain Rescue. Treat injuries as best you can and calculate your position on the map (or check on a GPS/phone). All hillwalkers should register their mobile phones with the emergency SMS service by texting 'register' to 999 – this allows 999 texts to be made and responded to in areas where there is insufficient signal to make a call.

Access

Scotland has traditionally had a more liberal approach to letting people walk on open ground than the rest of the UK. That's not to say that there haven't been access disputes, including the famous trespass at Jock's Road near Ballater, although the subsequent legal action bankrupted both the landowner Duncan MacPherson and the Scottish Rights of Way Society (is it always the lawyers that are the real winners?). It did, however, lead to the passing of the Scottish Rights of Way Act. More recently the Land Reform Act 2003 granted much more sweeping rights of access – comprehensively codifying what has become known as the Right to Roam. Like all these things the devil is in the detail and while generally there is a right of access on open land there are a number of restrictions and also responsibilities which are built into the accompanying Scottish Outdoor Access Code. In particular, there are no automatic access rights near buildings, in gardens, and in fields where crops are growing. Dogs must not be allowed to worry livestock or disturb groundnesting birds. Gates should be left as you find them, walls and fences should not be damaged and farming, forestry, shooting and stalking activities should be respected with minimal disturbance.

The Scottish stag stalking season runs from 1 July to 20 October, although many estates operate a much shorter season and will only be stalking on a few dates within that period. Once the preserve of wealthy landowners and industrialists, many of whom bought Scottish estates inspired by Queen Victoria's passion for the Highlands, stalking remains a profitable business which employs a small army of gamekeepers, ghillies and other staff. The Outdoor Access Code asks both walkers and land managers to respect each other's activities, and walkers heading for the hills during the stalking season should try and find out if stalking is taking place and whether they need to alter their planned route to avoid it. This is necessary for your own safety as well as avoiding the tweed-clad wrath of a stalker whose hours spent crawling through the heather have been made futile by an orange-Gore-Tex-wearing hillwalker. Some estates are more helpful at providing stalking information than others. The latest stalking information for a good number of estates is available online through Walkhighlands' route pages via the 'Heading for the Scottish Hills' web service; the latter website has further information if choosing a different route.

Grouse shooting takes place from 12 August usually to the end of

September. With grouse butts often marked on OS maps and the patchwork appearance of the heather grouse moors easily identifiable, it is often possible to spot a shooting party out on the hill and take measures to avoid walking into the line of the shoot or disturbing the beaters or dogs.

Accommodation

Nowadays there is accommodation to suit all budgets and comfort levels within easy reach of the majority of Munros. However, one of the joys of embarking on the challenge of the Munros is that, unless you are extremely fit, some of the peaks will involve expeditions which are best undertaken with a wild camp or a stay in a remote bothy. Whether walked in blissful isolation or in the company of like-minded walkers and climbers (or the axe-carrying starey-eyed bloke in the corner of the bothy) these nights are often the most memorable and can lead to more of these trips or at the very least a heightened appreciation of home comforts on return.

This guide is focused around good places to base yourself for Munro trips in each area, and a number of local accommodation options are highlighted. However, increasingly many B&B and hotel owners are welcoming walkers and providing early breakfasts, drying facilities and local knowledge which make them a good alternative to the network of hostels (the standard of which continues to rise each year), campsites and self catering cottages. Campervans are also increasingly popular, particularly for hire, and can provide a fun and convenient mobile base for climbing Munros.

The Access Code is generous towards wild campers, allowing camping on access land away from roads and buildings for a maximum of three days at the same site. In some areas where camping has caused a problem with anti-social behaviour, such as around Loch Lomond, local byelaws prohibit it. Wild camping should always be undertaken on the 'leave no trace' ethos, with any rubbish carried out. Care should be taken not to pollute rivers, water from pot washing should be poured onto the ground, not into the watercourse, and you should go to the toilet as far away from a watercourse as possible, burying faeces in a hole and burning or packing out toilet paper. In the Cairngorms the problem caused by the number of people camping out or snow-holing in the winter months led to the Cairngorms Snow White Project – special pots can be collected from the Ranger Service at the Cairngorm Mountain ski and snowboard centre near Aviemore to carry out human waste to disposal points.

Bothies, too, need to be used responsibly. Basically these are usually unlocked buildings which provide four walls and a roof but little else – the toilet facilities usually come in the form of a shovel. Some are provided by estates and any abuse is likely to see them locked, but many more are available through the permission of the estate but maintained by volunteers from the Mountain Bothies Association. The remote locations make keeping these places wind-and-water tight a major challenge – please do your bit by not only carrying out all your own rubbish and leaving the place tidy, but perhaps carrying out any litter other walkers may have left there as well. The MBA organise work parties which are great fun and a good way to give something back if you enjoy bothies. The Mountain Bothies Association publishes a Bothy Code on behaving responsibly.

Transport

Public transport in the remoter parts of the Highlands is sparse and often non-existent. Long-distance coaches do serve many of the walking areas such as Glencoe, and local buses can often be used to get from your accommodation to some of the routes, but access to the start of the walks from public transport is often pretty limited. The West Highland Railway running from Glasgow to Mallaig and its eastern partner from Edinburgh to Inverness do provide access to many of the ranges – this is noted in the text. The transport planner at *travelinescotland.com* is the best starting point. The Caledonian Sleeper running from London to Fort William, Aviemore and Inverness can be a great way of combining accommodation and transport, but fares can be mortgage jobs unless you are lucky enough to nab one of their elusive bargain berths. Car-sharing via clubs and websites can cut down on costs, and hitching is still commonplace in many of the remoter areas – make sure you take sensible precautions.

Resources

Aside from this volume, of course, the main friend of the Munroist has to be a map. The OS 1:25,000 Explorer series is now the bestselling range aimed at walkers and includes extra navigational features like walls and fences not shown on other scales. More confident navigators will swear by the pink 1:50,000 Landranger series, which certainly reduces damage to your wallet. Harveys also produces very high-quality mapping for many of the mountain areas and once familiar with their distinct look these are favoured by many hillwalkers. You can also print your own maps, either using mapping software on your PC or websites such as *walkhighlands.co.uk* – if doing this be careful to ensure you print a large enough area if you need to change your route, and remember that any water at all will cause the ink to run on home-printed sheets, quickly rendering the map useless – so it is probably best to have a professionally printed map as well.

GPS is a useful addition to knowing how

to use a map and compass – make sure you carry spare batteries and don't come to rely on it completely as it could pack up when you need it most. One of the most useful features of any GPS (including those on smartphones) is the ability to pinpoint your location as a grid reference. Whole routes or just spot points can also be pre-programmed into a GPS and used to keep you on the correct route while walking. Again, routes for all the Munros are available as downloads for GPS units and smartphones on Walkhighlands.co.uk. If using these, do so only in combination with mapping as batteries and electronic devices can fail, and some judgements are still needed – for instance a path along the rim of the cliffs may be enjoyable in summer, but in winter you would want to keep safely away from any cornices – snow which overhangs the edge and is prone to collapse.

Where to start

There are several Munros which are much more popular than others, usually those with shorter routes and good paths lower down. These easier hills are probably the best ones to tackle first; Ben Lomond sees scores of people reaching their first ever Munro on any decent day in the summer. Other peaks suitable for early in your bagging career would include Ben Lawers and Beinn Ghlas, Ben Chonzie, Schiehallion, Mayar and Driesh, or Ben Vorlich above Loch Earn. Once you have a few of these under your belt you'll be itching to begin exploring the rockier peaks of the west or the remote wilds of the Cairngorms.

The hardest Munro really depends on your perspective. For anyone with a fear of heights, routes such as the Aonach Eagach or Liathach in Torridon are likely to lead to many sleepless nights! The greatest of such difficulties are undoubtedly experienced on the Cuillin of Skye, an awesome ridge of naked rock contorted into crags and pinnacles – light years away from some of the rolling hills of the mainland. Worse (or best!) of all is the Inaccessible Pinnacle – the only Munro that calls for real rockclimbing – up a ridge with 'an overhanging drop over infinity on one side, and steeper and further on the other'. It also requires an abseil descent; most Munro-baggers will be calling on a guide for this one.

Others will have the climbing skills to confidently tackle these dramatic peaks, and such people are likely to regard some of the remoter Munros, requiring great physical effort, as the hardest. There are several peaks that will most likely require an overnight stay, none more so than the amazing mountains of the Great Wilderness – the Fisherfield and Letterewe Forests in the northwest.

Beyond the Munros

Climbing the Munros will mean exploring vast swathes of the most beautiful parts of Scotland, drawing you out into the wildest and yet varied landscapes and to undertake some great challenges – but, of course, the Munros are not the whole story. Whilst some people do become rather intensely focused on the list, a glance around from any summit should reveal that in bagging these hills you are really only scratching the surface of what Scotland has to offer. It is the focus on Munros to the exclusion of everything else that sometimes gives the Munro-bagger a bad name, but you'll soon realise that many of the very finest hills in Scotland are not Munros. Anyone climbing Beinn Narnain and Beinn Ime in the Arrochar Alps will be staring across at the dramatic rock peaks of The Cobbler – proof that highest is not necessarily the best. Take the time to dig a little deeper and explore more widely and your Munro trips will be all the more enjoyable.

Those who have come to love the idea of lists will soon find that these don't stop with the Munros either. Most popular are the Corbetts – summits between 2500 and 3000 feet – which provide every bit as much challenge, if not more, than the Munros themselves. Traditionally an objective for those who have completed the Munros, increasing numbers of hillwalkers are now taking on both lists at once. Although the Corbetts include some amazing lesser-known hills, many of them easily matching the Munros, there's still more! Some of the best hillwalking in the country is in Assynt, where incredibly dramatic hills such as Suilven and Stac Pollaidh don't even reach high enough for Corbett status. Scotland's many islands, too, offer much unforgettable wild walking, even on seemingly lowly hills.

There really is a lifetime of exploration and discovery out there waiting for you – so by all means climb the Munros, but do try to avoid becoming too blinkered by those damned lists!

Useful organisations and websites

Mountaineering Scotland (formerly the Mountaineering Council of Scotland) is the representative body for hillwalkers and climbers in Scotland. They were key in the fight for access legislation, are also involved in promoting safety, education and in conservation, and deserve every hill-goer's support. *mountaineering.scot*

The John Muir Trust, named after the Scottish father of the conservation movement, fight for the preservation of the environment and the sense of wildness that is so key to the satisfaction of heading out into nature. *jmt.org*

The Mountain Bothies Association is a group of volunteers who organise the maintenance and repair of around 100 unlocked shelters amongst the mountains and islands. They arrange regular work parties where you can help to keep these places open and available. *mountainbothies.org.uk*

Walkhighlands is a website for walking in Scotland, run by the authors of this guide. It includes routes, GPS files and mapping for all the Munros, as well as a guide to all types of accommodation. The site also enables you to register which hills you've climbed – marking them on your own 'bagging map' – and to share your experiences and photos with others, as well as read everyone else's accounts of each hill. *walkhighlands.co.uk*

The Scottish Outdoor Access Code is essential reading – the complete online guide to behaving responsibly in the outdoors. *outdooraccess-scotland.com*

The Mountain Weather Information Service provides detailed forecasts for hill conditions split into a number of areas and updated daily. *mwis.org.uk*

The Scottish Avalanche Information Service provides forecasts of the risk of avalanche in the Scottish hills – essential for planning in winter months. *sais.gov.uk*

Heading for the Scottish Hills gives up-to-date stalking information for many estates; the information is also shown where appropriate on the routes on Walkhighlands website. *outdooraccess-scotland.com/hftsh*

Arrochar Alps from Ben Lomond

Loch Lomond and the Arrochar Alps

The east side of Loch Lomond harbours only a single Munro, one of the best-known and most accessible of them all, Ben Lomond. Just beyond a low pass to the west over which the Vikings once hauled their longboats is Loch Long – a saltwater finger reaching far into the hills. Here rise the steep and rocky peaks of the Arrochar Alps. Within easy reach of Glasgow and the central belt, this area has been immensely popular since the first surge in the rise of hillwalking and mountaineering in the 1930s and remains so today, the remarkable outline of The Cobbler and its neighbours luring people from the city to head out and begin exploring the hills.

Rowardennan

A popular stop-off on the West Highland Way, Rowardennan sits at the far end of the public road up the east side of Loch Lomond. A good base for Ben Lomond, its facilities are limited to the Rowardennan Hotel, which is very welcoming to walkers and serves bar meals, the lochside youth hostel, and self catering lodges. The information centre also has toilets. Overnight camping or sleeping at the car park is prohibited and this is actively enforced, with wild camping banned along this section of the lochside during summer months.

The Oak Tree Inn in nearby Balmaha is recommended for meals and there are more accommodation options here also. Unless intent on just bagging the Ben, there is plenty of lower-level walking in the area, including an ascent of little Conic Hill, surely one of the best viewpoints around, and exploring the lochside on sections of the West Highland Way. There are boat trips out on the loch and a little ferry will take you across to Inchcailloch Island, a real gem and perhaps an escape from the crowds.

Arrochar and Loch Fyne

Strung out along the roadside at the head of Loch Long is the village of Arrochar, a popular destination for trippers since the days when the Clyde Paddle Steamers brought them in their thousands up the

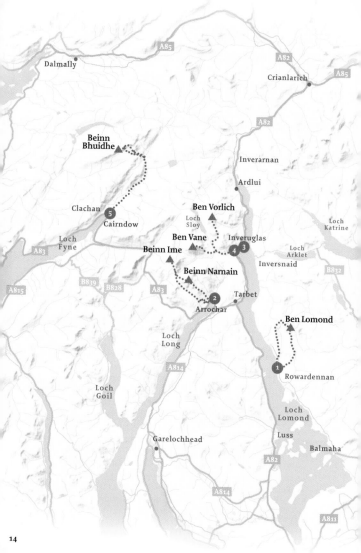

Dalmally

A85

Crianlarich

A82

A85

A82

Inverarnan

Ardlui

**Beinn
Bhuidhe**

Clachan

5

Cairndow

Loch
Fyne

A83

Ben Vorlich

Loch
Sloy

Ben Vane

Inveruglas

4 **3**

Loch
Katrine

Loch
Arklet

Inversnaid

B832

Beinn Ime

Beinn Narnain

B839

B828

A83

2

Arrochar

Tarbet

A815

Loch
Long

A814

Loch
Goil

Garelochhead

Loch
Lomond

Luss

Balmaha

A82

A814

A811

Ben Lomond

1

Rowardennan

lochs. By the 1930s a new influx of visitors was thronging Arrochar, as the hills – and especially their crags – provided a ready escape for workers from the Glasgow shipyards and the dole queues; a period captured perfectly in Alastair Borthwick's classic book *Always a Little Further*. The youth hostel that opened to serve these early climbers has long gone, though you can still emulate their antics by sleeping rough under the overhang at the Narnain Boulders. For those looking for a little more in the way of facilities the original Arrochar Hotel is still here, whilst the Village Inn has real ales as well as food and accommodation. There is also a good range of bed and breakfasts, a fish and chip shop and a general store.

Arrochar is the usual starting point for Beinn Narnain and Beinn Ime as well as The Cobbler (which misses out on Munro status but is nevertheless unmissable), but Ben Vane and Ben Vorlich are out of sight and mind and are usually climbed from the east.

Continuing west from Arrochar the A83 climbs through Glen Croe over the Rest and Be Thankful mountain pass before descending to reach the upper end of Loch Fyne. Beinn Bhuidhe is the solitary peak that draws Munro-baggers over here, although the area has much more to offer. At the very head of the loch is the original Loch Fyne Oyster Bar and seafood shop, and an excellent small brewery produces Fyne Ales. Nearby Cairndow has the beautiful Ardkinglas Woodland Garden and some accommodation, but there are many more places to stay and things to see at Inveraray, an attractive 18th-century planned town of whitewashed buildings set by the shores of the loch.

Ben Lomond

Ben Lomond

Ben Lomond (974m) *beacon hill*

Distance **12km**
Ascent **990m**
Time **4.5 – 5.5 hours**
Start point **OS Grid ref: NS359986**
Map **OS Explorer 364**
Public transport **no direct bus to start but linked by summer ferry from Tarbet Pier (bus to Tarbet from Glasgow)**
Terrain & hazards **excellent ascent path; return via Ptarmigan is rougher and rockier**

More than 30,000 people make it to the top of Ben Lomond every year – but any lack of solitude is compensated for by the fantastic views of Loch Lomond and its islands and the sense of achievement. Munro-bagging starts here for many with Ben Lomond a popular first Munro.

At the car park at Rowardennan there is an information centre and toilets. Ben Lomond is out of sight from here; venture down to the metal jetty by the shore for a glimpse of the mountain. Start the ascent along the signed path behind the information centre, ignoring the West Highland Way track towards the youth hostel. Climb steadily through oak woods at first, before passing an area of felled forestry now being regenerated as a native woodland. Cross a track and continue uphill, with the first views to Loch Lomond looking back.

A gate leads to the open hillside where cattle and sheep graze and the path continues its steady climb. Once a hideous 25m-wide scar on the hillside that could be seen from Glasgow, the path has been repaired by the National Trust for Scotland. Eventually the final peak comes into view with the prominent zigzag of the path visible on the right.

The path continues up the broad ridge of the mountain, leading to a steep climb to the summit ridge. The more exciting eastern flank of the mountain is revealed as the path skirts around the rim of the impressive eastern corrie. Any thoughts of this being a tame hill are dismissed with a glance down the craggy mountainside and possibly an icy blast of wind from the north. As one of Scotland's favourite mountains you are unlikely to be alone at the summit – Ben Lomond attracts everyone from large family groups to dedicated runners who number their yearly ascents in the hundreds.

For the easiest descent you can return by the outward route, but the Ptarmigan Ridge makes for a popular alternative to complete a circuit. Take the rocky path northwest from the summit to descend very steeply to a col before climbing southwest to Ptarmigan at 731m. From here the route follows a knobbly ridge for much of the descent with excellent views towards Loch Lomond. The distinctive shape of The Cobbler comes into view alongside the other peaks of the Arrochar Alps across the loch to the west. There is a clear path, although it is narrow and rocky in places;

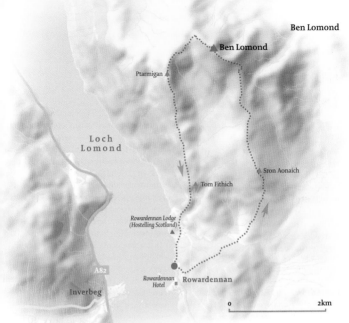

Ben Lomond

Ptarmigan

Loch
Lomond

Sron Aonaich

Tom Fithich

Rowardennan Lodge
(Hostelling Scotland)

A82

Rowardennan
Hotel

Rowardennan

Inverbeg

0   2km

the wettest areas have been improved with large stepping stones. About two-thirds of the way down, the path leaves the true ridge to descend below crags and continue on a direct line towards Rowardennan.

The path passes through a gate and descends more steeply. Before reaching some trees at the top of the woodland, bear left to go through another gate and descend alongside a burn. After an open gateway there is a good view of a waterfall. Continue down to a road, turning left to pass behind the youth hostel. For the last section it is possible to take the path on the right by the shore. This passes a modern sculpture, a war memorial made by Doug Cocker of Dundee. Ben Lomond

and the slopes down to the loch have been dedicated as a Memorial Park to commemorate those who have lost their lives for their country. The car park is a short distance beyond.

Alternatives

It takes a determined eccentric to ascend Ben Lomond from any other direction. However, it is possible to make a longer ascent from the east, starting along the forest tracks at the foot of Loch Chon. There is a fair amount of up and down along tracks until just short of Comer. From here the climb leads steeply over pathless ground to reach the rim of Coire a' Bhathaich, following this up to the summit.

2

Beinn Ime
Beinn Narnain

Beinn Ime (1011m) *butter hill*
Beinn Narnain (926m) *notched hill*

Distance **13.5km**
Ascent **1320m**
Time **6 – 7 hours**
Start point **OS Grid ref: NN294048**
Map **OS Explorer 364**
Public transport **Arrochar is served by trains and buses from Glasgow**
Terrain & hazards **hillpaths throughout; steep and eroded on the ascent of Beinn Narnain with some easy scrambling**

So close to Glasgow and yet so rugged, the Arrochar Alps have long attracted rockclimbers and walkers alike. The ascent of Beinn Narnain is rocky and full of character, providing a fine approach to the highest of the range, Beinn Ime. The return route passes The Cobbler which – though not a Munro – is undoubtedly the most dramatic mountain in the area and well worth a detour.

Start from the large car park (charge payable) at Succoth on Loch Long, just beyond Arrochar. Cross the main road and take the obvious path opposite into the woods. Keep a sharp eye out for a faint path heading up to the right after a very short distance. A little overgrown at the start, it soon becomes clearer and climbs steeply, passing a series of large concrete blocks left over from a hydro project. Walk straight across a track to continue up a rugged path which can run with water after heavy rain. There are good views back down to the loch and across to Ben Lomond. Eventually an obvious path traversing the hillside is reached; carry straight on – although the OS map shows the route up Beinn Narnain bearing left here, the easiest way is to keep ahead, bearing slightly right at first and then continuing the climb up rough ground.

Pass a couple of easy rocky sections and a boggy area where the path peters out temporarily. Soon there are great views to The Cobbler on the left and after a brief flatter section the route climbs to Cruach nam Miseag. After a short descent the prominent rock buttress of the Spearhead is reached. A narrow path leads right of the main buttress to ascend a rock-filled gully. The final climb to Beinn Narnain's summit, set on a small plateau, is easier.

Continue WNW to pick up the path which descends, steeply in places, to the Bealach a'Mhaim. Beinn Ime can be seen straight ahead. A steep and rocky mountain from most aspects, the climb from this side is up a broad and sometimes boggy slope. The summit of this, the highest point in the Arrochar Alps, is marked with a trig point.

Return to the bealach and aim right to traverse across to the slightly lower bealach between Beinn Narnain and the Cobbler. At the clear path junction you

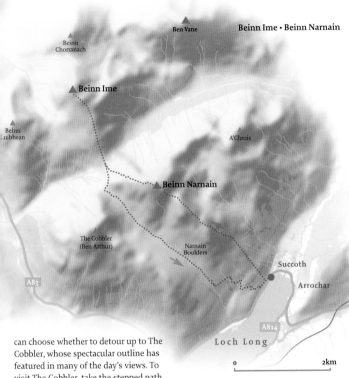

Beinn Ime

Ben Vane

Beinn
Chorranach

Beinn
Luibhean

A'Chrois

Beinn Narnain

The Cobbler
(Ben Arthur)

Narnain
Boulders

Succoth

Arrochar

A83

A814

Loch Long

0   2km

can choose whether to detour up to The Cobbler, whose spectacular outline has featured in many of the day's views. To visit The Cobbler, take the stepped path ahead. Otherwise take the left path to drop down past the impressive Narnain Boulders, with excellent views of the Cobbler's three summits. Shortly after passing the small hydro dam a path branches off left; ignore this to continue straight ahead, soon descending through trees. At a track near a mast, turn left and then take a right turn to follow a path past a bench; this makes a series of wide zigzags through a felled area before returning to the car park.

Alternatives

Ben Vane could be added to the route given above, though both the descent from Beinn Ime and the climb to Ben Vane from the intervening bealach is steep and pathless, requiring care in poor visibility.

It is also possible to climb Beinn Ime from Butterbridge. This route is shorter but steeper and less interesting than the more popular approach from Succoth, although it does give the opportunity to climb Beinn Luibhean along the way.

Beinn Narnain and The Cobbler

3

Ben Vane

Ben Vane (915m) *middle hill*

Distance **11km**
Ascent **930m**
Time **4 – 6 hours**
Start point **OS Grid ref: NN322098**
Map **OS Explorer 364**
Public transport **buses from Glasgow towards Fort William, Inverness and Skye**
Terrain & hazards **tarmac track for approach, then very steep and rocky path to summit**

Ben Vane only just reaches the magical 3000ft mark, but this fiercely steep wee mountain is the equal of any of its neighbours. The ascent gives a short day but there are several false summits; the climb is sustained enough for the top to come as a real relief.

Start from Inveruglas car park (charge payable) by the side of Loch Lomond on the A82, where there is a visitor centre with toilets and café. Cross the busy A82 and turn right passing the hydro-electric power station and follow the path then track (The Loch Lomond & Cowal Way). Return to the A82 pavement for a short distance before turning right up a gated tarmac lane which leads under the railway and climbs uphill.

The lane passes an electricity substation, with Ben Vorlich rising to the right and A'Chrois on the left above a dense blanket of forestry. Ignore the

tarmac track on the right. Ben Vane is the pyramid of rock and grass directly ahead. Beyond Coiregrogain, the tarmac road curves round to the right, heading for the Loch Sloy dam; branch left instead onto a track which crosses a bridge. After 400m, immediately after a small stream, turn right onto a clear path, climbing to reach a low shoulder at the foot of the ridge which leads up to Ben Vane. Cross the shoulder and follow the path that rises directly up the mountain. The route is steep in places but height is gained quickly and superb views soon open up behind you towards Loch Lomond and the mountains beyond.

This path avoids any difficulties although there is some optional scrambling. Higher up, the ridge becomes better defined and there are several false tops before the cairn at the true summit of Ben Vane is reached. The steepness of the hill gives great depth to the views, though the distant prospects are obscured by Ben Vane's neighbours. Retrace your steps to the start.

Alternatives
It is possible to continue the walk by descending the even steeper west ridge before dropping down to the Glas Bhealach and thus onto Beinn Ime; however, this route is very steep and demanding, with difficult route finding.

Loch Sloy

Ben
Vorlich

Little Hills

Ben Vane

Inveruglas

Loch
Lomond

Coiregrogain

Inveruglas Water

A82

Dubh Chnoc

A'Chrois

Beinn
Narnain

Cruach Tairbert

Succoth

Arrochar

*Arrochar
and Tarbert*

0   2km

Ben Vane

Ben Vorlich

Ben Vorlich (943m) *hill of the bay*

Distance **13.5km**
Ascent **940m**
Time **5 – 6.5 hours**
Start point **OS Grid ref: NN322098**
Map **OS Explorer 364**
Public Transport **buses from Glasgow to Fort William, Inverness and Skye**
Terrain & hazards **approach tracks, then very steep approach to the ridge**

This rugged mountain is the most northerly of the Arrochar Alps. This route describes the most direct and quickest way up, from Inveruglas via the Loch Sloy dam road; however, this is a hill with several alternatives.

Start from Inveruglas car park (charge payable) where there is a visitor centre, café and toilets. Cross the A82 and turn right, with views of the giant pipes running down the mountainside to drive the turbines of the Sloy hydro-electric power station. Built in the 1950s to supply electricity to Glasgow at times of peak demand, it was one of a number of hydro-power schemes developed throughout the Highlands at the time.

Follow the path, then track (The Loch Lomond & Cowal Way) and return to the A82 pavement for a short distance before turning right up a gated tarmac lane which goes under the railway and then steeply uphill. Soon the steep, featureless slopes of Ben Vorlich loom up on the right whilst the more elegant summit of A'Chrois is seen on the left, rising above a dense blanket of forestry. Ahead, Ben Vane stands as a rough pyramid of rock and grass. Stay on the tarmac road as it leads towards the Loch Sloy dam, keeping right when the track for Ben Vane turns left after Coiregrogain.

About 1km before the dam look out for a tiny cairn marking the start of a path off to the right, just after a small burn. The climb soon becomes steep and unrelenting before finally emerging on the south ridge of Ben Vorlich.

Follow the straightforward ridge at a more gentle angle to reach the trig point. The true summit of Ben Vorlich is 200m further on, atop a small crag. The views are excellent, with Ben Lui looking majestic to the north, and Loch Lomond winding away into the distance to the south. Unless you plan to extend the walk and have transport arranged, it is best to return down the outward route.

Alternatives

Further up the loch, park at Ardlui and start up the track to Garristuck cottage. Head up towards Stob an Fhithich and over Stob nan Coinnich Bhacain. Continue to the summit and the trig point beyond before descending via the ill-defined east ridge, passing over the Little Hills. From here head northeast for Stuc na Nughinn and carry on down the ridge to pass under the railway and emerge at Stuckendroin farm, about 1km from the start.

Stuckendroin

A82

Ben Vorlich

Little Hills

Loch Sloy

Ben Vane

Inveruglas

Loch Lomond

Coiregrogain

Inveruglas Water

A82

Dubh Chnoc

A'Chrois

0   2km

Ben Vorlich from Ben Vane

Beinn Bhuidhe

Beinn Bhuidhe (948m) *yellow hill*

Distance 21.5km
Ascent 1000m
Time 7 – 8 hours
Start point OS Grid ref: NN193127
Map OS Explorer 364
Public transport Glasgow Citylink service to Loch Fyne Oyster Bar
Terrain & hazards the walk in is on tarmac and rough tracks and can be cycled part way; steep ascent route including an avoidable scramble and some boggy ground above steep drops; descent is pathless but easier going

The thought of celebratory oysters and beer may spur you on to reach the remote and rather underrated solitary Munro of Beinn Bhuidhe. The long approach up Glen Fyne, whether on foot or bike, is a delight and whilst parts of the ascent are usually sodden, the summit views, both down Loch Fyne and past Ben Cruachan to the west coast, are nothing short of superb.

At the head of Loch Fyne a small horseshoe road leads off the A83; there is a car park on the west side of the bridge. Begin by crossing the bridge and turning left onto the private road up Glen Fyne, soon passing the Fyne Ales Brewery. The road passes pleasant farmland, crossing back over the Fyne after 3km. On the far side turn right to continue up the glen, passing the small settlement at Glenfyne Lodge. Ignore the bridge to the

power station and stay on the rough track on the west side of the water. At a gate in a deer fence, cyclists are asked to leave their bikes and the track becomes rougher as it passes through a rich area of coppiced hazel. From the old cottage at Inverchorachan there is a choice of routes. The main path bears left immediately after the gate; this route is eroded in places where it runs along the side of a steep gorge and there is a small scramble which those without a head for heights may prefer to avoid – the alternative is to stay high on the slopes above the north side of the gorge, following the descent route in reverse.

If taking the route up the south side of the gorge, go through another gate and follow the path uphill close to the waterfalls. Take care on some slightly scrambly sections as the path heads across the slope high above the attractively wooded Allt na Faing – one particularly awkward step could be avoided if necessary by traversing grassy slopes higher up. At the top of the valley the path climbs past a fine waterfall before reaching the gentler slopes of a boggy plateau above. Head WNW across this towards the craggy ridge of Beinn Bhuidhe which rises abruptly from the moorland. Look out for a grassy slope leading to a gully where a boggy path picks its way up onto the ridge. Reaching the crest is a great moment with a sudden superb view of Ben Cruachan and Loch

Beinn Bhuidhe

Ceann Garbh

Beinn Bhuidhe

Inverchorachan

Glenfyne Lodge

Clachan Hill

Maol Meadhonach

G l e n F y n e

River Fyne

Clachan Farm

Fyne Ales Brewery

A83

Loch Fyne

0   2km

Awe. A distinct path now bears southwest along the ridge, keeping very close to the steep left side at first before passing a lochan and then ascending to the summit with its cairn and disintegrating trig point. On a fine day you could spend a happy hour picking out the many mainland peaks in view as well as island summits on Mull, Jura or even Arran.

For the descent, return along the ridge; to vary the route follow the ridge for a further 300m to its lowest point and then descend east on a fairly gentle gradient over lumpy ground before aiming southeast as the ridge is left behind. Keep high above the gorge, crossing a couple of burns to reach a fence with a stile. From here aim for the gate on the right at the corner and accompany the fence to reach another gate on the left. Drop down just to the right of a sheep fank; from here the Glen Fyne track can be joined. Turn right to go back over the long walk in of earlier in the day – or smugly reclaim your bicycle and whizz down the glen, leaving time for a tasting session at the Loch Fyne Oyster Bar by the start.

Alternatives

It is possible to approach Beinn Bhuidhe via the neighbouring Glen Shira which has some fine woods lower down but more monotonous forestry in its upper reaches – fences make access more difficult. Follow the track to the bridge over the Brannie Burn at NN158165; from the far side of this the continuation directly uphill ENE involves passing through dense forestry, making best use of a burn and firebreak to reach the open ground above.

Crianlarich and Tyndrum Hills, Bridge of Orchy and Dalmally

North of Loch Lomond the mountains begin to tower up on all sides as the landscape takes on its full Highland stature. With both the West Highland railway and long-distance buses heading here from Glasgow, the latter along the tortuously windy Lomondside stretch of the A82, this area is both accessible and popular.

Inverarnan and Crianlarich

The Drovers Inn at Inverarnan has legendary status amongst Munro-baggers and West Highland Wayfarers alike. The decaying facade gives the impression that the place has been shut down for years, and the moth-eaten stuffed bear and his furry friends certainly seem to come from another era. That old man propping up the bar could be one of the locals – or is it Old George, a ghost who regularly turns up to haunt his old watering hole? Large bar meals are provided by the kilted staff. Love it or hate it, this is a place you have to experience at least once.

Within walking distance is the large campsite at Beinglas which also has a bar and restaurant open to non-residents, a shop selling some walking essentials and wooden wigwams for those less sure of the Scottish climate. Being within spitting distance of Glasgow, the well-run campsite can get very busy on summer weekends.

Further north is Crianlarich, set at the

junction of the A82 and the A85, where the two main routes from the Lowlands to the West Highlands converge. Though the tiny size of the village may come as a surprise given its prominence on far away roadsigns, Crianlarich also has a railway station which doubles as a welcome tearoom. Being set close by the West Highland Way, the friendly shop makes a real effort to cater for walkers. The village has an hostel (Hostelling Scotland), B&B and hotel accommodation and plenty of self-catering options, as well as the Rod and Reel for that well-deserved post Munro pint.

Tyndrum

Tyndrum may be somewhat lacking when it comes to attractive examples of Highland vernacular architecture, being blessed with various buildings that wouldn't look out of place in a motorway service station. However, it sits astride the main A82 road near the Oban junction and has two railway stations, and provides a convenient base. There is B&B accommodation, Tyndrum Lodge (also a pub with Paddy's Bar and grill), and the excellent By The Way Hostel, campsite and wooden wigwams. There is further camping and wigwams at Strathfillan just down the glen, whilst a shop on the northern edge of the village replenishes supplies.

Deservedly the most popular place to eat is the Real Food Cafe, usually packed to the rafters with Munro-baggers buzzing after

their successful ascents. It may have once been a Little Chef, but these days it serves up an ethical and extremely tasty take on all the fish-and-chip shop favourites – their vegan curry hits the spot too. Pies and everything else are all excellent quality, homemade and locally sourced; this really is a must-visit. Across the road the Green Welly Shop offers an alternative with an evening pizza takeaway; it also has a good outdoor gear shop.

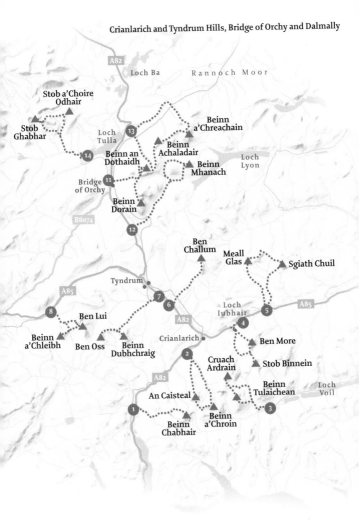

A82

Loch Ba

Rannoch Moor

Stob a'Choire
Odhair

Stob
Ghabhar

Loch
Tulla

13

Beinn
a'Chreachain

14

Beinn an
Dothaidh

Beinn
Achaladair

11

Loch
Lyon

Bridge
of Orchy

Beinn
Mhanach

Beinn
Dorain

B8074

12

Ben
Challum

Meall
Glas

Sgiath Chuil

Tyndrum

A85

7

6

Loch
Iubhair

5

A85

8

Ben Lui

A82

4

Ben More

Beinn
a'Chleibh

Ben Oss

Beinn
Dubhchraig

Crianlarich

2

Cruach
Ardrain

Stob Binnein

A82

An Caisteal

Beinn
Tulaichean

Loch
Voil

1

Beinn
Chabhair

Beinn
a'Chroin

3

Bridge of Orchy

Driving north from Tyndrum, the great conical mountain of Beinn Dorain soon appears; although grassy, its steep, regular form makes it one of the most arresting sights in this part of the Highlands. The hamlet of Bridge of Orchy is just a short distance further, and speeding motorists could pass through it almost without noticing. It is, however, a staging post on the West Highland Way and so is popular with walkers; the more remote location also gives it a more Highland character than Tyndrum or Crianlarich.

The dominating building is the whitewashed Bridge of Orchy Hotel. The bar here is walker-friendly with a good atmosphere, real fires and real ales; the food is fairly pricey but good. There is a hostel/bunkhouse, the West Highland Way Sleeper, at the railway station along the lane opposite. Finally, there is the remote Inveroran Hotel on the road to Forest Lodge, another popular spot for West Highland Wayfarers and conveniently placed for the Stob Ghabhar group.

Dalmally

Both the railway and the main A85 road to Oban run along the northern shore of Loch Awe, one of Scotland's largest freshwater lochs, and are crammed into a tiny space between the water and the steep slopes of Ben Cruachan as they head west through the Pass of Brander. It was the railway that led to the beginnings of the tiny village of

Lochawe, following the construction of the impressive Lochawe Hotel, a fine Scots Baronial pile with a superb outlook over the water to the ruins of Kilchurn Castle. The castle is well worth a visit – either by boat from Lochawe or on foot from the road to the east – as is St Conan's Kirk, the implausibly grand and eccentric creation of local landowner Walter Campbell and his sister Helen, who lived on a nearby islet, Innis Chonain.

Ben Cruachan itself is the site of one of Scotland's most remarkable feats of engineering. A kilometre underground is a gigantic man-made cavern – high enough to contain the Tower of London – which was hollowed out in the 1960s to house the turbines for a hydro-electric power station. There can't be many mountains with a wet weather alternative built in; you can take a tour deep into the heart of Ben Cruachan to see the workings of the massive power plant – look out for the tropical pot plants that thrive in the well-lit temperate conditions of the giant tunnels.

Besides the hotel, now used for coach tours rather than railway travellers, tiny Lochawe is also home to The Tight Line, a pub serving bar meals, as well as a village shop and bed and breakfast accommodation; further hotels and guest houses can be found in the neighbouring village of Dalmally. The nearest campsites and hostels are at Tyndrum and Inveraray.

View from Beinn Dorain

Beinn Chabhair

Beinn Chabhair (933m) *hill of the hawk*

Distance 15km
Ascent 940m
Time 5 – 6 hours
Start point OS Grid ref: NN318184
Map OS Explorer 364
Public transport use buses from Glasgow towards Fort William, Inverness and Skye
Terrain & hazards steep and stony start, very boggy section, but great path on the ridge

An enjoyable hill with good views down Loch Long, Beinn Chabhair is part of the Crianlarich group of hills, but the awkward terrain linking it to An Caisteal means it is usually tackled on its own. The summit ridge has an interesting collection of knolls and rocky bits, recompense for the bogs lower down and the initial steep climb alongside Beinglas Falls.

Start from the Drovers Inn at Inverarnan and head briefly north along the A82 before turning right for Beinglas Farm Campsite. Once over the bridge turn right to skirt the edge of the field rather than walking direct to the farm which is discouraged. Go through a gate at the edge of the campsite and pass the West Highland Way signs and wigwams to cross a stile over a stone wall. The stony path immediately begins a steep climb and is eroded in places. Pass the Beinglas Falls and then cross a stile over a deer fence to keep following the Bein Glas burn upstream. At a fork the higher path is the better option, though the two routes converge further on.

Keep on the north side of the burn as it heads over open moorland which is very boggy in places, before ascending again with the rugged ridge of Beinn Chabhair on the left. A faint path forks off to the left and is easily missed; if Lochan Beinn Chabhair comes into view then you have just passed it. The path leads over wet ground before rising alongside a burn to reach the ridge just west of Meall nan Tarmachan.

From here onwards the ridge is a delightful meander between and over rocky knolls, passing a couple of tiny lochans. The summit is situated at the far end. This is a great vantage point for looking down Loch Long on a clear day, with the Trossachs seen laid out to the east. The easiest descent is to retrace the outward route.

Alternatives

For a rougher, more demanding alternative descent, the ridge could be continued past Lochan a'Chaisteil before descending west and rejoining the outward route for the path next to the Bein Glas Burn.

It is also possible to combine Beinn Chabhair with the neigbouring Munros, but the slopes both down to and up from the bealach between this peak and An Caisteal are rocky and require experience and great care.

A82

Glen Falloch

River Falloch

Stob Glas

An Caisteal

Lochan a'Chaisteil

Meall nan Tarmachan

Beinglas Farm Campsite

erarnan

Drovers Inn

Bein Glas Burn

Lochan Beinn Chabhair

Beinn Chabhair

Ardlui

Loch Lomond

A82

0   2km

An Caisteal and Beinn Chabhair from Beinn Dhubhcraig

2

An Caisteal
Beinn a'Chroin

An Caisteal (995m) *the castle*
Beinn a'Chroin (942m) *hill of the sheepfold*

Distance **14km**
Ascent **1040m**
Time **6 – 7 hours**
Start point **OS Grid ref: NN369239**
Map **OS Explorer 364**
Public transport **use buses from Glasgow towards Fort William, Inverness and Skye**
Terrain & hazards **short section of track; path for most of the route, rocky at times**

These two Munros provide an enjoyable and fairly short ridge traverse. Their upper slopes are rocky and rugged, giving some character after the grassy terrain below.

Start from a lay-by 2km south of Crianlarich on the A82. From here climb a stile and cross the boggy field to reach the underpass that leads below the railway. Follow the track which crosses the River Falloch and heads upriver for around 1km. Pass through a gate in a fence and then leave the track, aiming straight up the grassy flank of Sron Gharbh seen up to the right. The climb is fairly easy going with a couple of short rocky sections. Higher up, a path emerges as the top of Sron Gharbh is reached.

From here the ridge is well-named as Twistin Hill. A meandering path rises steadily along it, at one point negotiating a rocky cleft that looks like a giant has whacked the mountain with a meat cleaver. Pass over or round a rocky knoll – the 'Castle' that gives the mountain its Gaelic name – before climbing up to the summit.

From the summit continue south along the ridge. A small path leads across a couple of easy rock steps before reaching the Bealach Buidhe. From here, traverse diagonally right (southeast) up the steep rocky slopes beyond. There is a big step up at one point – you may prefer to detour around to the right. The path then winds between rocky lumps and tiny lochans, passing a small cairn which marks the true summit of Beinn a'Chroin. Another cairn, sited just after a steep dip, was for many years thought to be the top. The views cover range after range of hills receding to far away Ben Nevis. Just before you reach the cairn a faint path leaves off to the left – this is the return route.

To descend, drop down the grassy north ridge on a narrow path. Further down aim for a point where the two burns meet, and cross just before the confluence. Now the path follows the west side of the River Falloch down the glen. There are some invitingly clear but very cold pools which may tempt on a hot day. After passing a massive boulder the route crosses boggy ground before regaining the outward track opposite a sheep fank. Follow this back to the bridge and through the sheep-creep under the railway to the start.

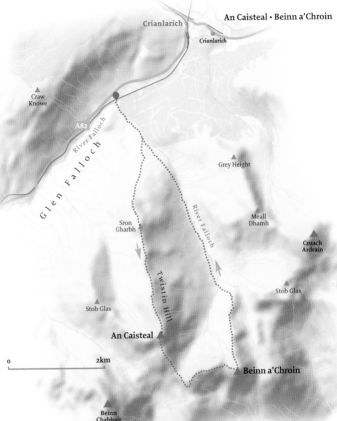

Crianlarich

Crianlarich

Craw
Knowe

A82

River Falloch

Glen Falloch

Grey Height

River Falloch

Sron
Gharbh

Meall
Dhamh

Cruach
Ardrain

Twistin Hill

Stob Glas

Stob Glas

An Caisteal

Beinn a'Chroin

0   2km

Beinn
Chabhair

Alternatives

It is possible to climb these hills together with Beinn Chabhair, though the bealach between them is fairly low and the terrain on both sides is very steep and tricky to negotiate. A less frequented approach is from Inverlochlarig to the east, using the track up the glen past the Ishag Burn before heading up the rugged slopes, passing to the left of an area of crags to reach the upper slopes of Beinn a'Chroin. An Caisteal is within easy reach but rather inconveniently placed for a return to Inverlochlarig; another option is to traverse to Cruach Ardrain and Beinn Tulaichean.

3

Beinn Tulaichean Cruach Ardrain

Beinn Tulaichean (946m) *hill of the hillocks*
Cruach Ardrain (1046m) *high stacked heap*

Distance **12.5km**
Ascent **1020m**
Time **5 – 7 hours**
Start point **OS Grid ref: NN445185**
Maps **OS Explorer 364 and 365**
Terrain & hazards **wet and pathless ascent and descent with better section between the two Munros**

Cruach Ardrain's distinctive outline can be seen clearly from the Crianlarich and Tyndrum area. However, the inclusion in the Munros list of Beinn Tulaichean – a peak on its south ridge – means that a circuit from the south tends to be more appealing.

Start from the car park at the end of the public road beyond Loch Voil; there is a shelter and information board here. Begin along the track on the north side of the glen to reach the farm at Inverlochlarig. This was the final home of infamous outlaw Rob Roy MacGregor, after he had been pardoned. He died here in 1736 and his grave can be seen in the Balquhidder churchyard down the glen. The track swings left and crosses the bridge; on the far side take the stile on the right and follow the path by the burn passing a small hydro building before turning right on a track. Once through the gate in the fence continue on the track until a bend

and then leave it to climb the slopes of Beinn Tulaichean on the left. The lower slopes are boggy but some rocky outcrops higher up help to relieve the otherwise monotonous uphill slog.

A short section of knobbly ridge leads to the summit of Beinn Tulaichean. At 946m and with only a short descent between this and Cruach Ardrain it is surprising that Beinn Tulaichean has managed to attain and hang on to Munro status. Head down the NNW ridge, following a path to the bealach before tackling the slightly rougher climb to Cruach Ardrain. The true summit is about 100m northeast from the first cairn – cross a dip and pass two small cairns and a second dip to attain the true top at 1046m.

Retrace your steps to the bealach with Beinn Tulaichean and then head down into the glen to the east on grassy slopes with some easily-avoidable rock slabs. Once you reach the track, follow it south back to Inverlochlarig Farm and the start.

Alternatives

The more popular approach to Cruach Ardrain is from the north. Begin from the car park near the bridge over the River Falloch, and follow the track up beside the Falloch to a fork where the left branch leads down to a bridge. Climb the often wet slopes to the right of the forestry to reach Grey Height, continuing to Cruach

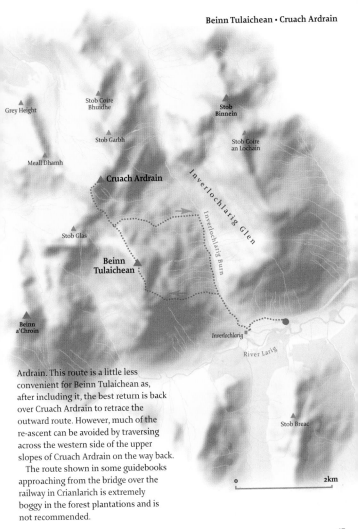

Grey Height

Stob Coire
Bhuidhe

**Stob
Binnein**

Stob Garbh

Stob Coire
an Lochain

Meall Dhamh

Cruach Ardrain

Inverlochlarig Glen

Inverlochlarig Burn

Stob Glas

**Beinn
Tulaichean**

Beinn
a'Chroin

Inverlochlarig

River Larig

Stob Breac

0   2km

Ardrain. This route is a little less
convenient for Beinn Tulaichean as,
after including it, the best return is back
over Cruach Ardrain to retrace the
outward route. However, much of the
re-ascent can be avoided by traversing
across the western side of the upper
slopes of Cruach Ardrain on the way back.

The route shown in some guidebooks
approaching from the bridge over the
railway in Crianlarich is extremely
boggy in the forest plantations and is
not recommended.

Ben More

4

Ben More
Stob Binnein

Ben More (1174m) *big hill*
Stob Binnein (1165m) *peak of the anvil*

Distance **12km**
Ascent **1330m**
Time **7 – 8 hours**
Start point **OS Grid ref: NN420263**
Map **OS Explorer 365**
Terrain & hazards **very steep on both ascent and descent**

Ben More dominates the Crianlarich area, a massive pyramid of green that reveals at once the unrelenting gradient of the direct ascent. Distant views show it to be one of a pair and the traverse across to the more elegant Stob Binnein makes for an enjoyable outing.

Just east of Benmore Farm there is limited parking on the verge of the A85, or a proper lay-by further along the road at the west end of Loch Iubhair. A small wooden sign indicates the start of a path which crosses the ditch to join a track just above the farm; turn left along the track which winds uphill and passes through a gate.

Soon after the gate, it's time to get those calf muscles going; head straight up the steep grassy slope. Boggy at first, the slope soon dries out, but the gradient doesn't get any easier. There are sections of path in places lower down and as you gain height these combine to form a clear path, keeping a little to the left of the ill-defined lower section of the Sloc Curraidh, a corrie high on Ben More.

Take care not to venture into the Sloc Curraidh as the headwall is steep and has seen fatalities; this side of Ben More has a reputation as an avalanche blackspot in winter. From around 800m there is a drystone dyke along the steep ridge bordering the north side of the corrie; the path keeps just to the left of this. Continue climbing by the dyke to gain the rocky shoulder of Cuidhe Chrom. After this the going becomes easier and the path swings left, giving a view of Loch Tay, before reaching the final slopes.

A large cairn marks the summit of Ben More which, as you might expect from such a dominant mountain, is a great viewpoint. The mountains of the Southern Highlands are arranged in a grand arc. The trig point is just beyond the cairn, atop a rocky outcrop, and from here you can assess the next stage, the ridge to the attractive peak of Stob Binnein.

There is a substantial 300m descent to the bealach between the two peaks. The going is rocky but with a clear path at first, with a short scramble that can be avoided by detouring a little to the left. Further down the slopes become grassy, leading eventually to the massive bealach that marks the Bealach Eadar da-Bheinn. The climb to Stob Binnein is straightforward and the path zigzags to relieve the

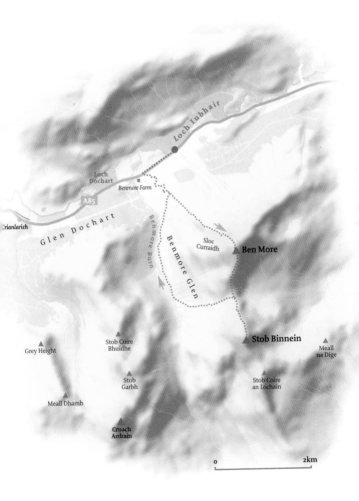

gradient en route to the summit at 1165m. Much more of the Trossachs can be seen from here. The south ridge looks tempting but if returning to the A85 you need to instead retrace your steps to the bealach.

Do not follow the cairned path heading across the slopes below Ben More as this leads to very steep rocky ground. Instead, descend directly from the bealach down boggy slopes, eventually picking up a path on the left side of the burn. Once down to the floor of the glen bear north to reach the end of a track by a bridge. Do not cross the bridge but follow the track to reach the gate passed earlier in the day. Go through it and carry on down to return to the start.

Alternatives

The south ridge of Stob Binnein was mentioned above; it provides a grand route of ascent, gained via a steep path from Inverlochlarig in the Trossachs. This route is much less convenient for Ben More as the return walk would involve either climbing back over Stob Binnein or a very boggy trudge through the pass between the glens to the west.

Another route which avoids the steep climb from Benmore Farm is to make a circuit around the glen of the Allt Coire Chaorach. The disadvantage of this route is difficulty finding a reasonable way through the forestry lower down; there has been a lot of felling in recent years. Once clear of the trees aim for Stob Creagach and continue over Meall na Dige for Stob Binnein. Traverse to Ben More and then descend via the Sron nam Forsairean ridge.

5

Sgiath Chuil
Meall Glas

Sgiath Chuil (921m) *corner wing*
Meall Glas (959m) *rounded green-grey hill*

Distance 15.75km
Ascent 990m
Time 7 – 9 hours
Start point OS Grid ref: NN448275
Maps OS Explorer 365 and 378
Terrain & hazards **steep pathless slopes between the two Munros; boggy areas on the approaches**

Meall Glas and Sgiath Chuil are set well back from Glen Dochart and their sprawling slopes draw little attention compared to their more impressive neighbours. The approach is boggy though pleasant lower down and the drop between the two hills is steep, but the summits themselves are excellent viewpoints.

The route starts from the A85 at the turning for Auchessan; parking here requires care on the grass verge of the main road. Start by following the lane towards Auchessan, crossing over the River Dochart. Both Munros can be seen from here, their summits rising above the moor. Pass a couple of houses to reach the old farmhouse and continue straight ahead through a gate (the other sign for 'Hill Path' pointing left is the return route). Keep to the right of a farm shed and pass through two more gates to reach the Allt Riobain. Do not cross the burn but

instead leave the track and take the path running between the burn and a fence.

Keep next to the burn as it swings left and the path climbs up beside it. This is a delightful tree-lined stretch with cascading falls and pools. The fence on the left encloses a large area that has recently been planted with native trees. As the path rises the views back over Glen Dochart to mighty Ben More make a good excuse for a breather. Go through a deer fence and after the corner of the plantation the path peters out.

Keep following the Allt Riobain, soon reaching a sleeper bridge over a tributary. From here continue to a small dam about 300m upstream. Cross the Allt Riobain just below the dam and bear directly northeast up the slopes of Sgiath Chuil, over boggy ground at first. The summit is atop the large crag ahead and can be accessed easily by passing the cliffs on either side. From here Ben Lawers is prominent with Ben Vorlich and Stuc a'Chroin visible further right. A dip between the rocks makes a great place to shelter from the wind and soak up the views.

Continue north along the broad ridge towards a shallow bealach. To get to Meall Glas there is no alternative but to descend steeply to the west, down to the Lairig a'Churain fully 300m below. Aim slightly to the west and descend gentle stony

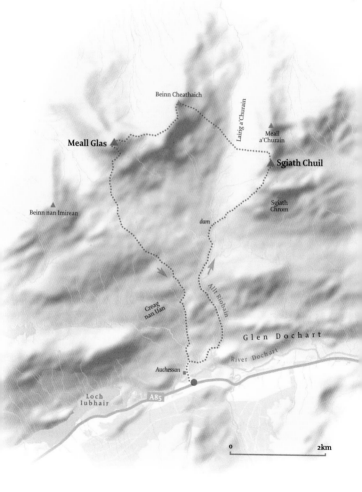

Beinn Cheathaich

Lairig a'Churain

Meall a'Churain

Meall Glas

Sgiath Chuil

Beinn nan Imirean

Sgiath Chrom

dam

Creag nan Uan

Allt Riobain

Glen Dochart

Auchessan

River Dochart

Loch Iubhair

A85

0   2km

slopes at first. Where the slope steepens, look for a patch of boulders and descend steeply through these to reach the bealach. On the far side aim northwest to reach the ridge of Beinn Cheathaich to the north of the top. From here a path leads towards the summit of Meall Glas which is just over 1km away. Ben Challum dominates the view west.

Start the descent by heading a short way southeast to pass some broken crags. Continue south, picking up a boggy path for a lengthy moorland traverse, eventually reaching a burn and following it downhill east of Creag nan Uan. Go straight ahead at a vague track and follow the path on the left side of the burn, soon reaching the fenced area. Bear right to a stile in the dip and continue through lovely woodland by the burn. Keep right of the sheepfolds to join a track and follow this behind the old farmhouse at Auchessan. Turn right to join the lane back to the main road at the start.

Alternatives

The approach from Glen Lochay to the north requires a little more driving, but does avoid the worst of the bogs. It involves a wade of the River Lochay – alternatively you could cross the bridge to the east if the river is in spate. Begin from the end of the public road up the glen; the river must be waded to reach Lubchurran as the bridge marked on OS maps does not exist. Follow the track up by the Lubchurran Burn before crossing it and striking off up Sgiath Chuil. Continue to Meall Glas as described above and return by descending north from Beinn Cheathaich. Lower down aim to rejoin the Lubchurran Burn track.

Summit of Sgiath Chuil

6

Ben Challum

Ben Challum (1025m) *Calum's hill*

Distance **11.5km**
Ascent **910m**
Time **5 – 7 hours**
Start point **OS Grid ref: NN355281**
Map **OS Explorer 364**
Public transport **Citylink buses from Glasgow to Fort William, Skye and Inverness run past the start**
Terrain & hazards **boggy gradual climb to start; some awkward stiles**

The most popular route up Ben Challum involves a rather boggy trudge up the broad lower slopes above Strath Fillan. The ridge and summit above are no disappointment, however, and on a fine day the views are superb.

Although the Glen Lochay side of Ben Challum is more attractive, the usual approach is via Kirkton Farm off the A82. Start from the lay-by on the west side of the A82 just north of the Kirkton Farm turning. Cross the road and follow the Kirkton lane, going over the bridge and then turning left just before the farm. After the briefest of acquaintances, leave the West Highland Way by taking the track to pass to the right of a cemetery flanked by two tall trees, and then using the level crossing at the railway.

Leave the track and follow a faint path uphill, continuing alongside a deer fence and crossing stiles. After a long slog up boggy ground the going improves on the approach to the south top from where the outlook to Ben Lui, Ben More and Stob Binnein is excellent on a clear day. In poor visibility the next section can be confusing as a cleft divides the ridge – head northwest a very short distance to cross it before continuing north. A short ridge descent leads to the final climb, and the summit rewards with expansive panoramas – including a grand sweeping view down Glen Lochay. Return by the outward route.

Alternatives
The alternative approach from Kenknock in Glen Lochay is longer and more remote, but from this direction Ben Challum takes on a finer, more conical appearance. From the head of Glen Lochay pass just south of the crags on Stob a'Bhiora to gain the east ridge.

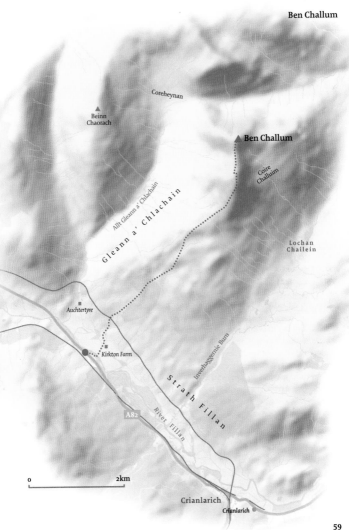

Ben Challum

Ben Challum

Coreheynan

Beinn
Chaorach

Coire
Challuim

Allt Gleann a' Chlachain

G l e a n n   a '   C h l a c h a i n

Lochan
Chailein

Auchtertyre

Kirkton Farm

Invelraggernie Burn

S t r a t h   F i l l a n

A82

River Fillan

0   2km

Crianlarich

Crianlarich

7

Ben Oss
Beinn Dubhchraig

Ben Oss (1029m) *elk hill*
Beinn Dubhchraig (978m) *hill of the dark crag*

Distance **17.5km**
Ascent **1200m**
Time **7 – 8 hours**
Start point **OS Grid ref: NN343291**
Map **OS Explorer 364**
Public transport **Citylink buses from Glasgow to Fort William, Skye and Inverness run past the start**
Terrain & hazards **the section through the pinewood is very boggy underfoot; higher up the slope is pathless, with broad ridges, rocky in parts, above; in poor visibility navigation on the upper slopes, particularly across to Ben Oss, can be difficult**

Ben Oss and Beinn Dubhchraig are rather in the shadow of the higher, and more elegant, Ben Lui. However, they should not be overlooked as there are stunning native pinewoods on the approach – a rarity in this part of the Highlands – and they provide a different perspective on their more illustrious neighbour.

The car park at Dalrigh is off the west side of the A82 between Crianlarich and Tyndrum. From here the summit of Beinn Dubhchraig can be seen over the tree tops. From the parking area follow the surfaced lane downhill, crossing the West Highland Way and then White Bridge before turning right onto a track. Cross the bridge over the railway and, after the gate, head right along a boggy path, aiming for a dilapidated footbridge over the Allt Gleann Auchreoch just above its confluence with the River Cononish. On the far side bear left upstream to enter Coille Coire-Chuilc, a beautiful mixed pinewood. After 300m a drier path to the right climbs through the trees away from the burn, or you could stay on the boggier path by the water. The paths unite higher up and, still very boggy, follow a branch stream, the Allt Coire Dubhchraig, which cascades down a series of waterfalls. Go through a fence and head towards a stile in the deer fence higher up. Soon the trees are left behind and after passing a third fence continue on the path near the burn, keeping in the same direction once the path gives out to reach the very broad ridge just above some lochans.

Bear southeast for an easy climb to the summit of Beinn Dubhchraig. To head for Ben Oss, first return down the ridge, aiming northwest and picking up an indistinct path to the left side of some lochans. Now descend rockier ground to the Bealach Buidhe, overlooking Loch Oss. Continue to the far side of the bealach and keep an eye out for a small cairn just before the path descends a little to cross a burn. Leave the path here and bear west up a grassy slope. Soon a faint path leads to the northeastern top of Ben Oss.

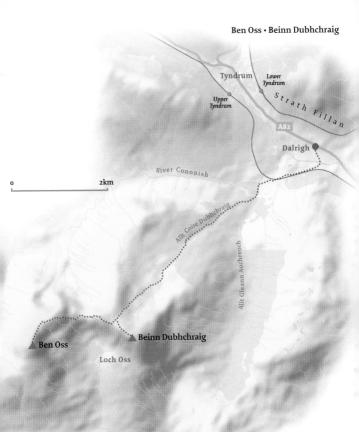

Ben Oss · Beinn Dubhchraig

Continue down to a bealach before the final easy climb to the summit. To return it is necessary to descend back to the bealach and up the ridge towards Beinn Dubhchraig until just past the lochans as there are crags to the north which bar a more direct return. Retrace the route of

ascent beside the Allt Coire Dubhchraig and back to Dalrigh.

Alternatives

The same approach is used almost invariably, although very fit walkers may combine these hills with Ben Lui.

61

Beinn Dubhchraig and Loch Oss

8

Ben Lui
Beinn a'Chleibh

Ben Lui (Beinn Laoigh) (1130m)
hill of the calf
Beinn a'Chleibh (916m) *hill of the creel*

Distance **9.5km**
Ascent **1080m**
Time **5 – 7 hours**
Start point **OS Grid ref: NN239278**
Map **OS Explorer 364**
Public transport **some Glasgow – Oban buses run along the A85 through Glen Lochy**
Terrain & hazards **the River Lochy must be forded at the start of the route; this could be impossible when in spate; the section through the forest is very boggy; there are crags on the upper slopes, with careful navigation needed, especially on Beinn a'Chleibh when the clouds are down**

Ben Lui, with its twin summits rising elegantly above the steep headwall of Coire Gaothach, must rank high on any list of the most impressive mountains in the Southern Highlands. The classic ascent via Glen Cononish offers the best views, but the route given here from Glen Lochy makes it much easier to include neighbouring Beinn a'Chleibh.

The car park is off the south side of the A85 from where a path leads to the River Lochy. This usually provides a chilling wade – head to the right to find the safest spot and do not attempt if the river is in spate. On the far side is the railway – crossing over the lines here is a criminal offence, so use the underpass – usually the metal walkway keeps boots out of the Eas Diamh which flows through here to join the Lochy. A path then rises into the forest beyond with the Eas Daimh on your right.

Keep a sharp eye out for a small cairn at the point where a burn meets the Eas Daimh. Leave the main path here, crossing the Eas Daimh onto a narrow path beside a burn. Be warned – if you miss this path you face an even boggier slog through the forest! Once out of the trees either make for the bealach between the two peaks or climb steeply and more directly to the east to join the northwest ridge of Ben Lui. On this route once the hard work of reaching the ridge is over it is an enjoyable walk along the ridge to the summit.

Don't be fooled by the cairn at the northwest summit – the true summit (1130m) is a wee bit further just beyond a dip. The cairn here teeters on the edge of Coire Gaothach, an impressive cliff-girt bowl which usually holds snow into the early summer. The classic winter mountaineering route of Central Gully climbs directly to the cairn from the corrie floor far below.

From the summit a path bears southwest down a broad ridge towards

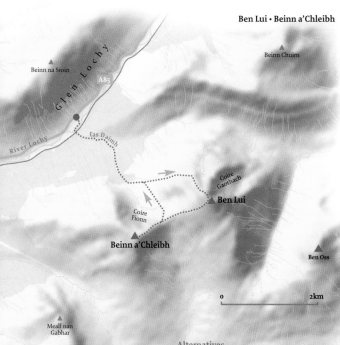

Beinn a'Chleibh. After the bealach the path winds up onto the plateau; the summit cairn can be hard to locate in poor visibility. For the descent return to the bealach above Coire Fionn. Drop down into the corrie; it is steep at first but easier lower down. Aim for the point where the path emerges from the forest and retrace your steps to the start.

Alternatives

The best views of Ben Lui are from the east, and the classic route takes these in on a longer approach from Dalrigh that passes an area known for its gold deposits – recently planning permission has been granted for further gold mining in this area. From the floor of Coire Gaothach head onto the ridge forming the right-hand rim; this route is steep and rocky but has a faint path. Including Beinn a'Cheibh from this side involves a traverse back across the slopes of Ben Lui; the very fittest walkers may include Ben Oss and Beinn Dubhchraig as well.

Ben Lui from Ben Oss

9

Beinn a'Chochuill
Beinn Eunaich

Beinn a'Chochuill (980m) *hill of the shell*
Beinn Eunaich (989m) *fowling hill*

Distance **13.5km**
Ascent **1220m**
Time **6 – 7 hours**
Start point **OS Grid ref: NN136287**
Map **OS Explorer 377**
Public transport **regular bus to Lochawe**
Terrain & hazards **track and then grassy slopes with a very steep final descent; no difficulties or exposure on the ridge**

Whilst no match for the higher and spikier Ben Cruachan, this enjoyable ridge traverse gives grandstand views of its glamorous neighbour as well as over Loch Etive and towards the peaks of Glen Coe.

The route starts from the B8077 which branches off the A85 at the head of Loch Awe; follow the sign for Stronmilchan. There is limited parking at the roadside near the bridge over the Allt Mhoille. Begin by walking along the road away from Loch Awe to turn left onto the Castle Estate Farm track, branching left at a fork, and left again when the track divides at the gate for the Castles Estate Farm. The track now leads up the glen; it was built as part of the Ben Cruachan hydro scheme which includes tunnels excavated all the way through Beinn a'Chochuill as well as Cruachan itself.

The track rises gradually across the hillside before a slight descent to cross the Allt Lairig Ianachain. Fork right at the next junction and continue on the track for 200m before striking off northwest up the grassy slope, which becomes a defined ridge with a small path higher up. Behind you the views over Loch Awe and Kilchurn Castle provide an excellent excuse for a breather. Once the main spine of the mountain is reached follow a narrow path west along it, passing a small rocky outcrop before the final rise to the summit of Beinn a'Chochuill.

From here it is necessary to return to the point where you joined the ridge and then continue east down to the bealach Lairig Ianachain at 728m. The route up Beinn Eunaich is well seen ahead – a straightforward grassy slope with some stones and a vague path aiming for the large cairn. This, the higher of the two Munros, is probably the best viewpoint for the Cruachan ridge, which looks wonderfully wild and rocky.

The descent aims WSW from the cairn down a broad and grassy ridge which is a delight on springy turf. Soon after a couple of peat hags, the small path bears to the right and begins an extremely steep descent to the hydro track. The path is loose and eroded so the descent requires great care; the track is likely to be reached with some relief. It is now a straightforward walk back to the start.

Alternatives

The route above is followed almost invariably; it is possible to extend it by following the northeast ridge of Beinn Eunaich over several lower summits to reach the Lairig Dhoireann; the path marked on OS maps here no longer exists, but its route can be retraced back to the track in Glen Strae to return to the start. Very fit walkers may attempt to link these Munros to the Cruachan ridge; this is possible by crossing the low bealach of the Lairig Noe, though the route – particularly the ascent up to Sron an Isean – is very steep, rocky and pathless.

Beinn Eunaich from Stob Garbh

10

Ben Cruachan Stob Diamh

Ben Cruachan (1126m) *hill of peaks*
Stob Diamh (998m) *peak of the stag*

Distance **14km**
Ascent **1380m**
Time **7 – 9 hours**
Start point **OS Grid ref: NN080267**
Map **OS Explorer 377**
Public transport **train (Falls of Cruachan station – only in summer months) and bus service to Ben Cruachan power station visitor centre.**
Terrain & hazards **steep and rocky paths; short section of scrambling, no real exposure, grassy descent can be boggy. Those with vertigo may find the dam ladder the scariest part!**

The huge bulk of Ben Cruachan is topped by a fine ridge and several distinctive pointed summits which help make it a landmark when seen from other hills across the region. The horseshoe route around the reservoir, taking in the second Munro, Stob Diamh, is one of the best walks in the Southern Highlands.

The visitor centre does not allow walkers to use its car park, so park instead near the station where there is space to pull off the A85 and park along the side of the road. Alternatively head 700m towards Oban where there is a proper lay-by, and walk back. Begin up the path to the station, passing under the railway and up steps before bearing left through trees,

steeply in places. As the trees thin, cross a deer fence at a stile and continue towards the Cruachan Dam.

At the track turn left, cross the burn and head up the zigzig path to the metal handrails and staircase which takes you up onto the dam itself. From the west end of the dam take the path which shortcuts up to the track leading along the west side of the reservoir.

Just before the end of this track, cross a burn and take a faint path on the left which rises steadily over the rough ground to reach Coire Dearg. From here the steep and eroded route leads to a bealach where there is a small lochan. Now head north up the stony path which leads all the way to Ben Cruachan's summit cairn and the stump that is all that remains of the trig point. This is the highest summit in a wide area and the views are very extensive, the best being over Loch Etive and west to the pointed subsidiary summit of Taynuilt Peak (Stob Dearg) with the island-dotted sea beyond.

From the summit follow the clear ridge northeast. The route soon crosses some rock slabs which are bypassed by a path below before climbing back up to the ridge. A steep short haul brings you to Drochaid Ghlas; many walkers have gone wrong here in mist by heading along the north ridge, but the correct route branches off from a cairn and drops

Aonach Breac

Glen Liver

Beinn a'Chochuill

Meall nan Each

Drochaid Ghlas

Sron an Isean

Stob Diamh

Ben Cruachan

Stob Garbh

Coire Dearg

Coire Cruachan

Meall Cuanail

Cruachan Reservoir

Lairig Torran

Beinn a'Bhuiridh

Pass of Brander

Power Station

Falls of Cruachan

A85

Loch Awe

0   2km

steeply down rockier ground onto the east ridge. The going becomes easy as the ridge leads to a final pull up to Stob Diamh. Here the great horseshoe of ridges facing Dalmally are well seen. Take the ridge to the south, with a small climb over Stob Garbh and then a descent to the Lairig Torran bealach beyond. The route now bears west to follow grassy slopes on the north side of a burn – there is a faint path at times. The path reaches the track at a tunnel entrance to the power station. Follow the track down to below the dam where a shortcut path links to the outward route which can then be retraced to the start.

Alternatives

Ben Cruachan is a popular ascent in its own right, but the above circuit is the classic route, likely to be preferred by Munro-baggers. Purists will want to include Meall Cuanail, Taynuilt Peak and the Corbett Beinn a'Bhuiridh, though the ascent of the latter is very steep and rocky from the final bealach.

There is a very fine alternative route to Stob Diamh; the Dalmally Horseshoe is a circuit of its eastern ridges, two arms enclosing the Allt Coire Chreachainn.

Loch Etive from Stob Diamh

11

Beinn Dorain
Beinn an Dothaidh

Beinn Dorain (1076m)
hill of the small stream
Beinn an Dothaidh (1004m)
hill of the scorching

Distance **14km**
Ascent **1110m**
Time **6 – 8 hours**
Start point **OS Grid ref: NN297396**
Map **OS Explorer 377**
Public transport **Bridge of Orchy is well served both by Citylink buses and by its train station**
Terrain & hazards **there are steep, boggy and eroded sections in places. In bad visibility navigation can be difficult**

The steep, regular cone of Beinn Dorain makes it a real landmark on the journey into the Highlands, dominating the view north from both the A82 and the West Highland Way north of Tyndrum. Combined with neighbour Beinn an Dothaidh – a superb viewpoint – it makes a satisfying outing.

Luckily the relentlessly steep slopes that Beinn Dorain presents to the A82 are not the usual route of ascent, which starts instead from Bridge of Orchy itself. There is a public car park by the Bridge of Orchy Hotel. Cross the main road and head up the lane to the train station. Pass through the underpass and then left onto a path uphill, keeping to the south of the Allt Coire an

Dothaidh into Coire an Dothaidh and continuing eventually up to the bealach at 744m. The view now begins to open up eastwards towards Loch Lyon in Perthshire.

Both Munros are climbed from here and it matters little which is tackled first. For Beinn Dorain, follow the wide path south up the ridge. Higher up the ridge becomes more defined and the path eventually reaches a large cairn. Carn Sasunnaich can easily be mistaken for the top in bad weather; perhaps the Gaelic name meaning 'the Englishman's Cairn' reflects the navigational skills of walkers from south of the border?

Continue downhill and across a bealach, ignoring a bypass path to the right to reach the true summit and its view down to a great arc on the West Highland railway.

Return to the 744m bealach and climb northeast at first to begin the ascent of Beinn an Dothaidh. Once past a steep section aim directly up more gentle slopes to the west top which has a stunning outlook over Loch Tulla to Rannoch Moor and the peaks of the Black Mount and Glencoe. From here the true summit is a short distance east along the plateau edge. Descend back across Coire Reidh to the bealach and retrace the outward journey before enjoying a well-earned pint in the bar at the Bridge of Orchy Hotel.

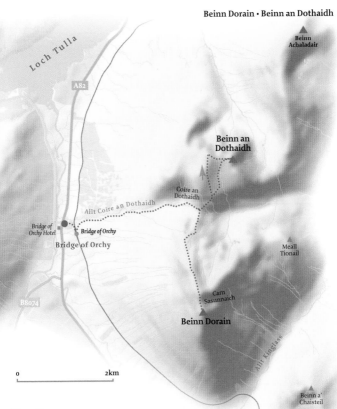

Beinn Dorain • Beinn an Dothaidh

Alternatives

The very fit can continue from Beinn an Dothaidh to take in Beinn Achaladair and Beinn a'Chreachain – a fine traverse with magnificent views; however, the descent to Achallader Farm would leave you a long way from the start at Bridge of Orchy.

Another possible extension would be to descend to the bealach east of Beinn an

Dothaidh and then traverse the east slope of Beinn Achaladair to eventually reach Beinn Mhanach. A descent could then be made down the Auch Glen and the West Highland Way followed back to Bridge of Orchy, but this would make a very challenging day of 28km with 1600m of ascent.

Beinn an Dothaidh

Duncan Ban MacIntyre

Donnchadh Bàn Mac an t-Saoir – known as Duncan Ban MacIntyre in English – was one of the most celebrated Gaelic poets. Writing during what is regarded as a golden era in Gaelic poetry, Duncan Ban drew inspiration from the landscape in which he grew up and worked in the local deer forests as a young man. He was born on the banks of Loch Tulla in 1724 and is best known for the poem 'In praise of Ben Doran', a work which anticipates the ecological outlook we know today.

As a gamekeeper he was no fan of the large-scale introduction of sheep to the Highlands and wrote this poem in celebration of the fox 'Song of the Foxes'.

> 'My blessing with the Foxes dwell
> For that they hunt the sheep so well.
> Ill fa' the sheep, a greyfaced nation
> That swept our hills with desolation.'

A large granite memorial sits high above the old military road from Inveraray to Dalmally in Glen Orchy. Queen Victoria visited it in 1875 and was said to be especially pleased with the view.

Beinn Dorain and Auch Glen

Beinn Mhanach

Beinn Mhanach (953m) *hill of the monk*

Distance **21km**
Ascent **820m**
Time **6 – 7 hours**
Start point **OS Grid ref: NN316353**
Map **OS Explorer 377**
Public transport **Citylink buses from Glasgow to Fort William, Skye and Inverness pass the start**
Terrain & hazards **the approach track fords the Allt Kinglass several times; wading is often necessary but may become impossible in spate conditions. The hill itself is pathless**

Beinn Mhanach is dismissed by many as a rather dull and shapeless hill. Whilst it is true that it lacks distinctive form, it is remote by Southern Highlands standards and the approach up the glen, idyllic on a fine summer's day, provides a real feeling of getting 'away from it all'.

Vehicles are not allowed down the private road to Auch, so use the rough informal lay-by on the east side of the A82 immediately south of the turning for Auch (signed for Auch Estate and holiday cottages) and tuck those wing mirrors in! Begin down the Auch road and, once over a bridge, pass the farm to reach a crossroads with the West Highland Way.

Continue ahead alongside the Allt Kinglass, fording a burn before passing underneath the impressive viaduct of the West Highland Line. You are now entering peaceful Gleann Achadh-innis Chailein,

popularly known as the Auch Glen. At a fork in the track keep left, soon crossing the ford over the main river where a chilly wade may be necessary. Less than 1.5km further, the track recrosses the river and repeats this a few more times, although at the final bend there is a rougher path to enable you to stay on the southeast side if needed. Where the river diverges, ford the Allt a'Chuirn to reach the old farm buildings at Ais-an t-Sidhean, once home to the 18th-century Gaelic poet Duncan Ban MacIntyre.

After one more river ford, the water is crossed for a final time on a railway sleeper bridge. Take the right fork to head east up the glen. After 1km cross a bridge over the Allt a'Chuirn and leave the track to head NNE straight up the slope on the left, keeping to the right of the burn and fence. The fence heads for the bealach between Beinn a'Chuirn and Beinn Mhanach. Cross the fence part way up and aim ENE directly for the summit, a muscle-stretching pull over good ground. Like being the shortest person at a rock concert, the views from the summit at 953m are somewhat restricted by the higher peaks around. A slight detour along the ridge brings Loch Lyon into view.

The return route could be made the same way; one way to vary it is to descend to the bealach with Beinn a'Chuirn. From here a short detour could be made to this top for a bit more exercise and a peaceful lunchstop. Otherwise follow the fence

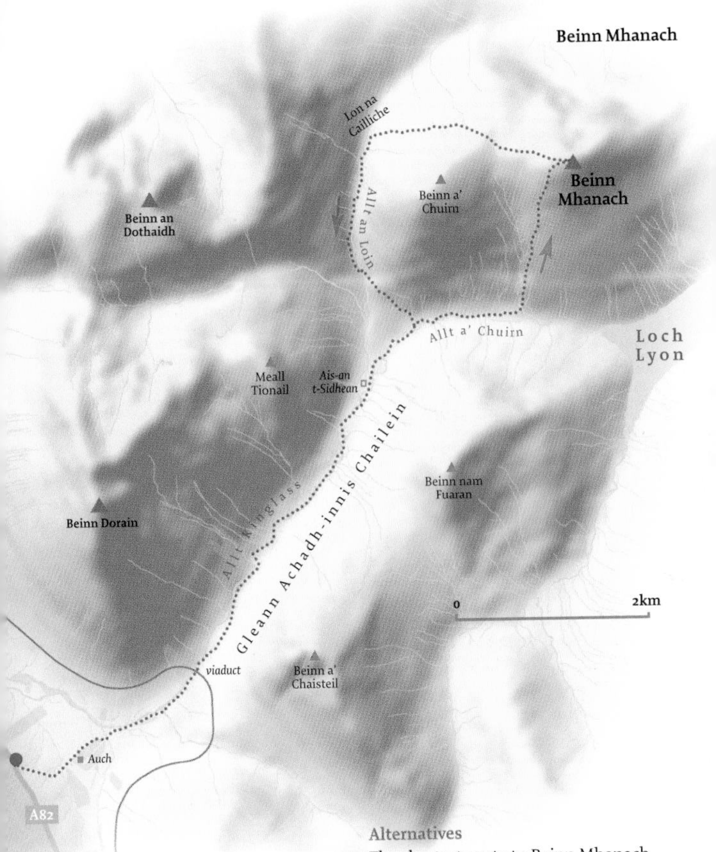

Beinn Mhanach

Beinn Mhanach

WNW across the usually wet hillside towards the bealach of Lon na Cailliche at NN354417. From here the glen of the Allt an Loin can be followed, soon picking up a track. Keep left at a fork to shortly rejoin the outward route for the return along the glen, with good views of the viaduct.

Alternatives

The shortest route to Beinn Mhanach is actually from Achallader Farm. This heads up Coire Achaladair to the bealach and then traverses under the eastern slopes of Beinn Achaladair to reach the Lon na Cailliche bealach, as mentioned as a possible addition to the Beinn Achaladair route.

Beinn Mhanach

Beinn Achaladair
Beinn a'Chreachain

Beinn Achaladair (1038m)
hill of the field by the hard water
Beinn a'Chreachain (1081m)
hill of the rocks

Distance **19km**
Ascent **1240m**
Time **6 – 8 hours**
Start point **OS Grid ref: NN322433**
Map **OS Explorer 377**
Public transport **Citylink buses pass along the nearby A82 en route to Fort William**
Terrain & hazards **mixed; some pathless sections and boggy areas, one very steep climb, faster going on some grassy sections of ridge**

The two most northern Munros of the Beinn Dorain group provide excellent ridge walking with superb views out over Rannoch Moor. The approach leads through the beautiful Caledonian pinewood of Crannach.

From the A82 it is a bumpy ride along the track to a parking area short of Achallader Farm. Continue on foot to the farm. Don't follow the 'Hill Path' sign; instead go left through a gate signed for Gorton. Follow the grassy track and ford the Allt Ur; you can usually keep your boots dry here, but in spate conditions there is a bridge 600m upstream. At the next fork stay on the track to cross the bridge over the Water of Tulla. The ruins

of Tom nan Grodh farm are ahead – stay on the main track by turning right. Around 2km further on leave the track to head right and cross the river once again on a rickety wooden footbridge.

The route now enters the Crannach pinewood – a magnificent relic of the ancient Caledonian Forest that once covered the Highlands; the granny pines are mixed with younger birches and hazel. The path keeps left, leading up away from the river before petering out in boggy ground. Head ESE to reach the top corner of a fenced area enclosing lush regenerated woodland. From here continue south to a gate and tunnel under the railway. Watching your head, pass under the West Highland Line and continue up the path beside a deer fence, ignoring the two stiles, and staying close to the cascading burn as it leads towards Coire an Lochain; Beinn Achaladair looks magnificent above the pines. Once in the corrie find a good place to cross and then aim southeast up the open slope to the left of the cliffs that bar the corrie headwall. Soon Lochan a'Chreachain, sheltered by the crags, comes into view with Rannoch Moor stretching away behind. Reach the ridge at 900m and bear right to follow the ridge southwest towards the summit.

At 1081m Beinn a'Chreachain is the highest peak in the Beinn Dorain range.

The views are very extensive, with Ben Nevis prominent across the great flatness of the moor. To the southeast Ben Lawers is the dominant peak in the distance. Descend west to the bealach with Meall Buidhe and stay on the ridge rather than be tempted by the contouring path to the left which peters out. The ridge descends to the Bealach an Aoghlain with a steep slope ahead. This is negotiated with the help of a path which begins slightly to the right and finds a reasonable way up. The

summit of Beinn Achaladair is perched right on the edge of high cliffs and has even better views, with the summits of the Black Mount rising above Loch Tulla and the peaks of Glencoe beyond.

Continue along the ridge which curves sinuously onwards to the bealach above Coire Daingean. From here a path descends north over rough ground. Eventually the route follows the east side of the burn below waterfalls before switching to the west bank after a steep section. The going can be very wet as the path descends along Coire Achaladair. Keep left of a fence and cross the railway bridge, continuing to the farmyard and car park beyond.

Alternatives

These two peaks are almost invariably climbed via the route described. It is possible for fit walkers to continue over Beinn an Dothaidh and Beinn Dorain if not returning to Achallader Farm. Perhaps a more practical extension is to detour to take in the solitary Munro of Beinn Mhanach by traversing round the east slope of Beinn Achaladair from the final bealach, returning the same way.

Above Coire an Lochain on Beinn a'Chreachain

Stob Ghabhar
Stob a'Choire Odhair

Stob Ghabhar (1090m) *goat peak*
Stob a'Choire Odhair (945m) *peak of the
dappled corrie*

Distance **16km**
Ascent **1190m**
Time **8 – 9 hours**
Start point **OS Grid ref: NN270418**
Map **OS Explorer 377**
Terrain & hazards **rough mountain route;
includes an extremely steep and loose
ascent over broken rocks and scree; above
there is a narrow but straightforward
section of ridge; the section by the
waterfall on the descent is badly eroded**

**The finest of the Black Mount peaks, Stob
Ghabhar is a steep and complex
mountain with great character; seen
across Rannoch Moor with its lower
neighbour Stob a'Choire Odhair it makes
one of the classic postcard views of
Scotland. Some of the secrets of its ridges
and corries are revealed on this rough
day's hillwalking with fabulous views.**

This route starts from Victoria Bridge at
the west end of Loch Tulla, 1km beyond the
Inveroran Hotel on the minor road from
Bridge of Orchy. There is a parking area
approximately 300m before the bridge on
the left. The bridge is part of the West
Highland Way; cross it but turn left just
before Forest Lodge along a track signed for
'Loch Etive by Glen Kinglass'.

Pass the hut at Clashgour – this may

look like a small toolshed, but it was once
the local schoolhouse; it is now owned by
the Glasgow University Mountaineering
Club. Don't cross the Allt Toaig but
instead turn right to follow it upstream.
The path leads up into Coire Toaig,
gaining height across the hillside opposite
slabby crags and a waterfall. Cross the Allt
Caolain Duibh and take the stalkers' path
on the right to climb northeast. The path
zigzags steeply upwards and peters out;
continue up gentler slopes to reach the
cairn of Stob a'Choire Odhair. The vast
watery expanse of Rannoch Moor looks
superb to the northeast.

From the summit aim west down the
broad ridge to the bealach at 668m. Keep
left on up the ridge at a faint fork, and
after another 300m leave the path and
start climbing directly up the slope to the
south, avoiding the temptation to
continue contouring the slopes into
Coirein Lochain. This part of the route is
extremely steep and tough; care is needed
to find the best line, avoiding the worst of
the scree and loose rocks. Reaching the
ridge of the Aonach Eagach tends to be a
bit of a relief. This is a superb ridge,
narrow for a time, but it has none of the
difficulties of its famous Glencoe
namesake. Follow it to the right, crossing
a notch and up a rocky section before it
curves round and picks up a line of
fenceposts to reach the summit of Stob

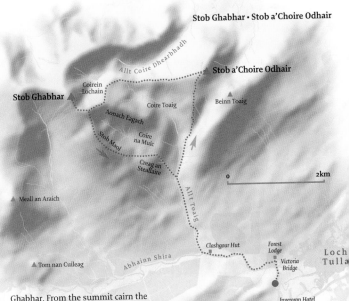

Stob a'Choire Odhair

Stob Ghabhar

Coirein
Lochain

Coire Toaig

Aonach Eagach

Coire
na Muic

Stob Maol

Creag an
Steallaire

▲ Meall an Araich

Allt Coire Dhearbhadh

Beinn Toaig

Allt Toaig

0   2km

Clashgour Hut

Forest
Lodge

Victoria
Bridge

Loch
Tulla

▲ Tom nan Cuileag

Abhainn Shira

Inveroran Hotel

Ghabhar. From the summit cairn the craggy northeast face plunges into Coirein Lochain far below.

Begin the descent by retracing your steps for 500m to a cairn and then forking to the right to follow the Stob Maol ridge SSE. The broad ridge is easier going; keep the steep ground on your left, eventually aiming east to reach the burn flowing from Coire na Muic. Cross this and keep to the far bank, descending past Creag an Steallaire (the Crags of the Falls); the steep path is badly eroded and requires great care. Once down on easier ground, continue by the burn to its junction with the Allt Toaig; cross this in its ravine to rejoin the outward path – this could be a problem in spate. Turn right along the path to return to Victoria Bridge.

Alternatives

The descent by the waterfall and the crossing of the Allt Toaig could be avoided by continuing the descent southwards to the former farm at Clashgour.

The classic longer day in these hills is the Clachlet Traverse of four Munros, a linear route linking the old inns at Inveroran and the Kingshouse. After climbing the hills above as described, this route continues along the ridges to the Bealach Fuar-chathaidh and up onto the summit of Clach Leathad. After following the ridge to Creise the route heads back across to Meall a'Bhuiridh before dropping down to the Glencoe Mountain ski centre car park.

Loch Tulla and Stob Ghabhar

Glen Etive, Glen Coe, Kinlochleven and Duror

You don't have to be a Munro-bagger to appreciate that Glen Coe is something special. The drive north over the empty vastness of Rannoch Moor cannot fail to impress, and no matter how many times you have seen it before, the magnificent rocky pyramid of Buachaille Etive Mor – the sentinel of a landscape of unsurpassed rocky grandeur – dangerously tempts the gaze of speeding motorists.

Glencoe village nestles at the foot of the eponymous glen – a magnet for thousands of mountaineers, climbers and hillwalkers. As a result it can feel a little busy during the high season, but the village is ideally placed for access to the hills. Check out the riverside Red Squirrel Campsite (fires are allowed so you can kipper yourself as a necessary midge deterrent), the Hostelling Scotland hostel and its excellent independent neighbour. All three of these are just a short walk away from the Clachaig Inn, probably the best-known hillwalkers' pub in the country. With a commitment to real ale that few places can match, this legendary hostelry is packed to the rafters with baggers glowing from their conquests, and features regular live music as a break from tales of derring-do.

Kinlochleven

For walkers on a budget nowhere can match the range of accommodation options in Kinlochleven. The town was

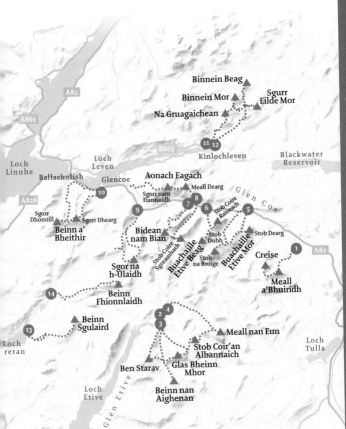

Binnein Beag

Binnein Mor
Sgurr
Eilde Mor

Na Gruagaichean

11 12
Kinlochleven

Blackwater
Reservoir

Loch
Leven

Loch
Linnhe

Ballachulish

Glencoe

Aonach Eagach

Meall Dearg

Glen Coe

Sgorr nam
Fiannaidh

10

7 **8**

6

Stob Coire
Raineach

9

Stob Dearg

5

Sgorr
Dhonuill

Sgorr Dhearg

Bidean
nam Bian

Beinn a'
Bheithir

Stob Coire
Sgreamhach

Buachaille
Etive Beag

Stob
Dubh

Buachaille
Etive Mor

Creise

1

A82

Stob
na Broige

Sgor na
h-Ulaidh

Meall
a'Bhuiridh

Beinn
Fhionnlaidh

14

2 **4**

3

Meall nan Eun

13

Beinn
Sgulaird

Stob Coir'an
Albannaich

Loch
Tulla

Loch
reran

Ben Starav

Glas Bheinn
Mhor

Loch
Etive

Glen Etive

Beinn nan
Aighenan

built to provide housing for the now defunct aluminium works and has stemmed its more recent economic decline by providing for the needs of West Highland Wayfarers and other walkers. The Ice Factor indoor adventure centre has been a key element in its recovery, providing the thrill of climbing on real ice in a giant refrigerated room as well as a large indoor climbing wall. Many walkers may be happier resting weary limbs in the sauna or enjoying a wood-fired pizza while watching beginners fall off the ice. There is also a useful gear shop here.

Try the excellent Blackwater Hostel where most rooms are small and ensuite, or the camping cabins at the Macdonald Hotel which also serves hungry-walker-sized bar meals. For local seafood you can do no better than find your way to the Loch Leven Seafood Café on the north side of the loch. Bolted onto a shellfish export business, the fare here is simply cooked at very fair prices – you can also buy cooked, raw or even live seafood at the adjoining shop if you are self-catering.

Glen Creran

Bypassed by the coastal road linking Oban with Fort William, Glen Creran is a glen for connoisseurs, its lower reaches clad in fine oakwoods, including the Glasdrum National Nature Reserve. At the head of the glen there are two Munros – amongst the least-visited south of the Great Glen – and few facilities. This is a place still very much as nature intended and only walkers can pass through from the head of the glen to Glencoe or Duror.

The Creagan Inn is the nearest hostelry but there are a string of places to stay and eat along the coastline. Perhaps the most attractive village is Port Appin, blessed by not one but two 'foodie' hotels, the Airds and the Pier House. If staying in the area the island of Lismore is well worth a visit on the passenger ferry; it well deserves its Gaelic name which translates as the Big Garden. If horticulture is your thing, Kinlochlaich has a well-stocked walled garden as well as extensive landscaped grounds and a respected nursery. Well seen from the coast road north is Castle Stalker, a medieval tower house; its setting on a tiny island has made it a mainstay of the postcard and calendar industry. It is open for limited days during the summer.

Sron na Creise

Creise
Meall a'Bhuiridh

Creise (1100m) *narrow*
Meall a'Bhuiridh (1108m)
rounded hill of the bellowing

Distance **10.5km**
Ascent **1120m**
Time **5 – 7 hours**
Start point **OS Grid ref: NN266525**
Map **OS Explorer 384**
Public transport **Citylink buses between Glasgow, Fort William, Skye and Inverness pass the start**
Terrain & hazards **a straightforward route with some boggy ground, large boulderfields on the climb up Meall a'Bhuiridh, and a steep rocky climb to the ridge of Creise**

Though little known by name, these mountains form a familiar sight on the drive north across Rannoch Moor; the view across the lochans beside the A82 being a classic. From the Glencoe ski centre Buachaille Etive Mor steals the scene; nonetheless, this is the quickest start point for this pair of Munros, with some fine ridgewalking once clear of the skiing bric-a-brac.

The Glencoe Mountain Ski Centre at White Corries is well signed along a minor road off the A82. The walk starts from the massive car park here and heads up the slope under the chairlift with the Allt na Giubhas to your right. It might be possible to catch a ride, but the slope is, in fact, relatively short and some might think ascending part of the hill with your legs swinging high above the heather defeats the purpose of hillwalking!

At the top of the slope aim to the right of the buildings and head west across a boggy area. Follow a minor burn at first, crossing some tributaries and aiming to reach the foot of Meall a'Bhuiridh's north ridge. Head SSW up onto the broad ridge, which becomes steeper and stonier higher up. The Creise ridge can be seen opposite above the Glas Choire. The slope eventually eases to reach the rocky summit of Meall a'Bhuiridh. Rannoch Moor stretches away to the east, and yes – that is the pointy cone of Schiehallion beyond. The West Highland railway line can be seen cutting across the southern edge of the moor, whilst looking west is the great ridge from Clach Leathad over Creise to Sron na Creise.

Follow the fine ridge WSW to a bealach and continue up rockier ground to gain a minor summit on the Clach Leathad/Creise ridge. Until 1981 Clach Leathad was regarded as the highest summit on this ridge – and hence the Munro. New surveys showed Creise to deserve the honour – so now walkers head to the right; enough for some to wonder at the sanity of Munro-bagging! If returning to the ski centre it is best to retrace your steps back over Meall a'Bhuiridh.

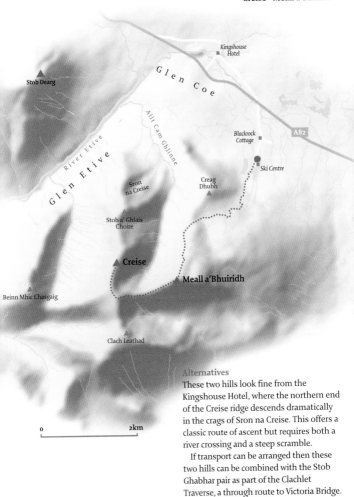

Kingshouse Hotel

G l e n   C o e

Stob Dearg

Allt Cam Ghlinne

River Etive

G l e n   E t i v e

Blackrock Cottage

A82

Ski Centre

Sron na Creise

Creag Dhubh

Stob a' Ghlais Choire

Creise

Meall a'Bhuiridh

Beinn Mhic Chasgaig

Clach Leathad

0 _____ 2km

Alternatives

These two hills look fine from the Kingshouse Hotel, where the northern end of the Creise ridge descends dramatically in the crags of Sron na Creise. This offers a classic route of ascent but requires both a river crossing and a steep scramble.

If transport can be arranged then these two hills can be combined with the Stob Ghabhar pair as part of the Clachlet Traverse, a through route to Victoria Bridge.

2

Ben Starav
Glas Bheinn Mhor

Ben Starav (1078m) *hill of the rustling noise*
Glas Bheinn Mhor (997m) *big grey hill*

Distance 16km
Ascent 1390m
Time 7 – 9 hours
Start point OS Grid ref: NN137468
Maps OS Explorer 377 and 384
Terrain & hazards fairly tough walk with
steep and rocky sections, easy scrambling
and boggy ground lower down

Ben Starav is a real brute of a Munro,
rising steep and impressive directly from
sea level at the shores of Loch Etive. The
direct ascent is a test of fitness, but
Starav has more surprises in store as a
fine rocky arête leads the way from the
summit towards Glas Bheinn Mhor.

Take the winding single-track road
down Glen Etive; there is a rough parking
area just east of the start of the track to
Coileitir. Begin down this track (SP: Hill
path), crossing the bridge over the
attractive River Etive to reach the building
at Coileitir. Follow the new path which
detours around the back of the building
before rejoining the track and crossing a
burn to reach the more substantial Allt
Mheuran. Head upstream to a bridge;
cross and then continue up the west bank
on a sodden path. Leave this after 500m to
head southwest and begin the climb up
the north ridge of Ben Starav; there is a
vague path in places. The slope eases

briefly before the ridge becomes stonier,
better defined and drier underfoot; the
ascent is helped by a clearer path. At
approximately 800m another ridge joins
from the northwest; continue up the
combined ridge as it undulates and then
narrows for the final pull to the summit.
It is quite a relief to reach the decaying
trig point at the summit. As the highest
Munro in the local area, there are
sensational views of Loch Etive, backed by
the pointed peaks of Ben Cruachan.

From the summit head to the southeast
summit at 1068m, keeping the cliffs on
your left. The route now drops steeply
onto an elegant rocky arête which leads
out to Stob Coire Dheirg. The crest
provides easy scrambling; any problems
can be avoided using a bypass on the
right. From Stob Coire Dheirg, do not be
led astray by the obvious north ridge but
instead aim ESE at first to find the east
ridge which descends more easily to
Bealachan Lochain Ghaineamhaich –
surely a test for any Gaelic spelling bee.

Unless adding Beinn nan Aighenan to
the day, continue east up the ridge over
Meall nan Tri Tighearnan. A dip and final
climb leads to Glas Bheinn Mhor – a
shapely peak, though somewhat
overshadowed by Ben Starav.

Continue along the ridge to the bealach
at 738m before descending northwest into
the glen, keeping to the right of the burn.

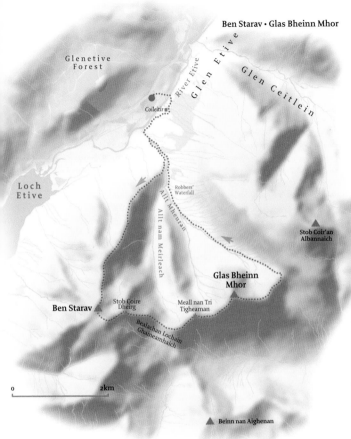

There is a path, but the going can be wet. Eventually the Eas nam Meirleach or Robbers' Waterfall comes into view; continue on the east bank across some very boggy terrain to reach the footbridge crossed near the start of the day. From here, retrace your steps to the start.

Alternatives

To include Beinn nan Aighenan in this route, detour from the Bealachan Lochain Ghaineamhaich; see following pages. Another option for the very fit is to continue the route from the final bealach by climbing onto Stob Coir' an Albannaich.

Glas Bheinn Mhor and Ben Starav

Beinn nan Aighenan

Beinn nan Aighenan (957m) *hill of the hinds*

Distance **16km**

Ascent **1320m**

Time **7 – 9 hours**

Start point **OS Grid ref: NN137468**

Maps **OS Explorer 377 and 384**

Terrain & hazards **rough and rocky hill path**

Beinn nan Aighenan is the forgotten Munro of the Starav range, being hidden away from Glen Etive by an intervening ridge. Although it can be included with an ascent of Ben Starav and its neighbours, that makes a very long day and many end up leaving it for an ascent on its own.

Parking in the lower reaches of Glen Etive can be problematic when busy. There is a small rough parking area on the right just before the start of the track to Coileitir. If this is full, look for a suitable section of grassy verge, taking care not to block any passing places. There are superb views of Ben Starav and Glas Bheinn Mhor. Head down the Coileitir track, signed 'Hill path', and soon cross a bridge over the picturesque River Etive. Bear right at a junction to reach a locked gate just short of Coileitir. This part of the route lies on an ancient droving route and used to pass in front of the cottage. However, following renovations to the building, the path has now been diverted up around the back. Turn left and keep the fence on your right to head up across boggy ground before dropping back down to rejoin the original track beyond Coileitir.

This track soon narrows to a path which runs close to the River Etive and then swings left alongside the Allt Mheuran. Cross a footbridge and continue up the far bank. At a fork take the higher route; the lower path ends up traversing across a very steep eroded slope above a gorge. Ignore a faint path bearing directly for Ben Starav and continue up the glen.

The route is boggy underfoot but there are great views of the Eas nam Meirleach or Robbers' Waterfall to compensate. The path soon crosses a tributary of the Allt nam Meirleach flowing down from Coire an Fhir-leith. After this the Meirleach flows through a succession of box canyons and care is needed in places (on the return it is natural to take a higher path which is further from the rim). The path follows a clear route as it climbs steeply to the Bealachan Lochain Ghaineamhaich at the head of the glen.

This is the low point of the ridge between Ben Starav on the right and Glas Bheinn Mhor to the left. Beinn nan Aighenan is ahead, but there is a drop of 150m before the ascent begins. Take the lower of the two small paths heading diagonally left down the far side of the bealach bearing southeast. This route is deceptive as Beinn nan Aighenan looks very close at first as much of the intervening drop is hidden from view. The path winds its way down rocky, slabby slopes to reach the low point.

The climb up the ridge beyond is rocky

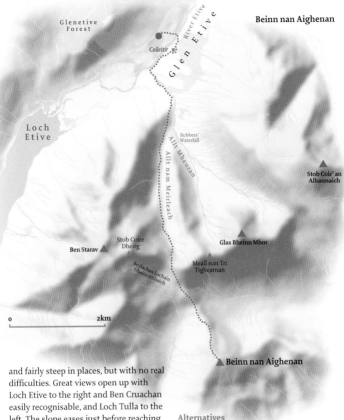

Glenetive
Forest

Beinn nan Aighenan

River Etive

Coileitir

Glen Etive

Loch
Etive

Robbers'
Waterfall

Allt Mheuran

Allt nam Meirleach

Stob Coir' an
Albannaich

Ben Starav

Stob Coire
Dheirg

Glas Bheinn Mhor

Meall nan Tri
Tighearnan

Bealachan Lochain
Ghaineamhaich

Beinn nan Aighenan

0   2km

and fairly steep in places, but with no real
difficulties. Great views open up with
Loch Etive to the right and Ben Cruachan
easily recognisable, and Loch Tulla to the
left. The slope eases just before reaching
the summit cairn.

The quickest return route is to retrace
your steps back to Glen Etive over the
Bealachan Lochain Ghaineamhaich.
However, from the bealach you could opt
to take in either or both of the Munros –
Ben Starav and Glas Bheinn Mhor – along
the ridge on either side.

Alternatives

A much longer approach is possible from
Victoria Bridge near Loch Tulla. Follow the
old path past Loch Dochard and over
moorland before crossing the River
Kinglass. The eastern slopes of Beinn nan
Aighenan rise very steeply ahead from
here, the gradient lessening a little if you
head further round to the left.

On Beinn nan Aighenan

4

Stob Coir'an Albannaich
Meall nan Eun

Stob Coir'an Albannaich (1044m)
peak of the Scotsman's corrie
Meall nan Eun (928m)
rounded hill of the birds

Distance **18km**
Ascent **1330m**
Time **7 – 9 hours**
Start point **OS Grid ref: NN137468**
Maps **OS Explorer 377 and 384**
Terrain & hazards **boggy approach, two descents down broken rocky slopes require navigational care**

Stob Coir'an Albannaich is often overlooked, but its fine pointed summit atop a steep crag has great character. Neighbouring Meall nan Eun contrasts as a broad dome, though ringed by precipitous slopes. This circuit gives a quiet alternative to the hordes which can throng the nearby peaks of Glencoe.

The start point is the same as for Ben Starav, a small parking area just east of the start of the track leading to Coileitir. Begin along the track (SP Hill Path), crossing the bridge over the River Etive before turning right and passing around the building at Coileitir on a boggy detour path. Although you can head diagonally across the relatively flat terrain to the Allt nam Meirleach, the intervening ground is often waterlogged and will ensure wet feet for the rest of the walk. Instead keep alongside the River Etive and then left beside the Allt nam Meirleach, ignoring the bridge and continuing on a faint path – it's still very boggy though. The Robber's Waterfall or Eas nam Meirleach can be seen above the confluence of the Allt nam Meirleach and the Allt Mheuran. Carry on upstream; the going gets easier after the route climbs above the small gorge, and higher up there are good views across to Ben Starav and the conical peak of Glas Bheinn Mhor. Continue to reach the bealach between Glas Bheinn Mhor and Stob Coir'an Albannaich.

Climb steeply north to gain the flat shoulder above and then detour around to the left to avoid a depression, before climbing to the ridge. Suddenly the dramatic side of the mountain is revealed as the ground falls away into the deep, slabby corries of the north face. Follow the rim of these cliffs to the right to reach the summit of Stob Coir'an Albannaich; there are two cairns offering a fantastic view of the Glencoe peaks.

The section between the two Munros can pose navigation problems in poor conditions. Start out down the initially steep east ridge until it starts to level off. Now it is necessary to aim north, taking care to find the correct rake that will bring you down to the bealach without being barred by cliffs. The first rake is just in front of a rocky knobble; continue a short way to a second rake which has a tiny cairn

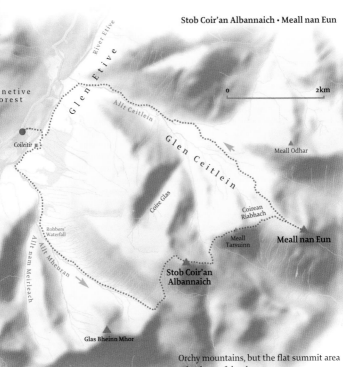

and a faint path heading down it. Start out on slabs before bearing slightly left further down to follow the grassy gully.

From here Meall Tarsuinn must be climbed before the second Munro can be tackled. A path winds down the far side avoiding some steep slabs. The final section up to the dome-like top of Meall nan Eun is straightforward. There are views over Loch Tulla to the Bridge of

Orchy mountains, but the flat summit area robs them of depth.

To start the descent aim northwest back over the plateau and head down the steep slopes into Coirean Riabhach. Broken crags make route finding difficult and care is needed to find a safe line. Further down the gradient eases but the ground becomes rough and tussocky as you aim for the Allt Ceitlein. Follow the muddy path on the north bank until it joins a track in Glen Etive. Bear left along it and then turn right at the next junction to cross the bridge over the Etive and return to the start.

Buachaille Etive Mor

5

Buachaille Etive Mor: Stob Dearg Stob na Broige

Stob Dearg (1022m) *red peak*
Stob na Broige (956m) *peak of the shoe*

Distance **13km**
Ascent **1100m**
Time **6 – 8 hours**
Start point **OS Grid ref: NN221563**
Map **OS Explorer 384**
Public transport **Citylink buses between Glasgow, Fort William, Skye and Inverness pass the start**
Terrain & hazards **steep scree and loose rocks on the scrambly ascent in Coire na Tulaich; the descent is little better, and can be slippery in the wet, care is needed**

Buachaille Etive Mor is probably the most photographed hill in Scotland. Resembling every child's drawing of a mountain, Stob Dearg, its main summit, is a great pyramid of rock whose height is emphasised by the flatness of Rannoch Moor at its base. Appearances are deceptive, however, as other viewpoints reveal that the Buachaille actually takes the form of a long ridge with several separate summits; their traverse is a hillwalking classic.

To anyone passing along the A82, Stob Dearg appears quite unclimbable at first glance. The usual route leads up Coire na Tulaich, a corrie with a headwall of steep scree. In winter this is a notorious blackspot for avalanches and there have been several fatal accidents involving hillwalkers. As it faces north the corrie holds snow late, the slopes are very steep and often iced, usually with a cornice at the top. The usual rules with all winter hill ascents apply even more so here – do not attempt it when there is snow lying unless you have a high level of winter skills and are equipped with crampons, ice-axe and awareness of the current avalanche risk.

The start is from the busy lay-by at Altnafeadh. Follow the track down to a footbridge and bear right on the far side to pass Lagangarbh hut. The SMC hut is famous for a spot of rebellious redecorating undertaken in the style of Jackson Pollock by the young Dougal Haston (later one of the first Brits to summit Everest), enraging the more staid members of the SMC. Continue to a fork and branch right, climbing up and crossing the Allt Coire na Tulaich.

Now climbing to the back of the corrie, the route becomes increasingly steep with the last section out on loose scree, although there is a faint path. The sudden arrival at the ridge is usually a relief. Bear left and climb up the fairly wide and boulder strewn ridge towards the summit.

Stob Dearg is the highest of the two

Glen Etive, Glen Coe, Kinlochleven and Duror

Stob Mhic
Mhatuin

Glen Coe

Altnafeadh

Bei
Chru

A82

River Coupall

Stob Coire
Raineach

Lairig Gartain

Coire na
Tulaich

Buachaille Etive Beag

Stob Dearg

Stob Dubh

Coire
Cloiche
Finne

Coire
Altruim

Stob na
Doire

Stob na Broige

Stob
Coire
Altruim

Glen Etive

Buachaille Etive Mor

River Etive

Stob a' Ghlais
Choire

Creise

Beinn Mhic
Chasgaig

0   2km

Munros on the Buachaille at 1022m. The ground falls away precipitously from here and in the right conditions, the mountain casts a massive triangular shadow onto Rannoch Moor. Return along the ridge and continue following it as it ascends slightly to reach a long level section, before a final climb up to Stob na Doire. Many walkers are surprised to find this isn't a Munro as it certainly feels like it could be! Care is needed with navigation at this point as the lie of the ground can lead onto the southeast spur when visibility is poor; keep to the main ridge which drops to a lower bealach before climbing over to Stob Coire Altruim and then continuing more gradually to reach Stob na Broige, which really is the second Munro of the ridge. Its promotion in 1997 has meant many more

hillwalkers complete the whole of this great ridge walk rather than just 'bagging' Stob Dearg.

Return to the low bealach before Stob na Doire and then descend a very steep path north into Coire Altruim. The slopes are a mix of slippery grass with some loose rock and the path is badly eroded, so take care. Once at the foot of the glen cross the River Coupall and follow the path northeast through the Lairig Gartain. This eventually emerges on the A82; all that remains now is a rather unpleasant 1km walk along the verge by the speeding traffic to return to Altnafeadh. Whenever you drive over Rannoch Moor in future you'll have the satisfaction of knowing you have stood at the top of that amazing pyramid of rock.

Summit of Buachaille Etive Mor

6

Buachaille Etive Beag: Stob Dubh Stob Coire Raineach

Stob Dubh (956m) *dark peak*
Stob Coire Raineach (925m)
peak of the bracken corrie

Distance **8km**
Ascent **900m**
Time **5 – 6 hours**
Start point **OS Grid ref: NN188563**
Map **OS Explorer 384**
Public transport **Citylink buses between Glasgow, Fort William, Skye and Inverness pass the start**
Terrain & Hazards **good path to the bealach, then fairly straightforward ridge**

Buachaille Etive Beag is rather overshadowed by the magnificent appearance of its neighbour at the head of Glencoe. Nonetheless it offers a wonderful shorter ridge traverse in its own right and when seen from Glen Etive is more than a match for its big Buachaille brother.

Start from the parking area opposite the cairn on the A82. From here Buachaille Etive Beag doesn't show her best side; begin by following the signed right of way through the Lairig Eilde. After 0.75km keep an eye out for a path to the left and turn up this. The National

Trust for Scotland, the local landowner, has recently undertaken extensive repairs to the once boggy footpath here.

The route continues diagonally up the hillside, aiming for the Mam Buidhe, the lowest point on the ridge. Don't be tempted to shortcut directly to the first Munro as the slopes are steeper than they look as well as loose and unpleasant. From the bealach, head left along the ridge and climb the bouldery slopes up to Stob Coire Raineach. This tiny summit plateau gives a wonderful grandstand view of the Aonach Eagach and over Rannoch Moor.

Return to the bealach and now ascend the ridge towards Stob Dubh. The climb levels out at 900m; the ridge then narrows to give an enjoyable traverse before the final curving ascent. The first cairn is the true summit of Stob Dubh, the higher of the wee Buachaille's two Munros. Do make the detour to the cairn at the far end of the ridge, however, as it gives an unbeatable view down Glen Etive, with Ben Starav looming massively over the loch. To return, head back to the bealach and retrace the outward route.

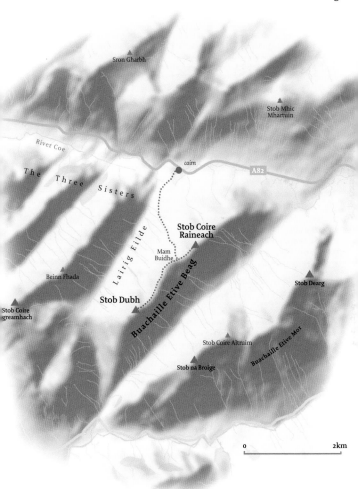

Sron Gharbh

Stob Mhic
Mhartuin

River Coe

The Three Sisters

cairn

A82

Lairig Eilde

**Stob Coire
Raineach**

Mam
Buidhe

Beinn Fhada

Buachaille Etive Beag

Stob Coire
greamhach

Stob Dubh

Stob Dearg

Stob Coire Altruim

Buachaille Etive Mor

Stob na Broige

0   2km

7

Bidean nam Bian
Stob Coire Sgreamhach

Bidean nam Bian (1150m)
peak of the mountains
Stob Coire Sgreamhach (1072m)
peak of the horrible corrie

Distance **11km**
Ascent **1315m**
Time **7 – 8 hours**
Start point **OS Grid ref: NN170569**
Map **OS Explorer 384**
Public transport **Citylink buses between Glasgow, Fort William, Skye and Inverness pass the start**
Terrain & hazards **steep, rocky and complex terrain; the descent into Coire Gabhail is down very steep eroded scree and often holds snow well into summer**

The Three Sisters are familiar from countless postcards and calendars, three blunt rocky buttresses which have been truncated by the ice-carved gash of Glen Coe. The summit of the great mountain of which they are a part hides behind them, but the massif of Bidean nam Bian ranks amongst the finest and most complex Scottish mountains.

Start from the large car park halfway up Glen Coe. From here, the Three Sisters look very impressive and the car park is a popular stopping point for coaches as well as those tackling the walk into the Lost Valley – there's often a bagpiper here in the high season. Begin the walk by taking the path down towards the old

track at the bottom of the glen – a part of General Wade's military road. Turn right along the track briefly before bearing left onto a path which leads to a footbridge over the River Coe.

Keep on the path as it climbs steadily into Coire nan Lochan, crossing a straightforward rocky section and keeping to the left of the burn. The path now climbs steeply up the side of the glen and the peak of Stob Coire nan Lochan rears prominently ahead. Near the top of Coire nan Lochan a waterfall cascades down a narrow box canyon; from this point the path climbs rougher scree up to the left to exit from the Coire before ascending the east ridge of Stob Coire nan Lochan with some easy scrambling. Alternatively the scree can be avoided by leaving the path just below the box canyon waterfall, crossing the burn and climbing up the grassy ground to the west and then aiming southwest into the upper coire. Towering above are the Pinnacle and South Buttresses of Stob Coire nan Lochan. Bear northwest to reach the foot of Stob Coire nan Lochan's north ridge and then follow this towards the summit, with spectacular views down the buttresses on the left. The two routes rejoin at Stob Coire nan Lochan; at 1115 metres high and with a fine outline many walkers feel that this Top should really be classed as a Munro in its own right.

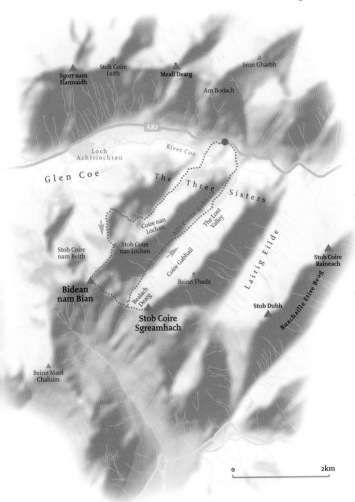

Sgorr nam Fiannaidh

Stob Coire Leith

Meall Dearg

Sron Gharbh

Am Bodach

A82

River Coe

Loch Achtriochtan

Glen Coe

The Three Sisters

Coire nan Lochan

Allt Coire Gabhail

The Lost Valley

Lairig Eilde

Stob Coire nam Beith

Stob Coire nan Lochan

Coire Gabhail

Stob Coire Raineach

Bidean nam Bian

Bealach Dearg

Beinn Fhada

Stob Dubh

Buachaille Etive Beag

Stob Coire Sgreamhach

Beinn Maol Chaluim

0   2km

119

Gently sloping scree leads down to a bealach from where a path keeps slightly to the left on the steeper section to reach the summit of Bidean nam Bian, the highest mountain in Argyll at 1150 metres. There are superlative views in all directions – Loch Etive can be seen to the southwest, with the sea and Mull beyond, whilst in the opposite direction Ben Nevis towers over the Aonach Eagach ridge.

Head along the southeast ridge towards the range's second Munro, Stob Coire Sgreamhach. This traverse is straightforward but with a spectacular outlook; the path crosses a couple of minor bumps before the final descent to Bealach Dearg. Beyond the path climbs again with a steep section on boulders to reach the summit of Stob Coire Sgreamhach, which was only promoted to Munro status in 1997. It is a great vantage point for the ridges of Buachaille Etive Beag and Buachaille Etive Mor as well as southwest to Ben Starav and Cruachan along Loch Etive.

Descents from Beinn Fhada are tricky to find as there are many cliffs unseen from above, so it is best to return to the Bealach Dearg before dropping steeply into Coire Gabhail. The upper part of this route has become a badly eroded scree slope; keep to the right side of the eroded gully at the top and a faint path avoids the worst sections. Further down the path improves greatly to head down the left side of the corrie, keeping above the stream before reaching the flat area known as the Lost Valley. Unseen from the floor of Glen Coe, this proved to be the perfect hiding place for cattle raiders and is a popular objective for a walk in its own right.

Pass the massive boulders to head down on the path out of the Lost Valley which is on the right-hand side on the lower flanks of Beinn Fhada. Follow a clear path which ascends a little before descending once more on sections of pitched footpath. There is one down scramble along a rake which can be avoided in descent by instead heading over the end of the boulder directly ahead. Beyond this obstacle, cross the burn using stones; on the far side the path continues down into Glen Coe. The river is crossed by a bridge over a ravine; continue through birchwoods and back to the car park.

Alternatives

Bidean nam Bian is such a complex mountain there are countless different routes and variants beside the one given here. One, suitable for confident scramblers, is the zigzag route which is on the east side of the middle sister, Gearr Aonach. The line of this can be clearly seen from the road further up Glencoe but is much harder to find on closer acquaintance. It begins from the top of a scree slope above lower Coire Gabhail and follows a series of rakes, the lower ones with small trees sprouting from them. The scrambling is modest and not very exposed if you find the right line – which is essential given the general steepness of this face. From the top of Gearr Aonach you can follow the ridge up to Stob Coire nam Lochan where the route described above can be joined.

A completely different route begins from the newly rebuilt parking area near the outflow of Loch Achtriochtan. A path begins here and climbs up amidst fine scenery into Coire nam Beitheach, with a little easy scrambling. From a confluence of burns you can either trace the left hand burn southeast into an upper corrie and find a route up the scree and boulders leading to the bealach between Stob Coire nam Lochan and Bidean nam Bian, or alternatively follow the other burn SSW at first and climb steeply up both grass and scree to gain the main ridge 500m west of Stob Coire nam Beith. If including the second Munro of Stob Coire Sgreamhach these routes are not so convenient, as you would either have to return over the summit of Bidean or follow the route down into Coire Gabhail, the latter leaving you faced with a long walk down Glencoe – including sections along the verge of the busy A82.

Slopes of Bidean nam Bian and Glen Coe

Aonach Eagach from Glen Coe

8

Aonach Eagach:
Meall Dearg
Sgorr nam Fiannaidh

Meall Dearg (953m) *rounded red hill*
Sgorr nam Fiannaidh (967m)
peak of the Fingalian warriors

Distance **9.5km**
Ascent **1080m**
Time **6 – 8 hours**
Start point **OS Grid ref: NN174567**
Map **OS Explorer 384**
Public transport **Citylink buses between Glasgow, Fort William, Skye and Inverness pass the start**
Terrain & hazards **hard, exposed scrambling along the ridge between Am Bodach and Stob Coire Leith – experience and a good head for heights is required; some walkers may prefer to accompany a friend with rockclimbing skills and a rope – or bring several spare pairs of pants!**

The very name of the Aonach Eagach strikes fear into many hillwalkers, but others will relish the thrilling and spectacular scrambling on the traverse of what is often claimed as the narrowest ridge on the mainland. The route links two Munros to make a day to be remembered long after the celebrations in the Clachaig have died down.

There is a small parking area on the north side of the A82, 300m west of the solitary house at Allt-na-Ruigh. If full, there is a larger car park a little way further west along the road. This walk ends near Glencoe village so transport may need to be arranged, or you could use the bus. Follow the initially rough path up the lower slopes of Am Bodach; higher up sections have been greatly improved. There are two variants; one heads up into Coire an Ruigh, emerging on the bealach northeast of Am Bodach and then along the ridge to the top. The second option is steeper and aims more directly up the steep spur to the top. From here the first real taste of the drama to come is revealed in a view of a rock pinnacle known as 'The Chancellor' below.

The first scrambling comes on the descent from Am Bodach, where there is a sloping, slabby cliff to tackle. Whilst not excessively steep and with plenty of holds, it can be slippery when wet. After this the ridge is narrow but fairly straightforward with a few short scrambly sections before the summit of Meall Dearg is reached. This was the last Munro to be climbed by the Reverend A E Robertson, the first man to complete the Munros back in 1901. On reaching the top he famously first kissed the cairn, and then his wife.

From Meall Dearg the ridge ahead looks very intimidating. There are no safe descent routes from the next section and several accidents have occurred when people have sought to leave the ridge to seek an alternative route. Initially there are several steep rocky chimneys and other short scrambling sections which must be climbed and descended; the ridge is very narrow in places, though with some wider sections. The trickiest part is near the end of the difficulties and is known as the 'Crazy Pinnacles'. Perhaps the most awkward move is right at the end where a very steep descent facing-in leads down onto an airy stance.

Once the Top of Stob Coire Leith is reached the scrambling is over and the ridge continues easily on a broad path to the second Munro, Sgorr nam Fiannaidh. This has a superb view of the lower reaches of Glen Coe.

Do not be tempted to descend the path above the Clachaig Gully; although it tempts some tired walkers it is in a very dangerous state and has become notorious as the scene of several fatalities. Looking up at the path from the Clachaig Inn it is clear where the dangers lie; lots of loose scree and rock on the edge of sheer drops. Instead take the longer but much more enjoyable route which continues along the ridge, passing a large cairn. After the Clachaig Gully path which heads left here, continue briefly along the ridge to two small cairns. Descend slightly northwest from here, following an initially indistinct path which becomes clearer before eventually meeting the main path to the Pap of Glencoe. Turn left here to follow this down to a track and emerge 1km east of Glencoe village.

Alternatives

If the phrase 'airy and exposed scrambling' brings you out in a rash it is possible to reach the summits of the two Munros without traversing the ridge. For Meall Dearg, start by the bridge over the Allt Gleann a' Chaolais on the B863 near Caolasnacon, just west of Kinlochleven, and head up the glen to the low bealach between Meall Dearg and the Corbett Garbh Bheinn. From here a rough ridge leads up to the summit of the Munro; return the same way.

Sgorr nam Fiannaidh can be reached by reversing the descent route given in the main description. Head up from Glencoe towards the Pap, but fork right before reaching the bealach. A path leads up to the ridge close to the summit; return the same way.

Glencoe

Meall Mor

Loch Leven

B863

Garbh
Bheinn

Pap of
Glencoe

**Sgorr nam
Fiannaidh**   Stob Coire
Leith   Crazy
Pinnacles   **Meall
Dearg**

Aonach Eagach   The Chancellor   Am
Bodach   Coire an
Ruigh

Glencoe
(lling Scotland)

Red Squirrel
Campsite

Clachaig Gully

er Coe

Signal
Rock   Clachaig Inn   Loch
Achtriochtan   Allt-na-Ruigh

A82   P a s s   o f   G l e n c o e

G l e n   C o e

Stob Coire
nan Lochan

Beinn Fhada

Bidean
nam Bian

0   2km

Aonach Eagach from Meall Dearg

9

Sgor na h-Ulaidh

Sgor na h-Ulaidh (994m) *peak of treasure*

Distance 16km
Ascent 1290m
Time 7 – 9 hours
Start point OS Grid ref: NN120563
Map OS Explorer 384
Public transport Citylink buses between Glasgow, Fort William, Skye and Inverness pass the start
Terrain & hazards some extremely steep ground on the ascent requires careful route finding

Out of sight from the Glencoe road, Sgor na h-Ulaidh is often out of mind – the forgotten Munro of the area. If you don't mind a very steep climb then this peak makes a superb hillwalk, especially if combined with the Corbett Meall Lighiche.

A short distance east of the bridge over the Allt na Muidhe on the A82 there is a car park. Sgor na h-Ulaidh cannot be seen from this spot; the ridge of Aonach Dubh a' Ghlinne is prominent and the more distant peak to the right is Meall Lighiche. Start by crossing the bridge (care with traffic) and turning left onto a track (SP Gleann Leac na Muidhe House). Follow this uphill; after 1km it crosses over the small gorge. Look back for a great view of the Aonach Eagach.

Pass a house and then a chalet, cottages and finally the farmhouse before passing to the right of a barn to continue up the glen. Climb a stile at the forestry plantation and continue along the path formed at the end of the track. To include the Corbett of Meall Lighiche in the walk, cross the river and the boggy ground beyond, climbing west to gain the start of the steep ridge which then leads south up to Creag Bhan. Bypass a large rocky knobble on the right and use a grassy gully to regain the ridge. The steep slopes ease as Creag Bhan is reached; continue to a line of fenceposts. From here detour to the right along a path close to the fenceposts to reach the summit of Meall Lighiche. Return to where you met the fenceposts and now follow them southeast to descend steeply to Bealach Easan, working your way around a few crags. (If omitting Meall Lighiche you would simply continue up the glen to reach this point.)

The bealach is a good place to examine the fearsome slopes opposite and try to pick the best line. The ascent from here requires careful route choice as it is easy to stray onto difficult ground. Head through a gate and bear right on the first part of the ascent, heading WSW to reach the shoulder of Corr na Beinne. Continue up steep grass, aiming slightly right to climb a broken area in a rock band before heading back left to tackle the final climb to Corr na Beinn. Reaching the ridge is a great relief; follow it east on a path, passing a false summit, to reach the true top right on the edge of the northern corries.

Sgor na h-Ulaidh is a fantastic viewpoint,

Glencoe

Sgorr nam
Fiannaidh

Glencoe
Independent
Hostel

Glencoe
(Hostelling Scotland)

Red Squirrel
Campsite

River Coe

Signal Rock

Clachaig Inn

Loch
Achtriochtan

A82

Glen Coe

Meall Mor

Allt na Muidhe

Gleann-leac
-na-Muidhe

Fionn Ghleann

Sgorr a'
Choise

Bidean
nam Bian

Creag
Bhan

Aonach Dubh a' Ghlinne

Meall an
Aodainn

Meall
Lighiche

Beinn Maol
Chaluim

Bealach
Easan

Stob an
Fhuarain

Corr na
Beinne

Sgor na
h-Ulaidh

Meall a'
Bhuiridh

Beinn Fhionnlaidh

0   2km

Aonach Dubh a'Ghlinne from Glen Coe

with Loch Etive well seen to the south and Ben Nevis rising behind dozens of lower peaks to the north. A great cleft in the crags splits the summit area; head around this before taking the path which leads down onto the notheast ridge. Zigzags ease the passage down steep rocky ground before the ridge rises to Stob an Fhuarain. From here aim north to reach the bealach at 798m on the Aonach Dubh a' Ghlinne ridge.

Descend directly into Gleann-leac-na-Muidhe from here, crossing scree higher up and steep grassy slopes lower down before picking up the stalkers' path in the glen. Follow this downstream; after 1km it rejoins the outward route – head for the gate leading to the track to the A82.

Alternatives

It is also possible to climb Sgor na h-Ulaidh from Invercharnan in Glen Etive. Take the forestry track up the glen of the Allt nan Gaoirean until it turns sharply to the right; from here follow a path ahead to the edge of the forest. Continue up the boggy open glen and up to the Bealach Clach nam Meirleach which lies between Sgor na h-Ulaidh and Meall a' Bhuiridh. From here follow the fenceposts at first, then a path up scree to the left before rejoining the posts as you climb up to the Munro summit.

10

Beinn a' Bheithir: Sgorr Dhearg Sgorr Dhonuill

Sgorr Dhearg (1024m) *red peak*
Sgorr Dhonuill (1001m) *Donald's peak*

Distance 15.5km
Ascent 1325m
Time 6 – 8 hours
Start point OS Grid ref: NN084584
Map OS Explorer 384
Public transport Citylink buses between
Glasgow, Fort William, Skye and
Inverness pass the start
Terrain & hazards start of climb is
pathless on steep heather and the
descent is muddy, but the ridge itself
gives excellent walking; rocky and
exposed to the summit of Sgorr Dhonuill

Beinn a' Bheithir rises grandly above the mouth of Loch Leven, living up to its dramatic name which means the Hill of the Thunderbolt. Though moated by dense forest plantations, the ridge itself offers excellent walking and the views stretch for miles of the western seaboard.

This route starts from Ballachulish; there is a large car park by the visitor centre and café. Ballachulish is famous for its slate; today the quarries are silent but the location by Loch Leven is as spectacular as ever. The eastern summit of Beinn a' Bheithir, Sgorr Bhan, forms an impressive backdrop to the village. Begin by walking along the road into the village; keep straight on onto Loanfern when the main road bends right beside a pub. Follow Loanfern until it crosses the river and immediately turn left on the far side to follow a lane past the school. Go through an iron gate on the right to take the boggy track which bears right through a field and past a stone wall. After the field the steep climb begins in earnest – head directly up the slope, carefully crossing the fence part way up to eventually emerge at a path running across the slope.

Turn right to follow the path more gently uphill, and then branch left at a fork to gain the Beinn Bhan ridge. There are views of Ballachulish Bridge and the narrows of Loch Leven. Head up the ridge which soon steepens; the path keeps to the slopes on the right. Leave the path just before it crosses a scree slope to regain the crest of the ridge. It leads to the Top of Sgorr Bhan; a graceful ridge now can be seen curving round to Sgorr Dhearg. This section is a delight, and the Munro summit at the far end is a superb spot to drink in the views, though there is little left of the trig point.

Descend WSW on a stony ridge down to the bealach at 760m. Follow the path up the far side; the slopes are grassy at first but become rockier with a very

Tom Meadhoin

Creag Bhreac

A82

A863

A828

Ballachulish Hotel

Loch Leven

A82

Visitor Centre

School

Ballachulish

River Laroch

Gleann a' Chaolais

Sgorr Dhonuill

Sgorr Dhearg

Sgorr Bhan

Beinn a' Bheithir

Gleann an Fhiodh

Sgorr a' Choise

0   2km

simple bit of scrambling in an exposed position just before the summit. The top of Sgorr Dhonuill is surprisingly spacious and is an even better viewpoint than Sgorr Dhearg – especially looking down Loch Linnhe to the islands of Lismore, Mull and even Scarba or Jura on a very clear day.

Return to the 760m bealach to begin the descent into the corrie to the north. Steep at first, it keeps fairly close to a line of fenceposts and avoids the crags; it is boggy though. As the slope eases and the first section of forestry is reached keep to the right of the posts, staying on the path until the edge of the forest rises across the hillside ahead. Ignore the start of the old, eroded descent path which is marked by a small cairn and enters the forest down a narrow clearing. There is a new, much better route a short distance further on, the start of which can be difficult to spot. Continue ahead, slightly uphill for a short way before slanting down into the trees and following the path down to eventually reach a forest track. Head across this and continue on a wide new path. At the next junction the route straight ahead leads to the Glenachulish forest car park, but to return to Ballachulish turn right. Follow the signs for St John's Church, ignoring a cycle route off to the left and other turnings on the right, and soon enough the A82 is reached near the church. Turn right and return to Ballachulish along the pavement beside the busy road, turning right at the sign for West Laroch to return through the village to the start.

Alternatives

Scramblers will prefer to begin the route by heading up the northeast ridge of Sgorr Bhan. This is a little loose and exposed in places but not difficult; when it narrows the way appears to be barred by rock steps but these can be avoided on the left before regaining the ridge.

It is also possible to continue along the ridge from Sgurr Dhonuill, making use of an alternative path through the forests below. However, the initial part of the descent into Coire Dearg is down very steep scree.

Beinn a' Bheithir from across Loch Leven

11

Binnein Mor
Na Gruagaichean

Binnein Mor (1130m) *big peak*
Na Gruagaichean (1056m) *the maidens*

Distance **15km**
Ascent **1140m**
Time **7 – 8 hours**
Start point **OS Grid ref: NN186630**
Map **OS Explorer 392**
Public transport **Citylink buses between Glasgow, Fort William, Skye and Inverness pass the start**
Terrain & hazards **paths for much of the way – not on the descent from Na Gruagaichean, steep ridges, mainly grassy with some rocky sections**

The Mamores give some of the best ridgewalking in Scotland. This superb circuit from Kinlochleven includes the highest, graceful Binnein Mor, combined with a traverse of the sharp twin summits of Na Gruagaichean.

This walk begins from the centre of Kinlochleven at the small car park beside St Paul's Church (signed 'Grey Mare's Tail' from the main road). Take the path from the car park, turning left at a T-junction and then right (red waymarkers). Stay right at the next junction, still following the markers; the path zigzags up the hill to reach open moorland.

Continue until a track is joined immediately east of the path to Sgor Eilde Beag, then take the stalkers' path which branches north at NN208634. Follow this,

soon crossing a burn and climbing around the southern flank of Sgor Eilde Beag. Follow the zigzags uphill; there is a branch path straight ahead that seems like a shortcut, but it peters out before the loch. At the top of the zigzag, ignore the path climbing to the left and instead follow the stalkers' path which flattens as it passes beneath the steep east face. From this vantage point, the isolated peak of Sgurr Eilde Mor looks formidable across Coire nan Lochan.

Take the path north to a junction; turn left here to follow another good stalkers' path which climbs across the north flank of Sgor Eilde Beag before doubling back to gain the ridge. A short detour left to Sgor Eilde Beag – a Top – is worthwhile for the views of Sgurr Eilde Mor. Otherwise head WNW up to point 1062m at a junction of ridges.

Follow the ridge running out towards Binnein Mor, seen backed by Ben Nevis and the Grey Corries. It drops briefly to a bealach before climbing to the summit, an airy perch with stunning views of the great mountain ranges in all directions. Looking down the steep cliffs, the outlier of Binnein Beag looks far too small to be a Munro.

Return to point 1062m and then follow the narrowing southwest ridge, soon climbing up to Na Gruagaichean, the second Munro of the day. The name

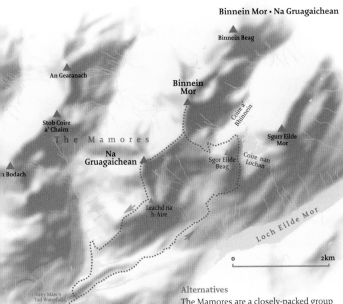

means 'The Maidens', a reference to the twin summits – the lower of the pair lies to the northwest across a very sharp drop. A quicker descent route leads along the south ridge of the main peak to Leachd na h-Aire which has good views down over Kinlochleven and Loch Leven. From here descend southwest down rough, pathless ground to eventually regain the track and then head back to either Mamore Lodge or the town.

Alternatives

The Mamores are a closely-packed group of Munros linked by ridges, so many different variations are possible. Descending from Binnein Mor to Binnein Beag is not recommended, but in the reverse direction the Sron a' Gharbh-Choire ridge gives a possible link route for competent scramblers on sometimes slippery and loose rocks.

More common is extending the walk along the main ridge from Na Gruagaichean. Cross the steep gap to the airy northwest summit and continue along the ridge to the bealach at 783m. From here there is a descent route into Coire na Ba, or you can continue along the main ridge to reach the next Munro, Stob Coire a' Chairn.

141

12

Sgurr Eilde Mor Binnein Beag

Sgurr Eilde Mor (1010m) *big peak of the hind*
Binnein Beag (943m) *small peak*

Distance **20km**
Ascent **1580m**
Time **8 – 10 hours**
Start point **OS Grid ref: NN188623**
Map **OS Explorer 392**
Public transport **Citylink buses between Glasgow, Fort William, Skye and Inverness pass the start**
Terrain & hazards **good on the long approach, boggy in places; the peaks are steep and stony with tough climbs**

Lying at the eastern extreme of the Mamores range these two Munros stand proudly apart. Their steep, scree-covered cones make for arduous climbs but also ensure they have spectacular views.

Starting from the car park by St Paul's Church in Kinlochleven, take the waymarked path into the woods. Go left almost immediately at a T-junction, then right by a red marker post. From here, keep to the main path, ignoring all branches and a path off to the left. There are good views back down Loch Leven. At another red marker post, keep right. The path – eroded in places – zigzags up onto the moorland. Join a vehicle track and turn left briefly before going right onto a stalkers' path at NN208634. This leads uphill, crossing a burn and traversing the steep flanks of Sgor Eilde Beag. The Blackwater Reservoir and dam can be seen behind Loch Eilde Mor. Keep on the main path as it turns sharp left at a zigzag, marked with a small cairn – the path which appears to continue ahead here soon peters out.

After gaining height the path contours round the east slopes of Sgor Eilde Beag, keeping high above the loch; the screes of Sgurr Eilde Mor look rather intimidating across the lochan. Binnein Beag is the first objective, however, so when a crossroads of paths is reached keep straight on, dropping slightly downhill and bending left before descending into the Coire a' Bhinnein via a series of zigzags. After crossing the burn head downstream briefly before a path on the left soon climbs again.

The ground is boggy in places as the path runs across the hillsides to reach the lochan at the bealach between Binnein Mor and Binnein Beag. Take the faint path on the near side of this lochan; the ascent of the south ridge soon begins. The route is littered with boulders and scree – there is a brief scramble which can be avoided. From the summit at 943m, Ben Nevis and the Grey Corries close the northern horizon but just as impressive is looking back down the way you just came. The lochan looks very far below with Binnein Mor towering impressively beyond.

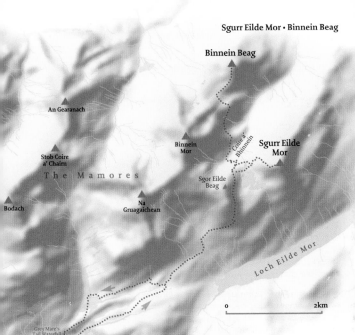

Return to the bealach and retrace your steps across the Coire a' Bhinnein valley and up the zigzag path opposite.

Before you reach the crossroads again, strike off left, aiming for the west ridge of Sgurr Eilde Mor. The path from the junction is picked up just below the first scree slope. Follow this to the left where it begins an ascent of the northwest face.

Higher up the crest of the ridge is gained via a steep and eroded scree slope. The summit of Sgurr Eilde Mor is now just a short distance away and reveals a breathtaking view across the lochan to the main Mamores ridge.

Retrace your route down the hill and follow the path to the crossroads mentioned earlier. Turn left here to begin the long walk back. If returning to Kinlochleven the route can be varied slightly by staying on the Loch Eilde Mor track until NN198633. From here a path can be followed back to the town, with a chance to visit the impressive Grey Mare's Tail waterfall.

Binnein Mor

13

Beinn Sgulaird

Beinn Sgulaird (937m) *hat-shaped hill*

Distance **13km**

Ascent **1220m**

Time **6 – 8 hours**

Start point **OS Grid ref: NN008451**

Maps **OS Explorer 377 and 384**

Terrain & hazards **sustained and strenuous ascent to reach the ridge; whilst the traverse that follows is very rocky it does not present any real difficulties**

The isolated position of Beinn Sgulaird on the west coast of Argyll makes it perhaps the most stunning viewpoint in this part of Scotland. The steep slopes give great depth to a wonderful prospect over the Firth of Lorne and the islands of Lismore and Mull, so save this strenuous ascent for a fine day.

The most scenic approach starts just northeast of Druimavuic where there is a small lay-by with an electronic road sign. Just west of this point, two tracks leave the road near the bend. Take the first track – the second one is the entrance to Druimavuic Gardens. Climb through the trees at first and through a gate to continue on the main track as it zigzags up the open slope above. Look out for a small cairn and a grassy path leading up the ridge to the left.

The lip of a deep cleft in the ridge is reached at point 488m. A small path runs left along the top of the cleft to a gap where a zigzag path eases the way down. Cross a fence and continue up the straightforward ridge. Soon Ben Cruachan can be seen peeping over a pass to the south whilst a glance over your shoulder reveals Loch Creran with Lismore and the rugged hills of Morvern and Ben More on Mull beyond. From the minor summit at 863m the top of Beinn Sgulaird looks to be within easy reach. However, the underfoot conditions make for very rough going and the route along the ridge takes longer than you might anticipate. Descend to a bealach over boulders and scree, aided by a path on the right of the ridge and then climb the dome of Meall Garbh. A faint path picks its way between rocky outcrops and smooth slabs to reach a cairn with good views of Beinn Sgulaird's summit. A steep and rocky descent leads to a second bealach and then the final climb up the south ridge. This section is excellent with a little very easy scrambling near the top where the path leads slightly left off the ridge. The views on a good day are unparalleled; Ben Nevis and the Glencoe peaks are easy to pick out as are the peaks of Cruachan which loom above Loch Etive. The easiest – especially for the knees – return route is to retrace your steps, enjoying the fabulous views ahead out over the sea. At the cleft below point 488m you can avoid the last bit of climbing by descending to the left to reach the landrover track in the glen below.

Beinn Sgulaird

Beinn Mhic
na Ceisich

Glen Ure

Loch Baile
Mhic Chailein

Stob Gaibhre

Beinn Sgulaird

Glen Creran

Meall Garbh

Loch
Creran

Druimavuic

Allt Buidhe

Coire
Buidhe

Beinn
Mheadhonach

0   2km

Alternatives

The northeast ridge looks a tempting
descent, but the slopes above Glen Ure
are forbiddingly steep with large
boilerplate slabs that are best avoided.
More practical is to descend WNW from the
summit down a steep, ill-defined ridge and
then continue westwards when easier
ground is reached, but this route too is
extremely steep.

Beinn Sgulaird

14

Beinn Fhionnlaidh

Beinn Fhionnlaidh (959m) *Finlay's hill*

Distance **14km**
Ascent **980m**
Time **6 hours**
Start point **OS Grid ref: NN036488**
Map **OS Explorer 384**
Terrain & hazards **mainly pathless but straightforward on a long, broad ridge with some boggy sections**

Beinn Fhionnlaidh is an extensive east-west ridge running from Glen Creran in the west towards Glen Etive in the east. It's a long time before the summit is revealed on this gradual ascent from Elleric; once there the reward is an unfamiliar angle on the great peaks of Glencoe.

Follow the public road along Glen Creran to the parking area at the end and start the walk along the track signed for Glen Etive and Glenure Lodge. This passes a house and crosses the River Creran before reaching a fork directly in front of Glenure Lodge. Keep left here, passing to the right of a white cottage and barn and heading through a farm gate. Immediately turn left through another gate to pass behind the cottage and follow the track to the pinewoods. Keep a careful eye out for a small track branching right uphill through the trees; when this ends at a turning area continue across open ground on a faint path and begin the climb ENE up onto the long ridge of Beinn

Fhionnlaidh. There is no clear path on the rough climb, but the gradients are steady. The steep mountain rising impressively to the south across the deep trench of Glen Ure is Beinn Sgulaird.

As the slope eases on the middle part of the ridge a couple of lochans are passed and then the terrain steepens for the final ascent. Some care is needed in poor visibility as the smaller peaks and undulating terrain can be confusing and the peaked summit itself, though marked with a large cairn and trig point, is not revealed until you are upon it. From here the views include Glen Etive to the southeast, steep Sgor na h-Ulaidh to the north with a peep into Glencoe. The return is via the same outward route with lots of opportunities to enjoy the sea views on the descent to Glen Creran.

Alternatives

Beinn Fhionnlaidh can be climbed equally well from Glen Etive. Start at Invercharnan and use the forestry road north of the Allt nan Gaoirean to gain the open slopes above. The burn is crossed (probably not using the very dilapidated bridge!) before aiming for the bealach north of Meall nan Gobhar. From there traces of a path lead north and then northwest up onto the east ridge of Beinn Fhionnlaidh. Follow this to the summit, with a little easy scrambling over a short rock step along the way.

Meall an
Aodainn

River Creran

G l e n   C r e r a n

**Beinn
Fhionnlaidh**

Elleric

Allt Bealach na h-Innsig

Glenure

River Ure

An Grianan

G l e n   U r e

Stob Gaibhre

Beinn Sgulaird

0   2km

Approaching the summit of Beinn Fhionnlaidh

'Praying Hands' in Glen Lyon

Loch Tay and Loch Earn

Loch Tay and Loch Earn

The mountains of Central Perthshire are at the heart of Scotland and within easy reach of the cities, ensuring their popularity with baggers even if many of the summits cannot stand comparison with their more northerly cousins. However, with attractive villages such as Killin and Fortingall, stone-built towns such as Aberfeldy or Crieff, and a glen as beautiful as Glen Lyon, there is little doubting the broad appeal of the area to visitors.

Crieff

On the fringe of the Highlands, Crieff is the nearest settlement to Ben Chonzie and the bustling market town has much to recommend it. Huge 'drovers' trysts' were once held here with thousands of cattle herded through the town. Today Crieff is better known as the home of the Famous Grouse Experience and has plenty of good places to stay and eat. Nearby, the smaller village of Comrie has bags of charm and between the two is Comrie Croft, a great hostel with friendly staff, camping facilities, Swedish 'kata' tents, mountain bike trails and an annual mountain bike challenge ride.

Loch Earn

Popular for watersports, Loch Earn is for many the gateway to the region. St Fillans at its foot is an attractive centre, whilst at the opposite end of the water Lochearnhead is probably the more convenient base for hillwalkers. The village has a shop, a pub serving meals, a watersports centre and a good number of B&B and self-catering options.

Killin

A short drive through Glen Ogle leads on to Killin. Often thronged by visitors in summer, this is a beautiful spot with an arched stone bridge overlooking the much-photographed Falls of Dochart. Set slightly back from the head of Loch Tay, Killin boasts a range of places to stay and to eat, as well as a supermarket and a well-stocked outdoor shop that also offers bike and canoe hire. Sadly the closure of the town's hostel has led to a shortage of budget accommodation, but The Bridge of Lochay and Killin Hotel provide reliable places to stay and there are numerous B&Bs and self-catering cottages nearby. The burger van which is located just off the A85 at the start of the long descent down Glen Ogle to Lochearnhead is also a popular stop with many walkers.

Aberfeldy

At the east end of Loch Tay, Kenmore, Weem and Aberfeldy all make good bases. Aberfeldy has a range of good B&Bs, hotels and self-catering options, as well as Munros outdoor gear shop. Be sure to check out the excellent Watermill to browse the bookshop, sample the goodies in the café or catch one of their regular events. On the edge of town Dewars World of Whisky provides a warming wet weather tour.

Kenmore enjoys a fine position at the foot of Loch Tay itself, and has a prime attraction in the excellent Crannog Centre

– a reconstruction of one of these ancient lake dwellings, the remains of which dot the lochs of the region. Fortingall, at the entrance to remote Glen Lyon, is famed for its ancient yew tree, reckoned to be the oldest living organism in Europe. The village has many picture perfect thatched holiday cottages, often with prices to match. The more budget-orientated can head to the caravan and campsite on Dunkeld road.

Loch Tay and Loch Earn

Loch Rannoch

Kinloch
Rannoch

Tummel
Bridge

Schiehallion

12

Meall
Garbh

Carn
Mairg

Carn
Gorm

Meall nan
Aighean

B846

Aberfeldy

11

Bridge of
Balgie

Mains of
Taymouth

A826

Meall a'
Choire Leith

Meall
Garbh

Meall
Greigh

Kenmore

An
Stuc

Meall Corranaich

Ball nan
Tnachan

Ben Lawers

5

Beinn
Ghlas

3 4

A827

Loch Tay

Ben Chonzie

lin

Loch
Lednock

Loch
Turret

1

A85

ochearnhead

Loch Earn

A85

2

Comrie

Crieff

A84

Ben Vorlich

Stuc
a'Chroin

157

Ben Chonzie

Ben Chonzie (931m) *mossy hill*

Distance **12.5km**
Ascent **710m**
Time **4 – 5 hours**
Start point **OS Grid ref: NN743273**
Map **OS Explorer 368**
Terrain & hazards **Landrover track, then boggy moorland path – indistinct in parts**

The highest point of an extensive area of rolling moorland hills, Ben Chonzie has often been slated as a dull hill. Although shapeless in form it offers a straightforward ascent, a great option for a shorter day or for practising winter skills; interest is added by a huge resident population of mountain hares.

Start from a small parking area opposite the old school at Coishavachan in Glen Lednock. Follow the track towards the houses at Coishavachan, turning right in front of the two cottages to pass through the gate and onto a rougher track. This curves left to pass the buildings and gently climbs uphill. Soon it crosses a bridge and through another gate, with the views back improving as height is gained. Further on, the route up the flanks of Ben Chonzie can be made out. Pass a small dam on the Invergeldie Burn and

continue up the other side, keeping left on the main track when it forks.

The track climbs more steeply and fords a burn. Ignore another track bearing left and, just before you reach the crest of the hill, keep an eye out for a small cairn on the left marking the start of the path at a sharp bend in the track. Although boggy at first this path soon becomes drier, though indistinct in places, as it follows the broad heathery ridge. Keep climbing steadily, reaching a line of fenceposts – a useful guide in poor weather as they lead to the summit – turning a right angle northeast for the final climb to the top at 931m. There is a large windshelter cairn just beyond the summit. The quickest return route is by the same outward path.

Alternatives

Whilst the route above is the easiest and quickest, Ben Chonzie shows its finest side to the east facing Loch Turret. It is possible to park below the dam and follow the track up the east side of this attractive reservoir to reach the wild head of the glen. From here the ascent to the plateau is quite steep and rough; after reaching Ben Chonzie a circuit could be completed by returning over Carn Chois.

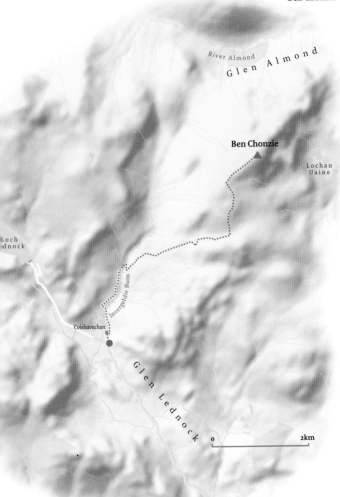

Ben Chonzie

Ben Chonzie

River Almond

Glen Almond

Lochan Uaine

Loch Lednock

Invergeldie Burn

Coishavachan

Glen Lednock

0   2km

2

Ben Vorlich
Stuc a'Chroin

Ben Vorlich (985m) *hill of the bay*
Stuc a'Chroin (975m) *peak of the sheepfold*

Distance **13.5km**
Ascent **1140m**
Time **7 – 8 hours**
Start point **OS Grid ref: NN633232**
Map **OS Explorer 368**
Terrain & hazards **good hillpath to Ben Vorlich; Stuc a'Chroin requires more experience with some scrambling, much steep ground and a boggy return**

In distant views these two Munros appear as identical twins; however, on closer inspection the sibling rivalry is more obvious. Ben Vorlich is one of the most popular Munros, a straightforward hill walk from Loch Earn and an excellent viewpoint. The extension to climb Stuc a'Chroin changes the character of the walk completely, with steep ground, crags and some scrambling bringing excitement to the day.

There is limited parking on the verge of the road along the south side of Loch Earn, just past the humpback bridge – arrive early to get a space. From here the first part of the walk is signposted; keep close by the Ardvorlich Burn and away from the farm. Beyond the farm the route follows a winding track high above the rushing waters.

After 1.5km fork right to continue climbing, soon crossing the Allt a'Choire Bhuidhe on a footbridge. A path, much improved in recent years, continues across open heather slopes before gaining the northern ridge of Ben Vorlich. Higher up the path is badly eroded in places with a final steep climb bearing left to reach the summit trig point at 985m. Its position on the southern fringe of the Highlands makes Ben Vorlich a superb viewpoint for much of central Scotland.

If Ben Vorlich has whetted your appetite for a meatier main course, Stuc a'Chroin will oblige. A much rockier and trickier peak, the ascent does involve some hands-on scrambling so is usually best left for decent weather – in winter conditions it should be tackled by experienced mountaineers only. Initially follow the ridge path to the west; it soon curves round to the left and descends to the intervening bealach. From here you'll find a choice of ascent routes. The main way takes the path to the bottom of the steep prow of Stuc a'Chroin from where it ascends a short boulderfield and then a zigzagging scrambling line beyond. The alternative is to descend a little into the corrie on the north side to climb a still-steep path up the grass and scree from there, before following the northwest ridge up to rejoin the scrambling route at the top of the prow where there is a memorial to the founder of the Falkirk Mountaineering Club.

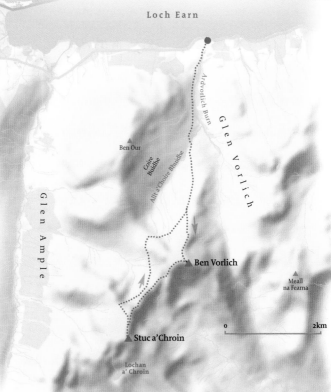

Loch Earn

Ardvorlich Burn

Glen Vorlich

Ben Our

Coire Buidhe

Allt a'Choire Bhuidhe

Glen Ample

Ben Vorlich

Meall na Fearna

Stuc a'Chroin

Lochan a' Chroin

0   2km

The actual summit is 500m further south along the ridge. With even better views than Ben Vorlich, Stuc a'Chroin plays host each May to a gruelling hill race, 22km long with approximately 5000ft of ascent. Acknowledged as Scotland's oldest hill race, the leaders regularly post times around the 2 hour 15 minute mark – something to chew over while enjoying a leisurely sandwich at the top.

To descend, the same choice of routes lead back to the bealach, with the steep scree path perhaps being preferred in this direction. Contour round below the

bealach and continue traversing until the northwest ridge of Ben Vorlich is reached. Here an eroded and soggy path contours around the head of Coire Buidhe to rejoin the route of ascent. Alternatively you can continue round the ridge to Ben Our and then descend east to the outward route from there. Once back on the main path, follow it down the hill to Ardvorlich and the start.

Alternatives

There are several less popular alternatives to the route above. One starts at the Falls of Edinample and ascends the glen before climbing up into Coire Fhuardaraich between the two peaks, though parts of the route through the forestry can be hard to locate. Another possible start point is to tackle both peaks as part of a longer horseshoe ridgewalk, beginning from the end of the minor road up Glen Artney.

If Ben Vorlich has already been climbed there are further options for Stuc a'Chroin. Starting from Loch Lubnaig in the Trossachs, it can be reached by traversing the rough connecting ridge from the Corbett Beinn Each. Finally the approach from the end of the road up the Keltie Water from Callander was once very popular, but following the loss of a bridge on the approach track it is now possible only after a spell of dry weather.

Loch Earn from Ben Vorlich

3

Meall nan Tarmachan

Meall nan Tarmachan (1044m)
rounded hill of the ptarmigan

Distance **12km**
Ascent **770m**
Time **5 – 7 hours**
Start point **OS Grid ref: NN604382**
Map **OS Explorer 378**
Terrain & hazards **good path for the ascent, steep near the top; ridge traverse is rocky with a short scramble on the descent of Meall Garbh; some pathless ground later on**

A high-level start makes Meall nan Tarmachan one of the shortest ascents amongst the Munros. However the summit is only the beginning of this rocky ridge walk with bags of character; it ranks amongst the best in the Southern Highlands.

Take the minor road which links Loch Tay with Glen Lyon and park at the Ben Lawers car park (charge payable). The walk begins from the track with the vehicle barrier; take this and then immediately turn right onto a well-made new path. This climbs gently uphill, with good views across to the Ben Lawers range, before reaching a track. Go straight across this onto a path which leads west up the slopes until it gains a ridge which is followed north to the minor summit at 923 metres.

Cross a slight depression and a flat grassy area before tackling the steep and rocky upper slopes, using a rising rake to reach the summit plateau of Meall nan Tarmachan a short distance north of the cairn. The summit is a great viewpoint, with the Ben Lawers range looking majestic across the deep trench of Lochan na Lairige.

Having bagged the Munro you could turn tail and return by the same outward route. However, this would mean missing out the best part of the day – the traverse of the knobbly, winding Tarmachan Ridge. Best tackled in good weather, it does have some steep sections and slight exposure in places.

The first objective on the ridge is the sharply pointed peak of Meall Garbh which is clearly visible. Descend the ridge to the south which curves to the right and passes a small lochan. The lumpy ground could make for difficult navigation if visibility is poor. Pass a hummock before a rougher climb leads up to the tiny summit of Meall Garbh, the finest top on the ridge. The ridge then descends steeply west, with the path negotiating a short rocky scramble; this can be avoided by taking a narrow and steep bypass path to the right just before reaching it.

Cross another minor hummock in the bealach before the ascent to the next top, Beinn nan Eachan, with its very steep south face. Bear right a little to avoid steep ground on the descent to the next bealach, a wide area of lumpy, grassy ground. A detour from here allows the

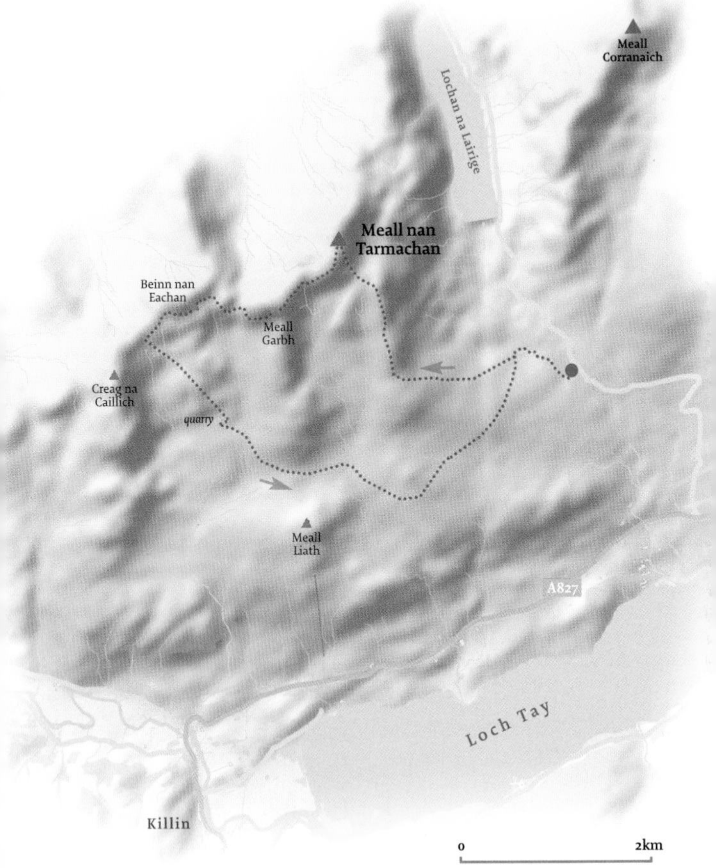

Meall nan Tarmachan

Meall Corranaich

Lochan na Lairige

Meall nan Tarmachan

Beinn nan Eachan

Meall Garbh

Creag na Caillich

quarry

Meall Liath

A827

Loch Tay

Killin

0   2km

final top – Creag na Caillich to be
included, but return to this spot
afterwards to take the easiest line of
descent. Aim southeast across rough

but mainly grassy slopes, boggy in places,
to reach the quarry shown on the OS map.
From here a track can be followed back
to the start.

Meall nan Tarmachan from Beinn Ghlas

4

Ben Lawers
Beinn Ghlas

Ben Lawers (1214m) *hill of the hoof*
Beinn Ghlas (1103m) *grey-green hill*

Distance **10.5km**
Ascent **960m**
Time **5 – 6 hours**
Start point **OS Grid ref: NN608378**
Map **OS Explorer 378**
Terrain & hazards **clear path to summit, very exposed in bad weather**

One of the ten highest mountains in Britain, Ben Lawers is the culmination of the sprawling range of hills on the north side of Loch Tay. It is very popular, due partly to the high-level start point and clear path, and partly to its location near the village of Killin. Beinn Ghlas, traversed en route to Ben Lawers, goes relatively unnoticed by many visitors, but is a Munro in its own right.

Ben Lawers is renowned for the rare alpine flowers on its slopes, and is owned by the National Trust for Scotland. Start at the dedicated car park on the west side of the high road linking Loch Tay with Glen Lyon; there is a voluntary donation. Begin the walk by heading through the walled interpretation area on the surfaced path to a gate. Go through this and cross the road to continue on the path, with views to Beinn Ghlas ahead. The deer fence protecting the flora of the Nature Reserve (from grazing sheep and deer) is reached;

enter it through the large gate. The nature trail, which can be added to the outward route at this point, leaves to the right; otherwise remain on the main path left of the burn at first.

The mountain in view is Beinn Ghlas, which continues to obscure Ben Lawers until you reach the summit. The path soon swings right, crossing the burn and eventually leaving the fenced area. Meall Corranaich is over to the left, whilst looking back is rocky Meall nan Tarmachan, also a very popular Munro. Pass some old shielings before beginning a steeper ascent, with the ground becoming rockier as the route zigzags up to a shoulder. A final climb reveals the small plateau at the summit of Beinn Ghlas.

A wide path leads along the grassy ridge, crossing a bealach before beginning the climb up Ben Lawers itself. The summit is marked by a trig point, but in the 1870s a massive cairn was built here to try and raise the mountain over the magic 4000ft threshold. However, this mammoth effort was in vain as the Ordnance Survey declined to include the structure in the height recorded.

To return, head back along the ridge to the bealach. From here a path on the right makes it possible to avoid the re-ascent of Beinn Ghlas and reach the bealach between it and Meall Corranaich.

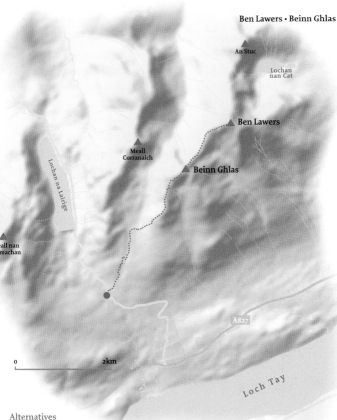

Ben Lawers · Beinn Ghlas

An Stuc

Lochan
nan Cat

Ben Lawers

Meall
Corranaich

Beinn Ghlas

Lochan na Lairige

eall nan
machan

A827

0   2km

Loch Tay

Alternatives

Experienced walkers could continue from
the summit over the further Munros of
An Stuc, Meall Garbh and Meall Greigh,
making a circuit around the fine corrie of
Lochan nan Cat. This involves much
trickier terrain (especially on An Stuc) and
requires return transport from the end
near the Ben Lawers Hotel on Loch Tay.

It is possible to complete all seven
Munros in the Lawers range from Glen
Lyon. Camusvrachan would be the start
point for this epic route completing
the horseshoe of peaks around the
headwaters of the Allt a' Chobhair,
though including Meall Greigh involves
a considerable detour.

Meall Garbh, An Stuc and Ben Lawers from Meall Corranaich

5

Meall Greigh
Meall Garbh
An Stuc

Meall Greigh (1001m)
rounded hill of the stud horse
Meall Garbh (1118m) *rough rounded hill*
An Stuc (1118m) *the peak*

Distance **16.5km**
Ascent **1235m**
Time **7 – 10 hours**
Start point **OS Grid ref: NN677395**
Map **OS Explorer 378**
Public transport **bus between Killin and Aberfeldy on schooldays**
Terrain & hazards **pathless in places on ascent and descent. The ridgewalk is mostly straightforward, but the ascent of An Stuc is a steep and loose scramble**

This excellent circuit links the hills encircling the corrie holding Lochan nan Cat, the finest feature of the Ben Lawers range. An Stuc became a Munro in 1997 and requires a steep scramble to reach the top – an ascent which may become technical in winter. Ben Lawers itself can easily be included by extending the walk.

Parking has in the past been problematic for this walk. However, the Lawers Hotel has now built a car park for walkers, giving the choice of whether to pay a charge or pop in to enjoy a drink or meal at the end of the walk. Start out by walking east along the main road for 0.5km to a white-painted cottage on the

left selling antler- and bone-carved products. Turn left up the track immediately beyond this to reach Machuim Farm; Meall Greigh can be seen ahead over the fields. At the farm follow the signed path to climb through the woods close by the Lawers Burn.

After leaving the trees, the path enters the Ben Lawers National Nature Reserve and passes an area dotted with old summer shielings. Don't follow the path which descends into the deep gully of the Lawers Burn, instead keeping high above the burn on its east side. The ascent to Meall Greigh from here is long and fairly featureless; either follow a minor tributary northwards to give a little interest during the climb, or aim more directly over Sron Mhor which has great views back over Loch Tay.

Meall Greigh is rather a sprawling and shapeless Munro, but because it is slightly detached from the main Lawers range it is an extensive viewpoint. The route ahead along the broad ridge to Meall Garbh is backed by steep An Stuc and massive Ben Lawers behind, with the tiny Lochan nan Cat cradled in front of them. Begin along the moorland ridge to reach the bealach of Lairig Innein. Ascending the slope beyond, the ridge then becomes better defined as it curves

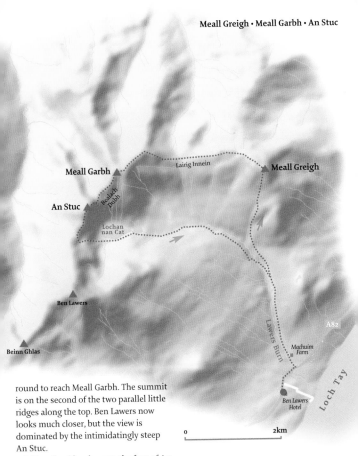

round to reach Meall Garbh. The summit is on the second of the two parallel little ridges along the top. Ben Lawers now looks much closer, but the view is dominated by the intimidatingly steep An Stuc.

Follow the ridge down to the foot of An Stuc to begin the steep and somewhat loose ascent. Care is needed, particularly in wet conditions, whilst in winter this climb is a more technical challenge. The summit cairn at 1118m may come as a

relief. An Stuc is exactly the same height as Meall Garbh and for many years this caused controversy in the rarefied Munro world as only the latter peak had Munro status. However, in 1997 this was rectified

173

as An Stuc became a Munro – rightly as it is the finest peak in the whole Lawers range.

Continue down the easier south ridge to reach Bealach Dubh where you can decide whether to include Ben Lawers in the circuit. If not, descend the very steep grassy gully close by the burn to reach the lochan. From here bear east following the burn to a dam, part of the Lawers hydro scheme. Pick up a track here for a short way before heading onto a clear path keeping high above the Lawers ravine. Further on, the path descends into the ravine and crosses a footbridge before rejoining the outward route and leading back to the start.

Alternatives

From the Bealach Dubh it is possible to continue and include Ben Lawers to make a fine circuit of Lochan nan Cat, descending along its east ridge and then northeast to regain the path up to the corrie. Another option is the massive round of the Lawers range from the north – see previous route for Ben Lawers.

Lawers range from the north

6

Meall Corranaich
Meall a'Choire Leith

Meall Corranaich (1069m)
rounded hill of lament
Meall a'Choire Leith (926m)
rounded hill of the grey corrie

Distance 9.5km
Ascent 755m
Time 5 – 6 hours
Start point OS Grid ref: NN593415
Map OS Explorer 378
Terrain & hazards rough going with some
pathless sections; very boggy

The western end of the great Ben Lawers ridge terminates in this pair of Munros. The high-level start makes these a short day for most, although the going is rough as the lower slopes are marred by extensive peatbogs.

Start just north of the summit of the Lairig an Lochain road that links Loch Tay with Glen Lyon, where there is parking marked by a large cairn. This road is often snowbound in winter. A well-made path leaves the road a short distance east of the cairn to head northeast onto the moors. In the bealach between Meall nan Eun and the rest of the range the path peters out. Follow a line of old fenceposts leading southeast over a small hillock (which can be avoided) and continue up the very broad ridge. The fenceposts finally leave the ridge to cut left across the slopes, taking a direct line towards Meall Corranaich.

As you join the steep southwest ridge of Meall Corranaich the going gets easier up to the summit cairn. Ben Lawers and its neighbouring peaks, An Stuc and Meall Garbh, close much of the horizon but Ben More and Stob Binnein are prominent to the southwest. Begin the descent on the north ridge, passing over a second, lower summit. It feels natural to mistakenly continue from here onto the NNW ridge so keep a keen eye out for the correct ridge which leads down to the bealach with Meall a'Choire Leith. Follow this as it curves round to the bealach with the crags of Coire Liath on the right. A short climb north then leads to the flat summit of Meall a'Choire Leith, the least distinguished of the Lawers Munros.

The return route is pathless for much of the way. At first descend southwest on steep grass to gain Coire Gorm and continue down to the concrete intake on the Allt Gleann Da-Eig. Continue southwest across the bogs to regain the outward path and return to the start.

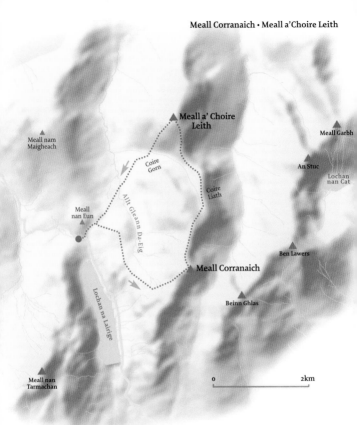

Meall a' Choire Leith

Meall nam Maigheach

Meall Garbh

An Stuc

Lochan nan Cat

Coire Gorn

Coire Liath

Allt Gleann Da-Eig

Meall nan Eun

Ben Lawers

Meall Corranaich

Lochan na Lairige

Beinn Ghlas

Meall nan Tarmachan

0   2km

Alternatives

The bogs can be avoided by starting the walk instead from the large Ben Lawers car park. Follow the clear path up to the bealach between Meall Corranaich and Beinn Ghlas before making a steep climb up to the summit of Meall Corranaich.

The disadvantage of this route is that after continuing to Meall a'Choire Leith it is necessary to climb back over Meall Corranaich to return to the start.

All seven Munros in the Ben Lawers range can also be tackled in an epic walk from Camusvrachan in Glen Lyon.

Meall Corranaich from the slopes of Beinn Ghlas

7

Meall Ghaordaidh

Meall Ghaordaidh (1039m)
rounded hill of the shoulder

Distance **9.5km**
Ascent **890m**
Time **5 – 6 hours**
Start point **OS Grid ref: NN526363**
Map **OS Explorer 378**
Terrain & hazards **mostly rounded slopes,
boggy at times**

Meall Ghaordaidh (Meall Ghaordie on
some OS maps) is a rounded and
undistinguished hill, with the usual
route of ascent from Glen Lochay being
up a broad grassy ridge, leaving its more
interesting northern side left unvisited
by most walkers. Its extensive views do
make the climb worthwhile, a good
option for a shorter day.

There is limited parking a short distance
past the bridge over the Allt Dhuin Croisg
on the Glen Lochay road from Killin. Start
by heading back along the road towards
the bridge and then turning left through a
gate signed for Meall Ghaordaidh. Follow
the rough track up through the fields,
climbing the stile over the grass-topped
stone wall.

The wooded ravine of the Allt Dhuin
Croisg is seen on the right and the scant
remains of old shielings are just beyond,
reminders of the days when women and
children would stay on the hill with the
grazing animals during the summer
months. Leave the track near a pole and
tiny cairn, bearing left, crossing a tiny
burn and ascending onto the initially
undefined southeast ridge of Meall
Ghaordaidh. The route is grassy and the
going can be boggy at times, eventually
leading up onto a shoulder at about 750m.
The climb then steepens for the final pull
to the trig point and wind shelter that
mark the summit at 1039m. Looking
northwest there is an excellent view over
the head of Glen Lyon and its loch.

The quickest return is to retrace your
steps down the ridge.

Alternatives
The less accessible Glen Lyon side of the
mountain has a more interesting
appearance; on this side Meall
Ghaordaidh is buttressed by two rocky
spurs, Creag Laoghain and Creag an
Tulabhain. The ascent from here is a little
tougher and requires more effort, usually
being made by heading from below the
Stronuich Reservoir, up into Coire
Loaghain between the two spurs.

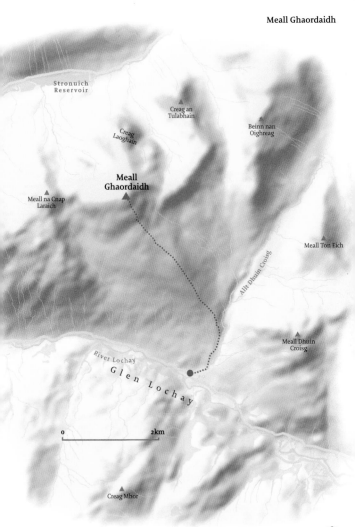

Stronuich
Reservoir

Creag an
Tulabhain

Creag
Laoghain

Beinn nan
Oighreag

**Meall
Ghaordaidh** ▲

Meall na Cnap ▲
Laraich

Meall Ton Eich ▲

Allit Dhuin Croisg

Meall Dhuin ▲
Croisg

River Lochay

G l e n   L o c h a y

0   2km

Creag Mhor ▲

Meall Ghaordaidh from Glen Lyon

8

Creag Mhor
Beinn Heasgarnich

Creag Mhor (1047m) *big crag*
Beinn Heasgarnich (1078m) *sheltering hill*

Distance **22km**
Ascent **1360m**
Time **7 – 9 hours**
Start point **OS Grid ref: NN476368**
Map **OS Explorer 378**
Terrain & hazards **rough hillwalking, often pathless; steep and craggy on ascent of Sron nan Eun; peatbogs on final descent**

These two Munros give one of the more challenging outings for baggers in this part of the Highlands, requiring experience as it crosses some potentially tricky pathless terrain. Creag Mhor is definitely the highlight of the day with a steep and craggy climb, whilst Beinn Heasgarnich (also known as Beinn Sheasgarnich) can be hard work as it is defended by acres of peat bog.

There is a car park in Glen Lochay around 1km short of Kenknock – it isn't possible to park at the end of the road. Instead reach the road end on foot, turning right at a crossroads onto a tarmac private road which leads eventually over a pass to Glen Lyon. Follow the road as far as NN461369 where a good track forks left. Take this as it passes a small dam and contours the slopes of Glen Lochay, heading west towards the hills. Ben Challum – more

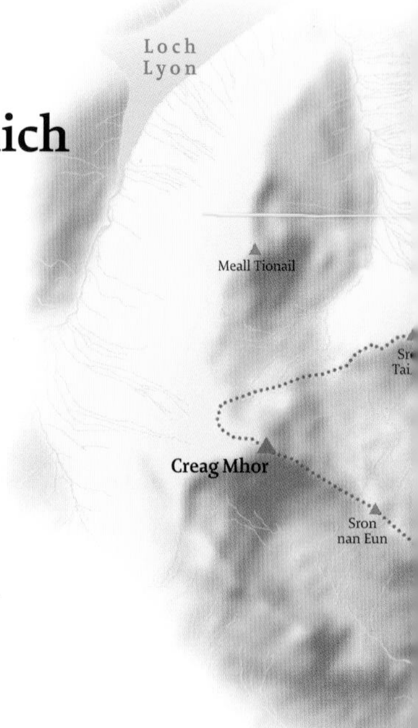

familiar when seen as a sprawling lump from Strath Fillan – appears as a fine peak from this side. The track crosses bridges over the Allt Badour and later the Allt Badavaime; after the latter leave the track and make for Sron nan Eun. The steep bluff at its southeast end can be avoided by heading just north of west to reach an easy gully giving access to the ridge above; alternatively a course slightly further north crosses easier ground.

Creag Mhor is revealed from Sron nan Eun; cross two small dips on the mainly grassy ridge to reach the large summit

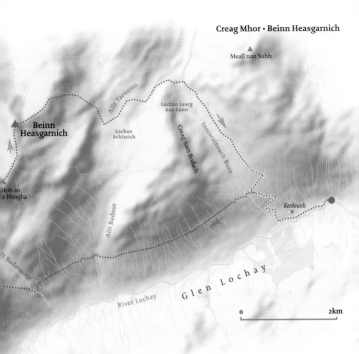

Meall nan Subh

Allt Tarsuinn

Lochan Learg
nan Lunn

**Beinn
Heasgarnich**

Lochan
Achlarich

Innisrainneach Burn

Creag nan Bodach

-tob an
r-Bhogha

Allt Badour

Kenknock

Allt Badavaine

River Lochay

G l e n   L o c h a y

0   2km

cairn. Crags block the direct route to the
bealach dividing Creag Mhor from Beinn
Heasgarnich, so it is necessary to head
down onto easier ground to the west at
first before descending briefly northwest
towards Meall Tionail and then cutting
ENE down to the peaty bealach once you
reach easier slopes. Once across the bogs
begin the ascent up the steep grass slope
to Sron Tairbh and onto Stob an Fhir-
Bhogha beyond. From here a very broad
grassy ridge leads to the summit plateau
and wind-shelter cairn on the summit of
Beinn Heasgarnich.

The descent route leads along the ENE
ridge for about 700m, then heads down
and aims to cross the headwaters of the
Allt Tarsuinn before it becomes
impassable. The area north of Lochan
Achlarich is a vast flat bog; follow the east
side of the Allt Tarsuinn before bearing
right to reach and cross another burn.
Continue down to flatter ground and
make for the high point of the private
Glen Lochay to Glen Lyon road. For once
most walkers will be glad of the tarmac
after all the bog; turn right and follow the
road back to the start.

9

Stuchd an Lochain

Stuchd an Lochain (960m)
peak of the little loch

Distance **8.5km**
Ascent **720m**
Time **3 – 5 hours**
Start point **OS Grid ref: NN511463**
Map **OS Explorer 378**
Terrain & hazards **steep ascent to the ridge, boggy and eroded in part; higher slopes are easier going**

A high-level start by the Giorra Dam greatly eases the ascent of Stuchd an Lochain, with the steep initial climb being rewarded with an enjoyable traverse above the rim of the corrie cradling Lochan nan Cat. Many Munro-baggers will combine this route with a visit to Meall Buidhe on the opposite side of the dam.

Take the minor road that branches off Glen Lyon to reach the Giorra Dam of Loch an Daimh. There is parking just before the bridge over the river below the dam. Start by crossing the bridge and following the track which climbs to the south end of the dam. The present-day loch was formed when the dam was built in the early 1960s as part of the Breadalbane hydroelectric scheme.

After 200m of track a cairn marks the start of the original path up Stuchd an Lochain. This route is fairly eroded and some find it easier to remain on the track until nearer to the boathouse before cutting up to rejoin the original route. The path then climbs very steeply to the ridge and can be wet. Once you reach the east ridge of Creag an Fheadain the walk improves as a line of old fenceposts steepen briefly before Creag an Fheadain's flat top is reached. Stuchd an Lochain looks fabulous with the steep cliffs of Coire an Lochain plunging down to jewel-like Lochan nan Cat.

The ridge descends to a minor bealach before rising to Sron a'Chona Choirein. After a slight dip, climb to the summit which is perched dramatically above the crags. Although only 960m high, Stuchd an Lochain enjoys an excellent position and the views are very extensive. Ben Lawers dominates to the southeast but it is the view north over Loch an Daimh that really impresses. Most people return the same way, leaving plenty of time to tackle Meall Buidhe.

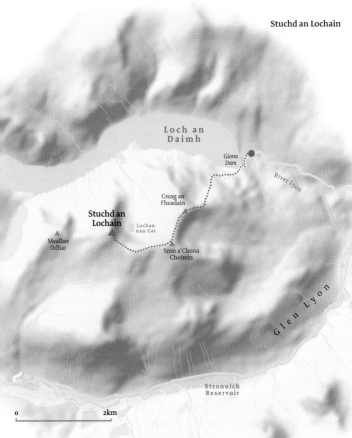

Loch an Daimh

Giorra Dam

River Lyon

Creag an Fheadain

Stuchd an Lochain

Lochan nan Cat

Meallan Odhar

Sron a'Chona Choirein

G l e n   L y o n

Stronuich Reservoir

0   2km

Alternatives

An approach from Pubil further up Glen Lyon is possible, but it lacks the attractiveness of the route given above. The very fit may be drawn towards making an epic traverse around all the hills above Loch an Daimh, starting with

Stuchd an Lochain and finishing on Meall Buidhe, passing over a couple of Corbetts en route. This would make for a very challenging day through little-visited terrain, 28km long but with a massive 1900m of ascent.

187

10

Meall Buidhe

Meall Buidhe (Glen Lyon) 932m
yellow rounded hill

Distance **8.5km**
Ascent **550m**
Time **3 – 4 hours**
Start point **OS Grid ref: NN511463**
Map **OS Explorer 378**
Terrain & hazards **short walk over rough moorland, boggy in places, with an easy final broad ridge to the summit**

Meall Buidhe ranks as one of the easiest ascents among the Munros. On a fine day the effort is well rewarded with views of its shapelier neighbour across Loch an Daimh, as well as over Rannoch Moor towards the great peaks of Glencoe.

Begin at the parking area just east of the Giorra Dam of Loch an Daimh, having taken the minor road branching off from Glen Lyon. Take the stony track uphill on the right near the sign, and keep left as it levels off and traverses above the reservoir. The easiest way to gain the ridge near Meall a' Phuill is to follow the track for 0.6km and then take a faint path up to the ridge – this avoids a very soggy section of ground. Further on the route crosses some peat hags which could be hard going after wet weather. Keep climbing the easy slope to reach the southern top at 917m from where there are great views along the easy, broad ridge – the summit cairn of Meall Buidhe is visible if the skies are clear. Head along the ridge to reach the cairn which marks the Munro at 932m. Loch Rannoch is seen spread out beyond, with Ben Nevis visible to the northwest and the impressive ranges around Glencoe easily identifiable.

Retrace your steps for the return, with a good view of Stuchd an Lochain and its fine corrie across the loch.

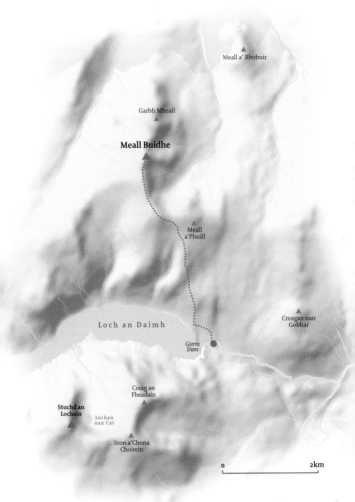

Meall a' Bhobuir

Garbh Mheall

Meall Buidhe

Meall a'Phuill

Loch an Daimh

Giorra Dam

Creagan nan Gobhar

Creag an Fheadain

Stuchd an Lochain

Lochan nan Cat

Sron a'Chona Choirein

0   2km

11

Carn Gorm
Meall Garbh
Carn Mairg
Meall nan Aighean

Carn Gorm (1029m) *blue rocky hill*
Meall Garbh (968m) *rough rounded hill*
Carn Mairg (1042m) *rusty rocky hill*
Meall nan Aighean (981m)
rounded hill of the hinds

Distance **18km**
Ascent **1310m**
Time **6 – 8 hours**
Start point **OS Grid ref: NN666482**
Map **OS Explorer 378**
Terrain & hazards **mostly rounded hills with some steeper ground on descent from Carn Mairg**

Few baggers can resist the chance to climb four Munros in a day, helping to make this range of fairly rounded summits one of the more popular walks in the area. Set on the north side of beautiful Glen Lyon, the mostly grassy terrain makes for fast walking with a wonderful feeling of space.

The route starts from Invervar where there is a small car park just below the phonebox. Go through a gate opposite the phone box and head up the track through another gate, entering the woods and following the Invervar Burn upstream. After 1.5km cross a rickety metal bridge and take the path up the opposite bank; it

leads around the edge of the forestry plantations until open ground is reached. From here continue up the straightforward moorland flanks of Carn Gorm. The route steepens before levelling out on a small plateau before a short final climb leads to the summit at 1029m.

From the small cairn descend along a broad ridge; the top of An Sgorr can either be traversed or bypassed on the left to reach a wide bealach marked with a cairn. From here head northeast, soon joining a line of rusty old fenceposts which lead in an easterly direction to the summit of Meall Garbh, its cairn bizarrely decorated with old iron posts.

The fenceposts are more intermittent as the route continues east to another wide bealach and then to the top of Meall a' Bharr at 1004m. As Carn Mairg is approached the ridge becomes stonier and better defined with some little cairns. A small tor has good views down Glen Lyon and across to the Ben Lawers range. When leaving Carn Mairg some careful navigation is needed if visibility is poor; from the summit aim east for around 200m and then southeast to avoid steeper, craggier ground before continuing down to the next col. From

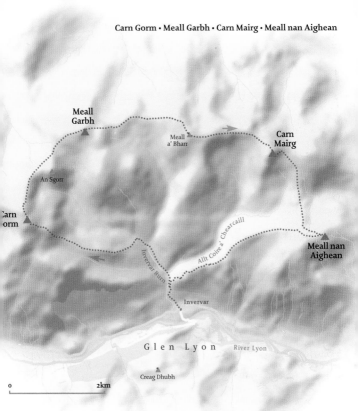

here the route climbs steadily to reach the summit ridge of Meall nan Aighean (also known as Creag Mhor in some guides). The actual Munro summit is a small tor about 500m along the summit plateau; from here the pointy peak of Schiehallion towers to the northeast.

From the summit retrace your steps briefly, ignoring the clear path to the nearby top. Descend the long west ridge, a pleasant route which soon has a clear path and superb views up Glen Lyon – one of Scotland's longest and most beautiful glens. A stalkers' path is crossed part way along; continue straight ahead down the crest of the ridge. Eventually the outward track is joined near the entrance to the wood; follow this back to Invervar.

From Carn Gorm looking down Glen Lyon

Schiehallion

Schiehallion (1083m)
fairy hill of the Caledonians

Distance **10km**

Ascent **730m**

Time **4 – 6 hours**

Start point **OS Grid ref: NN753556**

Map **OS Explorer 386**

Terrain & hazards **excellent path most of the way; final section crosses boulderfield**

One of Scotland's most popular hills, Schiehallion ranks amongst the easiest Munros to climb on a fine day. The classic view is from Loch Rannoch from where Schiehallion appears as an elegant cone, but the usual route of ascent mostly follows a fairly gentle, broad ridge. The final slopes to the summit are boulder covered and rough enough to ensure a proper mountain feel.

Start from the Braes of Foss car park, set on a minor road which links the B846 south of Tummel Bridge with Kinloch Rannoch. By 1999 Schiehallion had suffered from its great popularity, with the usual route up it eroded into a muddy scar visible for miles. The John Muir Trust then bought this flank of the hill and set about re-routing the path and undertaking remedial work on the old route. The new path makes for excellent going, passing some ruinous sheep fanks on its way to the base of the east ridge.

As the path climbs the ridge, the view opens up across Loch Tummel towards Beinn a'Ghlo, but as the gradient eases quartzite boulders litter the ridge leading to much slower progress. Care is needed in wet weather on this section and the summit is further along the ridge than many expect.

From the top you realise why pointy Schiehallion pops up in so many views, as a vista across a huge swathe of Scotland is revealed; most impressive is the view west across Rannoch Moor towards the peaks of Glencoe. Schiehallion is not just a pretty peak though – it has played its part in scientific endeavour and the evolution of mapping. In 1774 the Astronomer Royal Nevil Maskelyne used the mountain to take measurements of the deflection of a pendulum caused by its mass and thereby became the first person to measure the mass of the earth. As part of this experiment the volume of Schiehallion had to be calculated and for this purpose Charles Hutton invented contour lines which have been with us ever since.

Return to the start using the outward route, keeping to the new path to prevent further erosion.

Loch
Rannoch

Lochan an
Daim

Allt Strath Fionan

Braes of Foss

Cnoc nan
Aighean

Schiehallion

Gleann Mor

Allt Mor

Dun
Coillich

0   2km

Meall nan Eun

Schiehallion

A' Mharconaich

Pitlochry to Dalwhinnie

Pitlochry and Blair Atholl

A popular holiday destination for more than a hundred years, Pitlochry remains a magnet for visitors. Long famed for its theatre, more recently the Enchanted Forest festival in the autumn – when the trees are lit in spectacular displays of sound and music – has kept the town in the public eye. Nestled on the lower slopes of Ben Vrackie – which falls some way short of Munro status – it's not an obvious base for keen hillbaggers but as the main town for miles around it's still a key centre offering all services, from a wide choice of hotels and places to stay and eat to several outdoor shops. Deserving of special mention is the Moulin Inn, about a mile from the centre of town; it's been trading since 1695, forty years before the Battle of Culloden. Sometime Scottish Pub of the Year, the Moulin has its own brewhouse and a solid reputation.

Over the Pass of Killiecrankie, the small village of Blair Atholl is perhaps the more obvious haunt for the aspiring Munroist. Set off by a magnificent whitewashed castle, accommodation here is more limited, with the ancient Atholl Arms topping a list that includes several B&Bs and a huge caravan and campsite. It's the location which is the big draw of Blair Atholl, however, as the village is set right at the foot of one of Scotland's most stunning wild glens – Glen Tilt.

Drumochter Pass and Dalwhinnie

The bleak Pass of Drumochter has been a major route north through the Highlands since prehistoric times. Today it carries the busy A9, the railway and the Sustrans cycle route, and frequently features in severe winter weather reports. The mountains on either side look their best when under snow. To the west are four Munros, a series of broad ridges, whilst to the east a steep slope scored with gullies

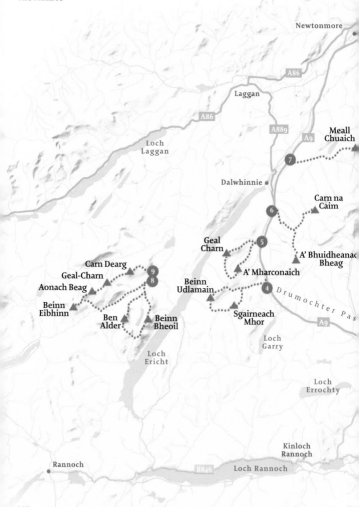

Newtonmore

A86

Laggan

A86

A889

A9

Meall
Chuaich

Loch
Laggan

7

Dalwhinnie

Carn na
Caim

6

Geal
Charn

5

A' Bhuidheanac
Bheag

Carn Dearg

Geal-Charn

Aonach Beag

9
8

A' Mharconaich

Beinn
Udlamain

4

Drumochter Pas

Beinn
Eibhinn

Ben
Alder

Beinn
Bheoil

Sgairneach
Mhor

A9

Loch
Ericht

Loch
Garry

Loch
Errochty

Kinloch
Rannoch

Rannoch

B846

Loch Rannoch

leads up to a vast plateau with two further Munro summits.

Just north of the pass is the straggling village of Dalwhinnie, reckoned to be one of the coldest in Britain with an average temperature of just 6.5°c. The village is best known for its distillery, the smoothness of Dalwhinnie making it one of the classic malts. There is also a mainline railway station – a great boon for walkers as this is also a jumping off point for longer trips into the remote Ben Alder region to the west. The great mountain of Ben Alder itself can be seen distantly along Loch Ericht. Facilities here are sparse, however; there is a shop at the petrol station and Crudenbeg House B&B is the best option for accommodation.

1

Beinn a'Ghlo:
Carn Liath
Braigh Coire Chruinn-bhalgain
Carn nan Gabhar

Carn Liath (975m) *rocky grey hill*
Braigh Coire Chruinn-bhalgain (1016m)
upland of the corrie of round lumps
Carn nan Gabhar (1129m)
rocky hill of the goats

Distance **22km**
Ascent **1240m**
Time **9 – 10 hours**
Start point **OS Grid ref: NN906671**
Map **OS Explorer 394**
Public transport **starting from Blair Atholl train station adds 5km each way**
Terrain & hazards **mostly good paths, steep descents between peaks and some rough ground**

Beinn a'Ghlo is a massive range of broad, sweeping ridges and hidden corries and is the dominant massif in a wide area. Its three Munro summits provide a strenuous but memorable walk; the summits themselves are rounded, but their steep flanks and sculpted forms give Beinn a'Ghlo real character.

Park in a rough lay-by on the left after a cattle grid, shortly before the end of the public road signed for Monzie. Begin by continuing on foot along the tarmac for a short distance to a junction beside the forest plantation. Take the right branch here, through a gate. The track gradually climbs to pass near a small hut with the great dome of Carn Liath as backdrop. Leave the track here to follow a clear path aiming directly for Carn Liath along a line of grouse butts.

The path is badly eroded as it steepens considerably up the heather slopes, but quickly brings you to the summit cairn, just beyond the trig point. The views are good but it's the sinuous ridgewalk ahead which is the real reward. It curves left, then right and then left again en route to the bealach. The eroded main path climbs across the slope to the right from here, or you can follow a smaller path more directly up the ridge from where the gradient lessens before reaching the summit cairn of Braigh Coire Chruinn-bhalgain, the middle of Beinn a'Ghlo's three peaks.

Finding the route to the next bealach requires more careful navigation if visibility is poor. Continue east round the corrie edge at first to reach the lower summit 1016m spot height. From here bear northeast along the plateau edge, keeping an eye out for a steep descent route to the right. Head east down to the Bealach an Fhiodha; on the far side a path makes a rising traverse up onto the ridge

Beinn a'Ghlo

Carn nan Gabhar

Carn Torcaidh

River Tilt

Braigh Coire Chruinn-bhalgain

Bealach an Fhiodha

Glen Tilt

Beinn a'Ghlo

Airgiod Bheinn

Meall na h-Eilrig

Meall Duibhinidh

Allt na Beinne Bige

Beinn Bheag

Carn Liath

Allt Coire na Saobhaidh

Allt Coire Lagain

Sron na h-Innearach

Loch Valigan

Meall Breac

Loch Moraig

0   2km

of Carn nan Gabhar. The going is gentler once on the ridge, though stony underfoot. Pass a cairn and then a trig point before finally reaching the large summit cairn of Carn nan Gabhar beyond. The highest of Beinn a'Ghlo's peaks, it offers a fine outlook into the wilds around the head of Glen Tilt.

Although the three Munros are now in the bag, the return route to Loch Moraig is long and tiring. Return to the Bealach an Fhiodha and then down the east side of the burn to the south. Cross the burn before it joins the Allt na Beinne Bige to pick up a stalkers' path which contours round the base of Beinn Bheag.

After crossing the Allt Coire na Saobhaidh the path begins to improve and eventually joins a track. Follow this track for several kilometres to rejoin the outward route, a short distance from Loch Moraig.

Beinn a'Ghlo from Ben Vrackie

2

Carn a'Chlamain

Carn a'Chlamain (963m)
rocky hill of the hawk

Distance 26km
Ascent 1020m
Time 7 – 9 hours
Start point OS Grid ref: NN874662
Maps OS Explorer 386 & 394
Public Transport train or bus to Blair Atholl, 1km from start
Terrain & hazards a straightforward but long walk on good paths and tracks

Carn a'Chlamain has a small peaked summit set on a vast and remote plateau. The lengthy approach is up Glen Tilt, one of the most beautiful and atmospheric of all Scottish glens – few are likely to regret the time spent hiking up this idyllic haven.

From Blair Atholl follow the road through Bridge of Tilt to reach the signed car park near the Old Bridge of Tilt. The walk begins by heading along one branch of the Glen Tilt circular walk, waymarked with yellow arrows – it leaves the car park near the information board. After crossing above the road on an old stone footbridge the path contours the steep slopes to join a track, bearing right along it. When a plantation is reached on the right there is a choice of routes; the easiest is remaining on the main track which soon crosses the Tilt and continues up the east

bank until Gaw's Bridge; alternatively an uphill path on the left climbs through silver birches and crosses a rifle range before continuing on the rougher path up the west side of the Tilt to the same point. The latter route requires more effort, but has the best views, though if long-range shooting is taking place at the rifle range there is no option but to stick to the track.

Whichever way you reach Gaw's Bridge you'll have a stunning 7km walk up the glen. From here keep to the north side of the Tilt, before crossing the Allt Craoinidh. On the far side take the intermittent path which climbs uphill through the heather to start the ascent proper. The path soon joins a bulldozed track which leads up the broad ridge, zigzagging to the right to pass a steeper section at 800m. Here, either stay on the track or branch left at a cairn and follow the line of the old path until the track is rejoined. It passes just to the right of the stony domed summit of Carn a'Chlamain so leave it for the final rough climb to the top. On a fine day this is a place to savour the feeling of remoteness and complete peace – the sky above seems immense.

The return is back down Glen Tilt, though you could vary the route by either sticking to the track or taking the route through the rifle range.

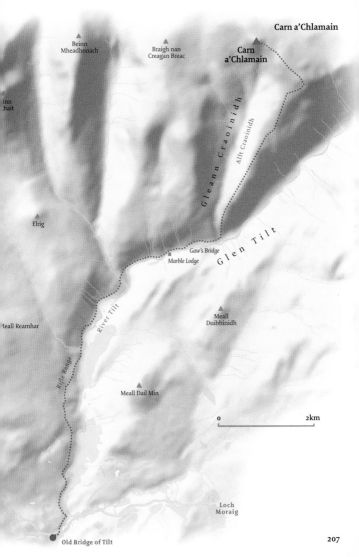

Carn a'Chlamain

Carn
a'Chlamain

Beinn
Mheadhonach

Braigh nan
Creagan Breac

Gleann Craoinidh

Alht Craoinidh

inn
hait

Elrig

Gaw's Bridge

Glen Tilt

Marble Lodge

Meall
Duibhinidh

Meall Reamhar

River Tilt

Rish Range

Meall Dail Min

0   2km

Loch
Moraig

Old Bridge of Tilt

Glen Tilt

3

Beinn Dearg

Beinn Dearg (1008m) *red hill*

Distance **29km**

Ascent **1030m**

Time **8 – 9 hours**

Start point **OS Grid ref: NN874662**

Maps **OS Explorer 386 and 394**

Public transport **train or bus to Blair Atholl, 1km from start**

Terrain & hazards **track on the approach, hillpaths on higher ground; the walk is long and exposed**

Although the terrain is relatively straightforward, the ascent of Beinn Dearg makes for a long day. This circular route is an enjoyable expedition with good views towards the Cairngorms.

Start from the signed car park near the Old Bridge of Tilt, just north of Blair Atholl – the car park is a fairly short walk from the train station. Start by following the black arrows, leaving the car park entrance and turning left along the road. Fork right to slope uphill and then keep straight when you come to a crossroads, passing a bungalow. Stay on the main track up the east side of the burn, ignoring the paths down to bridges on the left. After a stile at the end of the forestry the track continues across the open moorland, climbing away from Glen Banvie. Pass a prominent cairn, after which the track rises again, passing to the right of the hillock of Tom nan Cruach. The route winds above the eastern side of the Allt an t-Seapail

and climbs over a low bealach at 514m.

Descend to reach the Allt Scheicheachan bothy. This open shelter is maintained by MBA volunteers and makes a good base for a number of trips in this area. Cross the burn behind the bothy and follow a fainter track up its west side. Continue climbing for some distance – after which the track merges into an old stalkers' path, rising above the water and gaining height via a series of zigzags.

The path is eroded in places as it crosses the open, rolling slopes. Pass a minor cairned top from where the true summit of Beinn Dearg can be seen clearly ahead. The Munros were of little interest to the stalkers who built the path which passes to the left of the summit. Detour across the rounded granite stones to reach the large windshelter cairn which encloses a trig point.

Although it is quickest to return the same way there is an alternative that does not require much extra effort. After initially retracing your steps, leave the outward route once alongside the Allt Scheicheachan to follow a bulldozed track on the other side of the burn. The track climbs slightly and contours round the southwest slopes of Beinn a'Chait. After descending to reach the headwaters of the Allt Slanaidh it runs alongside its eastern side. When you reach a wooden shed, cross the water and carry on down the west side. The track eventually goes through a gate into forestry and passes

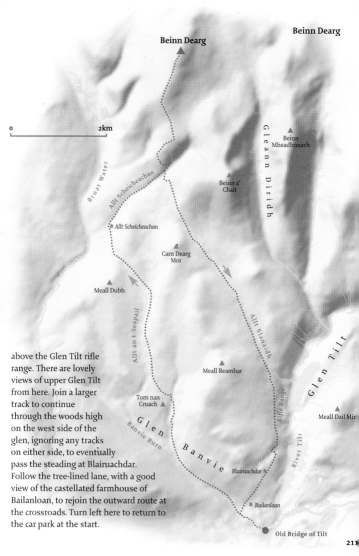

above the Glen Tilt rifle range. There are lovely views of upper Glen Tilt from here. Join a larger track to continue through the woods high on the west side of the glen, ignoring any tracks on either side, to eventually pass the steading at Blairuachdar. Follow the tree-lined lane, with a good view of the castellated farmhouse of Bailanloan, to rejoin the outward route at the crossroads. Turn left here to return to the car park at the start.

Beinn Dearg

Beinn Dearg

Gleann Diridh

Beinn Mheadhonach

Beinn a' Chait

Allt Scheicheachan

Bruar Water

Allt Scheicheachan

Carn Dearg Mor

Meall Dubh

Allt Slanaidh

Allt an t-Seapail

Meall Reamhar

Glen Tilt

Meall Dail Min

Tom nan Cruach

Glen Banvie Burn

Rifle Range

River Tilt

Blairuachdar

Bailanloan

Old Bridge of Tilt

0   2km

4

Beinn Udlamain
Sgairneach Mhor

Beinn Udlamain (1011m) *gloomy hill*
Sgairneach Mhor (991m) *big scree*

Distance **14.5km**
Ascent **805m**
Time **6 – 7 hours**
Start point **OS Grid ref: NN632755**
Map **OS Explorer 393**
Terrain & hazards **mostly straightforward hillwalking although the descent from Beinn Udlamain is very steep in parts**

Often dismissed as heathery lumps, it is true that these hills would not attract much attention if they did not reach the magic Munro height. However, the ascent is rewarded with expansive views over the remote Ben Alder massif.

Start from the lay-by right near the Drumochter Summit on the west (northbound) side of the A9. From here head south along the track, forking right to pass through a small tunnel under the railway. Bear right to follow a good track leading up into Coire Dhomhain. The steep, rounded hill on the left is the Sow of Atholl, a Corbett which can easily be added to the day's itinerary. Otherwise continue along the track for 2km or so; until recently it was then necessary to ford the burn, but now a bridge can be crossed before heading up the heathery slopes to reach the bealach between

Sgairneach Mhor and point 758m.

The ridge becomes better defined as height is gained, eventually passing above the broken crags of Coire Creagach. The trig point is a short distance further, marking the 991m-high summit. Ben Alder can be glimpsed ahead but the views are much better later in the walk. Descend to reach the bealach at the head of Coire Dhomhain and continue a short distance west before joining the broad south ridge of Beinn Udlamain. This leads directly up to the large cairn on the summit. At 1011 metres Beinn Udlamain is the highest of the four Munros on the west side of Drumochter; what it lacks in distinctive outline it makes up for with superb views over Loch Ericht into the wild mountains beyond.

Continue along the ridge until a short distance before the bealach at 860m, then strike off southeast steeply downhill over thick heather. Aim for the base of the burn which flows down from the bealach between Beinn Udlamain and A' Mharconaich, but keep to the right of the ravine it has worn down the hillside. The descent is tough going, requiring care, and it is a relief to reach the level floor of Coire Dhomhain. The walk now heads down the track to return to the railway and the start point by the A9.

Loch Ericht

Geal Charn

A' Mharconaich

Boar of Badenoch
(An Torc)

A9

Pass of Drumochter

Allt Coire Dhomhain

Coire   Dhomhain

Sow of Atholl
(Meall an
Dobharchain)

Allt Dubhag

Beinn
Udlamain

Coire
Creagach

Sgairneach
Mhor

Allt Coire Luidhearnaidh

0   2km

Mam Ban

Loch Garry

Alternatives

It is perfectly possible to combine this
walk with the following one (over
A' Mharconaich and Geal Charn) to
complete four Munros in a day; the return
can be done along the cyclepath.

Geal Charn
A' Mharconaich

Geal Charn (917m) *white hill*
A' Mharconaich (975m) *place of the horse*

Distance **11.5km**
Ascent **730m**
Time **4 – 5 hours**
Start point **OS Grid ref: NN627791**
Map **OS Explorer 393**
Terrain & hazards **straightforward hillwalk with a high start on heathery slopes**

A' Mharconaich is the most distinctive of the Drumochter Munros, projecting a steep nose to the northeast. The high start point means these two hills make for a straightforward hillwalk, easily extendable over the neighbouring Munros of Beinn Udlamain and Sgairneach Mhor for a longer day.

The route starts at Balsporran Cottages, a lonely spot on the north side of the Drumochter Pass. There is a parking area just off the west side of the A9. A 425m start cuts these hills down to size, but they look much more dramatic when under snow. This is hardly infrequent as even the main A9 is regularly blocked by winter snowfall, though the ploughs rush to clear it each time. The previous occupants of Balsporran Cottages (former railway cottages but now a B&B) once constructed an elaborate ice castle from blocks of ice hewn from the frozen River Truim.

Head over the level crossing and briefly follow the Landrover track by the burn. Soon a boggy path branches right and aims more directly up the heather slopes, eventually reaching a flat shoulder. Around 1km further on is the summit of Geal Charn. Often dismissed as a dull heathery lump, it nonetheless has a good view over Loch Ericht to Ben Alder, all the better for the minimal effort involved in reaching it.

From the summit, descend southwest and then south to reach the wide bealach at 739m. Continue up the featureless slopes beyond, aiming slightly left until you reach the summit plateau of A' Mharconaich. A short walk northeast brings you to the summit cairn at 975m. The descent down the nose of A' Mharconaich is the steepest ground encountered on this route and care should be taken in winter conditions. Follow the spur north, with the steep corrie on the right; the spur flattens and then bends northeast as it steepens again. Stay on the ridge until you come to the rougher lower ground. To shorten this section aim to the left to cross the burn and pick up the track leading back to Balsporran Cottages and the start.

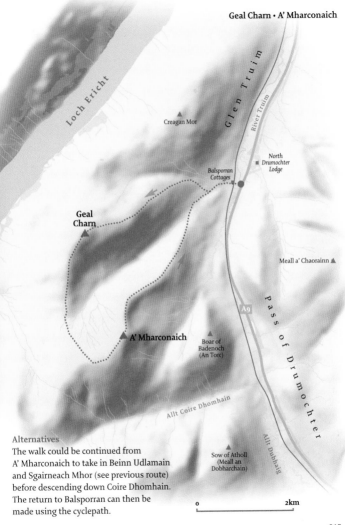

Loch Ericht

Glen Truim

River Truim

Creagan Mor ▲

North
Drumochter
Lodge ■

Balsporran
Cottages ●

**Geal
Charn** ▲

Meall a' Chaorainn ▲

A9

Pass of Drumochter

▲ **A' Mharconaich**

Boar of
Badenoch
(An Torc) ▲

Allt Coire Dhomhain

Sow of Atholl
(Meall an
Dobharchain) ▲

Allt Dubhaig

Alternatives

The walk could be continued from
A' Mharconaich to take in Beinn Udlamain
and Sgairneach Mhor (see previous route)
before descending down Coire Dhomhain.
The return to Balsporran can then be
made using the cyclepath.

0 _____ 2km

A' Mharconaich dawn

Carn na Caim
A' Bhuidheanach Bheag

Carn na Caim (941m) *rocky hill of the curve*
A' Bhuidheanach Bheag (936m)
the little yellow place

Distance **19km**
Ascent **825m**
Time **5 – 6 hours**
Start point **OS Grid ref: NN639820**
Map **OS Explorer 394**
Terrain & hazards **track to the plateau,
then soggy, indistinct paths and
moorland; good navigation skills needed
in poor visibility**

The steep slopes to the east of the
Drumochter Pass draw little attention
from passing traffic, marked only by a
series of gullies and some shallow
corries. Unseen above is a vast plateau
which extends across to Gaick; its two
major summits are Munros, both
included on this route.

There is parking at the lay-by on the
west side (northbound lane) of the A9
about 0.75km south of the turning to
Dalwhinnie. Carefully cross the road and
walk north along the verge for a
very short distance to reach a gate. Pass
through this and under the pylons to
follow a track north at first and then
east to start climbing. There are good
views across the pass to A' Mharconaich
and Geal Charn.

The track keeps to the wide slope
between two gullies and gradually gains
height. Near the top it reaches a very
small old quarry; little remains beyond a
dip in the ground and a few blocks of
quartzite – it could easily be missed in the
snow. Keep on the track beyond the
quarry and branch left onto the broad
ridge, continuing northeast. A line of
fenceposts aids navigation in poor
visibility on this section. After just under
2km leave the track to stay on the ridge
which curves right (still following the
fenceposts initially). Cross a shallow dip
which can be very wet underfoot unless
frozen, and climb the easy slope to the
summit of Carn na Caim. The views are
improved by its position near the
northern edge of the plateau.

Retrace your steps across the bealach
and back along the Landrover track to the
point where you first reached the plateau,
but now bear south rather than returning
past the quarry.

The plateau drops quite steeply at
A' Bhuidheanach – this can be avoided to
the east side on a path reached by bearing
left downhill a short way before meeting
the steeper slope. Cross another boggy
bealach to pick up a vague path and climb,
keeping a little to the right of a small
burn. The slope eases off as another flat
plateau is reached, just before the minor
top of A' Buidheanach Mhor. Bear
southwest and then south to reach the
trig point of A' Bhuidheanach Bheag. The

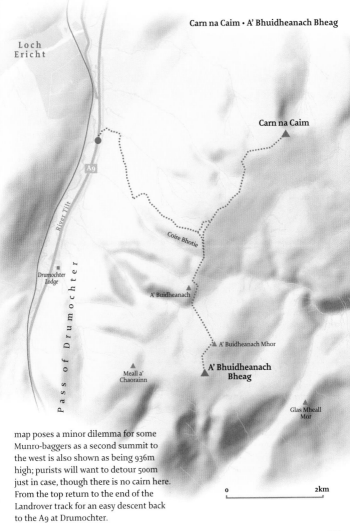

Loch
Ericht

Carn na Caim

A9

River Tilt

Coire Bhotie

Drumochter
Lodge

A' Buidheanach

A' Buidheanach Mhor

Meall a'
Chaorainn

**A' Bhuidheanach
Bheag**

Glas Mheall
Mor

map poses a minor dilemma for some
Munro-baggers as a second summit to
the west is also shown as being 936m
high; purists will want to detour 500m
just in case, though there is no cairn here.
From the top return to the end of the
Landrover track for an easy descent back
to the A9 at Drumochter.

0   2km

Meall Chuaich

Meall Chuaich (951m) *hill of the quaich*

Distance **14km**

Ascent **615m**

Time **4 – 5 hours**

Start point **OS Grid ref: NN654867**

Map **OS Explorer 394**

Terrain & hazards **a straightforward track leads to a path making this ascent fairly easy in most conditions**

Meall Chuaich is a rounded and fairly featureless hill whose position makes it a great viewpoint over Badenoch and upper Strathspey. It provides a good objective for a half-day or shorter hill walk.

Just south of Cuaich Cottages on the southbound lane of the A9 is lay-by number 94. Start from here, heading north along the verge until turning onto a gated track heading southeast. Soon a broader track is reached next to a water channel. This aqueduct is part of the extensive Tummel Hydro-Electric Power Scheme which opened in 1961. The channel carries water from the Allt Cuaich through the power station to eventually reach Loch Ericht beyond Dalwhinnie. Turn left to follow the track for about 2km to Cuaich Power Station. Cross the bridge

and continue on the track up the glen, ignoring a track which branches off next to the pipeline. Ignore another smaller track to the left and cross a bridge over the Allt a'Choire Chais.

Just before Loch Cuaich, turn right onto the track leading up the glen of the Allt Coire Cuaich. Pass a locked wooden bothy used by the estate for grouse shooting. Carry on over another bridge and watch out for a path bearing left where the track curves right. The path climbs the broad shoulder of Stac Meall Chuaich, keeping to the left of a line of grouse butts.

As the path gains height and becomes stonier it bypasses the summit of Stac Meall Chuaich to aim directly east to the summit of Meall Chuaich which is marked by a number of large cairns. Any lack of interest on the ascent itself is compensated by the excellent views; south and east are the vast featureless plateaux of the Drumochter and Gaick, whilst to the northeast the major Cairngorms summits can be picked out. The best vista, however, is to the north over Badenoch and Strathspey. The usual return route is to retrace your steps.

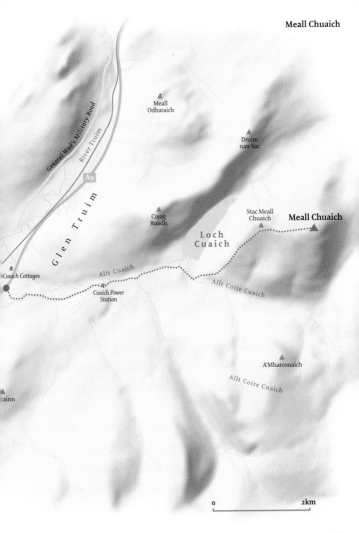

Meall Odharaich

Druim nan Sac

General Wad's Military Road

River Truim

A9

Glen Truim

Creag Ruadh

Stac Meall Chuaich

Meall Chuaich

Loch Cuaich

Cuaich Cottages

Allt Cuaich

Cuaich Power Station

Allt Coire Cuaich

A'Mharconaich

Allt Coire Cuaich

ainn

0   2km

Meall Chuaich

Ben Alder

8

Ben Alder
Beinn Bheoil

Ben Alder (1148m) *hill of rock and water*
Beinn Bheoil (1019m) *fore hill*

Distance 17km (plus 15km walk or
cycle each way from Dalwhinnie to Culra
and back)

Ascent 1030m

Time 7 – 8 hours (plus 3.5 hours walk
each way from Dalwhinnie to Culra
and back)

Start point OS Grid ref: NN522761
(no road access)

Map OS Explorer 393

Public transport train or bus to
Dalwhinnie

Terrain & hazards extremely remote;
several sections are pathless;
straightforward scrambling on the Long
Leachas ridge; navigation can be difficult
on the Ben Alder plateau, particularly
finding a safe descent to the bealach

Ben Alder is one of the great remote hill
massifs, a huge brute of a hill whose
spacious plateau is ringed by crags.
Wrapped around it are legends of a
poltergeist in a haunted bothy, all
adding to the appeal of this wild area.

The grassy areas around Loch Pattack or
the closed bothy at Culra make good wild
camping bases for this walk and would
also allow the four Munros of Beinn
Eibhinn, Aonach Beag, Geal-Charn and
Carn Dearg to be undertaken in a two- to
three-day trip. It is possible to cycle in
from Dalwhinnie and complete the walk

before returning, but this makes an
extremely long day.

Culra Bothy is reached by following the
estate road from Dalwhinnie Station
along Loch Ericht to Ben Alder Lodge and
then shortcutting onto a good solid path
on the left, before you reach Loch Pattack,
to a bridge over the Allt a'Chaoil-reidhe,
a short distance to the east of the bothy.
The bothy was one of the most popular
in the Highlands before it was closed in
2014 by the Mountain Bothies Association
(MBA) due to asbestos contamination.
Do not attempt to drive in and during the
stalking season please contact Ben Alder
Estate before climbing these hills.

Ben Alder presents its finest aspect to
Culra, with two narrow rocky ridges – the
Long and Short Leachas – enclosing a
steep corrie. The route described takes the
Long Leachas on the right (north) side.
From the bothy, return downstream to
reach the bridge and then start up the
stalker's path upriver on the far side.
After 2km the path curves away from the
burn and starts to head towards the
Bealach Beithe. A tiny cairn at NN515744
marks the best spot to leave the path and
strike out across the heather and bog on a
very faint path. This drops to cross the
Allt a'Bhealaich Bheithe, often possible
dryshod but impossible after heavy rain
or snowmelt. Continue across the rough
moor beyond, aiming to reach the Long
Leachas ridge just to the left of a small

An Lairig

Carn Dearg

Culra Bothy

Allt a' Chaoil-reidhe

Ben Alder Forest

Loch an Sgoir

Sgor Iutham

Allt a' Bhealaich Dhuibh

Allt a' Bhealaich Bheithe

Long Leachas

Short Leachas

Bealach Beithe

Loch a Bhealaich Bheithe

Ben Alder

Lochan a' Garbh Choire

Beinn Bheoil

Loch Ericht

Bealach Breabag

Sron Coire na h-Iolaire

0   2km

hillock on the ridge. Once on the ridge a path winds up between the crags and has no real difficulties, just two steeper sections. At the second of these the route bears to the right to avoid a crag and then ascends a small gully to regain the ridge at a narrower section with pinnacles. The path passes these before emerging on the stony plateau. Now continue above the head of the corrie, passing the top of the Short Leachas ridge (a steeper and more exposed alternative to the Long Leachas). There are good views down to Loch a' Bhealaich Bheithe and Beinn Bheoil. A boulderfield eventually leads to the summit, marked by a trig point and shelter cairn. The stone ruin just north below the summit is all that remains of a camp set up by Major General Thomas Frederick Colby on top of Ben Alder as part of the original Ordnance Survey mapping party.

Navigating around the plateau edge requires great care in poor visibility as it curves round from Lochan a'Garbh Choire, with great views over the Garbh Choire. From spot height 1103m (OS 1:25000 map, or marked with a 1100m contour ring on OS 1:50000) head down the steep and loose southeast slopes to the Bealach Breabag. Following the edge of the plateau any further east leaves you on a prow with no descent route. Once at the bealach a stalkers' path heads north for a quicker return to Culra. However, to continue to Beinn Bheoil head up the slopes of Sron Coire na h-Iolaire. Most walkers bypass the summit of this top on the left side, continuing onto a well-defined ridge to a bealach before climbing to the summit cairn at 1019m. Beinn Bheoil affords fine views of the length of Loch Ericht, with a glimpse of Dalwhinnie beyond.

Follow the ridge for another 1.5km before descending northwest after passing the screes. Cross the moor, aiming for the stalkers' path; once gained this leads back down to the bridge a short distance from Culra.

Alternatives

On the far side of these hills is Ben Alder Cottage, the bothy that was said to be haunted by a poltergeist (though the tales of a ghillie who hanged himself here are fictional). Above the bothy is one of the many caves in the Highlands said to have been used by Bonnie Prince Charlie. The bothy can be approached by a long walk either from Loch Rannoch or from Corrour Station (via the Bealach Cumhainn). From the bothy an old stalkers' path heads up to the bealach between the two Munros.

9

Carn Dearg
Geal-Charn
Aonach Beag
Beinn Eibhinn

Carn Dearg (1034m) *red rocky hill*
Geal-Charn (1132m) *white hill*
Aonach Beag (1116m) *little ridged mountain*
Beinn Eibhinn (1102m) *delightful hill*

Distance 18.5km (plus 15km walk or
cycle each way from Dalwhinnie to Culra
and back)

Ascent 1230m

Time 8 hours (plus 3.5 hours walk each
way from Dalwhinnie to Culra and back)

Start point OS Grid ref: NN522761
(no road access)

Map OS Explorer 393

Public transport train or bus to
Dalwhinnie

Terrain & hazards a remote route with a
long walk in and pathless sections of
rough, high-level moorland; steep climb
to Geal-Charn

This massive range is far less known than
neighbouring Ben Alder, but shares its
isolation and remoteness. The finest
feature, the exposed arête of the Lancet
Edge, gives a thrilling route for
scramblers but rather inconveniently for
Munro-baggers it reaches the ridge
halfway along. The best option if
returning to the start point is to climb the
hills from an overnight stay at Culra.

Culra is a 15km walk or cycle in
from Dalwhinnie – see the Ben Alder
route for details of the approach and the
bothy. From here there are fine views to
the Lancet Edge as well as Ben Alder, but
to include Carn Dearg it is necessary to
start up the rather less inspiring slopes
behind the bothy. Head west and then
northwest up the steep lower slopes;
any path soon peters out, leaving you to
continue up the heather or follow a
grassy gully if dry. When the gradient
eases carry on to gain the broad ridge
which gives a straightforward walk to the
first Munro of the day. Carn Dearg offers
excellent views across to Ben Alder and
the two Leachas ridges.

From the summit, descend to an initial
grassy bealach before crossing the Top of
Diollaird a'Chairn and continuing down
to a lower bealach. Here the majesty of
this group of mountains is revealed. On
the right is Coire Cheap with its circular
lochan, whilst on the left Loch an Sgoir is
cradled by the impressive Lancet Edge.
Now follow the path up the steep Aisre
Ghobhainn ridge, emerging suddenly on a
wide grassy plateau. Navigation requires
care in poor visibility – the summit of
Geal-Charn is approximately 1km WSW.

To continue the round, follow the edge of the plateau southwest, which leads down an obvious ridge, and make the straightforward climb up to the summit dome of Aonach Beag. From here continue southwest down the ridge to the next bealach. This dip is where the return route leaves the ridge but first make the steep climb up to the top of Beinn Eibhinn. The path is rocky but has no difficulties; there are two summits which the OS map shows as the same height so baggers will want to visit both to make sure.

Return to the bealach and take an indistinct path bearing south to avoid scree before heading down into Coire a'Charra Bhig on mostly grassy slopes. Further down, cross and keep to the left side of the burn. Just before you reach the bogs at the bottom of the corrie, traverse the rough slopes on the left, keeping below the crags of Sron Ruadh but above the worst of the peat. Once drier ground can be seen below, cross it to reach the Allt Coire a'Laobhair and aim for the stalkers' path a short distance up the far side. This excellent path comes as a great relief for tired limbs – head left along it to climb steadily over the pass (the Bealach Dubh) and then make for the steady 5.5km descent to Culra bothy, finding a good spot to cross the Allt Loch an Sgoir.

Alternatives

Most walkers will opt for an overnight stay on a visit to these hills; the classic route would be to complete the Munros from Culra as described above, but continue through to Corrour Station. It is possible for the fittest to approach the ridge in a single day from Luiblea near Loch Laggan to the north, either via the Allt Cam or even the stalkers' path across the east side of Beinn a'Chlachair.

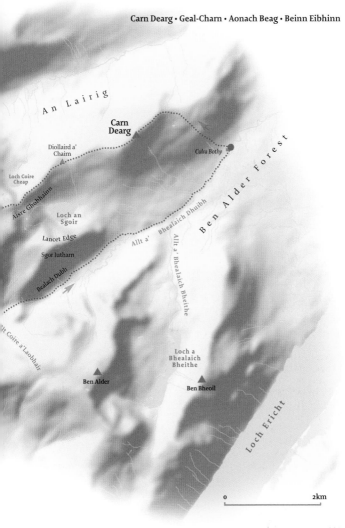

An Lairig

Carn
Dearg

Diollaird a'
Chairm

Culra Bothy

Loch Coire
Cheap

Aisre Ghobhainn

Loch an
Sgoir

Allt a' Bhealaich Dhuibh

Ben Alder Forest

Lancet Edge

Sgor Iutharn

Allt a' Bhealaich Bheithe

Bealach Dubh

Allt Coire a'Laobhair

Loch a
Bhealaich
Bheithe

Ben Alder

Ben Bheoil

Loch Ericht

0   2km

231

Ridge to Beinn Eibhinn, from Aonach Beag

Fords of Avon refuge

Badenoch and Strathspey

Kingussie and Newtonmore

These two fine old stone-built towns are clustered together at the heart of Badenoch, the uppermost part of the Spey Valley. Kingussie and Newtonmore grew up in the 19th century when the Highlands became a fashionable retreat for the wealthy, and their popularity remains today. If spending any time in the area, be sure to visit the superb Highland Folk Museum which features reconstructed buildings from a range of periods and is great fun for young and old.

Both towns offer a variety of facilities, with good general stores, fish and chip shops and a number of tearooms and pubs. The Glen Inn in Newtonmore does good homemade pub grub in the evenings. Those craving homemade cake and coffee should head for the friendly Sugar Bowl on Kingussie's High Street.

Apart from the hotels and many B&Bs, both towns have independent hostel accommodation, as does nearby Laggan. Finally there is a friendly no-frills campsite by the Spey on the southern fringe of Newtonmore. For wild campers or those returning from a bothy trip there are excellent public showers (charge) at the Bladnoch Centre on Spey Street. Coffee fiends can get a superb daily fix from the café at Ralia on the A9 just south of Newtonmore where you can also surf the internet and recharge your phone. The Coffee Bothy at Laggan, home to Kara the hillwalking parrot, is also excellent.

Aviemore

Once a tiny village, Aviemore's expansion began slowly, following the building of the railway, but it was in the 1960s that the modern town began as a purpose-built winter sports resort. Serving the UK's largest ski area, it initially brought an economic boom, but this proved to be short-lived. The grim architecture didn't help and by the early '90s the town was in real decline, memorably described by Muriel Gray as 'a gigantic concrete flypaper'. By the turn of the century,

however, the town was fighting back, with some of the ugliest buildings demolished and a new generation of vibrant outdoors businesses proving that a tacky Santa Claus Land was never going to be the best way to attract visitors to the Highlands. Aviemore is on the up once more.

The town has all the facilities you could need, from large hotels to scores of bed and breakfasts, supermarkets and a plethora of outdoor shops – ideal browsing fodder for a Munro-bagger on

a wet day. Deserving of special mention is the Aviemore Mountain Café, run by an enthusiastic Kiwi and serving some great local food, including home-baking that is just perfect for quickly replacing all those calories you've burnt off on the hills. Run by outdoors enthusiasts – and set above a gear shop – during the snowy season it hosts Winter Mountain Safety lectures from the Mountaineering Council of Scotland.

For the evenings the Old Bridge Inn is

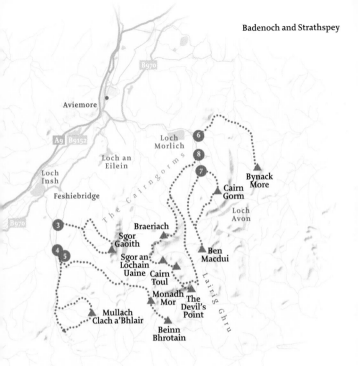

Aviemore

Loch
Morlich

6

8

Loch an
Eilein

7

Loch
Insh

Cairn
Gorm

Bynack
More

Feshiebridge

Loch
Avon

3

Braeriach

Sgor
Gaoith

4
5

Sgor an
Lochain
Uaine

Ben
Macdui

Cairn
Toul

Monadh
Mor

The
Devil's
Point

Mullach
Clach a'Bhlair

Beinn
Bhrotain

worth checking out; it has regular live music, a roaring fire, and the home-cooked food can be washed down by some excellent cask ales. If you leave a little worse for wear, there's the award-winning Aviemore Independent Bunkhouse just next door and a more traditional hostel in the centre of town. The large Macdonald resort provides a good wet weather distraction if you fancy a swim and a sauna.

Of course it isn't for Aviemore itself that visitors throng to the area. Rothiemurchus Forest extends for miles, a magnificent carpet of Scots pine dotted with jewel-like lochs such as Loch Morlich and Loch an Eilein, the perfect foreground for the looming wall of the Cairngorms beyond. It is also hugely popular, with a busy campsite and hostel at Loch Morlich. Scotland's National Outdoor Training Centre at Glenmore Lodge provides a range of courses aimed at walkers, including winter skills and avalanche training.

Geal Charn

Geal Charn (926m) *white hill*

Distance **12.5km**

Ascent **625m**

Time **4 – 5 hours**

Start point **OS Grid ref: NN521948**

Map **OS Explorer 401**

Terrain & hazards **paths faint and boggy at times**

Standing apart from the other Monadhliath Munros, Geal Charn is usually tackled on its own. Its finest feature is the craggy eastern corrie overlooking Glen Markie, but the most straightforward ascent is by the open slopes to the southwest.

To reach the start, turn off the A86 at Laggan and pass the Spey Dam; there is a parking area on the left immediately before Garva Bridge. General Wade built this double-span stone bridge as part of the Corrieyairack Pass route. Today the pass is a scheduled ancient monument and is still used by through-hikers, though the controversial Beauly to Denny powerline has resulted in a large substation being sited here.

For Geal Charn, cross the bridge and turn right up a track which aims north from the road, following the main route as it turns right to cross the Allt Coire Iain Oig. After the bridge turn left and soon fork left off the track onto a faint path which follows the burn upstream.

The path becomes clearer but remains very boggy in places, keeping to the southeastern side of the Feith Talagain. After 2km, where the Allt Coire nan Dearcag joins the main stream, cross the water and accompany it northeast uphill, before shortly leaving it to head up the broad ridge towards Geal Charn.

After a steeper section, you come to the flat southwest shoulder of Geal Charn. Continue northeast to reach the massive cairn on the summit. From here the vast, featureless plateau of the Monadhliath sweeps away to the north, but only the fittest will attempt to cross it to reach the three other Munros of the range. The easiest and quickest descent is to return the same way.

Alternatives

Another route up starts at the Spey Dam and follows the track by the east side of Glen Markie. The Markie Burn has to be forded shortly after the confluence with the Piper's Burn; this is not possible if in spate. The Piper's Burn is then followed until it branches at 480m before aiming up to reach the plateau, well to the northeast of the craggy headwall of the corrie. Finally cross the plateau, keeping back from the cliff edge, to reach the summit. This route and the one described above can be combined to give a circuit by walking 7.5km back along the minor road.

2

Carn Dearg
Carn Sgulain
A' Chailleach

Carn Dearg (945m) *red rocky hill*
Carn Sgulain (920m) *rocky hill of the basket*
A' Chailleach (930m) *the old woman*

Distance **25km**
Ascent **980m**
Time **8 hours**
Start point **OS Grid ref: NN693998**
Map **OS Explorer 402**
Public transport **none to start; buses and trains serve Newtonmore**
Terrain & hazards **tracks at lower level, then pathless and featureless hills**

The Monadhliath – or Grey Hills – are a vast area of rolling plateaux with acres of peat and bogs; the interior is rarely visited and all four Munros are along the southern fringe. Three of them are climbed on this circuit from Glen Banchor.

Take Glen Road out of Newtonmore; there is parking at the very end of the minor road in Glen Banchor. Begin by walking along the track up this attractive open glen which, though so close to Newtonmore, feels surprisingly remote. Cross the bridge over the Allt a' Chaorainn and pass a plantation and the site of a deserted township. Just before the bridge over the Allt Fionndrigh bear right onto a grassy track leading up Gleann Fionndrigh, with the outlier ridges of the Monadhliath closing in on both sides.

After 3km the track ends. Take the path on the left and cross the very rickety footbridge. Follow the stalkers' path as it zigzags out of the glen. As the ground flattens out, stay on the path which climbs and bends to the right; ignore the path branching left. Traverse the hillside to head alongside the Allt Ballach into upper Gleann Ballach. The path eventually peters out near the head of the glen.

From here Carn Dearg is directly west, but the route is barred by crags. Instead continue north into the upper bowl, where a wide grassy break gives an easy climb southwest. Keep to the north of the crags to reach the bealach between Carn Ban and Carn Dearg. A short detour southeast from this point brings you to the summit of Carn Dearg, the highest of the Monadhliath. The cairn teeters on top of the sheer drop to Gleann Ballach – a rare bit of drama for this range!

Return to the bealach and head north onto the stony ground around the summit of Carn Ban, a Top. The vast emptiness of the Monadhliath stretches to the north and west, one of the least visited of Britain's wild areas. Keep heading northeast, over the top of Carn Ballach and then Meall na Creugaich as the ground becomes boggy and less stony.

A line of fenceposts helps navigation

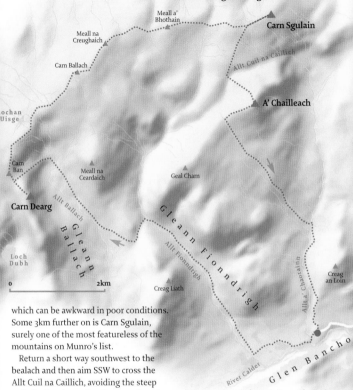

Carn Dearg · Carn Sgulain · A' Chailleach

Carn Sgulain

Meall a'
Bhothain

Meall na
Creughaich

Allt Cuil na Caillich

Carn Ballach

A' Chailleach

ochan
Uisge

Carn
Ban

Meall na
Ceardaich

Geal Charn

Carn Dearg

Allt Ballach

Gleann
Ballach

Gleann Fionndrigh

Loch
Dubh

Allt Fionndigh

0   2km

Allt a' Chaorainn

Creag
an Loin

Creag Liath

Glen Banchor

River Calder

which can be awkward in poor conditions.
Some 3km further on is Carn Sgulain,
surely one of the most featureless of the
mountains on Munro's list.

Return a short way southwest to the
bealach and then aim SSW to cross the
Allt Cuil na Caillich, avoiding the steep
gully further down. Continue southeast
on straightforward ground to reach the
third Munro, A' Chailleach with its
massive cairn and windshelter. This is a
popular objective in its own right and
there is a rough path for much of the
descent. Start by heading southwest
before the path curves left to descend
southeast into the glen with open views

of Newtonmore below. Part way down is
an old iron hut which offers some
protection on bad weather days. Cross the
Allt a'Chaorainn (if the burn is in spate,
there is a footbridge 0.5km downstream
which can be hard to spot). The better
path on the far side soon becomes a track,
leading directly down the glen to the Glen
Banchor road.

Looking across Badenoch to A' Chailleach and Carn Sgulain

3

Sgor Gaoith

Sgor Gaoith (1118m) *windy peak*

Distance **14km**
Ascent **910m**
Time **6 hours**
Start point **OS Grid ref: NH852012**
Map **OS Explorer 403**
Terrain & hazards **very good approach path, fairly gentle open slopes higher up, bouldery near summit; the cairn is right by the dramatic cliffs of the east face so great care is needed with navigation in poor visibility**

Sgor Gaoith makes for one of the best shorter ascents in the Cairngorms. The route climbs through the beautiful native pinewoods of Glen Feshie and then across the bare windswept upper slopes, but the highlight of this mountain is the peaked summit on the very edge of huge broken cliffs which plunge dramatically down to Loch Einich far below, making surely one of the grandest perches in the eastern Highlands.

This route starts from the minor road up the east side of Glen Feshie. There is a parking area off on the left just before a bridge over the Allt Ruadh; if you reach the hostel you've gone too far. Start by following the forest track east, cutting through a forestry plantation. This gives way to native trees, and soon a sign announces you are entering the Cairngorms National Nature Reserve.

When the track forks take the left branch to climb above the steep gorge of the Allt Ruadh amongst some fine Scots pines. As you gain height the views improve looking back over Badenoch to the Munros of the Monadhliath. At the next fork keep straight ahead onto a path which crosses the Allt nam Bo and leaves the trees, eventually also crossing the Allt Coire na Cloiche. A long traverse ends at the Allt a'Chrom Alltain; accompany this for a short while before crossing and aiming southeast up the slope. A path can be picked up from the flat shoulder at 810m which keeps a little south of east to reach the summit plateau just south of Sgor Gaoith.

On a fine summer's day keep near the eastern edge for great views across the crags as you head towards the summit, but when under snow keep well back as deep cornices form along the rim. The highest point is on the edge of broken cliffs which tumble directly to Loch Einich below, with stunning views across to Braeriach, its flanks scooped with a whole series of corries. On anything but the calmest day Sgor Gaoith lives up to its meaning as the 'peak of the wind'. It is the high point of a vast plateau stretching miles to the south which once held several Munros. Most of these are now relegated to the status of Tops, with only Mullach Clach a'Bhlair well to the south retaining its Munro status.

From Sgor Gaoith head north at first towards the next bealach, and then

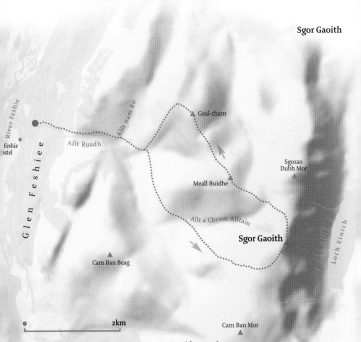

Sgor Gaoith

Sgoran Dubh Mor

Meall Buidhe

Geal-charn

Allt nam Bo

Allt Ruadh

River Feshie

Feshie ostel

Glen Feshiee

Allt a'Chrom Alltain

Carn Ban Beag

Loch Einich

0   2km

Carn Ban Mor

northwest along the broad ridge to Meall Buidhe, passing over a minor hillock. The going becomes bouldery in places; after the cairn continue to the next bealach, skirt another knoll and climb Geal-charn, which was once a Munro. From the summit keep heading northwest for 300m and then turn southwest down the heathery slope. Eventually the outward path is reached near the Allt Coire na Cloiche; turn right along it to return to the woods and retrace the outward route to the start.

Alternatives
There are many possible routes up to the plateau from various start points in Glen Feshie or even Loch an Eilein to the north. Perhaps the most popular alternative excursion is to combine Sgor Gaoith with Mullach Clach a'Bhlair; for this route it is best to use the car park 1km north of Achlean. The plateau is gained by forking left from the road onto a path signed for Carn Ban Mor. Once on the plateau, detour northwards to Sgor Gaoith before bearing south to the Mullach and then descending the track down the south side of Coire Garbhlach (see the following Mullach Clach a'Bhlair route).

Sgor Gaoith

4

Mullach Clach a'Bhlair

Mullach Clach a'Bhlair (1019m)
summit of the stony plain

Distance **22.5km**
Ascent **785m**
Time **7 hours**
Start point **OS Grid ref: NN850985**
Map **OS Explorer 403**
Terrain & hazards **the approach up Glen Feshie has two water crossings which may be impassable in spate; much of the ascent beyond is on a track, navigation on the plateau can be tricky in poor weather**

Glen Feshie is one of the most beautiful glens in Scotland, with some wonderful old Scots pines and a grand river. On a fine day it provides a sublime approach walk before a bulldozed track, detracting greatly from the wild feel of the area, leads up above twisting Coire Garbhlach to reach the plateau. The insignificant summit of Mullach Clach a'Bhlair can seem an anti-climax.

Follow the road up the east side of Glen Feshie (SP Achlean); there is an excellent car park on the left around 1km before Achlean. Walk to the road end and follow the path around the farmhouse to the left, continuing on the main path when two smaller routes branch off. At the edge of a plantation go through the gate and ford the burn, following the edge of a heathery bank above the River Feshie. The path dips steeply to cross the Allt Garbhlach which

can be impassable in spate conditions.

Bear right on a faint, grassy path that runs close to the Feshie; this gives easier walking than the top of the bank. Ancient pines are scattered across the wide floor of the glen; soon you pass the forestry plantation to the left and the landscape takes on a grand feel. This section can be boggy so the best bet is to stay amongst the trees on the left until a track is picked up. Turn right along this, branching left at a fork.

At a crossroads turn left onto a smaller track which starts to climb away from the glen, leaving the pinewoods behind. It climbs easily above Coire Caol and then aims for a small bealach on the ridge to the north, between Meall nan Sleac and Cadha na Coin Duibh. Whilst the track is a scar on a landscape of this quality, there are some fantastic views to be had into Coire Garbhlach by detouring left. Follow the track as it skirts the side of Cadha na Coin Duibh, revealing further dramatic views. Continue onto the flat plateau, and branch right when the track forks. After 0.75km leave the track and head south to reach the cairn at the summit of Mullach Clach a'Bhlair. The great size of the Moine Mhor plateau can really be appreciated from here, stretching across Braeriach and Cairn Toul.

The quickest descent is to return the same way; however, there is an alternative which adds variety and interest to the day. Descend southwest down the Druim nam

Carn Ban
Beag

Achlean

Allt Garbhlach

Glen Feshie

Coire Garbhlach
Meall nan
Sleac

Cadha na
Coin Duibh

Coire Caol

Carnachuin

Carn Dearg Beag

Allt Coire Chaoil

Ruigh
Aiteachain

River Feshie

**Mullach
Clach a'Bhlair**

Druim
nam Bo

Lochan
nam Bo

Creag na Gaibhre

0 2km

Bo ridge and traverse the north side of Lochan nam Bo before continuing to reach a large cairn on Creag na Gaibhre. From here an old and well-built but slightly overgrown path zigzags northwest downhill to cross the Allt Coire nam Bo and enter the forest of Upper Glen Feshie. The path emerges at Ruigh Aiteachain, a popular bothy maintained by volunteers from the Mountain Bothies Association. The location amongst the old granny pines is idyllic; Edwin Landseer painted *Monarch of the Glen* near here, as well as a fresco on the wall of an adjacent building which was visible until the 1930s. Please help to keep the bothy tidy and carry out any rubbish you find.

Head north along the glen, either fording a stream or detouring to a plank bridge on the right, to reach the crossroads passed earlier in the route. Go straight on to follow the outward route back to Achlean. Before a flood destroyed the bridge in 2009 you could cross the Feshie at Carnachuin and follow the private road on the far side before crossing back at a footbridge 1km south of Achlean.

Alternatives

A popular option is to traverse the rolling plateau to the north from the summit of Mullach Clach a'Bhlair to reach Sgor Gaoith before returning down the Hunter's Path from the south flank of Carn Ban Mor to Achlean. This route was much more popular before 1981 when the intervening Tops were classed as Munros in their own right.

5

Beinn Bhrotain Monadh Mor

Beinn Bhrotain (1157m) *hill of the hound*
Monadh Mor (1113m) *big hill*

Distance **29km**
Ascent **1500m**
Time **9 – 10 hours**
Start point **OS Grid ref: NN850985**
Map **OS Explorer 403**
Terrain & hazards **long section over featureless high-level plateau poses a considerable navigational challenge in snow or poor visibility, and is extremely exposed to storms; in good conditions the terrain gives fast going, apart from the boulders on Beinn Bhrotain; the two burns that cut through the plateau may require wading**

These two Munros are perhaps the least climbed of the Cairngorms giants, separated from the Cairn Toul group by the impressive glacial trench of Glen Geusachan. Reaching them from Glen Feshie involves a unique hillwalk, a long trek across the plateau of the Moine Mhor or 'the Great Moss'. This vast and empty space is serene on a perfect day, but could provide one of Scotland's toughest challenges in storm conditions.

Take the road up the east side of Glen Feshie and use the car park on the left about 1km short of Achlean where the road ends. Begin along the road towards Achlean, but turn left well before the farmhouse at a large stone inscribed 'Carn Ban Mor'. Follow the path to the forestry, passing through a gate and immediately forking left to climb steeply through the trees. Stunning views open up over the upper reaches of the Feshie as you gain height and leave the trees behind.

Follow the clear path as it rises towards the col between point 783m and Carn Ban Mor. From here it continues up the ridge, soon joined by a lower path. Looking back across Badenoch, a vast array of mountains are spread out with the cleft of The Window on Creag Meagaidh easily picked out on a clear day. Carry on by a burn before following the main path as it bears slightly left – the faint path ahead leads to a refreshing spring. At an obvious junction with a cairn, fork right – the left branch climbs Sgor Gaoith, a great option for a shorter day.

Once over the watershed the Cairngorm giants of Braeriach and Cairn Toul loom into view. Follow the wide path southeast, dropping down before a slight climb over point 957m to avoid a boggy area on the Moine Mhor, a great wild plateau. The feeling of being in the middle of a huge empty wilderness is rather spoilt as the path reaches a Landrover track. Follow this east until it ends above the small ravine containing the infant River Eidart. This can usually be crossed on stones – there is a better spot slightly upstream if needed. Cross a bog on the far side and

251

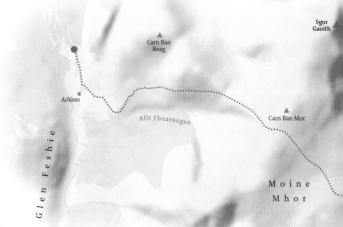

bear ESE across a slight bealach, continuing to the summit cairn of Tom Dubh, one of Britain's remotest Tops.

A short descent to the east leads to the Allt Luinneag. Despite the high altitude this is quite a substantial burn and usually requires a wade. Continue east, climbing onto the broad north ridge of Monadh Mor and following this to the summit cairn. The most striking view is looking east where dramatic crag-rimmed Glen Geusachan, overlooked by the Devil's Point, leads the eye to a prospect of Deeside and mighty Lochnagar. Beinn Bhrotain closes the right flank of the glen, a bouldery dome with crags on its northern flanks.

Check the daylight remaining and time taken so far, as the continuation to Beinn Bhrotain involves heading back over the Monadh Mor on the return. Pass left of the 1110m top and follow the path on a

steep descent to the bealach at 975m. Climb directly up the slope opposite, the last third of the way being slow going over boulders. At the summit are large shelter cairns, one of which rings the trig point. The views over Deeside are even better than from Monadh Mor. The quickest return to Glen Feshie is to retrace your steps all the way back, including a good deal of reascent.

Alternatives

Though already a long walk, the route could be extended by sticking to the landrover track on the return, detouring to take in Mullach Clach a'Bhlair before returning to the track for its descent above the spectacular defile of Coire Garbhlach, then following the path back up the east side of Glen Feshie; note, however, that the Allt Garbhlach has no bridge and may be impassable in spate.

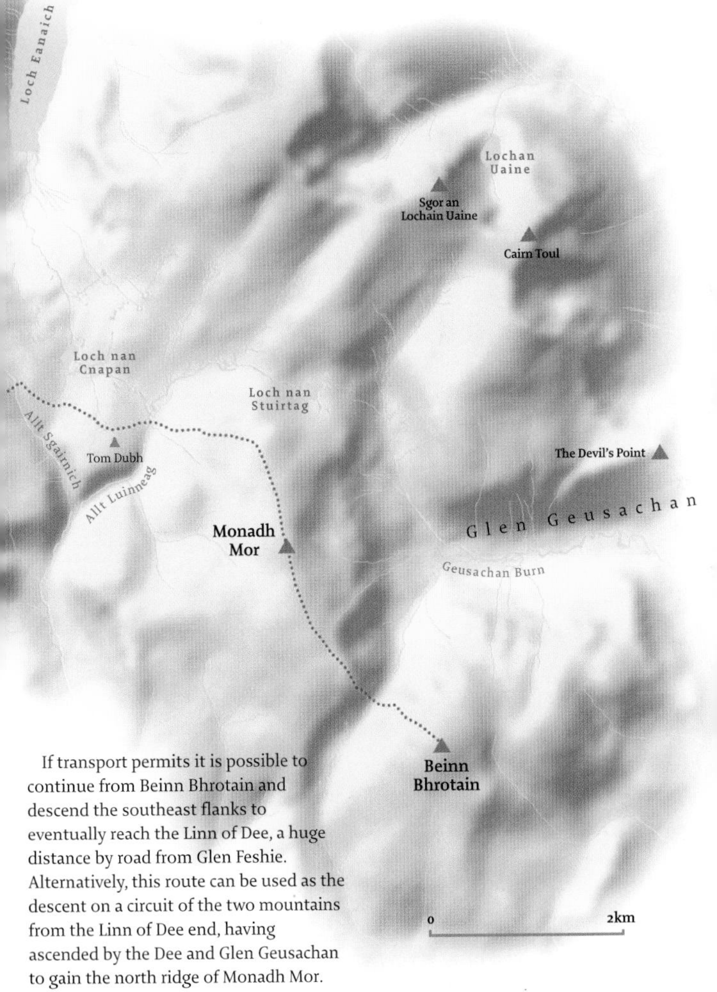

Loch Eanaich

Lochan
Uaine

Sgor an
Lochain Uaine

Cairn Toul

Loch nan
Cnapan

Loch nan
Stuirtag

Allt Sgairnich

Tom Dubh

Allt Luinneag

The Devil's Point

G l e n   G e u s a c h a n

**Monadh
Mor**

Geusachan Burn

**Beinn
Bhrotain**

If transport permits it is possible to
continue from Beinn Bhrotain and
descend the southeast flanks to
eventually reach the Linn of Dee, a huge
distance by road from Glen Feshie.
Alternatively, this route can be used as the
descent on a circuit of the two mountains
from the Linn of Dee end, having
ascended by the Dee and Glen Geusachan
to gain the north ridge of Monadh Mor.

0   2km

Looking down Glen Geusachan from Monadh Mor

6

Bynack More

Bynack More (1090m) *big cup*

Distance 19.5km
Ascent 785m
Time 6 – 7 hours
Start point OS Grid ref: NH988095
Map OS Explorer 403
Public transport none to start, but bus to Glenmore Visitor Centre
Terrain & hazards **a long walk, but the terrain underfoot can make for rapid progress in good summer conditions**

The most prominent of the Cairngorms when seen from distant Moray, Bynack More's position on the northeastern fringe of the main mountain group makes it a superlative viewpoint for North East Scotland. The ascent makes a popular excursion from Glenmore.

Although there is a limited parking area just beyond the National Outdoor Training Centre at Glenmore Lodge it is better to use the larger Glenmore Visitor Centre car park and follow the off-road path to the Lodge. Continue on foot along the track, keeping straight ahead at any turnings to soon emerge from the forestry and carry on up the glen towards the Ryvoan Pass. After 2km, you come to Lochan Uaine, the startling turquoise-green water reflecting the beautiful Scots pines. Continue climbing on the track before keeping right at a fork – signed for Braemar. The left-hand branch leads up via Ryvoan bothy and the stunning Abernethy Forest to Nethybridge. Pass to

the right of Loch a'Gharbh-choire, crossing the Allt a'Garbh-choire to reach the site of Bynack Stable. The iron hut which once stood here was useful only for those in desperate need of shelter; it had fallen into a state of decay and finally blew down in 2005. The flat green site left behind may be tempting for wild campers.

Cross the footbridge over the Nethy and follow the path up the moors beyond. This is part of the route of the Lairig an Laoith, an ancient cross-country drove road from Aviemore to Braemar. It is less well known than the higher Lairig Ghru and perhaps more challenging with the often tricky river crossing at Fords of Avon; however, the two Lairigs can be combined to make a fantastic two-day backpack. The path begins climbing more steeply until the broad shoulder of Bynack More is reached. Before the summit of the Lairig an eroded path, now more used than the pass itself, branches off to the right (south). Take this to climb directly towards the summit of Bynack More, keeping just to the right of the steep north ridge en route to the top.

Bynack More is a superb viewpoint; looking across from this position on the edge of the Cairngorm mountains, there is nothing to interrupt the view towards the Moray Firth and much of North East Scotland. The quickest return route is to retrace your outward steps. Perhaps Bynack More's most impressive features

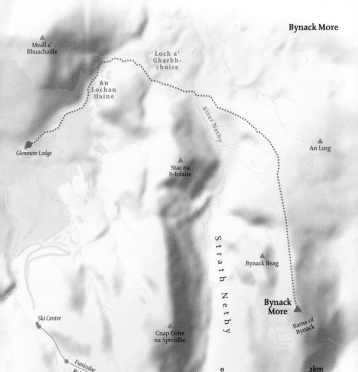

are the massive granite tors of the Barns of Bynack, around 500m from the summit but out of sight. To reach the largest of these, first head south to the Little Barns and then descend east on steeper ground.

Alternatives

Rather than returning to the summit from the Barns of Bynack, the walk could be extended by climbing A' Choinneach. This was a separate Munro until 1981, but now receives far fewer visitors. From here, bear southwest to the Saddle between Glen Avon and the headwaters of the Nethy. The fit may tackle the steep slopes west of the Saddle to include Cairn Gorm; these slopes are an avalanche blackspot in winter. Otherwise descend north into Strath Nethy and pick up a path on the east side of the burn to rejoin the outward route at the bridge next to the site of the Bynack Stable.

Bynack More summit, looking to Cairn Gorm

Ben Macdui plateau

7

Ben Macdui
Cairn Gorm

Ben Macdui (Beinn MacDuibh)
(1309m) *macduff's hill*
Cairn Gorm (1244m) *blue rocky hill*

Distance 17.5km
Ascent 934m
Time 6 – 8 hours
Start point OS Grid ref: NH989059
Map OS Explorer 403
Public transport bus from Aviemore to
Ski Centre
Terrain & hazards good paths lower
down; the section across the plateau is
one of the most exposed in Britain –
snow-covered for much of the year and
frequently blasted by extreme winds;
walkers should be confident of
conditions and their navigational skills
before setting out

Second in height only to Ben Nevis,
Ben Macdui is at the very heart of
the Cairngorms. Despite its lack of
immediate visual impact when seen
from afar, the long approaches, vast
exposed summit plateau, magnificent
crags and corries, and spectacular lochs
and lochans leave no doubt that this is a
mountain of real grandeur. The better-
known Cairn Gorm with its ski-
developments and funicular is really
little more than a bump on the Macdui
plateau's northern rim.

Macdui's central position ensures there
are many possible routes of ascent from
both north and south, but the route from
the ski centre is the shortest and most
popular, usually combined with Cairn
Gorm. It is possible to begin by trudging
quickly up to the Ptarmigan restaurant
from the ski centre and on to the summit
of Cairn Gorm in record time. However,
Cairn Gorm is a mountain where the
fastest route really should be avoided at
all costs – it keeps the more interesting
features of the mountain hidden and
leaves the walkers slogging uphill
amongst all the twisted metal of the
skiing paraphernalia.

Instead leave Cairn Gorm for the return
and head for the dramatic scenery of the
Northern Corries. From the ski centre car
park take the excellent path which bears
west, starting down some steps, over a
bridge and then quickly up and across the
slopes. When the path forks, keep right –
the upper path leads to Coire an t-
Sneachda – a mecca for ice-climbers and a
great destination for a shorter walk. Cross
the Allt Coire an t-Sneachda on stepping
stones and keep on the main path at
another fork, crossing the burn coming
down from Coire an Lochain.

The path now aims for the broad ridge
of Miadan Creag an Leth-choin; don't be
tempted by the smaller path cutting
across the slope. As you climb there are
good views across the cliff-girt bowl of
Coire an Lochain. Higher up, cross boggy

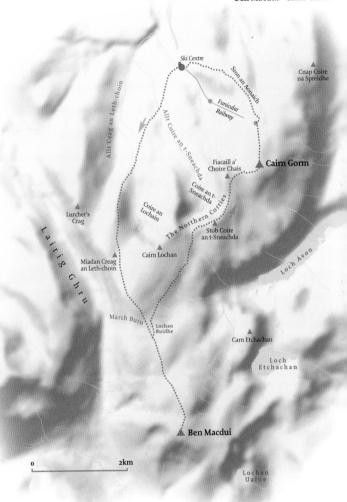

Ski Centre

Sròn an Aonaich

Cnap Coire
na Spreidhe

Allt Creag an Leth-choin

Allt Coire an t-Sneachda

Funicular
Railway

Fiacaill a'
Choire Chais

Cairn Gorm

Coire an t-
Sneachda

Lurcher's
Crag

Coire an
Lochain

L a i r i g   G h r u

The Northern Corries

Stob Coire
an t-Sneachda

Loch Avon

Cairn Lochan

Miadan Creag
an Leth-choin

March Burn

Lochan
Buidhe

Carn Etchachan

Loch
Etchachan

▲ **Ben Macdui**

0   2km

Lochan
Uaine

flatter ground before following a clear path which traverses the west flank of Cairn Lochan, high above the broken crags that plunge down to the Lairig Ghru. Pass between the headwaters of the March Burn and Lochan Buidhe to join a path coming across the plateau from Cairn Gorm.

After a slight descent, a long, gentle climb leads across the west slopes of Ben Macdui's north top to reach the massive main summit cairn and trig point. There is a view indicator to help identify the distant views from Britain's second highest mountain, which are very extensive – though the plateau robs them of depth. Retrace the outward route as far as the fork in the path south of Lochan Buidhe, and follow the right branch to reach the rim of the Northern Corries at the bealach between Cairn Lochan and Stob Coire an t-Sneachda. Continue over Stob Coire an t-Sneachda and then join the path coming up from Fiacaill a Choire Chais for the final broad slopes leading up to the summit of Cairn Gorm. Its position on the northern edge of the range makes this a better viewpoint than Ben Macdui, with a dramatic outlook over the Northern Corries and the great green expanse of Rothiemurchus below. To descend, head north to the Ptarmigan restaurant and down the Sron an Aonaich path which eventually curves round and down to the ski-centre car park.

Alternatives

Other approaches to the plateau from the north include the path up Fiacaill a'Choire Chais as already mentioned, and the Goat Track, though the latter is steep, badly eroded and holds snow into early summer – rocks and debris dislodged from the cliffs above have made this a blackspot for accidents. Keen scramblers can have a go at the ridge that divides Coire an t-Sneachda and Coire an Lochain; it is broad at first but narrows higher up and is composed of large blocks of granite – most of the difficulties can be avoided on the right.

Southern approaches begin from the Linn of Dee. Again there are many options, the most direct being up the Sron Riach ridge from Glen Luibeg. Queen Victoria, wearing huge skirts, made the ascent on foot from Loch Etchachan, following an approach up Glen Derry on a pony, but today's baggers are more likely to want to vary the route by taking in some of the subsidiary summits. An excellent route climbs over Carn a'Mhaim, continuing along a dramatic but straightforward arête before a final steep pull onto Ben Macdui; the return can then be made over the boulderfields of Derry Cairngorm, descending from the end of the ridge above Derry Lodge.

The Old Grey Man of Ben Macdui

One of the more persistent supernatural stories associated with the hills, the Old Grey Man was originally sighted by Norman Collie on Ben Macdui in 1891. Responsible for many of the first ascents in the Cuillin and an experienced Alpine and Himalayan climber, Collie was a respected mountaineer and research chemist, not known for an overactive imagination. However, he recalled his experience of the Grey Man at an address to the AGM of the Cairngorm Club in 1925. He had a real feeling of being followed, although he was alone – he estimated that the 'Grey Man' behind him was taking strides at least three or four times as long as his own. Although he didn't catch sight of his giant pursuer, Collie was so convinced of its sinister presence that he fled the mountain, not looking back until he was safely down in the glen. He never returned to Ben Macdui.

Later sightings have described a grey-haired man over 10 feet tall. In 1965 photographs were taken of huge footprints in the snow – possibly a hoax, this evidence has fuelled the ongoing rumour of an unearthly presence on the mountain. Some walkers and climbers have felt compelled to head towards the cliffs and others have speculated that the creature may have chased people to their death over Lurcher's Crag. More rational explanations have included the possibility of brocken spectres caused by the sun reflecting on low cloud. The presence of an imaginary companion in the hills has been reported many times elsewhere, such as on Everest. The mystery is best summed up in Norman Collie's own words, 'Whatever you make of it I do not know but there is something very queer at the top of Ben Macdui and I will not go there again by myself I know.'

Loch Avon basin and Shelter Stone crags

8

Braeriach
Cairn Toul
Sgor an Lochain Uaine
The Devil's Point

Braeriach (1296m) *grey upper part*
Cairn Toul (1291m) *rocky hill of the barn*
Sgor an Lochain Uaine (1258m)
peak of the little green loch
The Devil's Point (1004m) *originally Bod an Deamhain – penis of the demon*

Distance **36km**
Ascent **1980m**
Time **12 – 14 hours; can be done over two days with a camp or stay at Corrour bothy**
Start point **OS Grid ref: NH984073**
Map **OS Explorer 403**
Public transport **local bus from Aviemore**
Terrain & hazards **this route is extremely long, remote and exposed to severe weather, with very difficult navigation on the plateaux in poor visibility; in summer underfoot conditions are generally good, apart from an awkward boulderfield in the Chalamain Gap and more boulders on the Cairn Toul**

The archetypal Cairngorms outing, this yomp takes in four Munros, including three of the five highest mountains in Britain. Often split over two days, the approach is through the great trench of the Lairig Ghru, whilst the longer second section over the mountains runs around the rims of some awesome corries.

Start from the Sugar Bowl car park (charge payable) which is located on the left side of the road up to the Cairngorm ski centre, just before the zigzags. From here cross the road and take the path opposite, soon crossing the Allt Mor on a footbridge. Continue on the stone path which rises up and keeps north of the burn for 2km before crossing back to climb towards the Chalamain Gap, the obvious path ahead. At the gap the path peters out into a boulderfield which non-mountain goats will find slow and awkward to cross. On the far side of the gap, pick up the path again to head southwest and then WSW into the Lairig Ghru, climbing down to cross the burn on boulders before joining the main route on the far side.

The Lairig Ghru is a mighty glacier-carved trench running through the high Cairngorms, scattered with moraines of debris left by the retreating glaciers. First-time Lairig Ghru walkers cannot fail to be impressed by the majestic scale of Scotland's most famous hill-pass. Lurcher's Crag, with its immense broken cliffs, is up to the left and soon the Sron na Lairige walls can be seen on the right as the path continues up towards the summit of the pass.

Descend to the Pools of Dee, one of the two sources of the infant Dee which winds all the way to the sea at Aberdeen. The path keeps to the east side of the burn across the lower slopes of Ben Macdui to reach the Clach nan Taillear about 4km further on. This massive rock is named after a group of tailors who allegedly perished in a blizzard at this spot after trying to cross the Lairig as part of a bet – one of many tragedies that are testament to how fierce conditions can be here. Another 1km further on the path forks; head right to cross a footbridge and reach tiny Corrour bothy just beyond. This is the best known and one of the busiest of the open shelters maintained by the Mountain Bothies Association, a charity run by outdoors enthusiasts. As well as maintaining the building, their volunteers have taken on the unenviable job of carrying out and emptying the contents of the toilet installed to stop the pollution of the fragile environment caused by the high number of visitors to this spot. If you stay here, perhaps consider joining the MBA or at least helping by carrying out any rubbish you find inside the bothy.

The Devil's Point rises formidably as the guardian of the southern end of the Lairig Ghru, its name a euphemistic translation of the Gaelic *Bod an Deamhain* – 'the penis of the demon'. The ascent path climbs steeply beside the Allt a'Choire Odhair; the final zigzags can be banked out by hard snow into early summer. The plateau is reached suddenly and the summit of the Devil's Point is gained by a detour to the left with only 100m or so of ascent. Return to the bealach and begin the longer climb northwest, over the summit of Stob Coire an t-Saighdeir and around the rim of its namesake corrie. There is a gentle descent before the final steeper ascent to Cairn Toul. The views from this remote and airy summit are superb and it is especially satisfying to look northwest over the massive An Garbh Choire to Braeriach – the final and highest mountain on the route.

Keep the cliffs of Coire an Lochain on the right and continue to the next summit, Sgor an Lochain Uaine. Also known as the Angel's Peak, the Sgor was reclassified as a Munro in 1997, having previously been regarded as a subsidiary top of Cairn Toul. Continue along the headwall of the cliffs at first, dipping to a lower bealach before climbing to Carn na Criche above the great buttresses of Garbh Choire Mor. Now cut across the high plateau, keeping well clear of the crags, to reach the infant River Dee just below its second source, the Wells of Dee. Even at an altitude of 1200m it is already a fast-flowing stream. Cross it and aim directly for Braeriach – in poor visibility take great care on the approach to keep safely back from the plateau edge. The reward of the highest summit of the day is a fine view over Speyside and an even better one back

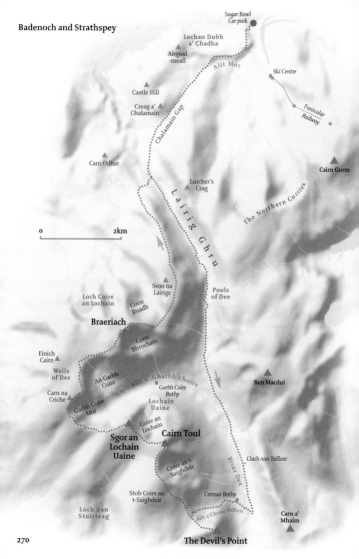

Badenoch and Strathspey

Sugar Bowl
Car park

Lochan Dubh
a' Chadha

Airgiod
-meall

Allt Mor

Ski Centre

Castle Hill

Creag a'
Chalamain

Chalamain Gap

Funicular
Railway

Carn Odhar

Lurcher's
Crag

Cairn Gorm

Lairig Ghru

The Northern Corries

0   2km

Loch Coire
an Lochain

Sron na
Lairige

Pools
of Dee

Coire
Ruadh

Braeriach

Coire
Bhrochain

Einich
Cairn

Wells of Dee

An Garbh
Coire

Allt a' Gharbh-choire

Ben Macdui

Carn na
Criche

Garbh Coire
Mor

Garbh Coire
Bothy

Lochain
Uaine

Coire an
Lochain

Cairn Toul

Sgor an
Lochain
Uaine

Coire an t-
Saighdeir

River Dee

Clach nan Taillear

Stob Coire an
t-Saighdeir

Corrour Bothy

Loch nan
Stuirteag

Allt a'Choire Odhair

Carn a'
Mhaim

The Devil's Point

across An Gharbh Coire to Cairn Toul. From the summit continue along the edge of the cliffs at first, then over Sron na Lairige and down its long north ridge, eventually following a path that cuts down to the Lairig Ghru. Once over the stream head back towards the Chalamain Gap – one final, tired tussle with the boulders being the last obstacle on the way back to the start.

Alternatives

Braeriach can be climbed by a circular route from the north. Start from Whitewell or Loch an Eilein and cross the Cairngorm Club footbridge to head up the start of the Lairig Ghru. Climb Braeriach via the Sron na Lairige and then start back by passing above the beautiful Coire an Lochain before making a long descent to Gleann Einich, joining the track back to Rothiemurchus Forest.

The other three Munros can be reached by a very long walk from the Linn of Dee; reach Corrour via Glen Luibeg and then follow the route as described. Braeriach is inconveniently located for this approach unless continuing to Speyside, as the Sron na Lairige descent route leaves you many kilometres from Corrour.

Cairn Toul, from Stob Coire an t-Saighdeir

The Devil's Point from the lochans below Carn a'Mhaim

Deeside

Deeside is often regarded as the more genteel side of the Cairngorms, probably because of its royal connections, plethora of castles and tearooms – enough for some to have dubbed it 'Royal Tea-side'. However, with long walk-ins, dramatic corries and some fine remnants of ancient forest, this side of the Cairngorms has a great deal to offer.

Braemar

Anyone attempting to complete the Munros is likely to get to know Braemar pretty well; it's the hub for an area packed with the coveted summits. The Munroists don't have the place to themselves, however, for this is one of the best known villages in the Highlands. A large part of its fame rests on the Braemar Gathering, the Royal-backed big daddy of Highland Games – if you are not attending this then it's best to avoid upper Deeside on the

last Saturday in September as it is packed to the rafters. But even without the Royals, Braemar would be a beautiful place, set on one of the Highland's finest rivers. The castle, managed by the local community, is well worth a visit, as is the wonderful Fife Arms; the giant winged stag flying above the public bar does a great job of reviving tired hillwalkers.

There are plenty of accommodation options around the village, including the well-run Invercauld campsite, two independent hostels (Rucksacks and the Braemar Lodge Bunkhouse), a large Hostelling Scotland hostel just on the edge of town, and many B&Bs and hotels. As well as The Fife Arms and other hotels serving bar meals, there is a chip shop near the river and the excellent Gordons, a café by day and bistro in the evenings. There are shops for all the essentials and a good independent outdoor shop and bike hire – very useful for making short work of some of the long walk-ins on these routes.

Ballater

Some 17 miles down the Dee from Braemar is Ballater, one of the most attractive small towns in the Highlands. Its streets are lined with Victorian granite houses, overlooked by the oak-clad Craigendarroch and centred on a large green. Many of the shops and services here are adorned with the insignia of members of the Royal Family, a reminder if any were needed of the close proximity of Balmoral. Deserving of special mention is Chalmers Bakery which has no less than three coats of arms outside – the pasties from here make ideal fodder for a day on the hill and may well have fuelled more than one Royal stalking party.

To slake your post-bagging hunger there is a fish and chip shop and several pubs serving food, as well as The Auld Kirk, which serves good lunches, and The Bothy, attached to the local outdoor shop, serving breakfast and lunch. Ballater tends towards the sedate and evening entertainment is usually limited to a quiet drink, although the place gets livelier at the weekends when it becomes a popular getaway spot for Aberdonians. There are lots of beautiful short walks to round off a visit to Balmoral or the Royal Lochnagar distillery. Try a jaunt up

Craigendarroch which has a great view of Lochnagar or a ramble around the Seven Bridges which takes in sections of the Dee riverbank to the west of town. If you really are in the mood for putting your feet up there is a choice of tearooms – try the old railway station. The line may be sadly long gone, but there is a replica of Queen Victoria's carriage on the platform inside, as well as the perfectly preserved waiting room complete with royal cludgie.

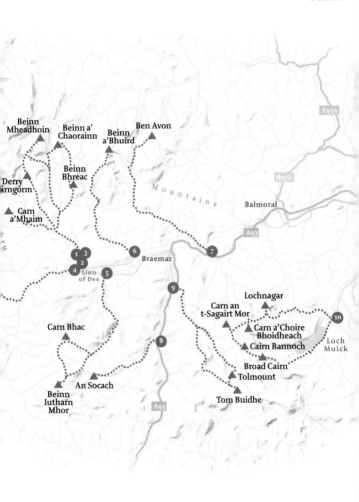

1

Carn a'Mhaim

Carn a'Mhaim (1037m)
cairn of the rounded hill

Distance **22.5km**

Ascent **650m**

Time **6 – 7 hours**

Start point **OS Grid ref: NO062898**

Map **OS Explorer 403**

Terrain & hazards **good tracks and paths
on approach, stony ascent and rocky
summit but fairly easy going throughout**

**Carn a'Mhaim is a southern satellite of
Ben Macdui; unusually for the
Cairngorms, it is linked to its giant
neighbour by a long, narrow arête. The
route below describes it as a single hill
ascent from the Linn of Dee – a
worthwhile walk that could easily be
extended to take in Ben Macdui.**

Start from the large car park at the Linn
of Dee, where there is a charge. Take the
path heading north out of the car park,
soon crossing a boardwalk before meeting
the main track heading up Glen Lui – turn
left here; after just over 1km it crosses the
Lui Water; turn left again to continue up
the glen.

After passing a small plantation the
lovely pinewoods around Derry Lodge are
reached. Once a shooting lodge, the
building is no longer used and is owned
by the National Trust for Scotland – part
of the huge Mar Lodge Estate. Pass the
lodge and cross the bridge over the Derry
Burn. This open area is often busy with
grazing red deer. Continue up towards
Glen Luibeg, passing a fenced area.

Approaching the Luibeg Burn, the path
forks. The left branch leads to a ford, but
in wet weather continue upstream for
about 400m to reach a bridge before
returning down the far bank. The path
leads round the low shoulder of Carn a'
Mhaim en route to Corrour. In a few
hundred metres fork right onto a path
which begins the ascent, crossing the deer
fence and continuing northwest up the
increasingly steep slopes. The ground
levels off above the level of the Coire na
Poite crags; bear slightly left to join the
south ridge heading up towards Carn
a'Mhaim. After gaining the first summit,
keep heading northwest to cross a
shallow col to reach the true summit
500m further on.

This gives dramatic views across the
great trench of the Dee to the Devil's
Point and Cairn Toul. If Carn a'Mhaim is
to be the only Munro of the day then the
best return route is via the outward path.

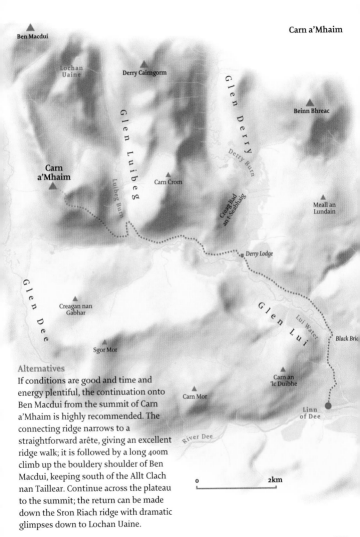

Alternatives

If conditions are good and time and
energy plentiful, the continuation onto
Ben Macdui from the summit of Carn
a'Mhaim is highly recommended. The
connecting ridge narrows to a
straightforward arête, giving an excellent
ridge walk; it is followed by a long 400m
climb up the bouldery shoulder of Ben
Macdui, keeping south of the Allt Clach
nan Taillear. Continue across the plateau
to the summit; the return can be made
down the Sron Riach ridge with dramatic
glimpses down to Lochan Uaine.

0   2km

279

Carn a'Mhaim

Glen Derry and Beinn Mheadhoin

2

Derry Cairngorm
Beinn Mheadhoin

Derry Cairngorm (1155m)
blue rocky hill of Derry
Beinn Mheadhoin (1182m) *middle hill*

Distance **31km**
Ascent **1210m**
Time **9 – 10 hours**
Start point **OS Grid ref: NO062898**
Map **OS Explorer**
Terrain & hazards **good approach tracks and paths; bouldery and exposed plateaux higher up**

Head deep into the wild heart of the Cairngorms on this long route to reach the dramatic granite tors of Beinn Mheadhoin. The southern approach is up beautiful Glen Derry and the return can be made over Derry Cairngorm.

Start from the large car park at the Linn of Dee (charge). If you've never been before, it's worth detouring at the start to the Linn of Dee itself, a waterfall below the roadbridge where water surges through a narrow gouge in the riverbed; amazingly the climber John Menlove Edwards swam down the Linn when it was in spate in the early 1930s. Otherwise, start the walk along the Glen Luibeg path from the back of the car park, which is boardwalked in part, turning left after a gate to follow the Landrover track up the glen. After crossing the Lui Water turn left again, soon emerging in the wide strath and eventually reaching the shelter of the old Scots pines at Derry Lodge. The Mar Estate now belongs to the National Trust for Scotland, although the granite-built lodge has been boarded up for years. Continue past it, but turn right immediately before the bridge over the Derry Burn onto a path through the woods up Glen Derry.

The gradual climb gives good views to the day's objectives, eventually leaving the beautiful woods and continuing up the more open upper glen. There is no bridge across the Glas Allt Mor which could be difficult or even impassable in spate. Around 400m beyond the crossing, take the left-hand fork in the track, crossing the Coire Etchachan Burn on a footbridge to head towards the Hutchison Memorial Hut. The massive vertical cliffs of Creagan a' Choire Etchachan which loom behind the bothy make it look tiny, but it is well placed as an emergency shelter for those caught out by bad weather. It is also a popular stopover on climbing and walking forays in this part of the Cairngorms; please help to keep it clean and tidy.

There is a good path to the bealach and Loch Etchachan, the highest substantial loch in Britain at 927m. Cross the outflow of Little Loch Etchachan and follow a path which branches up Beinn Mheadhoin to the right. This steepens higher up before levelling off onto the summit plateau at

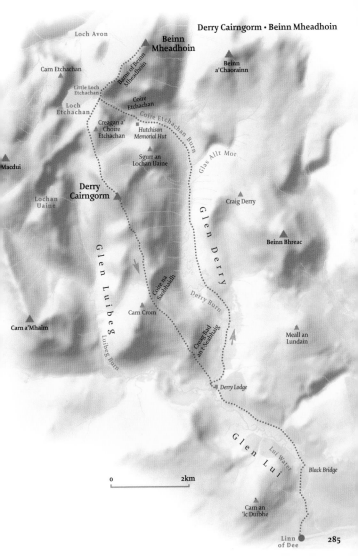

Loch Avon

Beinn Mheadhoin

Carn Etchachan

Beinn a'Chaorainn

Little Loch Etchachan

Barns of Beinn Mheadhoin

Coire Etchachan

Loch Etchachan

Coire Etchachan Burn

Creagan a' Choire Etchachan

Hutchison Memorial Hut

Glas Allt Mor

Sgurr an Lochan Uaine

Macdui

Craig Derry

Lochan Uaine

Derry Cairngorm

Glen Derry

Beinn Bhreac

Glen Luibeg

Coire na Saobhaidh

Carn a'Mhaim

Derry Burn

Carn Crom

Luibeg Burn

Croeag Bad an Seabhaig

Meall an Lundain

Derry Lodge

Glen Lui

Lui Water

Black Bridge

Carn an 'Ic Duibhe

Linn of Dee

0   2km

over 1100m. The stony plain ahead is decorated by several massive granite tors, the Barns of Beinn Mheadhoin. A path leads on to the highest of these where an easy scramble leads up to the top, the summit of the Munro.

Return to Loch Etchachan and follow the path WSW, heading towards Ben Macdui at first. After about 600m leave the path to the south, crossing the bealach to the west of Creagan a'Choire Etchachan and eventually picking up the faint path that links Derry Cairngorm and Ben Macdui. Pick your way across the large boulderfields on the upper reaches of Derry Cairngorm, which make for slow progress to the two summit cairns. Carry on over the boulders at first, passing another cairn and continuing towards the bealach before Carn Crom. This final rise is bypassed by a path on the left above the impressive crags of Coire na Saobhaidh. Follow it as it descends the east side of Creag Bad an t-Seabhaig and leads down to the footbridge at Derry Lodge. From here retrace the outward route to the Linn of Dee.

Alternatives

A shorter route to Beinn Mheadhoin – though it involves crossing the great ice-scoured basin of Loch Avon on both the outward and return journeys – is from the Cairngorm ski centre. Head up the Fiacaill a'Choire Chais and then down Coire Raibeirt, with a final steep and eroded section of path descending to the north shore of Loch Avon. Pass round the west end of this magnificent loch, fording the burn (may be impassable in spate) and passing the famous Shelter Stone howff – a cave used as a sleeping chamber, hollowed out under a massive fallen block. A path leads up to the bealach towards Loch Etchachan; leave this for the final ascent up to Beinn Mheadhoin.

Derry Cairngorm could be conveniently included with Ben Macdui on an ascent of the latter from the south; Carn a'Mhaim could also be visited to make a grand circular route.

3

Beinn a' Chaorainn
Beinn Bhreac

Beinn a' Chaorainn (1083m)
hill of the rowan
Beinn Bhreac (931m) *speckled hill*

Distance **28.5km**
Ascent **850m**
Time **8 – 9 hours**
Start point **OS Grid ref: NO062898**
Map **OS Explorer 403**
Terrain & hazards **good paths on the lower ground; exposed route with tricky navigation in poor visibility; care is needed crossing the Glas Allt Mor**

These two Munros are a little overshadowed by Beinn a'Bhuird and Ben Avon to the east and the Ben Macdui massif to the west. However, their ascent reaches into the heart of the Cairngorms and includes a beautiful walk through the pinewoods of Glen Derry.

From the back of the Linn of Dee car park (charge), take the footpath (SP Glen Lui) into the woods to reach a track. Turn left and continue through forestry and pinewoods before crossing the Black Bridge over the Lui and reaching the main Derry Lodge track – turn left here. The walk up the open glen is always enjoyable – each footstep taking you further from civilisation as you head into one of the UK's wildest areas.

Derry Lodge is a sturdily-built Victorian shooting lodge but is boarded up; along with the rest of the Mar Lodge Estate it is now owned by the National Trust for Scotland. Stay on the east side of Glen Derry rather than crossing either of the bridges beyond the lodge. A path leads up the glen through beautiful pine forest for 2km, reaching a high point before descending slightly. Turn right onto a vague path here, aiming for the bealach between Meall an Lundain and Beinn Bhreac. A straighforward but stony climb leads to the summit of Beinn Bhreac, the more easterly of its two tops at 931m. There is a great view back over the pinewoods of Glen Derry, whilst looking ahead the vast plateau of the Moine Bhealaidh stretches for several kilometres with Beinn a' Chaorainn visible beyond. Avoid the worst of the boggy ground by keeping to the east side of the plateau, where cottongrass grows in the summer months. Although only 4km separates the two Munros, it can feel much further on this bumpy open ground which is very exposed in poor weather.

Eventually the steeper slopes of Beinn a' Chaorainn are reached, leading up to the large summit cairn at 1083m. The view is much more extensive than that from Beinn Bhreac, with Ben Macdui towering to the left of the many granite tors of Beinn Mheadhoin. For the descent, the most pleasant route is by the southwest shoulder, continuing down steep slopes to a point just south of the summit of the

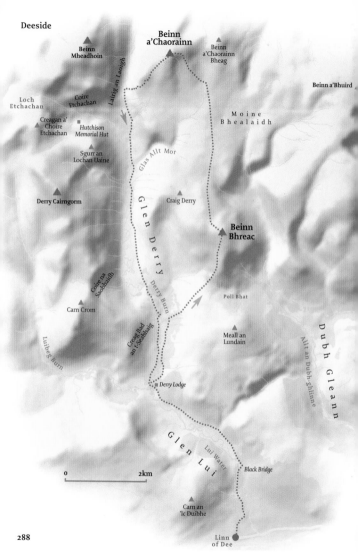

Deeside

Beinn
a'Chaorainn

Beinn Mheadhoin

Beinn a'Chaorainn Bheag

Beinn a'Bhuird

Loch Etchachan

Coire Etchachan

Lairig an Laoigh

Moine Bhealaidh

Creagan a' Choire Etchachan

Hutchison Memorial Hut

Sgurr an Lochan Uaine

Glas Allt Mor

Derry Cairngorm

Craig Derry

Glen Derry

Beinn Bhreac

Coire na Saobhaidh

Carn Crom

Derry Burn

Poll Bhat

Meall an Lundain

Dubh Gleann

Luibeg Burn

Creag Bad an t-Seabhaig

Allt an Dubh-ghlinne

Derry Lodge

Glen Lui

Lui Water

Black Bridge

0   2km

Carn an 'Ic Duibhe

Linn of Dee

288

Lairig an Laoigh. From the Lairig bear south along the path into Glen Derry, with fine views across the upper glen into Coire Etchachan. At the floor of the glen the path widens. Follow it to reach the Glas Allt Mor; there is no bridge and the crossing could be difficult in spate.

The bare upper glen continues for several kilometres until you come to the edge of the Derry pinewoods. Here you can either stay on the east bank of the Derry Burn or cross the bridge and head down the west side. The two routes meet at Derry Lodge; retrace your steps from here to the Linn of Dee.

Alternatives

These Munros are almost invariably climbed as a pair by the route given. The most obvious potential extension would be to cross the high exposed ground eastwards to link Beinn a' Chaorainn to the Beinn a'Bhuird massif.

Approach to Derry Lodge

Geldie Lodge

4

Carn an Fhidhleir
An Sgarsoch

Carn an Fhidhleir (944m)
rocky hill of the fiddler
An Sgarsoch (1006m) *place of sharp rocks*

Distance **42km**
Ascent **1060m**
Time **11 – 12 hours**
Start point **OS Grid ref: NO063897**
Maps **OS Explorer 394 and 403**
Terrain & hazards **good track for the long approach – suitable for mountain bikes; the hills are domes of pathless heather, boggy in parts; two river crossings which can be impassable in spate**

These two rolling domes lie more than 14km from the nearest public road as the crow flies – surely amongst the remotest of Munros. Carn an Fhidhleir and An Sgarsoch would be forgettable lumps if they were situated by the A9, but their isolated position between the main Cairngorm and Atholl ranges ensure they have a unique feeling of emptiness and space.

Start at the Linn of Dee car park where there is a parking charge (National Trust for Scotland). Head back along the road towards the Linn of Dee bridge but keep ahead when the road bends left, taking the track signed as a right of way to Blair Atholl (via Glen Tilt) and Kingussie (via Glen Feshie) – both fantastic long-distance through-walks. The route leads through mature pines with glimpses of

the Dee down to the left, before passing out into open countryside dotted with the remains of former townships.

The track makes for fast progress and has a good surface – a mountain bike would cut the length of the day, though the track gets stonier further on. Just before White Bridge a path branches off to the right, bound for Corrour Bothy; ignore this and cross the Dee on the track, passing some plantations. After another 2km there is a fork – the track ahead follows the Bynack Burn towards Glen Tilt; instead, turn right to pass a building and follow the north side of the Geldie.

After another 2.5km the track reaches the Allt Dhaidh Beag – there is a footbridge just to the right of the ford. Further on the Allt Dhaidh Mor can be an obstacle – it has no bridge and may require a wade. Do not attempt it in spate – and if running high, bear in mind that the Geldie itself will also have to be waded 1km further on. Ignore a branch off to the right to reach the ford across the Geldie – just after it there is another smaller tributary.

Follow the track up to the ruins of Geldie Lodge where a small, doorless shed at the rear provides unappealing shelter. From here the route continues along a well-maintained stalkers' path which aims west, greatly easing passage over the rough moorland. It extends further than is shown on OS maps, petering out just before the the Allt a'Chaorainn. Cross this burn and head up onto the moorland beyond. There is a faint path at first but it is soon lost amongst the bogs, so keep aiming for the north ridge of Carn an Fhidhleir. Here the walking becomes easier, following the ridge to reach the summit cairn. On a calm day this is a fine spot to enjoy the perfect silence.

Bear southeast along a ridge path which traverses the left flank of the minor bump of point 906m before dropping steeply down to the bealach to the east, a morass of wet peat at 702m. Continue up the far side, through heather, then more open ground, to reach the large summit cairn of An Sgarsoch, just beyond a rocky outcrop with a small shelter.

The long walk back begins by descending northwards. Apart from a short, steep section part way, this is a straightforward descent down an open slope towards the bealach with Scarsoch Bheag. A path avoids this hillock on the west side,

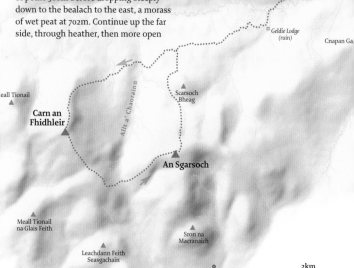

eventually swinging round to the right before petering out. Continue northwards downhill to rejoin the excellent stalkers' path used on the approach. You now need to retrace your steps all the way back to the Linn of Dee. The distance will seem even further if you are passed by fit, lycra-clad mountain bikers or even elderly gents on folding Bromptons who seem to appear at these moments as if to taunt the folly of preferring two legs rather than two wheels.

Alternatives

The central position of these hills ensures a variety of possible approaches. One option is heading up the east side of Glen Feshie from Achlean, passing the bothy at Ruigh Aiteachain. Parts of the old path at An Claigan have collapsed into the Feshie in a landslide and this section requires care, but once beyond the route continues on to the bridge over the River Eidart. The two hills can be approached across the peat bogs from here.

Another alternative – via Glen Tilt – is even longer. One option is to climb Carn a'Chlamain and continue down the far side to the bothy at Feith Uaine – a potential spot for an overnight halt. The two hills could then be reached after fording the river.

Beinn Iutharn Mhor

5

Beinn Iutharn Mhor
Carn Bhac

Beinn Iutharn Mhor (1045m) *big hell hill*
Carn Bhac (946m) *rocky hill of the peat banks*

Distance **32km**
Ascent **980m**
Time **8 – 9 hours**
Start point **OS Grid ref: NO089892**
Map **Explorer 387**
Terrain & hazards **good track for the long walk-in, grass and heather slopes with peat hags between the two hills; steep ascent and descent on Beinn Iutharn Mhor; it is possible to use a mountain bike as far as Altanour Lodge**

These remote hills in the heart of the Mounth have been decried as dull in some guidebooks. Many walkers, however, may welcome the peace and solitude they still offer and the long approach up fine Glen Ey.

Start from the small village of Inverey where there is a small car park on the south side of the road. There used to be a basic youth hostel here, but this is now closed; the nearest hostels are in Braemar. Inverey was also the last place in eastern Scotland where Gaelic was spoken as a first language, finally dying out in the 1930s.

Start the walk by heading southwest up the track from Meikle Inverey, passing several buildings and then following the Ey Burn. After 1km both the burn and the track fork; branch left to cross the Ey Burn

and then zigzag uphill before continuing along the west side of the glen. To the left down by the burn is the partially collapsed rock shelter known as the Colonel's Bed where a 17th-century colonel, outlawed for the murder of a laird, hid for many years, aided and abetted by old servants and a lover. The rim of the gorge can be visited by making a short detour, though the day ahead is a long one and care is needed by the slippery edge.

Continuing up the glen, pass the ruins of a remote farmstead at Auchelie. Further up, Piper's Wood can be seen opposite; after another 500m the track crosses the burn before crossing back 2.5km further on. The track ends at Altanour, a beautiful spot though the shooting lodge is completely ruinous. Continue up the glen following vehicle tracks for 400m, keeping right at a fork. A maze of muddy tracks and paths lead on up the glen, eventually crossing the Alltan Odhar and then climbing the ill-defined ridge between it and the Allt nan Clach Geala: at the flattening there are a series of grouse butts. Continue northwest and then eventually north, leaving the wet ground beyond for the final short pull to reach the cairn on the stony top of Carn Bhac.

From the top head southwest, passing below the 920m top and aiming for the

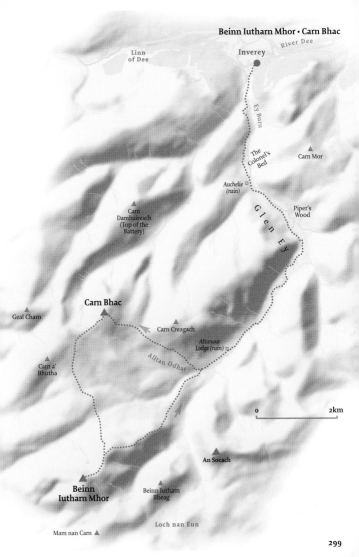

Beinn Iutharn Mhor • Carn Bhac

Inverey

River Dee

Linn
of Dee

Ey Burn

The
Colonel's
Bed

Carn Mor

Auchelie
(ruin)

Piper's
Wood

G l e n   E y

Carn
Damhaireach
(Top of the
Battery)

Carn Bhac

Geal Charn

Carn Creagach

Altanour
Lodge (ruin)

Alltan Odhar

Carn a'
Bhutha

0   2km

An Socach

**Beinn
Iutharn Mhor**

Beinn Iutharn
Bheag

Mam nan Carn

Loch nan Eun

bealach to the south (marked at 789m on Explorer maps). Continue over the peat-hagged and boggy ground for a further 0.5km to reach the base of the steep slopes which tower up to Beinn Iutharn Mhor. The worst of the scree on this punishing ascent can be avoided by taking a line slightly to the left. Once on the main ridge above, follow it to the right across rounded stones as it curves left and then right to reach the summit.

To return, head back along the ridge and follow it ENE on a steep descent to the boggy moorland far below. Cross this to the northeast, keeping to the higher ground as much as possible to then cross the Alltan Odhar and return along the glen past Altanour Lodge. The walk back down Glen Ey is likely to seem a long way with tired legs.

Alternatives

The very fit might extend the route above by including An Socach; from Beinn Iutharn Mhor head to Mam nan Carn and then along to the bealach below Beinn Iutharn Bheag. Descend to Loch nan Eun and then contour the hillsides to reach An Socach.

Beinn Iutharn Mhor could alternatively be approached from the Spittal of Glenshee, as an addition to the route given for Glas Tulaichean and Carn an Righ. From Carn an Righ traverse to Mam nan Carn, then detour to Beinn Iutharn Mhor before heading to Loch nan Eun as described above.

6

Beinn a'Bhuird

Beinn a'Bhuird (1197m) *table hill*

Distance **28km**
Ascent **960m**
Time **8 – 10 hours**
Start point **OS Grid ref: NO118911**
Map **OS Explorer 404**
Terrain & hazards **excellent going to the plateau, but navigation on the hill itself can be difficult and conditions are very exposed to poor weather; the river crossing may require a wade and should not be attempted when in spate**

Few outside of the hillwalking fraternity have heard of Beinn a'Bhuird, but this massive hill incorporates a vast area of high ground. The long approach up Glen Quoich leads through magnificent pinewoods whilst the plateau itself rewards with extensive views and a great feeling of space.

There is a parking area (charge payable) on the left just before the vehicle barrier which marks the end of the public road. From here, walk towards the barrier and take the path on the left which doubles back and climbs steeply.

You can take the next right turn for the short detour down to see the famous, stone-gouged Punchbowl in the Quoich Water below – legend has it that it held the drink for a toast as a precursor to the first Jacobite rebellion. Returning to the path, take the next right onto a track, passing through some particularly beautiful ancient pinewoods.

The footbridge visible after 2km can be used to vary the return route if leg muscles allow. Continuing on the track, Beinn a'Bhuird looms ever larger ahead. After crossing a burn ignore the path branching left which leads through the Clais Fhearnaig to Derry Lodge, instead continuing for another 1km to reach the ford over the Allt an Dubh-Ghleann. This usually requires a wade – it may be impassable if the water is in spate.

Before your feet have had a chance to warm up again, the track forks. Branch left here towards the spur of Carn Allt na Beinne. The original bulldozed track was once a notorious reminder of the lack of planning controls on such developments, creating an eroded scar visible from afar. In recent years the National Trust for Scotland has successfully reduced the width of the track and begun the restoration of the hillside. At a zigzag, a new path leaves the track to head for the bealach of An Diollaid.

Continue the climb up the ridge, which broadens out as the gradient eases, up onto the vast summit plateau. The final section is a real test of navigation skills in poor visibility to find the summit cairn whilst avoiding the cliffs which plunge so dramatically on the eastern edge.

In kinder conditions the views down into Coire an Dubh-lochain and its neighbours are superb, and you can continue by the rim or take a more direct line to regain the edge above Coire nan

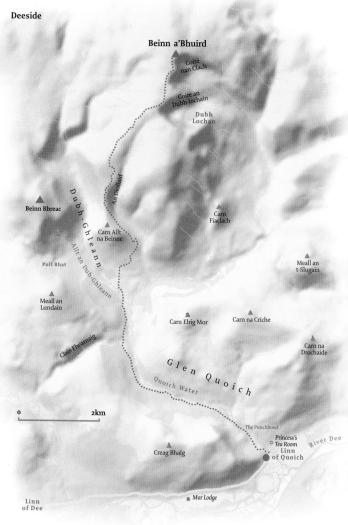

Deeside

Beinn a'Bhuird

Coire nan Clach

Coire an Dubh-lochain

Dubh Lochan

Beinn Breac

Dubh-Ghleann

An Diollaid

Carn Fiaclach

Carn Allt na Beinne

Poll Bhat

Allt an Dubh-Ghleann

Meall an t-Slugain

Meall an Lundain

Carn Elrig Mor

Carn na Criche

Clais Fhearnaig

Carn na Drochaide

Glen Quoich

Quoich Water

0   2km

The Punchbowl

Princess's Tea Room

River Dee

Creag Bhalg

Linn of Quoich

Linn of Dee

Mar Lodge

302

Clach and on to the summit with its massive cairn. Unless intent on a traverse or a much longer route, the return is the same way.

Alternatives

Whilst Glen Quoich gives the finest approach, it is also possible to climb Beinn a'Bhuird from Invercauld. Follow the route as described for Ben Avon as far as the Sneck, then climb west onto the plateau, crossing Cnap a'Cheirich to reach the summit. The fit could include Ben Avon as well.

Beinn a'Bhuird from above the Sneck

7

Ben Avon

Ben Avon (1171 m)
probably from abhainn – river

Distance **33km**
Ascent **1000m**
Time **8 – 10 hours**
Start point **OS Grid ref: NO188912**
Map **OS Explorer 404**
Public transport **Aberdeen – Braemar bus to Bridge of Dee**
Terrain & hazards **much of the route is on excellent paths, but the plateau is very exposed and navigating to the summit can be difficult in poor visibility**

The most easterly of the main Cairngorm ranges, Ben Avon is – by area – the biggest hill in Britain. Its huge summit plateau and ridges are scattered with an amazing array of granite tors, making it easy to identify from afar. The summit, reached by a scramble up one of those remarkable tors, is a superb viewpoint for North East Scotland.

Start from the car park at Keiloch on the Invercauld Estate just off the A93 between Crathie and Braemar (parking charge). The estate welcomes walkers – check out the toilets which are wallpapered with copies of hillwalkers' fanzine *The Angry Corrie*. Begin along the surfaced road signed for the Linn of Quoich, passing the estate cottages. In clear weather Beinn a'Bhuird is visible in the distance ahead before the road dives into the pines and passes the rear of the very grand Invercauld House.

Keep right at a fork before taking the next left beyond (signs for Slugain). The route runs through forestry until reaching a signposted fork; the main left branch here goes across the river and leads to the Linn of Quoich; instead keep ahead, again signed for Slugain. The track soon leaves the forestry behind to reach the open glen. Further up the Gleann an t-Slugain there is a choice of routes; the lower path through the delightful Fairy Glen is far more enjoyable than the track above it on the north side. Hidden from view, this is a magical place and is the supposed location of the infamous 'hidden howff' – a shelter used by hillwalkers – its exact whereabouts have long been a well-kept secret. Pass the ruins of Slugain Lodge and soon the two routes rejoin; continue north, eventually crossing the Glas Allt Mor. After the crossing the route zigzags to the left before heading sharply right to reach the prominent boulder of Clach a'Cleirich. From here the path continues a gentle climb to the bealach known as the Sneck which has a great view out over the wilderness of Slochd Mor and the impressive climbing grounds of the Garbh Choire.

Bear east and then northeast to follow the edge of the corrie and ascend to the vast plateau of Ben Avon. In good weather you can't fail to spot the huge granite tor of Leabaidh an Daimh Bhuidhe which forms the true summit, a short way northeast across a shallow depression, but finding it in low cloud or a whiteout

Slochd Mor

Leabaidh an Daimh Bhuidhe

Garbh Choire

Ben Avon

The Sneck

Carn Drochaid

Glas Allt Mor

Clach a' Cleirich

Carn Eas

Carn Liath

Carn Fiaclach

Carn Eag Dhubh

Carn na Craoibhe Seileich

Meall an t-Slugain

Meall Glasail Mor

Meikle Elrick

Gleann an t-Slugain

Fairy Glen

Allt an t-Slugain

Little Elrick

Meall Gorm

Carn na Criche

Carn na Drochaide

Creag a' Chleirich

Altdourie

Craig Leek

Braemar Castle

Invercauld House

Creag Choinnich

A93

Keiloch

Braemar

0   2km

is a serious challenge. Climbing to the top requires a hands-on approach – although the scramble is straightforward in good conditions; aim for the dip in the centre of the tor before scrambling to the top. As the tor is visible from so many distant hills it is quite satisfying to have visited it. The easiest return is by the same outward route.

Alternatives

The route above could be extended to take in Beinn a'Bhuird which lies on the other side of the Sneck.

Much less frequented is the ascent from Tomintoul, cycling or walking up a minor road and track to Inchrory. From near the Linn of Avon pick up a stalkers' path that climbs to the bealach just west of Meall Gaineimh before crossing the plateau. This route is an epic at 19km each way, but does give the opportunity to visit many more of Ben Avon's most spectacular tors, especially Clach Bhan which has been carved into fantastic shapes by the weather. By the tor is the Pool of the Women, said to relieve labour pains, though what someone in the early stages of labour would be doing in such a remote location is anyone's guess.

Approaching the summit of Ben Avon

8

An Socach

An Socach (944m) *the snout*

Distance 15.5km
Ascent 645m
Time 5 – 6 hours
Start point OS Grid ref: NO139832
Map OS Explorer 387
Terrain & hazards mostly pathless but
straightforward slopes

**An Socach is a rounded ridge between
Glen Clunie and Glen Ey with two
summits. Whilst it is unlikely to thrill, it
does give a fairly short and
straightforward hill walk.**

This route starts from the A93, 5.5km
north of the Cairnwell ski centre. Parking
can be found beside the edge of the
forestry plantations towards the head of
Glen Clunie. Begin by going through the
large gate on a landrover track and keep
left at a fork to follow the track past an
old farmhouse and into the Baddoch
Glen. Cross the bridge over the Baddoch
Burn and continue on the track. This soon
fords the Allt Coire Fhearneasg; the
crossing is usually easy enough. On the
far side leave the track to climb the slope
beside the burn; the going is steep at first.
When the gradient eases, bear left away

from the water, aiming for a cairn at the
base of the southeast ridge of An Socach.
Continue up the ridge towards the steeper
slopes ahead; a faint path climbs up these
just over to the right.

The broad, stony ridge leads to the
eastern summit of An Socach. The true
Munro summit is, however, actually the
western Top, a further 2km away, so keep
following the ridge to cross a bealach
between the two summits. The higher of
these is marked by a cairn and
windshelter, with the Cairngorms laid out
to the northwest. For the return, either
retrace the outward route or alternatively
descend from the bealach between the
two summits to reach the head of the
landrover track.

Alternatives

Although out of sight and probably out of
mind, An Socach can be climbed from the
Cairnwell ski centre. Cross the bealach
between Carn Aosda and the Cairnwell
and descend to the north side of Loch
Vrotachan before crossing the upper part
of the Baddoch Glen. Then simply head
up the slopes towards the summit.

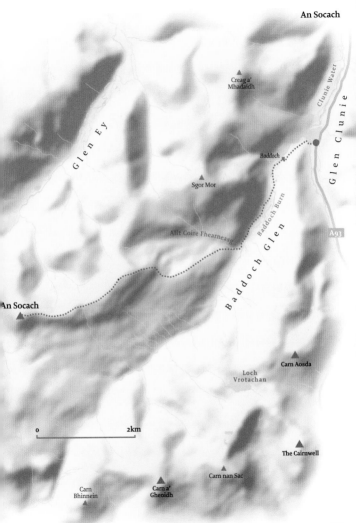

An Socach

Creag a' Mhadaidh

Glen Ey

Sgor Mor

Baddoch

Clunie Water

Glen Clunie

A93

Allt Coire Fhearneasg

Baddoch Burn

Baddoch Glen

An Socach

Carn Aosda

Loch Vrotachan

0   2km

Carn Bhinnein

Carn a' Gheoidh

Carn nan Sac

The Cairnwell

Looking into Glen Callater from above Coire Kander

Tolmount
Tom Buidhe

Tolmount (958m) *meaning unclear*
Tom Buidhe (957m) *yellow hill*

Distance **26.5km**
Ascent **840m**
Time **7 – 8 hours**
Start point **OS Grid ref: NO155881**
Maps **OS Explorer 387 and 388**
Terrain & hazards **excellent track up to Loch Callater, after which the going can be boggy; navigation on the plateau can be difficult in poor conditions and it is fairly exposed**

These two Munros rise as rather insignificant domes in the middle of the vast, wild Mounth plateau. The tops give fast walking and it is possible to reach them from several directions. The finest – though not the shortest – approach is the one given here from Glen Callater; from this direction Tolmount rises much more impressively at the head of the glen.

South of Braemar on the A93, there is a parking area (charge) just off the main road on the south side of the Callater Burn bridge just beyond Auchallater Farm. From here walk up the track (SP Clova), following the Callater Burn upstream. The Right of Way sign is a reminder of the importance of this route in the struggle to establish access rights in Scotland. The hill route from Braemar to Glen Clova is known as Jock's Road in

memory of John (Jock) Winter. In the late-19th century one Duncan MacPherson bought the Glen Doll Estate and tried to restrict access to the public. John Winter defied the ban and took his fight for access to the courts, supported by the Scottish Rights of Way Society. In the way of these things, a lengthy legal process culminated in a House of Lords ruling in favour of Winter, but by then both MacPherson and the Scottish Rights of Way Society were bankrupt. The case led to the passing of the Scottish Rights of Way Act, the most important piece of legislation for walkers until the Land Reform Act of 2003 which has granted increased access rights and responsibilities in the Scottish countryside.

Stay on the main track, crossing a bridge over the cascading Callater Burn at one point and continuing up the glen. Pausing to look back, the prominent granite tors on Ben Avon can be seen in the distance. Keep on the main track until the buildings at Loch Callater Lodge come into view. At the next fork, branch left but ignore the stalker's path to the left which leads to Lochnagar; instead head through a gate and pass between the lodge and Callater Stable. The Stable is now a bothy maintained by the MBA which makes a good place to get out of the weather for a break. Callater Lodge,

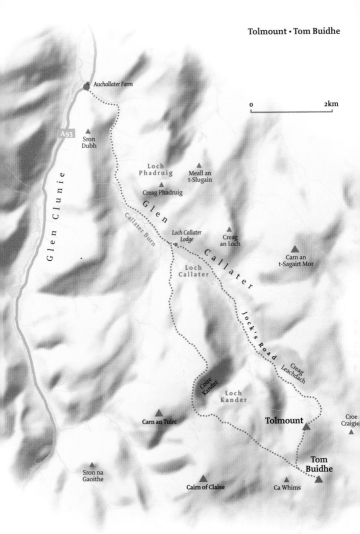

0   2km

A93

Glen Clunie

Auchallater Farm

Sron
Dubh

Loch
Phadruig

Meall an
t-Slugain

Creag Phadruig

Glen

Callater Burn

Loch Callater
Lodge

Creag
an Loch

Carn an
t-Sagairt Mor

Loch
Callater

Glen Callater

Jock's Road

Creag
Leachdach

Coire
Kander

Loch
Kander

Carn an Tuirc

Tolmount

Croc
Craigie

Sron na
Gaoithe

Cairn of Claise

Ca Whims

Tom
Buidhe

315

once used for shooting parties on the Estate, has seen better days but it still commands an excellent position at the foot of the loch.

Carry on along Jock's Road, now simply a path which heads away from the buildings to cross a small footbridge and a stile before following the northern shores of Loch Callater. Tolmount can at last be seen at the head of the glen. Once past Loch Callater continue up the glen, crossing minor burns on stones. The path becomes increasingly boggy, but there are great views into Coire Kander over to the right. As the path fades, carry on to pass under the crags of Creag Leachdach before beginning to climb out the eastern side of the glen at the lowest point. The ascent is steep, but once on the plateau the gradients ease again. Jock's Road is left behind here as you aim for Tolmount across the plateau.

The straightforward climb ends at the summit cairn which is set just back from the craggy north face on the seemingly endless plateau; this area is very exposed in poor weather and Jock's Road has seen fatalities in the past. On a clear day, Tom Buidhe is easily visible across a depression to the south and takes only about half an hour to reach. Maintain height by bearing SSW at first before curving round and up to the summit, which is almost the same height as Tolmount.

For the quickest return, retrace your steps, or it is possible to instead make a fine circuit around the head of Glen Callater. Return towards the bealach with Tolmount at first and then climb across the slopes of Cairn of Claise, aiming for the bealach between that hill and Carn an Tuirc. In poor visibility ensure you keep away from the steep cliffs that tumble down into Coire Kander. At the bealach are the remains of a drystone wall and a track; follow the track to the right as it curves above Coire Kander below the summit of Carn an Tuirc. The track passes a cairn and turns left to begin the descent, leading all the way down to Loch Callater where you cross the bridge over the river to retrace your steps to the start.

Alternatives

Two further Munros, Cairn of Claise and Carn an Tuirc, could easily be included in the route above with only short detours. Alternatively, Tolmount and Tom Buidhe could be climbed from the Cairnwell Pass to the west, probably as an extension to the route given over the Glas Maol Munros. Finally, if the Angus Glens make a more convenient start point, Jock's Road could be followed through Glen Doll to approach these Munros from the southeast.

Lochnagar
Carn a'Choire Bhoidheach
Carn an t-Sagairt Mor
Cairn Bannoch
Broad Cairn

Lochnagar (1155m) *small loch of noise*
Carn a'Choire Bhoidheach (1110m)
rocky hill of the beautiful corrie
Carn an t-Sagairt Mor (1047m)
rocky hill of the big priest
Cairn Bannoch (1012m) *broad rocky hill*
Broad Cairn (998m)

Distance **29km**
Ascent **1130m**
Time **9 – 10 hours**
Start point **OS Grid ref: NO309851**
Map **OS Explorer 388**
Terrain & hazards **a long and exposed mountain route, though straightforward in good conditions; the Ladder on Lochnagar is a notorious avalanche blackspot in winter conditions**

Celebrated in poetry by Byron and giving its name to both a whisky and a book by Prince Charles, Lochnagar is one of the best known Munros. Mountaineers would agree with all the attention, as its northeastern corrie is a masterpiece of rock architecture. For baggers this is just the first stop on a long yomp across the Mounth plateau, visiting a total of five Munros.

There is a car park at the end of the public road up Glen Muick (with a charge made for footpath maintenance). The Spittal of Glenmuick has toilets and a small but informative visitor centre. The route starts by heading directly towards the first mountain, Lochnagar, though it is out of sight. Follow the track past the visitor centre and turn right at the junction towards a bridge over the River Muick to the northwest. At the forestry on the far side of the glen go straight across the track and take a path up through the woods, soon reaching a track and continuing alongside the Allt na Guibhsaich. After 1km the track crosses the water, and a further 1km sees it pass above the Clais Rathadan ravine before bearing right and then reaching a fork. Branch left onto the well-built path which rises towards the bealach between Lochnagar and Meikle Pap. Although the main path bears left for Lochnagar it is worth continuing to the bealach to enjoy a superb view of Lochnagar towering above its northeastern corrie. Lochan na Gaire nestles in the middle, its Gaelic name means 'little loch of the noisy

sound' and has given rise to the modern name of the whole mountain as Lochnagar; the original name of the hill was Beinn Chiochan – 'the mountain of breasts'. There is a long day ahead, but if time and energy permit it is worth a short detour to the summit of Meikle Pap on the right, the classic viewpoint for the corrie.

From the bealach climb south straight up the boulder-strewn slope known as the Ladder; this holds snow late and has seen some fatal avalanches. Once on the plateau above, head round the back of the great cliffs; a peek down the gullies reveals a dramatic aerial view of the lochan below. Pass the small cairn at Cac Carn Mor and continue to the outcrop at Cac Carn Beag which marks the true summit of the mountain and has a view indicator. The Gaelic names on OS maps should really be Cadha Carn Mor and Beag (the big and small slope of the rocky hill), not Cac Carn Mor and Beag, which actually mean 'the big and small shitty cairn'. Queen Victoria tramped and rode over much of the Balmoral Estate with her faithful servant John Brown; she recorded that the summit of Lochnagar was 'cold, wet and cheerless, and the wind was blowing a hurricane'.

Return to Cac Carn Mor and follow the path southwest across the plateau. It is worth visiting the prow known as The Stuic for a great view to Loch nan Eun and across Deeside. The Munro summit of

Carn a'Choire Bhoidheach is 0.5km south. From here bear northwest to regain the stalkers' path, turning left and following its descent across the flanks of Carn an t-Sagairt Beag, crossing two small burns. After the second of these leave the path to gain the summit of Carn an t-Sagairt Mor, the third Munro of the day; the debris of a

Lochnagar

Meall Coire Saobhaidhe

Conachcraig

Glen Muick

River Muick

c Carn Beag

Meikle Pap

Clais Rathadan

Allt na Guibhsaich

Lochan na Gaire

Cac Carn Mor

Lochnagar

An t-Sron

Visitor Centre

Spittal of Glenmuick

Boat House

Loch Buidhe

Loch Muick

Black Hill

Black Burn

0   2km

Sandy Hillock

crashed aircraft lies on its northern slopes. Descend SSE to a featureless bealach where navigation skills will be tested in poor visibility, and then curve round to aim for the small conical summit of Cairn Bannoch, Munro number four. The Cairn of Gowal can be bypassed as the path improves on the way to the final summit, Broad Cairn. The popularity of Munro bagging can be seen in the clearer path to the summit in comparison to the original stalkers' path that passes it on the south side.

The route descends east from the summit, soon joining a bulldozed track across the plateau. Follow this briefly southeast and then along the top of the steep slopes above Loch Muick. It zigzags down to cross the Black Burn and eventually passes the boathouse on the way back to the Spittal of Glenmuick.

Alternatives

Whilst the above route enables all the hills to be tackled in a single day, there are many alternative approaches to climb them separately. The most popular circuit of Lochnagar is by the route described, descending by the Glas Allt to the royal lodge on the shores of Loch Muick. A longer approach is possible via Glen Gelder and Gelder Shiel, with the advantage that the best side of Lochnagar is in view for much of the way.

An old stalkers' path heads for Lochnagar from Glen Callater; this is a convenient approach for climbing Carn an t-Sagairt Mor and Carn a'Choire Bhoidheach. Broad Cairn and Cairn Bannoch are within range from Glen Doll in Angus, with an ascent via Bachnagairn. The most scenic approach to this pair, however, is up the glen above Loch Muick to the Dubh Loch, overlooked by the gigantic beetling crags of Creag an Dubh Loch. From here, continue up the glen, then bear south into Coire Uilleam Mhor and up onto Cairn Bannoch, returning over Broad Cairn by the main route given above.

Lochnagar plateau

Lochnagar's northeastern corrie

Glenshee and the Angus Glens

The five glens running north from Strathmore into the great Mounth plateau each have a distinct character and an array of walking opportunities. Their proximity to Dundee ensures they can be busy, but the wealth of routes mean that it is still easy to get away from it all. Options for baggers are more limited, as Glen Clova provides access to Driesh and Mayar (as well as a back route to Tolmount and Tom Buidhe) whilst Glen Esk is used as the approach to the most easterly Munro, Mount Keen.

Accommodation is provided at the Glen Clova Hotel which also serves meals and has a bunkhouse and self catering lodges. The Hostelling Scotland hostel at Glendoll at the head of the glen closed some years ago, as did the nearby Forestry Commission campsite. Bed and Breakfast can be found at Muirhouses Farm near Cortachy and in Clova, and there are more accommodation options in nearby Kirriemuir as well as the hostel in Glen Prosen. There are a few B&Bs

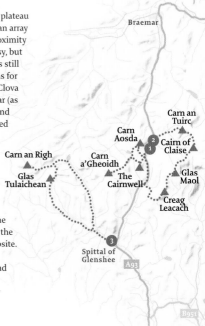

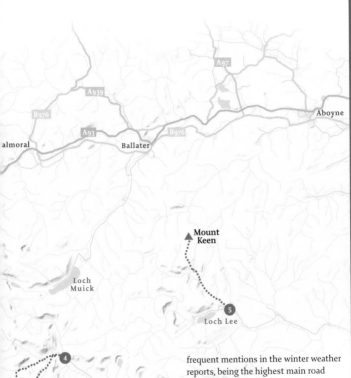

frequent mentions in the winter weather reports, being the highest main road in the UK and frequently snow-bound. Ecocamp Glenshee near Blacklunans boasts a number of glamping options and also offers Llama trekking, while the well-appointed Gulabain Lodge at Spittal of Glenshee provides hostel-style accommodation, outdoor activities and a welcoming café. Both serve the ski centre at the head of the pass where lifts extend into the hills on both sides.

in Glen Esk and nearby Edzell has a hotel and shops.

Glenshee – which is actually just inside Perthshire – is the through route to Braemar. It may be familiar from its

The Cairnwell from the south

1

The Cairnwell Carn Aosda Carn a'Gheoidh

The Cairnwell (933m) *rocky hill of bags*
Carn Aosda (917m) *ancient rocky hill*
Carn a'Gheoidh (975m)
rocky hill of the goose

Distance 11.5km
Ascent 595m
Time 4 – 6 hours
Start point OS Grid ref: NO138781
Map OS Explorer 387
Terrain & hazards **the route out to Carn a'Gheoidh requires careful navigation when visibility is poor; the final descent from the Cairnwell is pathless and steep**

This group of three Munros rises above the western side of the Cairnwell Pass, giving a high-level start to a straightforward hill-round. The Cairnwell looks impressive when driving up the pass from the south; its northeastern slopes have been developed as part of a skiing area that extends round to Carn Aosda, making the latter into perhaps the least attractive hill in Scotland in the summer months. The higher Carn a'Gheoidh is set apart to the west and remains unspoilt.

This route starts from the Glenshee Ski Centre at the summit of the high road to Braemar. The area became popular for winter sports in the 1930s when more people began venturing abroad for

holidays and wanted to be able to practise their new found skiing skills back home. At first basic rope pulls, powered by tractors, were used on the slopes as the sport gained popularity after the Second World War. The first T-bar lift was installed in 1957 by the Dundee Ski Club and in the early 1960s the chairlift became operational and the centre started to operate on a commercial basis. As with all Scottish ski resorts it is prone to the vagaries of the weather, but so far Glenshee has managed to weather financial crises; a management buy-out in 2004 allowing the continued operation of the site.

On the far side of the road is a sculpture of taciturn writer and painstaking chronicler of the Lake District fells, Alfred Wainwright and his wife Betty. Head past the far end of the main ski building, crossing a gravelled yard to join a track. Follow this diagonally to the right to reach a ski-lift and the restaurant. Turn right here, taking a track steeply uphill between two ski-lifts. The track bends left; at a fork branch right to pass under the ski-lift to a junction on the summit ridge. Bear right here and keep an eye out for a path which goes off left uphill leading directly to the summit of Carn Aosda. It seems amazing after so little exertion to

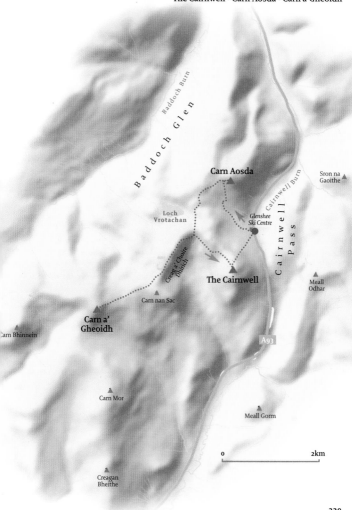

be at the summit of a Munro – this must be the easiest ascent of them all.

From the summit return along the broad ridge and follow it round to the bealach between Carn Aosda and the Cairnwell, with Loch Vrotachan down to the right. Ignore a path down from here; instead you can either continue up the ridge before forking right or save a short section of uphill by cutting across to a slightly higher bealach to the south (point 808m on OS Explorer maps). The ski paraphernalia is now out of sight, giving a much wilder and quieter feel to the walk. Climb the grassy slope and continue above the broken crags of Creag a'Choire Dhirich, passing a couple of lochans before reaching the small plateau of Carn nan Sac.

Head west across flat, featureless ground to reach the final short climb to the summit cairn of Carn a'Gheoidh, which – at 975m – is the highest of the day's three peaks. Now retrace the route back to the bealach below the Aosda – Cairnwell ridge. From here take the right fork to gain the northwest ridge of the Cairnwell.

Pass the top of the chairlift to reach the summit beyond, which suffers the indignity of being crowned by a pair of transmitter masts. A better position away from the metalware can be found by continuing a short distance until you find a peaceful spot to admire the view down Glen Shee. To return to the start, walk back over the summit of the Cairnwell and down the track until a point where you can leave the ridge to the right and head towards the ski centre; the descent is steep.

2

Glas Maol
Carn an Tuirc
Cairn of Claise
Creag Leacach

Glas Maol (1068m) *grey-green hill*

Carn an Tuirc (1019m)
rocky hill of the wild boar

Cairn of Claise (1064m)
rocky hill of the grassy holly

Creag Leacach (987m) *slabby crag*

Distance 19.5km

Ascent 1035m

Time 7 – 8 hours

Start point OS Grid ref: NO150978

Map OS Explorer 387

Terrain & hazards **approach can be
boggy; then high exposed plateau
lacking in features**

**A high-level start eases access to these
four rounded Munros on the east side of
the Cairnwell Pass. The highest, Glas
Maol, has been developed for skiing, but
the wide summit ridges and rolling
plateax have remained a wild place with a
great feeling of space. The fertile soils
have led to these hills being rivalled only
by Ben Lawers for their array of rare
arctic-alpine plants.**

There is limited parking in a lay-by on
the side of the A93, 2km north of the
Glenshee Ski Centre. A clear grassy path
leads down to an old stone bridge, once
part of the old military road from Perth to
Braemar. Cross this and turn right to
follow a path leading up the north side of
the Allt a' Gharbh-choire. The path is
indistinct in places and can be very boggy
after wet weather; it passes two ruined
sheilings. After the second set of ruins,
where the burn curves right, leave the
glen to aim directly for the dome of Carn
an Tuirc. Heather and grass soon give way
to stones before you reach the summit
cairn on the spacious plateau.

From the top, aim east, then southeast
to a featureless bealach, joining a track
here. The descent is so short that it is a
surprise that Carn an Tuirc is regarded as
a separate Munro. In good weather a
detour northeast can reveal a stunning
view into Corrie Kander, a classic ice-
scoured bowl with craggy walls.
Otherwise continue SSE to ascend Cairn
of Claise, following a line of fenceposts
and later a drystone wall which marks the
old county boundary.

From Cairn of Claise follow the broad
ridge southwest by a track and fenceposts.
The feeling is of overwhelming space as
the immense rolling mountains meet the
wide skies. Cross the route of the old
Monega Road and continue to the large
cairn and trig point at the summit of Glas

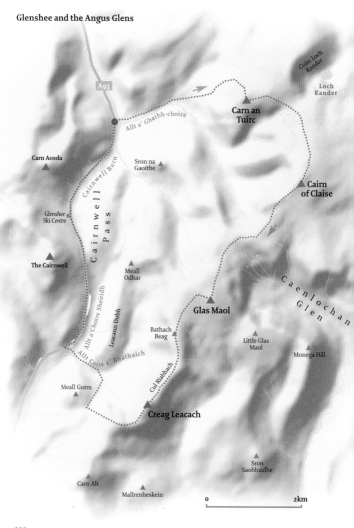

Glenshee and the Angus Glens

Coire Loch Kander

Loch Kander

A93

Carn an Tuirc

Allt a' Ghaibh-choire

Carn Aosda

Sron na Gaoithe

Cairn of Claise

Cairnwell Burn

Glenshee Ski Centre

C a i r n w e l l   P a s s

The Cairnwell

Meall Odhar

C a e n l o c h a n   G l e n

Allt a 'Choire Sheiridh

Glas Maol

Leacann Dubh

Bathach Beag

Little Glas Maol

Allt Coire a' Bhathaich

Monega Hill

Meall Gorm

Cul Riabhach

Creag Leacach

Carn Alt

Mallrenheskein

Sron Saobhaidhe

0   2km

Maol. The highest of this group of Munros, the plateau here extends for miles to the east and north, eventually merging with the Lochnagar range.

Follow the old county boundary west and then southwards over Bathach Beag to the bealach. Nearby is a tiny stone howff, only really suitable for those desperate to get out of the wind. The ridge becomes much better defined as it is followed over Cul Riabhach and then on up to the stony summit of Creag Leacach, the final and most shapely of the four Munros.

Continue along the stony ridge to the southwest top (943m) before descending steeply northwest to reach the bealach below Meall Gorm. At the bealach, head northeast down to the floor of Coire a'Bhathaich. Here, cross the burn and bear left down the glen – retaining some height above the water will enable you to pick up a path coming down the Leacann Dubh. Follow this and cross the footbridge over the Allt a'Choire Sheiridh to eventually reach the A93. All that remains now is a 4km plod along the roadside verge back to the start. It is possible to divert onto old sections of the 'Devil's Elbow' road and the military road to keep away from the speeding traffic as much as possible.

Alternatives

The walk could be made longer or shorter by either climbing Carn an Tuirc and Cairn of Claise as one pair and Glas Maol and Creag Leacach as another, or by detouring across the flat plateau to include Tolmount and Tom Buidhe.

Whilst the vast majority of walkers opt to make use of the Cairnwell Pass for a high-level start, the finest approach to Glas Maol is from the head of Glen Isla, using the route of the old Monega Road. Carn an Tuirc and Cairn of Claise can be included in a fine round with Tolmount and Tom Buidhe from Glen Callater.

Glas Maol and Creag Leacach from Ben Gulabin

3

Glas Tulaichean
Carn an Righ

Glas Tulaichean (1051m) *green grey hillocks*
Carn an Righ (1029m) *rocky hill of the king*

Distance **27.6km**
Ascent **1085m**
Time **8 – 10 hours**
Start point **OS Grid ref: NO105701**
Map **OS Explorer 387**
Terrain & hazards **track almost to summit of Glas Tulaichean, rougher moorland to Carn an Righ and on descent**

This pair of Munros lie in the empty lands of the Mounth between Beinn a'Ghlo and Glen Shee. Glas Tulaichean has the indignity of a Landrover track almost to the summit, but Carn an Righ, hidden behind, retains its wild feel.

There is a small parking area at the start of the private drive to the Dalmunzie Castle Hotel. The first 2km of the walk follow the driveway to the hotel, where it is possible to pay to park at reception to shorten the day if required. The hotel is a magnificent pile, built in the Scots baronial style, and welcomes walkers. Continue past on the track to the right which leads to Glenlochsie Farm.

Keep on the track to head west up Glen Lochsie until the track crosses the river at NO079717. There are two options here; either remain on the track which twice crosses the river, or alternatively follow a faint zigzag to the right and then back left at a higher level to walk along the line of

an old railway which was used to move stone for extensions to Dalmunzie in the 1920s. The two routes rejoin near the ruins of Glenlochsie Lodge. From here the track winds up the slope onto the broad ridge of Breac-reidh and then the high dome of Glas Tulaichean. The extensive views are compensation for the monotony of the track; at its highest point leave the main track to follow fainter trails and fenceposts to the right, which, after a short distance, reach the summit at 1051m. The ground falls away on the east side into the great bowl of Glas Choire Mor.

Descend around the rim of this corrie, then bear north from the shoulder. At a convenient point break left for a final steeper descent to to the boggy ground below Mam nan Carn before picking up a stalkers' path on the slopes just beyond. Follow this to the 771m bealach beneath Carn an Righ before tackling the slopes opposite, keeping left at first to avoid the steeper ground. Finally, aim more directly to the summit across short grass and stones. Carn an Righ feels much wilder than its neighbour, with range after range of empty hills receding into the distance, Beinn a'Ghlo looking most noble to the west.

Return to the bealach and along the stalkers path below Mam nan Carn. When this peters out, pass south of Loch nan

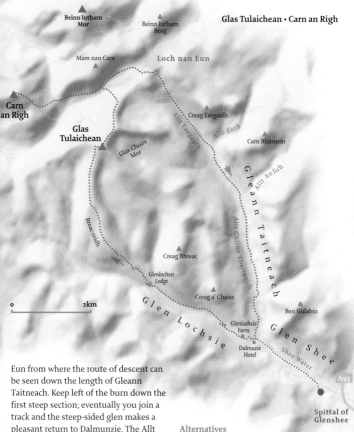

Beinn Iutharn Mor

Beinn Iutharn Beag

Mam nan Carn

Loch nan Eun

Carn an Righ

Creag Easgaidh

Allt Easgaidh

Allt Eng

Carn Bhinnein

Glas Tulaichean

Glas Choire Mor

Allt Aulich

Gleann Taitneach

Allt Ghlinn Thaitnich

Breac-reidh

Creag Bhreac

Glenlochsie Lodge

Creag a' Chaise

Ben Gulabin

Glen Lochsie

Glenlochsie Farm

Glen Shee

Dalmuzie Hotel

Shee Water

0   2km

A93

Spittal of Glenshee

Eun from where the route of descent can be seen down the length of Gleann Taitneach. Keep left of the burn down the first steep section; eventually you join a track and the steep-sided glen makes a pleasant return to Dalmunzie. The Allt Aulich must be crossed, but there is a footbridge just to the left on the Allt Coire Shith. Beyond this, cross the bridge over the main burn and take the path down the west bank to rejoin the outward route near the hotel. Turn left at the road to return to the start.

Alternatives

Although Glas Tulaichean is most readily climbed by the route given above, Carn an Righ can be reached from several directions. Linked at a high level to Beinn Iutharn Mhor, it is often included in a round of the Glen Ey hills, whilst an epic approach up Glen Tilt may also appeal.

Carn Bhinnein and Creag Leacach from Glas Tulaichean

4

Driesh
Mayar

Driesh (947m) *thorn bush*
Mayar (928m) *meaning unknown*

Distance **14.5km**
Ascent **835m**
Time **5 – 6 hours**
Start point **OS Grid ref: NO284760**
Map **OS Explorer 388**
Terrain & hazards **excellent path to back of Corrie Fee, short pathless moorland section, then rough path with navigation aided by fence posts; parking charge**

For Dundonians, Driesh and Mayar are amongst the best known and loved of the Munros. Rounded on their uppermost slopes but scoured by craggy corries on their flanks, they rise steeply above Glen Doll at the head of Glen Clova.

The head of Glen Clova is a beautiful spot and deservedly popular in summer. A number of shorter walks have been waymarked from the ranger station next to the Glen Doll car park; this route follows one initially up to Corrie Fee before heading off to the hills above. The ranger service operates a route card safety system during certain hours. From the car park (charge payable) take the track (SP Forest Walks) past the farm at Acharn, keep left at a fork and then follow signs for Corrie Fee, ignoring Jock's Road, the ancient route to Braemar that leaves on the right. The main track soon crosses the White Water; ignore another

track to the right and soon you are walking on a path through the woods, winding uphill to reach the deer fence at Corrie Fee.

Just beyond the fence is a great viewpoint where the huge glacier-carved bowl of the corrie with its waterfall at the back can really be appreciated. The bumpy corrie floor is formed by debris left behind by the retreating ice. Corrie Fee is designated as a National Nature Reserve, particularly for its large variety of rare plants, but it is also a good place to spot birds of prey.

Follow the path across the bottom of the corrie. The well-made path climbs steeply, eventually reaching the waterfall. From here climb directly towards Mayar; the summit only becomes visible towards the end of the ascent. From the top follow a line of old fence posts briefly northeast and then east for 1.5km until you reach a large corner fencepost (where another line of posts heads south). This is where the Kilbo Path drops down the Shank of Drumwhallo into Glen Prosen. Keep straight ahead on the right side of the fence. Ignore the path that descends across the Shank of Drumfollow, which is used on the descent, and instead continue to the bealach at the head of Corrie Kilbo. Climb the rough slope

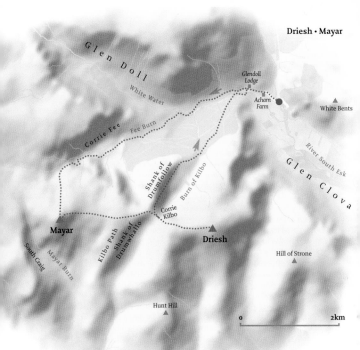

ahead, passing a couple of small cairns to reach Driesh's wide summit plateau with a trig point and shelter.

This return route retraces your steps back over the col above Corrie Kilbo before taking the clear path to the right which shortcuts to the main path heading down the Shank of Drumfollow. At the forestry, follow the fence for a while to a gate in the deer fence. Descend through the forest, crossing the Burn of Kilbo on stepping stones and, after skirting a felled area, go straight across a track to carry on downhill. At the next track continue ahead on a smaller path and turn right at

the bottom alongside the White Water. Further on turn left to reach Acharn Farm and then right to follow the track back to the car park.

Alternatives

The approach to these hills from Glen Prosen is far less frequented. Park near Glen Prosen Lodge and walk up to Kilbo near the head of the glen. Take the Shank of Drumwhallo up onto the plateau and detour to the summit of Mayar. Return to the top of the path and then cross to Driesh before descending via the Shank of Driesh and Lick.

341

Driesh from Loch Brandy

5

Mount Keen

Mount Keen (939m) *smooth hill*

Distance **17.5km**
Ascent **810m**
Time **5 – 6 hours**
Start point **OS Grid ref: NO446803**
Map **OS Explorer 395**
Public transport **bus (913) from Brechin on school days**
Terrain & hazards **track and clear hill path over exposed ground**

Mount Keen is the most easterly of the Munros, its domed summit rising above a vast swathe of featureless moorland and rewarding with extensive views. The shortest route is the southern approach given here from Glen Esk via Glen Mark.

At the head of Glen Esk is a car park at Invermark. From here walk along the road past the church, soon turning right onto a track (SP Mount Keen and Queen's Well). Bear left just before the house to go through a gate onto a track leading out into the glen. The remains of Invermark Castle can be seen on the left through the trees – a high sandstone tower that provided protection from cattle raiders.

Pass through an old metal gate to continue along the open glen, sometimes crowded with red deer during the autumn. Eventually the granite arches of the Queen's Well can be seen ahead. A popular destination for a short walk, the ornamental well was erected at the site of a spring where Queen Victoria rested during a pony expedition from Balmoral. A narrow path on the right leads to the well; from it continue ahead to soon reach a track just left of Glenmark Cottage. Turn right to pass the cottage and follow the track uphill, crossing the Easter Burn and then the Ladder Burn. The former has no bridge, but stepping stones usually make a dry feet crossing possible. The track leads up the Ladder Glen, eventually leaving the burn behind to zigzag up onto the higher moorland.

The track becomes a path aiming north; at a fork, branch right, the left route being the line of the ancient Mounth Road, a popular cattle droving and trade route between the glens. The path to the summit has been improved in recent years to try and alleviate the erosion on this popular hill. A short section of boulders leads to the summit and trig point. The view is very extensive, with craggy Lochnagar breaking up miles of rolling moors. Most walkers retrace the outward route, unless transport can be arranged from Glen Tanar which would make a fabulous through walk.

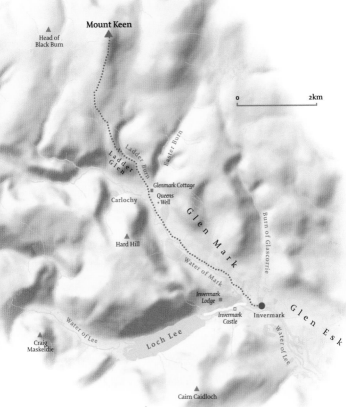

Mount Keen

Head of
Black Burn

Ladder Burn

Easter Burn

Ladder Glen

Glenmark Cottage

Queens
Well

Carlochy

Hard Hill

Glen Mark

Water of Mark

Burn of Glascorrie

Invermark
Lodge

Invermark
Castle

Invermark

Glen Esk

Water of Lee

Loch Lee

Water of Lee

Craig
Maskeldie

Cairn Caidloch

0   2km

Alternatives

To the northeast of Mount Keen, Glen
Tanar boasts some of the most beautiful
Caledonian pinewoods in Scotland,
making for a fine, if longer, approach from
Deeside. Park at the end of the public road
up the glen and follow a track round the
estate buildings and then up the glen.
Higher up the old Mounth Road forks and
the left branch leads up to the summit
(the right branch being a shortcut
through to Invermark).

Looking to Clachan Yell from Mount Keen

Spean Bridge and Roybridge

For those who want to hedge their bets with the weather on a trip to the Highlands, Glen Spean is perfectly situated. Close enough to Fort William for ascents of Ben Nevis and the Mamores, the Grey Corries are close at hand, and if the weather looks better in the east you can easily speed across to Creag Meagaidh or even the Cairngorms. Being on the West Highland Line it is also a useful jumping-off point for rail trips to Corrour Station or Rannoch.

Position is everything with Spean Bridge, as the dip around the junction of the A82 and A86 has a cluster of buildings, including a Spar shop and woollen mill with good café. The Commando Bar at the Spean Bridge Hotel has a roaring fire in winter and serves substantial pub fare, as well as fish and chips to take away. The fine dining option is Russell's Restaurant (which also has self-catering and rooms at the Smiddy House). The eco-friendly Old Pines Hotel and Restaurant on the road to

348

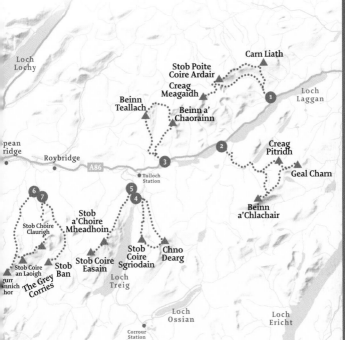

Gairlochy also justifies a detour.

Just along the road is Roybridge, also with a coffeeshop, an excellent campsite and a couple more pubs, of which the Roy Bridge Hotel has a bunkhouse. A couple of other noteworthy hostels in the area include The Great Glen Hostel not far away on the A82 and Aite Cruinnichidh just east of Roybridge.

Coire Ardair, Creag Meagaidh

1

Creag Meagaidh
Carn Liath
Stob Poite Coire Ardair

Creag Meagaidh (1130m)
crag of the boggy place
Carn Liath (1006m) *grey rocky hill*
Stob Poite Coire Ardair (1054m)
peak of the point of the high corrie

Distance **21km**
Ascent **1080m**
Time **8 – 9 hours**
Start point OS Grid ref: **NN482872**
Map OS Explorer **401**
Terrain & hazards **the open summit plateau and great cliffs mean that careful navigation is needed in poor visibility**

The massive vegetated cliffs of Coire Ardair have made Creag Meagaidh into one of Scotland's finest venues for winter climbing. They make a great spectacle for hillwalkers too on this superb circuit which also passes through some fine natural woodland.

The walk starts from the signed Creag Meagaidh car park at Aberarder on the north side of the A86 opposite Loch Laggan. Follow the path that starts alongside a track, ignoring two branches to the left. Further on cross the track to reach the farm buildings which are now the base for the Creag Meagaidh National Nature Reserve run by Scottish Natural Heritage. Like much of the Highlands, the estate was once heavily grazed by an

overpopulation of red deer and the agency carried out controversial large-scale culls to bring the numbers down to sustainable levels. The results have been spectacular as the native birchwoods began to regenerate and are now thriving.

Follow the path uphill to the right of the buildings; after a turning area at the end of the all-abilities section it steepens. Further on look out for a small cairn and a faint path striking off to the right. Take this much rougher route and climb up to the minor hillock of Na Cnapanan. From this point continue northwest, then NNW for the longer pull up the broadening hillside. The going is easy underfoot and there are fine views of the great crags of Creag Meagaidh which relieve any boredom with the more monotonous terrain underfoot. Eventually a wide plateau is reached; carry on past a first cairn to the larger one at 1006m which is the summit of Carn Liath.

Cross the open slopes west towards the lump of Meall an t-Snaim; from here the ridge starts to become better defined. Old fenceposts lead the way to the trench-like bealach of Uinneas Min Choire. Cross this and climb to Sron Coire a'Chriochairein; the ridge now curves sinuously, providing an enjoyable traverse around the edge of a corrie on the left. A long flat section then

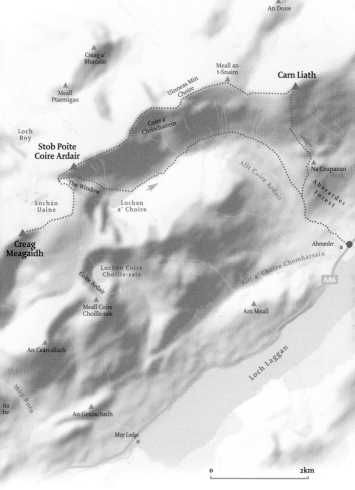

Creag Meagaidh · Carn Liath · Stob Poite Coire Ardair

An Doire

Creag a' Bhanain

Meall an t-Snaim

Carn Liath

Meall Ptarmigan

Uinneas Min Choire

Coire a' Chriochairein

Loch Roy

Stob Poite Coire Ardair

Na Cnapanan

Aberarder Forest

The Window

Allt Coire Ardair

Lochan Uaine

Lochan a' Choire

Aberarder

Creag Meagaidh

Allt a' Choire Chomharsain

A86

Lochan Coire Choille-rais

Coire Ardair

Meall Coire Choille-rais

Am Meall

An Cearcallach

Loch Laggan

Moy Burn

na he

An Geurachadh

Moy Lodge

0   2km

353

leads on to the summit of Stob Poite Coire Ardair which looks out over the awesome bowl of Coire Ardair.

From this second Munro head WSW down into the Window – a distinctive deep bealach which helps to identify Creag Meagaidh in views from miles around. Climb steeply up the far side – a winding path makes easier work of the loose ground. The slope eases into a vast plateau. The first objective is Mad Meg's Cairn, a large and ancient cairn at its centre. This isn't the summit, however; continuing west, the ground soon narrows and descends slightly to form a ridge. A short climb along this takes you to the much smaller summit cairn of Creag Meagaidh.

To descend, return to the Window and descend steeply to the east, keeping to the left of the burn lower down to reach the lochan in Coire Ardair. A wonderful destination for a walk in its own right, the tiny sheet of water is utterly dominated by the towering bulk of the great cliffs behind it – a mecca for ice-climbers in winter. An excellent path now leads back to the start; it begins along the north bank of the Allt Coire Ardair and descends through beautiful birchwoods to eventually return to the car park.

Alternatives

A far less popular route to Creag Meagaidh starts at Moy above Loch Laggan. It heads up the west side of the Moy Burn, crossing moorland initially before breaking off to find a way up the steep, rocky nose of Creag na Cailliche, making use of some grassy ramps. From there a long ridge sweeps round and up to Creag Meagaidh, intially accompanied by a stone dyke.

2

Beinn a'Chlachair
Creag Pitridh
Geal Charn

Beinn a'Chlachair (1087m)
stonemason's hill
Creag Pitridh (924m) *Petrie's crag*
Geal Charn (1049m) *white hill*

Distance **26km**
Ascent **1275m**
Time **8 – 9 hours**
Start point **OS Grid ref: NN432830**
Map **OS Explorer 393**
Terrain & hazards **track for the approach, then pathless with very steep sections**

This route takes you into the wild and relatively remote area south of Loch Laggan. Beinn a'Chlachair is a massive, steep-flanked whale of a ridge; Geal Charn is less shapely but redeemed by its peaked summit, whilst their smaller neighbour Creag Pitridh laps up the best of the views.

This route starts from the A86; there is a lay-by just east of the track heading over the bridge to Luiblea. Take this track and just before some trees fork left onto a track across the moor. After 1km turn sharp right at a junction, then keep left when the track forks to pass a small reservoir. In just over 1km the track crosses a bridge to reach the southern end of Lochan na h-Earba. There is a stunning sandy beach here and superb views across the water.

Keep an eye out for a cairn on the right indicating the start of a grassy path which cuts across to join the stalkers' path climbing by the Allt Coire Pitridh. Pass some ruined sheilings and cross a small burn coming down from the east. After a further 0.5km leave the excellent path behind in favour of crossing the Allt Coire Pitridh and ascending the steep grassy bank beyond. Head directly south across boggy ground and then steepening slopes, bearing slightly to the southwest to meet the eastern rim of Coire Mor Chlachair. There is a dramatic view across the corrie to the summit of Beinn a'Chlachair.

Continue up above the corrie rim, crossing (or bypassing on the left) a rocky lump to eventually emerge on the wide plateau; cross this to reach the summit. From here Chno Dearg dominates to the west, backed by the impressive Easains and the Grey Corries. To the east the rest of the day's route can be seen, with Geal Charn looking a long way away (it is!). Retrace your steps over the stony plateau and continue across it to the far northeastern end. Here it comes to an abrupt halt above steep cliffs which plunge down to Loch a'Bhealaich Leamhain. The descent route is to the north, either directly down the corner of

Spean Bridge and Roybridge

Binnein Shios

A86

Loch Laggan

An Geurachadh

Moy Lodge

Creag a' Mhaig

River Spean

uiblea

Binnein Shuas

Lochan na h-Earba

Creag Pitridh

Abhainn Ghuilbinn

Mullach Co
an Iubha

Geal Charn

Allt Coire Pitridh

Bealach
Leamhain

Loch
a' Bhealaich
Leamhain

Coire Mor
Chlachair

Beinn
a'Chlachair

Allt Cam

An Lairig

0   2km

356

the slopes towards the Bealach Leamhain (requiring great care with route finding and some scrambling) or start approximately 200m further west where it is possible to find a route down mostly steep grassy ground. If taking this option bear right once easier ground is reached to meet the stalkers' path from the bealach, rather than continuing directly over the bogs.

Follow the path briefly northwest to reach a junction and then turn right to take an excellent path which leads to the col between Creag Pitridh and Geal Charn. Trace this path for just 500m before striking off ENE up the stony slopes towards Geal Charn. There are a couple of false summits before the cone of Mullach Coire an Iubhair is revealed with the trig point just beyond and good views looking back to Beinn a' Chlachair.

To reach the third Munro return along the ridge for 700m before bearing WNW to the bealach below Creag Pitridh. From here the ascent looks steep, but shortly after crossing the stalkers' route there is a path to help. It aims directly for the top before doglegging left and then right to cross the quartzite which covers the summit. Creag Pitridh can seem a rather inconsequential hill compared to its much higher neighbours, but it has the finest view of the day, looking down onto Lochan na h-Earba and past the two Binneins to Loch Laggan.

A path heads west at first, leading down the steeper upper section, but once on the flatter shoulder aim southwest off the ridge to reach the confluence of the burn from the bealach with the Allt Coire Pitridh. Cutting down here avoids some very boggy ground further east. Now simply retrace your steps along the stalkers' path and the approach tracks to return to the start.

Lochan na h-Earba from Creag Pitridh

3

Beinn a' Chaorainn
Beinn Teallach

Beinn a' Chaorainn (1050m)
hill of the rowan
Beinn Teallach (915m) *hill of the hearth*

Distance **16km**
Ascent **1170m**
Time **6 – 8 hours**
Start point **OS Grid ref: NN377814**
Map **OS Explorer 400**
Terrain & hazards **very boggy terrain lower down and the Allt a'Chaorainn needs to be forded near the end of the walk; careful navigation required on Beinn a' Chaorainn in poor visibility**

Beinn Teallach is one of the less significant Munros; however, its neighbour Beinn a' Chaorainn offers excellent walking along the rim of its eastern corries. Both hills have rather boggy lower slopes.

There is a small parking area on the north side of the A86 at Roughburn. Start by following the forestry track just east of the bridge over the Allt a' Chaorainn, passing through dense plantations; it curves first left and then right after a quarry. Soon after this is a junction. Turn left here; after 100m or so a small cairn marks the start of a path on the right which leads through the trees up an overgrown firebreak. This path, though short, is exceptionally boggy; an alternative is to continue along the track to the edge of the forestry

and then turn right up open ground.

Either way, aim for the shoulder of Meall Clachaig and continue the long pull up the almost featureless hillside to reach the southern top of Beinn a' Chaorainn. From here the walk changes tempo with some excellent views down into the eastern corries with Creag Meagaidh beyond. Cross a slight dip to reach the central Munro summit. Straightforward in summer, there have been several accidents along here in winter conditions, possibly caused by walkers taking a direct bearing between the two summits and ending up on a collapsing cornice as the corrie bites into the plateau between them. On one occasion in 1994, two separate walkers (and a dog) fell at the same spot within an hour of each other; luckily all survived. In snow, ensure you can navigate safely away from the edge.

Continue around another fine curving corrie rim to the northern summit. From here descend north at first before aiming down to reach the cairn at Tom Mor on the very boggy bealach between Beinn a' Chaorainn and Beinn Teallach. Head to the right around the steep lower slope of Beinn Teallach before embarking on the direct ascent up the NNE ridge to reach the summit at 915m. Until 1984 Beinn Teallach was one of the highest Corbetts; after a resurvey it is now one of the lowest Munros.

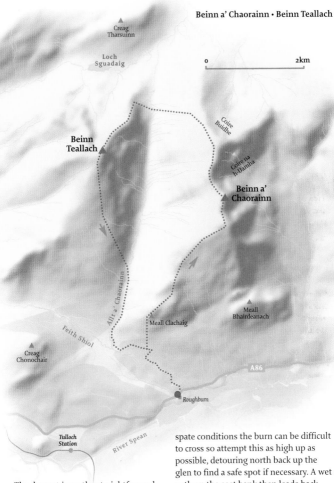

Beinn a' Chaorainn · Beinn Teallach

0   2km

Creag
Tharsuinn

Loch
Sguadaig

Beinn
Teallach

Coire
Buidhe

Coire na
h-Uamha

Beinn a'
Chaorainn

Allt a' Chaorainn

Feith Shiol

Meall Clachaig

Meall
Bhairdeanach

Creag
Chonochair

A86

Roughburn

Tulloch
Station

River Spean

The descent is on the straightforward
southern slopes, aiming for the Allt a'
Chaorainn once easy ground is reached. In

spate conditions the burn can be difficult
to cross so attempt this as high up as
possible, detouring north back up the
glen to find a safe spot if necessary. A wet
path on the east bank then leads back
down the glen, eventually meeting the
forest track to return to the start.

4

Chno Dearg
Stob Coire Sgriodain

Chno Dearg (1046m) *red nut (likely to have been a map-maker's error – it should be red hill)*
Stob Coire Sgriodain (976m)
peak of the scree corrie

Distance 13km
Ascent 930m
Time 5 – 7 hours
Start point OS Grid ref: NN350782
Map OS Explorer 393
Terrain & hazards **steep climb up Sron na Garbh-bheinne, very wet underfoot in places**

Chno Dearg is a rounded, boggy lump, though somewhat redeemed by decent views. Neighbouring Stob Coire Sgriodain may be lower, but it is also steeper and rockier; it enlivens this circuit from Fersit.

There is a parking at the track junction at the end of the public road to Fersit; take care to leave space for turning. Follow the track towards Fersit, crossing the river and railway, keeping right at a fork and passing the cottages. At another fork go right with the track that climbs up and passes to the right of a large metal barn. Pass through a gate onto the open moorland ground, and continue along the track until a branch on the right heads for a hut and pens.

Cross the boggy moorland aiming for the steep nose of Sron na Garbh-bheinne. As the ascent gets steeper several gullys cut across the slope; these aid progress at times, but generally just keep uphill until the rocky nose is gained. Pass over Sron na Garbh-bheinne and descend slightly before the final easy climb to the summit of Stob Coire Sgriodain. This is a fine viewpoint for Loch Treig and towards the vast expanse of Rannoch Moor to the southwest.

Now it's time to tackle the big lump. Chno Dearg is only 2km distant, but the ground in between is surprisingly rough. At first aim south from the summit to the trench of the Glac Bhan, and then follow the undulating ridge southeast. The going gets easier after 1km and a direct route to the top of Chno Dearg can then be taken. From the large summit cairn the Creag Meagaidh range can be seen looming massively to the north and the direct descent route down to Fersit can also be made out. The slopes are very wet underfoot, but otherwise straightforward; at their foot a track makes an easy return to the start.

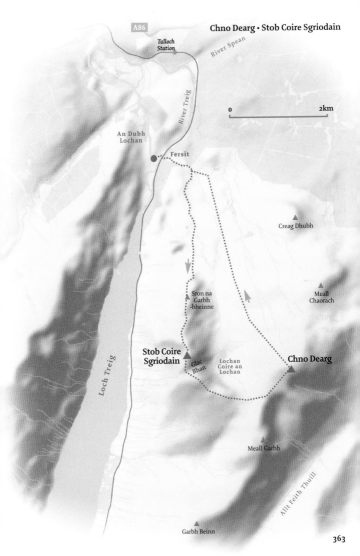

A86

Tulloch
Station

River Spean

River Treig

An Dubh
Lochan

Fersit

0   2km

Creag Dhubh

Sron na
Garbh
-bheinne

Meall
Chaorach

**Stob Coire
Sgriodain**

Glac
Bhan

Lochan
Coire an
Lochan

Chno Dearg

Loch Treig

Meall Garbh

Allt Feith Thuill

Garbh Beinn

Chno Dearg and the Easains from Glen Spean

5

Stob Coire Easain
Stob a'Choire Mheadhoin

Stob Coire Easain (1115m)
peak of the corrie of little waterfalls
Stob a'Choire Mheadhoin (1106m)
peak of the middle corrie

Distance 15.5km
Ascent 1230m (returning the same way)
Time 6 – 8 hours
Start point OS Grid ref: NN349789
Map OS Explorer 392
Terrain & hazards **the lower ground can be boggy, there is a path on the higher rocky slopes**

Popularly known as the Easains, this graceful pair of peaks are climbed on a long ridgewalk high above the glacial trough of Loch Treig.

Park at the end of the public road which leads to Fersit, leaving space for turning. Begin along the track from the far end, signed as a private road. Pass through a gate and birchwoods towards the Loch Treig dam. Stay on the main branch at two forks – first right, then left. Almost 1km beyond the dam two tracks branch off right in quick succession; take the second one, which climbs uphill and leads to a sheepfold. Very muddy ATV tracks lead on up the moorland; keep to the right of a burn before crossing it and swinging left below a small waterfall shaded by birches. The very muddy and rough tyre tracks emerge up on the moor just to the left of a concrete hydro pillar.

From this angle Meall Cian Dearg can look intimidating, but there is a path which bears slightly to the left of the steep nose and allows the top to be reached without any real scrambling. As the ridge levels take the chance to enjoy the great views; to the left Stob Coire Sgriodain rises across the other side of Loch Treig whilst to the right is the skyline of the Grey Corries. After a brief flatter section the ridge climbs above Coire Shomhairle and along the rim of Coire Aluinn before reaching the summit of Stob a'Choire Mheadhoin.

From the large summit cairn the slightly higher and more shapely twin Munro of Stob Coire Easain is revealed across a bealach. Make the steep descent to this col and then an equally steep pull up the other side; a path helps. At 1115m Stob Coire Easain has expansive views in all directions, but the outlook over the Grey Corries really stands out.

The easiest descent is by the outward route. The obvious alternative is to return to the bealach and then descend to the northwest. A path helps on the initial steep section before the going becomes boggier down into Coire Lair. Follow the south side of the Allt Laire before picking up a path much further on and finally rejoining the old railway to return to the start; this route is boggy and can feel rather long and tedious.

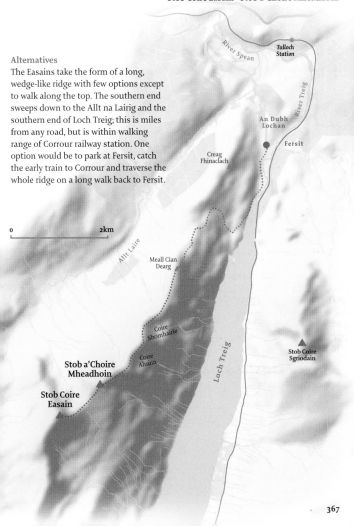

Alternatives

The Easains take the form of a long, wedge-like ridge with few options except to walk along the top. The southern end sweeps down to the Allt na Lairig and the southern end of Loch Treig; this is miles from any road, but is within walking range of Corrour railway station. One option would be to park at Fersit, catch the early train to Corrour and traverse the whole ridge on a long walk back to Fersit.

River Spean

Tulloch Station

River Treig

An Dubh Lochan

Fersit

Creag Fhinaclach

0   2km

Allt Laire

Meall Cian Dearg

Coire Shomhairle

Coire Aluinn

Loch Treig

Stob Coire Sgriodain

Stob a'Choire Mheadhoin

Stob Coire Easain

Creag Fhinaclach from An Dubh Lochan

Stob Choire Claurigh from Stob Coire an Laoigh

6

The Grey Corries:
Stob Choire Claurigh
Stob Coire an Laoigh
Sgurr Choinnich Mhor

Stob Choire Claurigh (1177m)
peak of the corrie of brawling
Stob Coire an Laoigh (1116m)
peak of the corrie of the calf
Sgurr Choinnich Mhor (1094m)
big peak of the moss

Distance **20km**
Ascent **1505m**
Time **8 – 9 hours**
Start point **OS Grid ref: NN255788**
Map **OS Explorer 392**
Public transport **nearest bus and rail at Spean Bridge – adds 5km each way**
Terrain & hazards **this route involves rough, rocky and steep mountain ridges in a remote area**

The Grey Corries provide one of the classic long hill traverses. This demanding route takes in the three Munros on the main spine of the range and has everything; an airy ridge, remoteness and superlative views.

Lying east of the Nevis Range, the Grey Corries are well seen from the Commando Memorial near Spean Bridge, their flanks covered in sparkling silver quartzite screes. To reach the start of the walk it is possible to drive up a very rough gated private track from Corriechoille, reached via the minor

road past the railway station at Spean Bridge. If your car survives the potholes then there is limited parking where the track meets the former line of a disused narrow-gauge railway at NN255788. The railway was used during the construction of the aluminum works tunnel that links Fort William to Loch Treig.

From here continue on foot up the track, passing an area of felled forestry and the 'Wee Minister' – a wooden sculpture that could give a real fright in the dark. After the forestry is left behind go through two gates before turning right beside the fence, rounding an enclosed area and then climbing the grassy slope beyond with the trees and a fence on your right. Veer south onto the open slopes that eventually lead up to Stob Coire Gaibhre. This section is something of a slog, but the reward is a dramatic view across the corrie on the left with its tiny lochan to the outlying top of Stob Coire na Ceannain and the prospect of the magnificent ridgewalk ahead.

Follow the broad ridge, keeping the cliffs and corrie on the left, and after a small descent, climb up to a knobbly summit. From here a branching ridge leads ENE out to Stob Coire na Ceannain to the left. Unless detouring to take in this extra summit climb steeply up onto the crest to reach Stob Choire Claurigh. The fifteenth highest mountain in Britain, it has excellent views of the ridge snaking away to the west as well as to Stob Ban, a pointy outlier of the Grey Corries described in the following route.

The ridge soon leads on to the Top of Stob a'Choire Leith. A worn path over the quartzite scree makes the going fairly straightforward. The ridge curves left here and descends on grass before a stony climb to a rocky top just before the summit of Stob Coire Cath na Sine, with a sharp drop on the left. Continue west to Caisteil; the ridge then descends to a bealach before rising to the second Munro of the day, Stob Coire an Laoigh.

Continue to Stob Coire Easain, a Top at 1080m. For the third Munro, Sgurr Choinnich Mhor, head SSW to the wide Bealach Coire Easain. A very steep pull up a narrow arête leads up the pyramid-shaped peak and the finest summit of the day.

From here retrace your steps back to Stob Coire Easain, and now descend the north ridge on wide slopes which soon narrow to a defined ridge as the route crosses Beinn na Socaich. The slopes open out again after this minor peak; once near the edge of the forestry, aim for a pedestrian gate in the forest fence. From here an ill-defined path leads through a gap between the trees. Continue ahead until a minor hillock; the path leads down

to the left of this. Turn right at a forest track, following this as it leads over a bridge; ignore the track branching left on the far side, continuing instead to reach a T-junction. Turn left, following the track downhill. At a track junction (with Spean Bridge signed ahead) follow the main track which bends right. Ignore a track off to the left, and at a second junction take the left fork downhill (ignoring the track climbing slightly right). This eventually leads back to the access track from Coirecoille and the start.

Alternatives

The basic route given above is almost invariably used for Stob Choire Claurigh and Stob Coire an Laoigh. The day could be extended further by ascending Stob Ban first and then reaching Stob Choire Claurigh from the south.

Sgurr Choinnich Mhor can be climbed from Glen Nevis. Park at the end of the public road and walk through the Nevis Gorge to Steall Falls. Continue up the glen for 2km beyond the Steall ruins before heading NNE up the open slopes by a burn. High above, traverse the grassy ridge of Sgurr Choinnich Beag before continuing to its higher parent.

The Grey Corries ridge is linked at a high level to the Aonachs to the west. However, the direct climb up onto the Aonachs from the bealach is blocked by crags; it is possible to instead ascend via a grassy gully well to the left.

The Grey Corries

Leanachan Forest

former tramway

Allt Leachdach

Cruach Innse

Allt Coire Chiomhlidh

Stob Coire Gaibhre

Allt Coire an Eoin

Stob Coire na Ceannain

Stob a'Choire Leith

Stob Choire Claurigh

Beinn na Socaich

The Grey Corries

Stob Coire Easain

Caisteil

Stob Coire Cath na Sine

Bealach Coire Easain

Stob Coire an Laoigh

Stob Ban

Allt Coire Rath

Sgurr Choinnich Mhor

Sgurr Choinnich Beag

0   2km

373

Stob Ban

Stob Ban (977m) *white peak*

Distance 18km
Ascent 870m
Time 6 – 8 hours
Start point OS Grid ref: NN255788
Map OS Explorer 392
Public transport nearest bus/rail at
Spean Bridge – adds 5km each way
Terrain & hazards good track for
approach, then boggy lower slopes and
steep ground near summit

Stob Ban is hidden away behind the main Grey Corries ridge. Although it can be combined with its big neighbours, this shapely cone makes a fine objective in its own right.

The approach is the same as the main Grey Corries route above, driving up the very rough and pot-holed track from Corriechoille, heading through a gate and continuing as far as NN255788 where there is space to park. Carry on along the track, through another gate, and passing the Wee Minister – a wooden figure who stands sentinel beside this part of the ancient right of way over the Lairig Leacach.

Cross the Allt Leachdach and continue uphill into a pass between the Grey Corries on the right and the Corbetts of Cruach Innse and rocky Sgurr Innse on the left. After reaching the high point of the Lairig Leacach at 515m, continue gently downhill to the tiny Leacach Bothy – with Stob Ban now looking very majestic behind. This volunteer-maintained Mountain Bothies Association shelter is small but perfectly formed and provides a good rest spot. From here cross the bridge over the Allt a'Chuil Choirean and continue briefly to reach a fork in the path; turn right here to begin the climb towards the northeast ridge of Stob Ban. Boggy at first, the route improves as the gradient eases, reaching a flatter area about halfway up. The summit remains in view for the final climb with the last section on quartzite. From the summit cairn there are excellent views over a mass of wild land, though there are higher mountains all around, with the Grey Corries, Aonachs and Ben Nevis dominant.

The quickest return is by the outward route; however, it is possible to descend a steep and loose scree slope WNW before turning north to a bealach with a lochan. From here you could either continue up onto the main Grey Corries ridge, or descend into Coire Claurigh over quartzite slabs which involves some scrambling, before aiming for the bothy and a final return on the outward route.

Stob Ban

Leanachan
Forest

Allt Leachdach

Cruach
Innse

Stob Coire
Gaibhre

Sguar
Innse

Stob Coire
na Ceannain

Lairig Leacach

Stob Choire
Claurigh

Leachach
Bothy

Stob
a'Choire Leith

The Grey Corries

Allt a' Chuil Choirean

Stob Coire
Cath na Sine

Caisteil

Coire
Clarigh

Stob Coire
an Laoigh

Stob Ban

Sgurr
ìnnich Mhor

Allt Coire Rath

0   2km

Meall a' Bhuirich

375

Stob Ban seen from the main Grey Corries ridge

The CIC Hut and Tower Ridge on Ben Nevis

Fort William

At the foot of Britain's highest mountain, Fort William is the natural base for anyone tackling the Ben or any of the Munros stretching from Glencoe to Invergarry or as far as Creag Meagaidh to the east. As the finale of the West Highland Way and also the start of the Great Glen Way to Inverness, there are always groups of footsore walkers tottering round the Morrisons supermarket here, lugging outsize rucksacks as they try to agree on provisions.

Despite its fine setting, stretched out along the banks of Loch Linnhe, Fort William is blighted by the busy A82 dual-carriageway bypass which runs between the centre and the waterfront, presenting the driver with a rear view of some spectacularly ugly buildings. The town's superb position, however, and efforts to brand itself the 'Outdoor Capital of the UK' mean it is packed with businesses catering for walkers, with a growing community of guides and instructors offering every outdoor activity under the sun (or rain!).

The town has good public transport with regular trains on the dramatic West Highland Line, as well as coaches from Glasgow which head on to Skye or Inverness. Taking the train to Mallaig or south across Rannoch Moor is a great option for a day off – however, the Jacobite steam train which strikes a Harry Potteresque pose as it crosses the impressive Glenfinnan Viaduct does get heavily booked up. Also on offer for a rest day are seal trips and cruises on Loch Linnhe, canoeing and other watersports on the Caledonian Canal and nearby Loch Oich, or testing your bravery and bones on the world-championship mountain bike trails at Nevis Range. The Range also has skiing and snowboarding in the winter and a high-level zip wire course in the summer. Those needing a proper rest for aching limbs can seek out the swimming pool with sauna and steam room on the north side of town, or try some retail therapy along the high street which is packed with outdoor gear shops.

As you'd expect there are tons of places to stay. Of note is the massive Glen Nevis Campsite, beautifully situated in the glen, a 3.5km walk from the town centre. Often packed in the summer, it has excellent facilities (including, on occasion, Handel's Water Music piped into the showers) and zero-tolerance of rowdy groups. The nearby Hostelling Scotland hostel can get very noisy and busy in the summer, as can the independent options in Fort William itself and at nearby Corpach. There are B&Bs to suit every budget as well as self-catering and hotels, but despite the plentiful accommodation it can be hard to find last-minute options in high summer.

Filling that hungry stomach is also not a problem with many cafés, pubs and restaurants. The Grog and Gruel is perhaps the pick of the pubs, run by the owners of the Clachaig Inn in Glencoe and providing reliable and large-portioned fare. More upmarket options include the Crannog, which specialises in seafood, jutting out into Loch Linnhe on the old pier. At the other end of the scale, the cheap and cheerful café in Morrisons, near the train station, is always an option and opens early for breakfast.

Glenfinnan and the Road to the Isles

The road leading onwards from Fort William to Mallaig passes through classic West Highland scenery, with mountains, forests, rugged coastline and sandy beaches. This huge chunk of the Highlands stretches beautifully for miles out to the mainland's most westerly point at Ardnamurchan, but contains only three Munros, all east of the Road to the Isles. Two of these are set back beyond the spectacular viaduct at Glenfinnan, where Bonnie Prince Charlie first unfurled his standard at the beginning of the ill-fated Jacobite rebellion of 1745. A monument commemorating this enjoys a superb outlook along Loch Shiel, and the tiny village here does offer some facilities with two hotels and a hostel set in old railway carriages beside the West Highland Line.

Further north the landscape becomes increasingly rugged with only a tiny roller-coaster of tarmac threading an unlikely passage along the north shore of Loch Arkaig into the interior, and serving as a jumping-off point for a couple of Munro epics.

Invergarry and Glen Garry

Like Spean Bridge, Invergarry has one of those strategic positions from which you can easily be off and away up to the Munros in several different directions. It sits where Glen Garry reaches the Great Glen; a lonely single-track road makes a tortuous course up by Loch Quoich before terminating at Kinlochhourn, starting point for the walk-in to Knoydart for many, and where there is also a B&B which often serves basic refreshments.

The Invergarry Hotel is always a popular port of call and the Drynachan B&B is also a reliable walker-friendly option. For those on a tighter budget, the independent Invergarry Lodge hostel is on the side road to Mandally, whilst the Great Glen Hostel is beside the A82 at Laggan.

Knoydart

With no road access to link it to the outside world, Knoydart is the remotest inhabited corner of mainland Scotland. There are two main options for climbing the spectacular peaks of this area, with overnight stays either at Barrisdale Bay on Loch Hourn or in Inverie. Home to most of the peninsula's inhabitants and facilities, Inverie is easily accessible from Mallaig by boat, whereas Barrisdale involves an arduous hike from Kinlochhourn, although it is also possible to get a boat here from Arnisdale.

Accommodation at Barrisdale is limited to camping, or the estate bothy; nominal fees are paid to the ghillie in the mornings. Inverie by contrast has a choice of facilities, including several B&Bs, a small shop, a pub in The Old Forge, a bunkhouse and self catering cottages, and offers the chance to see how the community buy-out is progressing first hand. The spanking-new pier is testament to the influx of money to the remote peninsula and locals understand that welcoming visitors is key to their economic success. The Knoydart Foundation Bunkhouse could not be more friendly and this is continued at the good value waterside tearoom. The main Bruce Watt ferry provides a scheduled service every weekday in summer, less frequently at other times, and Knoydart Seabridge provides alternative sailings including at weekends.

The Munros

Loch Hourn

Knoydart

Ladhar
Bheinn

Luinne
Bheinn

Sgurr a'
Mhaoraich

Gleouraich Spid
Mial

14

13

12

Loch
Quoich

Inverie
Bay

16 15

Meall
Buidhe

Sgurr na
Ciche

Sgurr nan
Coireachan

Garbh Chioch
Mhor

Sgurr
Mor

Gairich

Loch
Nevis

Loch Morar

Morar

Sgurr nan
Coireachan

Sgurr
Thuilm

10 11

Loch Arkaig

Gulvain

Lochailort

● A861

Glenfinnan   8

A830

7

Locheilside   Loch Eil

Loch
Shiel

Loch Eil

A861

Loch
Linnhe

A82

382

Fort William

Loch Cluanie

Loch Loyne

A87

Loch Garry

Invergarry

A82

Sron a' Choire Ghairbh

9

Meall na Teanga

B8004

Loch Lochy

Spean Bridge

B8004

A82

A86

Tulloch Station

Loch Laggan

Torlundy

ort William

1

Carn Mor Dearg

Aonach Mor

Glen Nevis

Aonach Beag

Loch Treig

Ben Nevis

3 2

Sgurr a' Mhaim

An Gearanach

The Ring of Steall

Beinn na Lap

Loch Ossian

6 5

Corrour Station

Carn Dearg

Sgor Gaibhre

llach an rean

Stob Ban

Stob Coire a' Chairn

Am Bodach

Kinlochleven

Ben Nevis above Caol

Ben Nevis
Carn Mor Dearg

Ben Nevis (1344m) *venomous hill*
Carn Mor Dearg (1220m) *big red rocky hill*

Distance **17.5km**

Ascent **1560m**

Time **10 hours**

Start point **OS Grid ref: NN144763**

Map **OS Explorer 392**

Public transport **rail and coaches to Fort William; Citylink bus between Fort William and Torlundy 1km from start**

Terrain & hazards **the arête between Carn Mor Dearg and Ben Nevis is airy but any actual scrambling is minimal; the whole route is long and strenuous, with very careful navigation needed for the descent from Ben Nevis when there is snow and poor visibility**

Any fine day in the summer sees hordes of visitors swarming up the 'Mountain Track' from Glen Nevis to the top of Ben Nevis – for many it will be the only hill they will ever climb. For the experienced, however, there is a more exciting option which starts from Torlundy that does real justice to Britain's highest mountain. The spectacular Carn Mor Dearg arête gives an airy traverse along its elegant curving crest, whilst providing grandstand views of the awesome north face.

Start from the North Face car park which is found 1km along a track from Torlundy. Start by walking along the track past the vehicle barrier. At a bend turn right onto a path (The North Face Trail). Head uphill, keeping left at a fork, and further up keep straight on when another path joins to eventually emerge from the trees. A bench here provides good views of Fort William and Ben Nevis. Keep left on the path passing a small dam to your right. At the next path junction turn right (following sign for Allt a'Mhuillin and CIC Hut).

Keep straight ahead to join a track, eventually turning right at a junction of tracks to head directly towards Ben Nevis. At the end of the track climb the stile and follow the moorland path keeping to the left of the Allt a'Mhuillin (plenty of pools for a cooling dip on the way back if its a hot day) and watching the impressive north face of Ben Nevis getting nearer. Take the smaller path on the left to start climbing the ridge of Carn Mor Dearg. The path is boggy to start with but becomes drier and rockier as height is gained.

The route doesn't climb directly to the ridge but cuts across the southern slope of Carn Beag Dearg, a magical vantage point for the climber's paradise that is Ben Nevis's north face. Gain the ridge at Carn Dearg Meadhonach. From here it is a spectacular but straightforward grassy ridge walk to the summit of Carn Mor Dearg at 1220m.

Although this is the ninth highest Munro, it is overshadowed by the majesty of the north face of Ben Nevis across the way. The arête can also clearly be seen curving between the two peaks.

Leave the summit in a southwesterly direction at first and then bear south along the clear ridge. There are some sections of fairly easy scrambling, but the large stable slabs of rock provide reassurance and any difficulties can usually be overcome by resorting to shuffling if you are not bothered about your dignity or style, or using a path just below the crest. This is one of the best ridge walks in Britain.

Eventually the arête starts to ascend as it nears the bulk of Ben Nevis. Finally, a faint path zigzags up the bouldery slopes to reach the summit plateau just a short way from the trig point. There is a great sense of satisfaction and some smugness at having climbed the longer and more involving route, but everyone's ascent of Britain's highest mountain is a personal achievement – you are very unlikely to be alone at the top.

To descend, follow the main route down. Great care is needed with navigation in poor visibility and snowy conditions – there have been many fatal accidents to those who, in trying to avoid Gardyloo Gully on the north face, fall into the trap of Five Finger Gully on the other flank of the Ben. To steer a course between these two gullies when the route cannot be seen, follow a bearing from the summit of 231 degrees for 150m, and then keep on a bearing of 282 degrees

– remember to allow for current magnetic variation, and be careful to stay on this bearing during the 100m steepening known as Maclean's Steep. This will help you pass the most dangerous area. If visibility is good you can follow the well-worn path which zigzags down the slope. This leads towards Lochan Meall an t-Suidhe, crossing the Red Burn and soon reaching a path junction. Go straight ahead here to leave behind most walkers who will be heading left down into Glen Nevis. Bear left at the next path to follow the clear path to the outflow of the loch. From here the route is pathless as it descends over rough ground (don't be tempting to take the path much further right which leads to the CIC hut and the bottom of the climbing cliffs) instead bear NNE aiming for the Allt a'Mhuillin. There are a number of places where the burn can be easily forded unless in spate conditions. It's only a few steps up on the far side to rejoin the outward path. Turn left to retrace the route back to the North Face car park at Torlundy.

Alternatives

The vast majority of those climbing 'The Ben' will use the main track throughout. This begins at the car park and visitor centre in Glen Nevis, crosses the footbridge and heads right to soon join the other main path to the summit from Achintee Farm. At around 160m the brutally steep path which heads directly

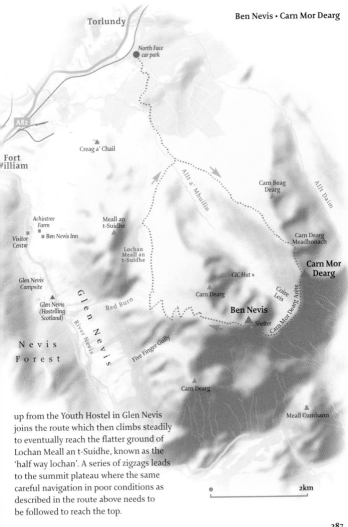

Torlundy

North Face
car park

A82

Fort
William

Creag a' Chail

Allt a' Mhuillin

Carn Beag
Dearg

Allt Daim

Achintree
Farm

Ben Nevis Inn

Meall an
t-Suidhe

Carn Dearg
Meadhonach

Visitor
Centre

**Carn Mor
Dearg**

Lochan
Meall an
t-Suidhe

CIC Hut

Glen Nevis
Campsite

Coire
Leis

Carn Dearg

Glen Nevis
(Hostelling
Scotland)

Red Burn

Ben Nevis

Shelter

Carn Mor Dearg Arête

River Nevis

N e v i s
F o r e s t

Five Finger Gully

G
l
e
n
N
e
v
i
s

Carn Dearg

Meall Cumhann

up from the Youth Hostel in Glen Nevis
joins the route which then climbs steadily
to eventually reach the flatter ground of
Lochan Meall an t-Suidhe, known as the
'half way lochan'. A series of zigzags leads
to the summit plateau where the same
careful navigation in poor conditions as
described in the route above needs to
be followed to reach the top.

0   2km

388

Carn Mor Dearg seen from the North Face of Ben Nevis

2

Aonach Beag
Aonach Mor

Aonach Beag (1234m) *little ridged mountain*
Aonach Mor (1221m) *big ridged mountain*

Distance 16.5km
Ascent 1375m
Time 7 – 8 hours
Start point OS Grid ref: NN168691
Map OS Explorer 392
Public transport bus (41) from Fort
William (very limited in winter)
Terrain & hazards **good navigation skills
are needed on the wide summit plateau
which has very steep flanks; the descent
from Aonach Mor is steep with boggy
ground at lower levels**

An approach from beautiful Glen Nevis
avoids the ski developments on this
ascent of two of Britain's highest
mountains. The route gives a feeling of
wildness which may be lacking if these
summits are tackled using the Nevis
gondola on their northern slopes.

Start from the car park at the end of
the public road up Glen Nevis, beneath a
massive waterslide coming down from
the Ben. From the car park follow the
main path into mixed woodland; the
glen soon narrows into the dramatic
Nevis Gorge. Eventually the path emerges
from the trees onto a picturesque green
pasture with the dramatic cascades of the
Steall Falls backed by the peaks of the
Mamores – surely one of the most
enchanting spots in Scotland and a world

away from the bustle of the lower glen.

Stay on the main path which follows
the glen round to the left into more
desolate country. After 1km cross a bridge
to reach the ruins of a small settlement.
Turn off the main path here to follow a
faint path up rough ground to the right of
the Allt Coire nan Laogh, eventually
gaining the ridge leading up to Sgurr
a'Bhuic to avoid difficult ground at the
back of Coire nan Laogh. This Top has
good views of the Mamores and Grey
Corries. Continue along the ridge to a
bealach before climbing steeply by the
cliff edge to gain the Top of Stob Coire
Bhealaich. There is then a slight
depression before continuing up onto the
great dome of Aonach Beag.

Despite *beag* meaning 'small' and *mor*
meaning 'big', Aonach Beag is actually
higher than Aonach Mor; the name of the
latter refers to its sheer bulk. Head down
the northwest slopes which soon steepen
and narrow to reach the bealach with the
wider slope of Aonach Mor. Take care in
poor visibility when navigation is
difficult; to both east and west are
massive sweeps of broken crags. Aim
north where the slopes soon widen onto
the long summit plateau, which has
impressive cliffs falling to the east. The
summit is right in the middle of the
plateau and can take some finding in
mist. For the descent, head back across

Carn Beag Dearg

Coire an Lochan

Aonach Mor

Stob an Chul-Choire

Carn Dearg Meadhonach

Carn Mor Dearg

Aonach Beag

Stob Coire Bhealaich

Ben Nevis

Coire Guibhsachan

Coire nan Laogh

Sgurr a'Bhuic

Allt Coire nan Laogh

Meall Cumhann

Steall (ruins)

Water of Nevis

Steall Falls

G l e n   N e v i s

0   2km

An Gearanach

the plateau for around 750m to near a small cairn; from here an ill-defined ridge descends steeply to the west. There is an eroded path which aids progress down to the bealach at 830m. Now bear south down into Coire Guibhsachan and follow the rather soggy glen down to the Steall ruins. From here, retrace the outward route to Glen Nevis.

Alternatives

Walkers looking for a quick way to the summit of Aonach Mor can ride the Nevis Range Gondola to the Snowgoose Restaurant at an altitude of 650m. From there the summit plateau is within much easier reach, though if including Aonach Beag you will have to return back over Aonach Mor.

Aonach Beag and Aonach Mor from Carn Mor Dearg

3

Stob Ban
Mullach nan Coirean

Stob Ban (999m) *white peak*
Mullach nan Coirean (939m)
summit of the corries

Distance **13km**
Ascent **1155m**
Time **6 – 8 hours**
Start point **OS Grid ref: NN145683**
Map **OS Explorer 392**
Public transport **bus (41) from Fort William (very limited in winter)**
Terrain & hazards **steep ridges with scree; rocky sections on Stob Ban; boggy in the forest on the descent**

One of the most distinctive peaks in the Mamores, Stob Ban is an instantly recognisable backdrop to many beautiful Glen Nevis views. This excellent ridge walk links it to Mullach nan Coirean to make a grand circuit.

Start from the car park up to the right just before the bridge at Polldubh on the Glen Nevis road. The bridge offers a good view of the falls on the Allt Coire a' Mhusgain; do not cross but instead take a track – which soon becomes a path, leading south. It climbs steadily and passes along the flanks of Sgurr a' Mhaim, keeping a fair way above the deep ravine of the burn and passing through scattered woodland before reaching upper Coire a'Mhusgain. The path continues rising to reach an upper level before finally emerging on the bealach. Stob Ban looks a little intimidating – bear west along the ridge. Grassy at first, the upper slopes consist of scree and loose rocks. The summit is dramatically set above the northeastern corrie and, as might be expected from its prominent position, has spectacular views of both Glen and Ben Nevis.

Follow the north ridge to reach a knoll at a junction of ridges. From here, take the west ridge towards Mullach nan Coirean; there are scree slopes on the flanks, but the ridge itself is straightforward and the final ascent to the flat summit is gentle.

To return to Glen Nevis head north at first, following the rim of the steep eastern corrie to the right to gain the northeast ridge. This leads down towards an area of forestry, now clear felled. At the high fence, turn left and follow it steeply down to the stream. Cross a stile and follow a new path through the felled area to gain a forest track. Head along this, forking left downhill when a junction is reached. At the sharp bend ahead, take the good path which descends more directly through the trees to return to Polldubh.

Stob Ban • Mullach nan Coirean

Ben Nevis

Nevis
Forest

Carn Dearg

Sgorr Chalum

Polldubh

Water of Nevis

Glen Nevis

Sron
Riabach

Allt Coire a' Mhusgain

Allt Coire Dheirg

Mullach
nan Coirean

Sgurr a' Mhaim

Meall a'
Chaorainn

Coire a'
Mhusgain

Stob Ban

Sgurr an
Iubhair

Am Bodach

Allt Nathrach

0   2km

Beinn na Caillich

Stob Ban from Ben Nevis

Sgurr a' Mhaim and the Devil's Ridge

4

The Ring of Steall:
An Gearanach
Stob Coire a'Chairn
Am Bodach
Sgurr a' Mhaim

An Gearanach (982m) *the complainer*
Stob Coire a'Chairn (981m)
peak of the corrie of the cairn
Am Bodach (1032m) *the old man*
Sgurr a' Mhaim (1099m)
peak of the rounded hill

Distance 16km
Ascent 1675m
Time 9 – 11 hours
Start point OS Grid ref: NN168691
Map OS Explorer 392
Public transport **bus (41) from Fort William to Lower Falls car park**
Terrain & hazards **a long and tough day; although the route follows a path for much of the way, there are many sections of easy scrambling which some may find more difficult because of the exposure**

This horseshoe of spectacular ridges is undoubtedly one of the finest hillwalks in Scotland. Four Munros linked by airy sections of arête, including some scrambling. Best kept for a fine day to enjoy it to the full, the Ring of Steall is a highlight in any Munro-bagger's diary.

Start from the car park at the very end of the public road up Glen Nevis. Follow the main path which leads through the trees and passes through the very impressive Nevis Gorge. The gorge suddenly opens out into a green meadow backed by the Steall Falls – a stunning sight. Fork right from the main path to reach the wire bridge over the Water of Nevis. The bridge consists of three cables – one for the feet and two as handrails – and requires a fine sense of balance to cross. When the river is low, it is possible to paddle across if you don't want to risk tumbling from the bridge, even if you are mocked by children crossing and re-crossing the three strands of wire for fun. Turn left on the far side to pass the Steall Hut, property of the Lochaber Mountaineering Club, and cross the rocks at the base of the Falls themselves – this could be impossible after heavy rains.

After passing the base of the next buttress, cross a smaller burn, then join an old stalkers' path which climbs up to the right beside an eroded gully. Further on, the route gains height through a series of zigzags before swinging to the right to join a ridge. After a steep section the ridge leads on more easily to the summit of An

The Ring of Steall

Gearanach, the first Munro of the day; there are superb views looking back to Ben Nevis.

Screw on your head for heights for the next section which leads along the rocky arête of An Garbhanach, a Top. The easy but airy scrambling is comparable to the Carn Mor Dearg Arête. After descending to a bealach climb up towards Stob Coire a'Chairn; there is some loose scree near the top. At this point the main spine of the Mamores ridge is joined and there are good views to the east along it towards Binnein Mor.

Descend the grassy southwest ridge, traversing a minor summit before climbing much more steeply to Am Bodach. There are some loose rocks and very mild scrambling before the summit is reached. From here follow the west ridge down to a high bealach and continue to Sgurr an Iubhair. This summit was a Munro from 1981, when it was promoted from being a humble Top, until 1997 when it was demoted again. You'll have to ask the Scottish Mountaineering Club what is going on with that one! From here the route turns towards the intimidating-sounding Devil's Ridge – don't dwell on the mindset of those who give these worrying nicknames to mountain features. Instead, set out to descend easily northwest to a wide bealach before tackling the traverse of Stob Coire a' Mhail. Although exposed and narrow, the crest is mainly grassy with a path. Shortly after the summit there is a rockier section; the trickiest section of ridge crest can be avoided by following a bypass path which descends a short distance to the left. Even the bypass option involves a rather awkward step around a projecting boulder – perhaps worse in anticipation than in reality. Once back on the ridge it continues without further difficulty up to Sgurr a' Mhaim, whose upper slopes are covered with quartzite scree. This is the highest summit of the day and a magnificent viewpoint. Stob Ban looks particularly fine to the southwest, but the highlight is undoubtedly looking back along the Devil's Ridge – now viewed with smug satisfaction rather than a knot in the stomach.

The most obvious descent would appear to be down the northeast ridge, heading towards Steall. However, there is precipitous ground lower down which has seen several fatal accidents – do not be tempted to head this way as there is no safe route from the corrie floor to the glen below. Instead, follow the northwest ridge from the summit, over quartzite at first and then steeply over grass. This is still a relentless descent and is hard on the knees, eventually leading down to the path by the Allt Coire a'Mhusgain. Accompany this to reach the road near Polldubh Falls. Unless you're catching a lift, cross the bridge and follow the road for 2.5km to the start. It is possible to avoid some tarmac by taking a path on the south side of the river before crossing the bridge at NN158684 to rejoin the road.

Alternatives

The Mamores are packed with fine ridges, providing a multitude of options. One great variation would be to ascend Sgurr a' Mhaim and follow the Devil's Ridge to Sgurr an Iubhair, but then descend to the bealach to the west, perhaps continuing to include Stob Ban and maybe even Mullach nan Coirean.

Non-scramblers could tackle An Gearanach by the ascent route given and return the same way; likewise Sgurr a' Mhaim could be ascended out-and-back from Polldubh Falls using the descent route described above. If taking these options then Am Bodach and Stob Coire a'Chairn could then be climbed on their own from the Kinlochleven side of the range.

5

Sgor Gaibhre
Carn Dearg

Sgor Gaibhre (955m) *goat's peak*
Carn Dearg (941m) *red rocky hill*

Distance **21.75km**
Ascent **975m**
Time **7 – 8 hours**
Start point **OS Grid ref: NN356664**
Map **OS Explorer 385**
Public transport **train to Corrour Station on West Highland Line (no road access)**
Terrain & hazards **tracks, hillpaths; pathless on the main climb and descent**

Though their outlines are unspectacular, the remote setting of Sgor Gaibhre and Carn Dearg above beautiful Loch Ossian more than makes up for any lack of character. This route from Corrour Station has the advantage of a high-level start to minimise the effort. Rather than completing the hills between trains, the trip is greatly enhanced by an overnight stay at the idyllic eco-hostel on the shores of the loch.

Start with the train journey on the West Highland Line to Corrour Station. Whether approaching from the north or south, the rail journey is a memorable one, running through magnificently remote countryside. With no public road access, Corrour is the most isolated station on Britain's rail network and may be familiar from its role in the film *Trainspotting*. The Station House is part of the Corrour Estate and is now home to a

small three-room hotel and a seasonal restaurant – a useful refuge as you wait for the return train. For an atmospheric overnight stay try the original Loch Ossian Hostel which comes into view as you start the walk along the vehicle track towards the loch. This enjoys perhaps the most perfect setting of any hostel, right down by the water's edge amongst a group of pines. It was once the waiting room for private guests of Corrour Estate; here they would await the steamer which would take them along the water to the shooting lodge. The hostel was given an eco-makeover by the SYHA (now known as Hostelling Scotland) in the 1990s and now – with composting toilets, but no showers – it can cater for up to 20 guests.

At a fork in the track keep right and, further on when it branches left to the hostel, turn right instead onto a recently improved path. This forms part of the ancient Road to the Isles route which leads eventually to Rannoch Station. The path gradually gains height, but becomes very wet underfoot as it crosses the flat ground east of Meall na Lice. It meets another path by Peter's Rock – a memorial to Peter Trowell, a warden at the hostel, who died nearby in 1979.

Leave the paths behind and head directly up the open slope over moorland to Meall na Leitire Duibhe. Now follow the broad, bumpy shoulder around Coire

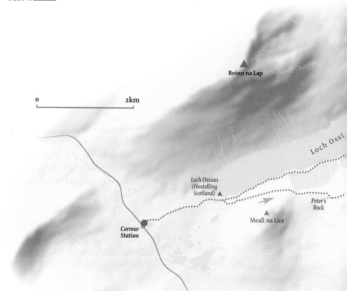

Creagach to reach the fine cairn which marks the summit of Carn Dearg. Although lower than many of the surrounding mountains its central position makes it a wonderful vantage point over the wild country at the heart of the Highlands.

The route down to Mam Ban is not immediately obvious, though the grassy cone of Sgor Gaibhre and its twin Top, Sgor Choinnich, can easily be seen on a clear day. Bear northeast over a small intervening hillock and on down a steeper section to reach the boggy bealach. From here the route up Sgor Gaibhre is much clearer, with a path leading directly up to the summit which sports a much smaller

cairn. The eastern side of the mountain falls away steeply to give depth to the massive bulk of Ben Alder beyond.

Take care in poor visibility on the descent to the Bealach nan Sgor as there is steep ground on the right – head northwest initially to avoid this. From the col steep slopes lead up to Sgor Choinnich, a twin to Sgor Gaibhre though only classified as a Top. It can be bypassed by making a rising traverse to the left from the bealach, or climbed direct. Either way, head over gentle slopes to cross Meall Nathrach Mor, and continue down the pathless heather towards the foot of Loch Ossian, aiming just to the right of the plantations. Make for the gate in the

404

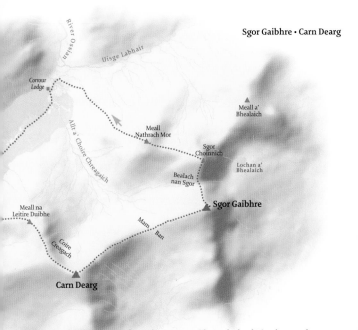

River Ossian

Uisge Labhair

Corrour
Lodge

Allt a' Choire Chreagaich

Meall a'
Bhealaich

Meall
Nathrach Mor

Sgor
Choinnich

Lochan a'
Bhealaich

Bealach
nan Sgor

Sgor Gaibhre

Meall na
Leitire Duibhe

Mam
Ban

Coire
Creagach

Carn Dearg

fence beside a burn and, once through, keep just right of a felled area to eventually pick up a clear path. Turn left onto this, crossing a bridge to reach Loch Ossian. Immediately on the right is the futuristic Corrour Lodge; completed in 2003 at a rumoured cost of over £20 million, the granite and glass structure was commissioned by an heir to the Tetrapak fortune. It looks like the lair of a Bond villain, although more mundanely it currently provides a country retreat for paying guests.

Turn left along the track for the long but beautiful walk along the edge of Loch Ossian. Keep right at the fork and head through forestry where rhododendrons provide a splash of Himalayan colour during the spring. The conifers eventually give way to birches and finally open ground before Loch Ossian hostel is reached. If not staying here, continue to the station.

Alternatives

If you don't like trains, one alternative is an approach from Loch Eigheach on the lonely road from Kinloch Rannoch in Perthshire to Rannoch Station. The walk from here is a long horseshoe of humpy ridges around the headwaters of the Allt Eigheach, though for bagging-fiends there is the advantage of including a Corbett, Meall na Meoig, along the way.

Looking over Loch Ossian from the slopes of Meall Nathrach Mor

Beinn na Lap

Beinn na Lap (935m) *dappled hill*

Distance **10km**
Time **3 – 5 hours**
Start point **OS Grid ref: NN356664**
Map **OS Explorer 385**
Public transport **train to Corrour Station on West Highland Line (no road access)**
Terrain & hazards **boggy lower slopes; pathless, indistinct ridge higher up**

Beinn na Lap – otherwise in the middle of nowhere – is easily accessed from Corrour Station, the most remote stop on the fabulous West Highland Line. A starting height of 400m helps to make the ascent one of the quickest amongst the Munros. The hill is unspectacular, but the views – over Rannoch Moor and the nearby mountains – are excellent. Soak up the unique atmosphere of the area with a stay at the waterside Loch Ossian hostel.

Taking the train to Corrour Station is a real treat. The timetable from the north (Tulloch is the nearest station) is better for day walkers, but the remote rail trip is enjoyable from any start point. There is no vehicular access unless you are staying on the Corrour Estate and even then your suspension will be tested by miles of Landrover track to reach Loch Ossian from the north.

Corrour Station House is now run as a seasonal restaurant and small hotel, whilst the hostel at nearby Loch Ossian provides accommodation. The Ossian hostel is a converted steamer waiting room and provides a cosy and characterful place to stay with a wood-burning stove and ecofriendly composting loos.

From the train station follow the track east across the moor. Loch Ossian soon comes into view with the tiny hostel visible amongst a stand of trees by the water. Before reaching it, branch left at a fork and then left again at the next junction, past a vehicle barrier. Almost immediately, leave the track where it bends left to follow an indistinct boggy path heading directly for the west ridge of Beinn na Lap. The climb soon steepens with improving views back down over Loch Ossian.

Once on the broad ridge of Ceann Caol Beinn na Lap the gradient eases. The rocky ground crosses a number of rounded lumps before the summit comes into sight. At this point a square windshelter cairn on the right edge of the ridge provides commanding views over the loch below.

The effort required to reach the top really is negligible by Munro standards because of the high-level start and it can be a surprise to arrive at the summit cairn. Beinn na Lap gives a fine perspective on the arc of higher summits around as well as the more open sweep towards Rannoch Moor. The easiest return is by the same outward route. If time allows Beinn na Lap makes a good combination with the horseshoe Corbett Leum Uilleam on the other side of the railway line.

Garbh-bheinn

Allt Feith Thuill

Sron na Cloiche Sgoilite

Lochan Ruigh Phaill

Beinn na Lap

Ceann Caol Beinn na Lap

Loch Ossian

Loch Ossian (Hostelling Scotland)

Meall na Lice

Corrour Station

Loch na Sgeallaig

0   2km

Alternatives
To make a longer circular route, follow the Sron na Cloiche Sgoilite ridge and then take the path and track back through Strath Ossian and along the north shore of Loch Ossian to pick up the outward track back to the station.

Gulvain

Gulvain (987m) *hill of noise*

Distance **21km**
Ascent **1230m**
Time **7 – 10 hours**
Start point **OS Grid ref: NM960794**
Maps **OS Explorer 398 and 399**
Terrain & hazards **long walk in to remote hill with grassy but steep ascent**

The solitary Munro of Gulvain may be far from roads, but Gleann Fionnlighe makes for a pleasant, if lengthy, approach. The lower slopes give a long pull up steep grass, but the final ridge above and its stunning views are an ample reward.

The walk starts from near the junction of the A830 and the A861, but the best place to leave a car is a short distance along the A861 at a lay-by on the right. Return to the A830 and briefly turn right beside it and then left onto a track to some houses. Turn right at the houses and cross a bridge; the walk now turns up the gated track on the left (SP Footpath to Strathan). The track leads up the east side of the glen at first, climbing slightly through the birchwoods. After 2km it crosse back over the Fionn Lighe and continues up the glen.

Pass the deserted building at Uachan, after which the track becomes much rougher; some cyclists may want to abandon their bikes here. When the track forks, keep right, staying near the river.

Some 2km beyond Uachan, the forest is left behind as the track continues up the now open Gleann Fionnlighe, eventually becoming a path. After 2km cross a bridge over the Allt a'choire Reidh; a chance to stop and examine the steep and featureless grassy slopes of Gulvain ahead. Shortly after crossing the burn, look out for a small cairn which indicates a path forking off to the right. After around 0.5km further a hill path heads left to begin the ascent, which is continuously steep up to a minor hump at 855m. Here the gradient eases and the walk continues pleasantly along the ridge to the trig point on the south top. This is not the Munro summit, however; the higher cairn on Gulvain is just over 1km further along the ridge. It descends slightly to a level bealach before a fine narrower section leads up to the true summit, from where the lochs and mountains of West Lochaber spread out as far as the eye can see. Return by the same route – it may seem a very long way!

Alternatives

It is possible – if you are very fit – to head up Glen Mallie and then climb northwest to a bealach at 536m which is crossed by a drystone dyke. Alternatively, this point could be reached by traversing Mullach Coire nan Geur-oirean – a tongue-twisting Graham. The route then ascends the ridge to arrive directly at the summit cairn.

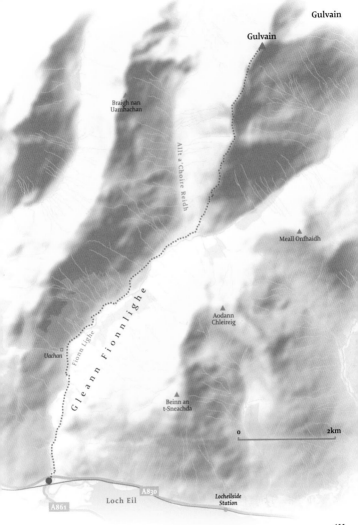

Gulvain

Gulvain

Braigh nan
Uamhachan

Allt a'Choire Reidh

Meall Onfhaidh

Aodann
Chleireig

Gleann Fionnlighe

Fionn Lighe

Uachan

Beinn an
t-Sneachda

0   2km

A830
A861   Loch Eil   Locheilside
                                    Station

Sgurr Thuilm
Sgurr nan Coireachan

Sgurr Thuilm (963m) *peak of the hillock*
Sgurr nan Coireachan (956m)
peak of the corries

Distance 23km
Ascent 1445m
Time 9 – 10 hours
Start point OS Grid ref: NM906808
Map OS Explorer 398
Public transport train or bus to Glenfinnan
Terrain & hazards **excellent track on approach could be cycled; the summits and ridges are steep, rugged and rocky**

The viaduct, monument, and views down Loch Shiel from Glenfinnan make it one of Scotland's most celebrated locations. Its two Munros are set well back, however, and receive far less attention. Nonetheless, the traverse of these very rugged, steep peaks makes for a superb but demanding day.

Turn north onto a tarred track off the A830 at Glenfinnan, just northwest of the bridge over the River Finnan; there is then a parking area on the right-hand side. (This can get very busy and you may need to arrive early to bag a space.) The walk begins along the private tarmac road which leads up the glen, soon passing under the impressive railway viaduct.

The viaduct carries the celebrated West Highland Line from Fort William to Mallaig and has been made even more famous due to its starring role in the first *Harry Potter* film. Continue up the glen, ignoring any turnings, and after 3km cross the Allt a Chaol-ghlinne. Once over the bridge turn right onto a rougher track to reach the old cottage of Corryhully. The estate maintains this shelter which can be used as a bothy outwith the stalking season. Follow the track up the west bank of the River Finnan for 2km before crossing a bridge and continuing on the track to the right.

After 250m strike off northeast; there are traces of a rough path at first, but this becomes indistinct as you climb steeply onto the Druim Coire a' Bheithe ridge just to the right of a burn. Once the ridge becomes better defined follow it; after a flat shoulder it turns north and crosses a minor lump, passing some fenceposts before the final short pull up to Sgurr Thuilm. The ground falls away steeply to the north and west, making for spectacular views into Knoydart.

Retrace the route as far down as the fenceposts and then bear west along the ridge that leads to Sgurr nan Coireachan. The ridge passes over four intervening lumps and the rough ground makes it slow going, but traces of a path help before it eventually climbs to the trig point at the top of Sgurr nan Coireachan. This second Munro of the day is, if anything, an even finer viewpoint than the first. To descend take the southeast

Sgurr nan Coireachan

Meall an Tarmachain

Beinn Gharbh

Sgurr Thuilm

Coire Odhar Mòr

Sgurr a' Choire Riabhaich

Coire Thollaidh

Allt Coire a' Bhaithe

Druim Coire a' Bheithe

Allt Guirnean

Glean Cuirnea...

Coire Carnaig

Streap

Sgurr an Fhuarain Duibh

Glenfinnan Lodge

Corryhully

River Finnan

Meall an Uillt Chaoil

Allt a Chaol-ghlinne

Beinn an Tuim

Fraoch-bheinn

Glen Finnan

Loch na Carnaich

A830

viaduct

0   2km

Glenfinnan

Visitor Centre

Glenfinnan

Monument

Loch Shiel

413

ridge towards the minor peak of Sgurr a' Choire Riabhaich. Cross the narrow ridge with care and head steeply downhill, eventually picking up a stalkers' path when the slope eases. This heads to the left, diagonally cutting across the east flank of the ridge before eventually leading down to the track in the glen. Turn right to retrace your steps for the long walk back to Glenfinnan.

Alternatives

It is also possible to approach these peaks from the end of the public road near the head of Loch Arkaig. This way is even rougher and involves a tricky crossing of the River Pean near the end, making it impossible if the water level is high. Pass through Strathan and then cross a bridge over the Pean at the foot of Gleann Cuirnean. Strike off up Meill an Fhir-eoin, avoiding a couple of craggy sections, and continue up the ridge to Sgurr Thuilm.

After traversing to Sgurr nan Coireachan as described above, return to the last bealach on the ridge between the summit and Meall nan Tarmachan. From here it is possible to make a steep descent northeast at first, then traverse the rough ground of an indistinct ridge above Coire nan Gall to reach point 406m. Finally, aim to reach the floor of the glen near the Glen Pean Bothy at the edge of the forestry. The river itself is the final obstacle; on the far side the path can be picked up for the return to the start.

Glenfinnan Viaduct

9

Sron a' Choire Ghairbh
Meall na Teanga

Sron a' Choire Ghairbh (937m)
nose of the rough corrie
Meall na Teanga (917m)
rounded hill of the tongue

Distance **19km**
Ascent **1260m**
Time **7 – 8 hours**
Start point **OS Grid ref: NN278958**
Map **OS Explorer 400**
Public transport **bus to Laggan Lochs – just over 1km from start**
Terrain & hazards **straightforward hillwalking on mainly grassy hills – a long day**

Sron a' Choire Ghairbh and Meall na Teanga rise steeply above Loch Lochy and are a familiar landmark on a drive through the Great Glen. The ascent from Kilfinnan approaches through forestry plantations, but the views are excellent and the going fairly straightforward.

There is limited parking on a grassy area just before the road crosses the bridge over the Kilfinnan Burn. Take care not to obstruct any passing or turning spaces. Start by crossing the bridge and following the Great Glen Way in the direction of Fort William. Pass the farm and follow the track running along the edge of the woodland, passing some chalets before entering the forest.

At a fork, the Great Glen Way heads left downhill towards the loch. Branch right here and follow the gently rising track. After about 2km, at a large boulder, turn right. The path climbs steeply through the forest. Once above the trees it continues along the north flank of the valley of the Allt Glas-Dhoire, aiming for the narrow pass between the two hills. This route is an old 'Coffin Road', once used by crofters to carry the dead to the graveyard at Kilfinnan.

On reaching the bealach you have a choice of which Munro to tackle first. For Sron a' Choire Gairbh follow the well-engineered stalkers' path on the north side of the bealach to eventually gain a grassy ridge. It is then a short walk along the edge of the broken cliffs to the summit cairn. There are impressive views up the Great Glen and towards the wilderness of Knoydart, and the next Munro, Meall na Teanga, is profiled against a backdrop of Ben Nevis.

Retrace your steps to the bealach. The route for Meall na Teanga is less obvious; climb across the slopes of Meall Dubh to reach the bealach to its right. Now aim for the broad north ridge of Meall na Teanga, which levels off before the summit cairn. Ben Nevis is seen to better effect from here. Return to the bealach and retrace your steps to Kilfinnan.

10

Sgurr na Ciche
Garbh Chioch Mhor
Sgurr nan Coireachan

Sgurr na Ciche (1040m) *peak of the breast*
Garbh Chioch Mhor (1013m)
big rough place of the breast
Sgurr nan Coireachan (953m)
peak of the corries

Distance **26km**
Ascent **1520m**
Time **10 – 12 hours**
Start point **OS Grid ref: NM988916**
Map **OS Explorer 398**
Terrain & hazards **boggy lower ground; the walk crosses exceptionally rugged, rocky terrain which can be exhausting**

This route traverses one of the most rugged and magnificent mountain ridges in Scotland, culminating in the steep, pointed summit of Sgurr na Ciche at the head of Loch Nevis. The tough, rocky terrain gives this very remote route an epic feel.

The single-track road along beautiful Loch Arkaig has bumps, twists and turns to match any rollercoaster before it ends near the head of the loch, where there is a car park on the left. Start the walk along the private track, branch right at a fork (signed for Tomdoun and Morar) and keep on the main route when the Tomdoun path goes off to the right. Pass Glendessary Farm and the Lodge before reaching Upper Glendessary.

Two paths continue from here; take the one to the right, an ancient right of way which climbs towards the top corner of the forestry seen ahead. It then carries on across the hillside just above the trees and is very wet in places. When you eventually reach the Allt Coire nan Uth, look out for the bridge and, once across, a small cairn which indicates the start of the climb directly up the steep slopes that lead onto the south ridge of Sgurr nan Coireachan. The pull up is unrelenting, but as the ridge becomes better defined the gradient eases for the final more pleasant approach to the summit cairn.

Descend the very steep west ridge, continuing down to the Bealach Coire nan Gall. There is a path which follows the remains of a drystone dyke; it rises steeply and traverses Garbh Chioch Bheag to reach the larger Garbh Chioch Mhor. The ridge is rocky and contorted, making for slow going, but the views of the magnificently rugged landscapes from the cairn at the second Munro of the day repay any amount of effort.

Keep following the wall as it drops steeply down to the bealach with the impressive cone of Sgurr na Ciche ahead. On all but the stillest day the bealach lives up to its name 'Feadan na Ciche' – the Whistle of the Breast – as the wind can tear cruelly through this gap. The ascent to Sgurr na Ciche appears intimidating. However, a path winds first to the left before making a series of zigzags to reach the shapely summit and its classic view along the length of Loch Nevis.

The return is energy-sapping – so be prepared. Return to the Feadan na Ciche and then aim southwest down into a gulch. This is steep and requires care with some straightforward scrambling. Keep heading down once out of the gully until, at about 650m, you can bear southeast across the shoulder of Garbh Chioch Mhor. Keep going in the same direction to pick up the path from Sourlies (on Loch Nevis) to Glendessary. Turn left along this boggy path. At a fork there are two options; either branch left above the forestry to rejoin the outward route, or turn right to head down through the trees. If taking the latter option the terrain is often sodden; you eventually come to the River Dessary which you accompany downstream to reach the end of a track. This leads through an open section and then close to A' Chuil Bothy before re-entering the trees. After a further 4km, turn left at a junction to cross the river at Strathan and return to the start.

Alternatives

This is a great area for wild camping or staying overnight in one of several bothies; doing this opens up many different combinations and possibilities. One option is to stay at the tiny, basic shelter at Sourlies at the head of Loch Nevis and then ascend Sgurr na Ciche along its long western ridge. Sourlies, like A' Chuil, is maintained by volunteers from the Mountain Bothies Association; if visiting any of the bothies please help by keeping them tidy and carrying out any rubbish you find there.

Fort William

Ben Aden

Meall a'
Choire Dhuibh

River Carnach

**Sgurr
na Ciche**

Feadan
na Ciche

**Garbh
Chioch Mhor**

**Sgurr nan
Coireachar**

Garbh
Chioch Bheag

Bealach Coire
nan Gall

Loch
Nevis

Sourlies

Allt Coire na Ciche

Finiskaig River

Lochan a'
Mhaim

G l e n

Sgurr na
h-Aide

Bidein a'
Chabair

0   2km

Sgurr Mor

Sgurr an
Fhuarain

Sgurr Beag

G l e n   K i n g i e

An Eag

Druim a'
Chuirn

a Coire nan Uth

Sgurr Cos na
Breachd-laoidh

Fraoch
Bheinn

Upper
Glendessary

Glendessary
Lodge

River Dessary

Glendessary Farm

A' Chuil

D e s s a r y

Loch Arkaig

Monadh Gorm

Strathan

G l e n   P e a n

Garbh Chioch Mhor and Sgurr na Ciche from Sgurr an Fhuarain

11

Sgurr Mor

Sgurr Mor (1003m) *big peak*

Distance 24km
Ascent 1510m
Time 9 – 11 hours
Start point OS Grid ref: NM987916
Map OS Explorer 398
Terrain & hazards rough and remote walking on pathless ground with some steep and some boggy sections; the River Kingie may be impassable in spate

Sgurr Mor, a rocky and steep peak between Loch Quoich and lonely Glen Kingie, must rank as one of the remotest Munros. Unless you have a kayak or boat to cross the loch, the quickest ascent involves a long walk from Glendessary to the south.

After the tortuous but beautiful drive up Loch Arkaig, park up in the car park on the left near the head of the loch. Go through the gate and branch right (signed for Morar and Tomdoun) when the track forks. Keep straight ahead when the Tomdoun path leaves to the right and continue on the track beside the Allt na Feithe. Immediately after crossing the Allt na Feithe turn right (north) onto an indistinct path, soon passing through a gate and climbing towards the pass. Sgurr Mor comes into view across Glen Kingie as the gradient eases, but the going becomes increasingly boggy as the top of the pass is reached; aim directly north across pathless ground to descend into the glen.

Glen Kingie is one of the Highlands' emptiest glens, with the solitary bothy at Kinbreak being the only building for many miles down the glen. The river must be forded – this usually presents no problem, but if in spate it can be impossible to cross safely without a long detour.

Bear directly north up the hillside opposite, aiming for the bealach between Sgurr Mor and Sgurr an Fhuarain. Though very steep, the pathless slope is grassy and has no difficulties. Once at the ridge there are sudden views down to Loch Quoich. Sgurr Mor is to the west, but having come so far it is worth considering a detour to the east first to climb the Corbett of Sgurr an Fhuarain. Back at the bealach, begin the ascent to Sgurr Mor using a stalkers' path which heads to the right of the ridge crest part way up the slope, gaining height in a series of old zigzags before rejoining the ridge high up. A false summit is crossed before the final cairn comes into view. From here the mountains of Knoydart provide a sensational backdrop to the pointed summit of Sgurr na Ciche.

The quickest return is to retrace your steps, but there is a fine alternative route as far as the pass. Head down the steep and rocky southwest ridge of Sgurr Mor; the going is made much easier by the stalkers' path. This descends to a first bealach and then traverses Sgurr Beag before a long descent to the lowest

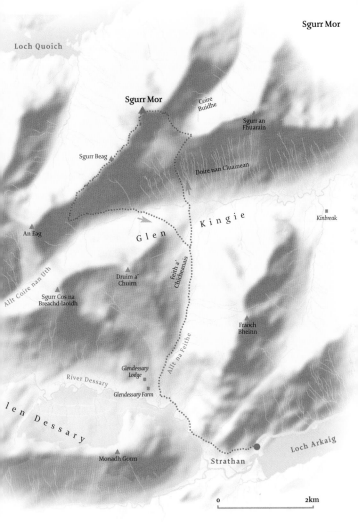

Sgurr Mor

Loch Quoich

Sgurr Mor

Coire Buidhe

Sgurr an Fhuarain

Sgurr Beag

Doire nan Cluainean

Kingie

Kinbreak

An Eag

Glen

Allt Coire nan Uth

Druim a' Chuirn

Feith a' Chicheanais

Sgurr Cos na Breachd-laoidh

Fraoch Bheinn

Allt na Feithe

Glendessary Lodge

River Dessary

Glendessary Farm

len Dessary

Monadh Gorm

Strathan

Loch Arkaig

0   2km

bealach on the ridge at 662m. Cross this bealach and continue a very short distance up the far side to pick up another stalker's path which gradually descends across the south flank of the ridge before doubling back to drop down into Glen Kingie.

At the floor of the glen cross the fence and the River Kingie to contour round the boggy slopes on the far side before climbing gradually up into the Feith a' Chicheanais pass crossed earlier in the day. Take a last look back at these remote hills before retracing the outward route to Glen Dessary.

Alternatives

Hillwalkers who are also kayakers can reach the foot of the northern side of Sgurr Mor by paddling across Loch Quoich.

Sgurr Mor

12

Gairich

Gairich (919m) *the roaring*

Distance **15km**
Ascent **870m**
Time **6 – 7 hours**
Start point **OS Grid ref: NH070025**
Map **OS Explorer 399**
Terrain & hazards **extremely boggy initially, with short and very easy scramble near the top**

Gairich is the final peak of the great ridge that extends from Sgurr na Ciche. Despite its diminutive size it is far enough from its neighbours to have great character, and the relatively short ascent is rewarded with superb views.

Start from the Loch Quoich Dam; there is parking just west of the dam on the south side of the road. The dam is a massive 320m long and 38m high. It was built in 1962 in one of the largest of the hydro-electric schemes which brought electricity to much of the Highlands for the first time. Start out by crossing the top of the dam from where you can examine the craggy northeast face of Gairich.

Follow the rough and very boggy path, keeping close to the water at first. After 1km the path climbs away from the reservoir and passes the southern end of Lochan an Fhigheadair. Underfoot conditions improve as it crosses a low bealach before heading down towards the forestry below the Bealach na Faire to join another old route. Don't be tempted by the gate here; instead bear right onto a rough trod which rises alongside the forest fence to reach a stalkers' path from Glen Kingie.

Climb Druim na Geid Salaich in a series of zigzags to reach the extensive plateau of Bac nam Foid where the path becomes indistinct. Bear west towards Gairich; the path becomes clear again on reaching steeper ground. It keeps to the left of the ridgeline at first before zigzagging sharply right to ascend to the foot of a steep section. A path worn by Munro-baggers now leads up the ridge and gets very steep higher up; there's a tiny bit of simple scrambling before reaching the summit. Gairich is one of the smallest of the Munros, but its isolated position gives it a superb outlook over the waters of Loch Quoich and towards the rugged peaks of Knoydart and Glendessary. Return by the same outward route.

Gleouraich

Spidean
Mialach

Loch
Fearna

dam

Gearr Garry

Loch Quoich

Lochan an
Fhigheadair

Bealach
na Faire

Gairich

Bac nam
Foid

Druim na Geid Salaich

River Kingie

G l e n   K i n g i e

Lochan
nan Sgud

0   2km

Loch Quoich and Gairich

Gleouraich
Spidean Mialach

Gleouraich (1035m) *the roaring*
Spidean Mialach (996m) *lousy peak*

Distance **12km**
Ascent **1130m**
Time **6 – 8 hours**
Start point **OS Grid ref: NH032028**
Map **OS Explorer 414**
Terrain & hazards **good stalkers' paths are a great aid on these steep and rocky peaks**

With splendid rocky corries on their northern flanks these two Munros offer superb hillwalking. Access is eased by some good stalkers' paths; the one used on the descent in particular being a remarkable monument to the skill of its builders.

This route starts from the tiny road which runs along the north side of Loch Quoich. There is parking opposite the end of the stalkers' path coming down from Gleouraich at NH029029. Begin by heading east along the road for 400m until a small cairn marks the start of another stalkers' path on the right, this time heading for Spidean Mialach, which slopes up the hillside to the right and passes beneath the electricity pylons.

The going becomes quite boggy in Coire Mheil; continue to the Allt Coire Dubh where the path begins to fade out. Heading upstream until the burn diverges, cross the left branch and trace the right

one upstream. Choose a good point to strike off directly up the open slopes, aiming directly for Spidean Mialach. The large summit cairn is perched on the edge of the dramatic northern cliffs.

Ahead is the most spectacular part of the walk. Follow the ridge, with a whole series of steep, rocky corries forming the northern edge, soon descending quite steeply to the Fiar Bhealach. After a slight dip, tackle the final rocky climb to the cairn and trig point of Gleouraich, the second Munro of the day. There are good views of the little-known grassy side of the Glen Shiel Ridge and also into Knoydart.

Continue to a junction of ridges and take the path which leads down the left branch. The pointy top of Sgurr na Ciche can be seen across Loch Quoich as the path crosses a flat shoulder and then runs just below the crest of the Druim Seilleach ridge on its western flank. The path is good, but you can't help but be aware of the great gulf on the right where the slopes drop straight into a finger of Loch Quoich far below. After heading back onto the ridge itself the path descends the nose of Sron a' Chuillin via a series of zigzags and leads southeast downhill, soon joining the Allt Coire Peitireach down to the road.

Gleouraich • Spidean Mialach

Maol
Chinn-dearg

Aonach
air Chrith

River Quoich

Easter Glen Quoich Burn

Glenquoich
Forest

Glen Quoich

Glen Quoich

Gleouraich

Creag Coire na
Fiar Bhealaich

Fiar
Bhealach

Spidean
Mialach

Druim
Seilleach

Coire Dubh

Allt Coire Dubh

Sron a'
Chuilinn

Allt Coire Peitireach

Coire Mheil

Allt a' Mheill

Loch
Fearna

Loch Quoich

dam

Gearr Garry

0   2km

433

14

Sgurr a' Mhaoraich

Sgurr a' Mhaoraich (1027m)
peak of the shellfish

Distance **14km**
Ascent **1025m**
Time **6 – 8 hours**
Start point **OS Grid ref: NH014040**
Map **OS Explorer 414**
Terrain & hazards **good stalkers' path eases the first part of the ascent; the steep and rocky return over Am Bathaich can be avoided by returning the same way**

The location of this solitary Munro between Loch Quoich and Loch Hourn makes it an outstanding viewpoint. On its own the mountain can be climbed quickly, but the longer, circular route given here is well worthwhile.

There is space to park just after the concrete bridge over the northern leg of Loch Quoich on the road to Kinloch Hourn; if full, park carefully on the verge a little further on. Start by following the road west, looking out for the start of a stalkers' path at NH010034. Follow this up the lower slopes, passing under the pylons to reach the wide ridge of Bac nan Canaichean. Follow the ridge across the two summits of Sgurr Coire nan Eiricheallach; it falls steeply on the northern side into Coire a' Chaorainn. Pass a drystone dyke, after which the ridge narrows for the final rocky climb up Sgurr a' Mhaoraich. In calm conditions the panorama deserves a lengthy break.

The entire South Glen Shiel Ridge stretches out to the northeast, but it cannot compete with the view towards the great peaks of Knoydart, with the sea and the Cuillin of Skye beyond. In the opposite direction is Loch Quoich; the current waterline was created in 1962 when the loch was dammed as part of the largest of the hydro-electric schemes which first brought electricity to the Highlands.

If looking for a short day or the weather is closing in, the quickest descent is back down the outward path. However, the route can be made into a circuit by heading around Coire a' Chaorainn before making a steeper descent. Follow the summit ridge NNW for about 350m before descending the steep NNE spur to the Bealach Coire a' Chaorainn. The best line up the craggy slopes opposite is to keep to the left initially before traversing back to the right once safely above the difficulties.

Continue ENE over the bumpy summits of Am Bathaich before the ridge starts to descend more steeply. Pick up a stalkers' path which starts on the south side of the ridge. This eventually zigzags down to the Allt Coire a'Chaorainn; cross this and head downstream by the boggy south bank. After 1km the path meets the track coming down the glen from the abandoned farm at Alltbeithe. Turn right to emerge on the road near the start.

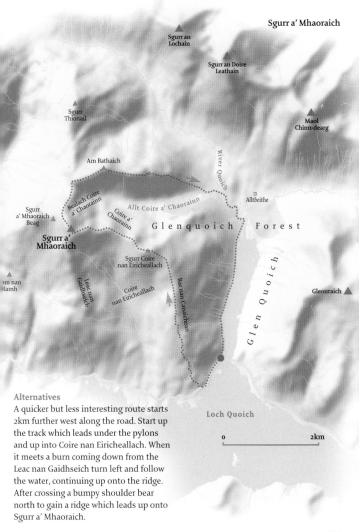

Sgurr a' Mhaoraich

Sgurr an
Lochain

Sgurr an Doire
Leathain

Maol
Chinn-dearg

Sgurr
Thionail

River Quoich

Am Bathaich

Bealach Coire
a' Chaorainn

Allt Coire a' Chaorainn

Alltbeithe

Sgurr
a' Mhaoraich
Beag

Coire a'
Chaorainn

G l e n q u o i c h   F o r e s t

Sgurr a'
Mhaoraich

Sgurr Coire
nan Eiricheallach

om nan
Ramh

Leac nan
Gaidhseich

Coire
nan Eiricheallach

Bac nan Canaichean

Gleouraich

G l e n   Q u o i c h

Loch Quoich

Alternatives

A quicker but less interesting route starts
2km further west along the road. Start up
the track which leads under the pylons
and up into Coire nan Eiricheallach. When
it meets a burn coming down from the
Leac nan Gaidhseich turn left and follow
the water, continuing up onto the ridge.
After crossing a bumpy shoulder bear
north to gain a ridge which leads up onto
Sgurr a' Mhaoraich.

0   2km

435

Gleouraich, from Sgurr a' Mhaoraich

Climbing the ridge onto Luinne Bheinn

15

Luinne Bheinn
Meall Buidhe

Luinne Bheinn (939m) *sea-swelling hill*
Meall Buidhe (946m) *yellow rounded hill*

Distance **27km**
Ascent **1585m**
Time **10 – 13 hours**
Start point **OS Grid ref: NG765002**
Map **OS Explorer 413**
Public transport **bus or train to Mallaig, then ferry to Inverie (no road access)**
Terrain & hazards **extremely rugged, steep and rocky terrain throughout, with odd bits of very simple scrambling**

These two superb hills are at the heart of the remote Knoydart peninsula. They provide a challenging walk amidst a stunning landscape of sea and some of the finest mountains in Scotland. (NB: There is no road access into Knoydart from outside the area – see the area introduction).

From the pier at Inverie turn right to pass the Old Forge pub. Follow the road by the loch shore but when it bends right, take the track ahead signed for Kinlochhourn and Strathan. This climbs through the trees; at the top edge of the woods bear right through a gate, following the track which now slopes downhill, eventually passing the Brocket Memorial high on a knoll on the left. Lord Brocket was an absentee landlord, MP and Nazi sympathiser who evicted many tenants to ensure the continued use of

the land as a shooting retreat. The uneasy relationship between residents and landowners continued until the community buyout in 1999 – since then the population has grown to around 100.

Take a track branching right to cross the glen, soon reaching a footbridge over the Inverie River. Beyond this is Druim Bothy – this locked bothy is owned by the Kilchoan Estate and is available to rent, a lovely if very midgy spot at times. Cross another footbridge, this time over the Allt Gleann Meadail, and follow the path below the crags at the lower end of the Druim Righeanaich. Once beyond the crags leave the path and find a way up the steep slope on the left to gain the ridge. There are faint bits of path in places but in high summer bracken makes this ascent a real struggle; at such times it is worth considering the alternative of continuing up the path to the head of the glen before making a steep and rocky climb to Meall Buidhe from there. Otherwise, once the ridge is gained the going is relatively easy to the top of An t-Uiriollach. There are magical views looking back to Inverie Bay, the islands of Eigg and Rum and the Sleat Peninsula of Skye beyond.

The short descent leads to a straightforward climb up the ridge to reach the Munro summit of Meall Buidhe. From here, continue to the east top and follow the clear path which descends steeply through the crags and avoids any real difficulty. Without the path a safe descent to the Bealach Ile Coire would be very tricky to find.

A rough ascent leads to the grassy top of Druim Leac a' Shith, the summit of which is bypassed on the west side. A spectacular view of craggy Ben Aden and the length of Loch Quoich is revealed.

Descend via Meall Coire na Gaoithe'n Ear to reach the lowest point between the two Munros, the Bealach a'Choire Odhair. From here a sustained climb involves some straightforward scrambling to gain the east Top of Luinne Bheinn. The aerial view of Barrisdale Bay and Loch Hourn with Beinn Sgritheall towering beyond is heart-stopping. Continue past the summit cairn to descend the ridge,

steeply in places, to Bachd Mhic an Tosaich where the path peters out. Before the end of the ridge bear west down boggy slopes to reach an even wetter path. This follows a line of old fenceposts to reach the cairn marking the high point on the Mam Barrisdale pass.

You can join any hikers heading to Inverie from Barrisdale by turning left here to follow the old, well-graded path downhill. By the time Loch an Dubh-Lochain is reached, the path has deteriorated into a boggy mess in places, but it improves once beside the loch. After the ruin a track soon rejoins the outward route below the Brocket Memorial with a final gentle climb to return to Inverie.

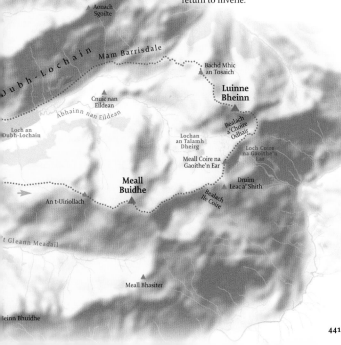

Ladhar Bheinn from Luinne Bheinn

16

Ladhar Bheinn

Ladhar Bheinn (1020m) *hill of the hoof*

Distance 22.5km
Ascent 1400m
Time 9 – 12 hours
Start point OS Grid ref: NG765002
Map OS Explorer 413
Public transport bus or train to Mallaig then ferry to Inverie (no road access)
Terrain & hazards rough, rugged and remote, with pathless ascent to ridge and some straightforward scrambling

A stunning and challenging circuit on what must rank as one of the very finest Scottish hills. Breathtaking mountain and sea views, dramatic ridges and vast crags falling into Coire Dhorrcail all add up to make a truly memorable Munro ascent. (NB. There is no road access into Knoydart from outside the area – see the introduction).

From the pier at Inverie head right to pass the Old Forge pub. Follow the waterside road past the village and then turn up a track at a bend, signed for Kinlochhourn and Strathan. At the next bend go right through a gate and follow the track, eventually passing below the prominent Brocket Memorial. Ignore the branch for Gleann Meadail to the right and continue towards Loch an Dubh-Lochain. From just before the loch up to the Mam Suidheig bealach is a pathless ascent over awkward ground, particularly in high summer when much of the ground is covered in bracken. The climb is

Mam Uidhe

The Old Forge

Inverie

Inverie Bay

Inverie R

A' Cruach

Lo
Bh'ao

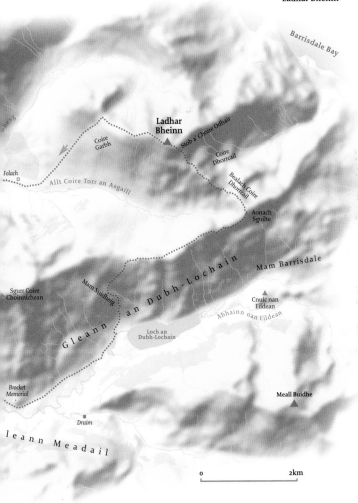

Ladhar Bheinn

Barrisdale Bay

Ladhar
Bheinn ▲ Stob a' Choire Odhair

Coire
Garbh

Coire
Dhorrcail

Allt Coire Torr an Asgaill

Bealach Coire
Dhorrcail

Folach

Aonach
Sgoilte

Mam Barrisdale

Sgurr Coire
Choinnichean

Mam Suidheig

G l e a n n   a n   D u b h - L o c h a i n

Cnuic nan
Eildean ▲

Abhainn nan Eildean

Loch an
Dubh-Lochain

Brocket
Memorial

Meall Buidhe ▲

Druim

l e a n n   M e a d a i l

0   2km

445

often a hard slog and reaching the bealach is a relief. Follow the ridge east towards Aonach Sgoilte, with ever improving views in all directions. Bypass point 636m on a grassy rake and rejoin the ridge on the climb beyond.

At the top of the next rise, at point 758m, the ridge divides into two crests. Keep in the gap in the middle to descend a grassy gully before traversing right to pick up the next section of ridge; the left-hand crest ends in crags. On the next climb a rocky section is avoided on the left before reaching the flat summit of Aonach Sgoilte, marked by a small cairn.

The path widens here as walkers coming up from Barrisdale join the route. Head northwest down the grassy slope to the Bealach Coire Dhorrcail. The steep climb beyond involves a couple of easy scrambles, with the views becoming ever more impressive with dramatic glimpses down into Coire Dhorrcail. An awkward step is needed to surmount a further rocky band, where shorter or less confident walkers may need a helping hand, before the final walk up the summit cone.

Ladhar Bheinn has three summits; the Stob a' Choire Odhair ridge, the final arm of the circuit of Coire Dhorrcail from Barrisdale Bay, sweeps away to the right from the first summit, providing a fantastic background for posing photos. The true summit is the second top, marked by a small cairn, whilst the third has what remains of a trig point. The whole ridge has some of Scotland's best views, with the Cuillin of Skye providing the final touch of magic.

The descent continues along the ridge, easily at first, becoming steeper before reaching a bealach just short of a lochan. From here, aim southwest down steep slopes of grass and rock into Coire Garbh. As the gradient lessens, a clear but soggy path keeps to the left of the forestry before following the river downstream, passing the ruins at Folach. Go through a gate to cross the bridge and join the track for the long plod back to Inverie. At the T-junction at Folach Gate turn left to follow the track on through the Mam Uidhe. On the far side it descends through more forestry to return to Inverie; keep straight on at a cross-tracks to emerge near the Old Forge pub – and after such a walk you deserve a pint!

Alternatives

A classic round of Ladhar Bheinn can be done from Barrisdale Bay on the shores of Loch Hourn. This is reached by a long up-and-down approach path from Kinloch Hourn; it is possible to camp at Barrisdale or pay to stay in the private bothy. This route involves some steep scrambling to gain Stob a'Chearcaill before following the route described above to the summit. The descent is made via the Stob a'Choire Odhair ridge.

The Seven Men of Knoydart and the Knoydart Foundation

Like many places across the Highlands, the Knoydart Peninsula was cleared of tenants in the mid-19th century, following a period of misery caused by potato blight and the failure of herring stocks; the tenants were forced to emigrate to Canada and were replaced by sheep. By the 1930s the estate was owned by Lord Brocket – a former Conservative MP with strong Nazi sympathies; he was reportedly friendly with Ribbentrop and attended Hitler's 50th birthday party in 1939.

Knoydart was requisitioned during World War Two for the training of commandos and SOE agents, but was returned in 1945 to Brocket who sacked many of the local staff and discouraged anyone who tried to enter the peninsula. Tensions increased, and in 1948 the Seven Men, some of them returning soldiers, launched a land raid on the estate and staked out new crofts. Despite public sympathy the Seven lost the eventual legal battle – and the land. A giant memorial still commemorates Lord Brocket in the glen behind Inverie, and it wasn't until 1981 that a second smaller memorial was built in the village itself to remember the Seven Men and their fight for the land.

In 1999 the estate was bought by the Knoydart Foundation, a partnership between local residents, Highland Council, neighbouring estates and the John Muir and Chris Brasher Trusts. Since then the community's fortunes have been revived strongly, and a new pier was opened to ease boat access in 2006.

Ladhar Bheinn and Loch Hourn

Kintail

A mecca for hillwalkers who like to record their summits, Kintail offers the chance to pick off plentiful Munros on both sides of the main road. These linear ridgewalks are amongst the most enjoyable in Scotland. Transport back to the start can be a problem, although Citylink buses run regularly along the A82 and provide an alternative to car sharing. The Cluanie Inn at the top of the glen offers refreshments and

accommodation, as would be expected from such an ancient staging post, whilst, where the glen reaches the sea, the Kintail Lodge Hotel has a reputation for filling meals.

Shiel Bridge has a shop, a basic campsite (many prefer nearby Morvich) and several self-catering options. Further along the A82 Dornie offers more of a village feel with a pub and general store. The Schoolhouse also offers self catering

rooms by the night. The hostel (Hostelling Scotland) at Ratagan has a fantastic view of the Five Sisters across the water. Glenelg itself, isolated by the Mam Ratagan Pass, is an attractive village en route to Beinn Sgritheall. When heading this way, ensure you make time to visit the impressively-preserved Iron-Age brochs nearby as well as Sheena's Tea Hut at Corran – the very end of the road – for tea and cake.

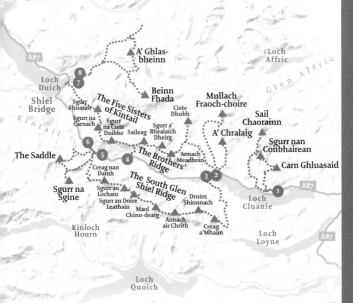

1

Carn Ghluasaid
Sgurr nan Conbhairean
Sail Chaorainn

Carn Ghluasaid (957m)
rocky hill of movement
Sgurr nan Conbhairean (1110m)
peak of the keepers of the hounds
Sail Chaorainn (1002m) *heel of the rowan*

Distance 17km
Ascent 1320m
Time 7 – 9 hours
Start point OS Grid ref: NH144103
Map OS Explorer 414
Public transport Citylink coaches on A87 from Glasgow and Inverness to Skye
Terrain & hazards a good stalkers' path makes the approach to these mountains fairly easy going – more rounded than other Kintail peaks

With a good stalkers' path up the first hill, this round of three Munros provides a gentler alternative to the celebrated ridges of Kintail.

The walk starts from the large parking area below the A87 at Lundie, which is marked on OS maps although there is no settlement here. Seen from here, the mountains are foreshortened, so don't be fooled into thinking these are just moorland lumps – the grand dome on Sgurr nan Conbhairean is only revealed from further down Glen Moriston. Cross the road and follow the section of the old road on the other side, but turn up the

obvious stony track which climbs steeply to reach a mast. Just beyond, a cairn marks the start of the stalkers' path on the right. This path is a delight, being well-graded and almost dry underfoot. It rises to reach the shoulder of An Cruachan before tackling the steeper slope on the left of Coire nan Clach via a series of zigzags. The west ridge of Carn Ghluasaid is then joined, leading up onto the bouldery plateau.

The level terrain can make it hard to find the summit of Carn Ghluasaid, but the cairn sits on the northern rim above the steep crags of Toll Creagach Beag. Keep the impressive cliffs of the corrie on your right for a very short descent and a longer ascent up to the top of Creag a'Chaorainn, where the ridge turns west.

Cross the shallow Glas Bhealach before the ridge climbs more steeply to the summit dome of Sgurr nan Conbhairean. At 1110m this Munro is one of the giants of the area and offers correspondingly extensive views, particularly to the east. From the top, bear northwest for a short distance before the north ridge leads down to the col at 914m.

A short climb leads to Sail Chaorainn; the third Munro of the day. Return to the bealach and continue part way back up Sgurr nan Conbhairean until you come to

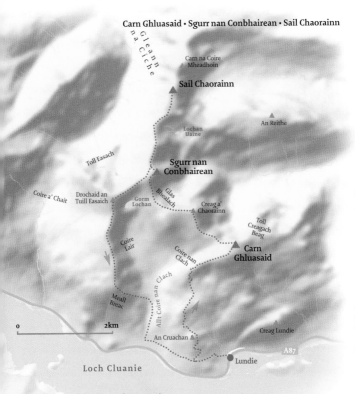

Gleann na Ciche

Carn na Coire Mheadhoin

Sail Chaorainn

An Reithe

Lochan Uaine

Toll Easach

Sgurr nan Conbhairean

Coire a' Chait

Drochaid an Tuill Easaich

Glas Bhealach

Gorm Lochan

Creag a' Chaorainn

Toll Creagach Beag

Coire Lair

Coire nan Clach

▲ **Carn Ghluasaid**

Allt Coire nan Clach

Meall Breac

0   2km

An Cruachan

Creag Lundie

Lundie   A87

Loch Cluanie

a faint path which bypasses the summit on the west side. This leads onto the initially broad southwest ridge, soon narrowing to a fine arête with views to the Gorm Lochan to the left and Toll Easach to the right. Continue ahead to Drochaid an Tuill Easaich; the top can be bypassed before heading down the south ridge.

The ridge leads down to the ill-defined shoulder of Meall Breac. Descend southeast from here and then east towards the Allt Coire nan Clach. Cross this and carry on down the far side to reach the old military road. Follow this east back past the transmitter mast to return to Lundie.

Alternatives

These summits can be climbed as part of a horseshoe of ridges from the Glen Affric side – see following route.

453

2

A' Chralaig
Mullach Fraoch-choire

A' Chralaig (1120m) *the basket*
Mullach Fraoch-choire (1102m)
summit of the heathery corrie

Distance 13km
Ascent 1150m
Time 6 – 8 hours
Start point OS Grid ref: NH092121
Map OS Explorer 414
Public Transport Citylink coaches on A87
from Glasgow and Inverness to Skye
Terrain & hazards steep terrain with
some mild scrambling; bogs on the
return route

**A' Chralaig rises massively above Glen
Cluanie and its ascent involves a long,
steep grind. The reward is the superb
ridgewalk that leads on to reach Mullach
Fraoch-choire – as fine as any in Kintail.**

Start from the long lay-by on the north
side of the A87, a short distance east of
the Cluanie Inn. Begin by walking east
along the road for a while to a rough
signposted track on the left into the An
Caorann Mor. After around 200m, strike
off to the right directly up the steep grassy
slopes to the northeast. The gradient
eases at about 750m as you emerge on the
south ridge of A' Chralaig.

Bear left along the ridge which
continues much more enjoyably uphill.
At about 1000m the ridge turns northwest
and leads easily to the huge cairn on the

summit of A' Chralaig. A commanding
view of the whole length of Loch Cluanie
and the surrounding mountains is spread
out behind you. The ridge continues
briefly north before a steeper rocky
northwesterly descent and then a
northerly continuation down to a col.
A clear path from the col continues across
the 1008m Top before a right turn to a
second bealach. From here the ridge
narrows and is broken into a series of
rocky towers, which may be enjoyed by
keen and experienced scramblers. Most
walkers will opt to use the bypass path
which keeps to the right side at first
before switching across to the left.

Soon you reach the summit of Mullach
Fraoch-choire. This offers a fine vantage
point for the wild upper reaches of
Glen Affric, whilst the view back along
the ridge is very satisfying. Return to
the last bealach and then descend a
steep scree path into the grassy bowl
of Coire Odhar.

Continue WNW down the open slopes,
bearing left at around 500m to shorten
the route back and reach the path near the
high point of the pass between Cluanie
and Affric. Follow this to the left; it is very
boggy underfoot and the start of the
Landrover track further down may come
as a relief. This leads back to the road near
the start.

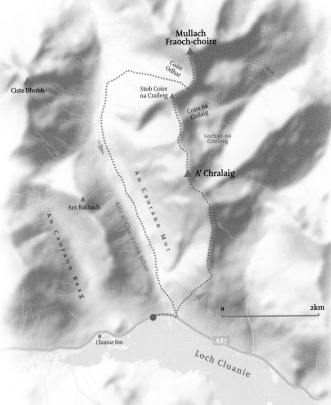

Mullach Fraoch-choire

Coire Odhar

Ciste Dhubh

Stob Coire na Craileig

Coire na Cralaig

Lochan na Craileig

A' Chralaig

An Caorann Mor

Am Bathach

Allt a Chaorainn Mhor

An Caorann Beag

Cluanie Inn

A87

Loch Cluanie

0   2km

Alternatives

A quick glance at a map shows that a fine alternative route to these mountains is from the head of Loch Affric, perhaps during a stay at the remote Alltbeithe Youth Hostel or Camban Bothy. The difficulties of access mean that this is not the obvious choice, but it is possible to include Sgurr nan Conbhairean and Sail Chaorainn (with a detour to Carn Ghluasaid) to complete a grand horseshoe of ridges around Gleann na Ciche.

A' Chralaig

An Cnapach on Ciste Dhubh

3

The Brothers' Ridge: Saileag Sgurr a'Bhealaich Dheirg Aonach Meadhoin Ciste Dhubh

Saileag (956m) *the little heel*
Sgurr a'Bhealaich Dheirg (1038m)
peak of the red pass
Aonach Meadhoin (1001m)
middle ridged hill
Ciste Dhubh (979m) *dark chest*

Distance **16km**
Ascent **1857m**
Time **9 – 10 hours**
Start point **OS Grid ref: NH009135**
Map **OS Explorer 414**
Public transport **Citylink coaches on A87 from Glasgow and Inverness to Skye**
Terrain & hazards **steep ascent to the ridge, then clear paths on sometimes narrow grassy ridges**

This is the eastward extension of the Five Sisters ridge, but only the very fittest would attempt to combine the two routes. Often known as the Brothers of Kintail, these Munros give their more famous siblings a run for their money in terms of fine ridgewalking. The route continues to reach the intriguing outlying peak of Ciste Dhubh.

Start from the Glenshiel car park at NH009135. This is a linear route, requiring two cars, the use of public transport or an additional 9km of road walking to return to the start. Walk briefly west along the road for a short distance to find a path that starts close to a burn and leads steeply up the grassy slopes. The 550m climb to the bealach is less than 1km in distance – a real steep pull. Above the top of the forestry the path bends east; after a short distance, leave the main path (which contours above the forestry) and turn left on a fainter path leading more directly uphill. The route zigzags up to reach the bealach; here turn east to begin the ridge walk.

The climb up to Saileag is quite straight-forward and the descent to the double bealach beyond is short. After passing a tiny lochan, the ridge rises to the western shoulder of Sgurr a' Bhealaich Dheirg, a much more substantial mountain. The ridge levels off before the gentle ascent to the 1030m cairn. This is not the true summit, however, which involves a short detour along a very slender arête to the northeast. After visiting the massive cairn, return to the main ridge.

Descend the wide southeast slopes,

keeping steep ground to your left, until the ridge becomes better defined once more as it turns east and drops to the col at 827m. A good path now leads over a top and, after a small dip, climbs to the Munro summit of Aonach Meadhoin. From here, descend steeply at first before following a fine ridge over the prominent Top of Sgurr an Fhuarail.

Drop down the NNE ridge to boggy Bealach a' Choinich to reach the foot of Ciste Dhubh. The slope above is wide and grassy at first and a soggy path heads up just to the right of some crags. Above the steep section, the climb becomes much more pleasant as the ridge narrows. A prominent peak, An Cnapach, sits astride the ridge and is flanked by very steep slopes; the path bypasses this on the west side, though purists may traverse it. Beyond, the ridge rises slightly before levelling off, with a great view of the summit dome of Ciste Dhubh ahead. The final slopes are rocky, but there are no real obstacles; the views back to An Cnapach are superb.

Return to Bealach a' Choinich. The return to Glen Shiel can be made down the boggy An Caorann Beag, but a much finer and drier option is to traverse along the ridge of the Corbett Am Bathach. A path then descends the southeast slopes, passing a newly felled area to reach a lay-by on the A87 around 1km east of the Cluanie Inn, 9km from the start.

Sgurr na Ciste Duibhe

Saileag

Bealach an Lapain

Alternatives

The route given makes for a long day, and Ciste Dhubh could be omitted by descending the southeast ridge of Sgurr an Fhuarail, keeping on the ridge over a couple of minor summits. From point 843m head south, keeping the steepest ground to your left, before bearing southeast to join the A87 opposite the Cluanie Inn. Ciste Dhubh and Am Bathach can then be climbed in a separate outing.

Ciste Dhubh

An Cnapach

Sgurr a' Bhealaich Dheirg

Bealach a' Choinich

Sgurr an Fhuarail

An Caorann Mòr

Am Bathach

Allt a' Chaorainn Mhòir

Aonach Meadhoin

An Caorann Beag

Glen Shiel

A87

Cluanie Inn

Loch Cluanie

0   2km

Ciste Dhubh seen from the Brothers' Ridge

Sgurr Fhuaran, with the Cuillin of Skye beyond

4

The Five Sisters of Kintail: Sgurr na Ciste Duibhe Sgurr na Carnach Sgurr Fhuaran

Sgurr na Ciste Duibhe (1027m)
peak of the dark chest
Sgurr na Carnach (1002m) *rocky peak*
Sgurr Fhuaran (1067m) *peak of the spring*

Distance 15km – for linear walk, assuming transport is available back to start
Ascent 1385m
Time 8 – 10 hours
Start point OS Grid ref: NH009135
Map OS Explorer 414
Public transport Citylink coaches on A87 from Glasgow and Inverness to Skye
Terrain & hazards steep climb to the ridge; ridgewalk involves some simple scrambling and rocky terrain

The Five Sisters provide an elegant backdrop at the head of Loch Shiel. Their traverse is a classic and surprisingly strenuous ridgewalk, taking in three Munros with magnificent views.

This is a linear route, so either arrange to leave a car near the end or use public transport to link up the start and finish – the road is very busy. Start from the Glenshiel car park at NH009135 on the A87. Head briefly west on the road before a path by the tiny burn leads steeply up the grassy slopes to the north. 550m of height is gained in under 1km before reaching the Bealach an Lapain, so there is no denying the steepness of the climb. Above the level of the forestry the path bends east above the trees; after a short distance, leave the path which seems to contour above the forestry and head left, more directly uphill on a fainter path. The route zigzags up to reach the bealach.

The reward for this slog is the magnificent ridge walk now stretching ahead. A long, undulating section leads to the pointed Top of Sgurr nan Spainteach (named 'the peak of the Spaniards' in honour of the defeated Jacobite-supporting soldiers who fought on the battlesite far below in June 1719). On the descent beyond there is a small rock scramble to descend before a bealach, and then the ridge splits into two crests with a depression between – very confusing in poor visibility. Head first along the right-hand crest before changing to the left following the faint path. A steep climb then leads up to the huge summit cairn of Sgurr na Ciste Duibhe, the first Sister and a Munro. For the best views continue just beyond to reveal the full length of Loch Duich. The ridge now broadens as you descend to the Bealach na Craoibhe.

The path winds up the rough and stony

Loch
Duich

**Allt a'
Chruinn**

Kintail Lodge ■

**Shiel
Bridge**

▲
Sgurr an
t-Searraich

▲
Sgurr na
Moraich

Allt a' Chruinn

*Fasach an
t-Searraich*

Loch
Shiel

River Shiel

Biod an
Fhithich

slopes to reach Sgurr na Carnach, which only became a Munro in 1997. The route down to the Bealach na Carnach beyond has some slight scrambling on rocky flakes; beyond, the climb up to Sgurr Fhuaran is steep and bouldery. This is the highest of the Five Sisters and the last of the three Munros.

From here, it is possible to descend the steep west ridge right down to Glen Shiel. The footbridge across the river just east of Loch Shiel is gone, so if following this descent it is necessary to continue along the north side until you come to the road.

A much better option is to carry on along the ridge. Descend the west ridge from Sgurr Fhuaran's summit for 300m to avoid steep ground, but then follow the path which cuts off right to join the north ridge below the difficulties; the descent to the Bealach Buidhe then continues without incident. The main path bypasses the fourth sister, Sgurr nan Saighead, but in spite of its lack of Munro status keep to the ridge – the slopes on the right are the steepest and most impressive in the whole Five Sisters range. There are great views down some fearsome gullies into Coire na h-Uaighe.

Before reaching the steep peak of Beinn Bhuidhe a path heads left to reach its northwest ridge. If taking this option, follow the path down the ridge, descending steeply at one point beside a burn, to reach the flat bog of Fasach an t-Searraich. From here, head north and cross the Allt a'Chruinn before following the path down its north bank. The other option is to scramble to the top of Beinn Bhuidhe, and then down its rocky NNE ridge to the next bealach. From here the purist can ascend the fifth sister, sprawling Sgurr na Moraich, before returning to the bealach and descending to the start of the path down the north bank of the Allt a' Chruinn, soon passing a waterfall. Continue down the path on the north bank, which soon improves and follows the line of a stalkers' path. Eventually the burn falls into a gorge; the path swings right here before making a winding descent of the hillside. It emerges at Allt a' Chruinn beside the waterworks, approximately 13km from the start of the walk.

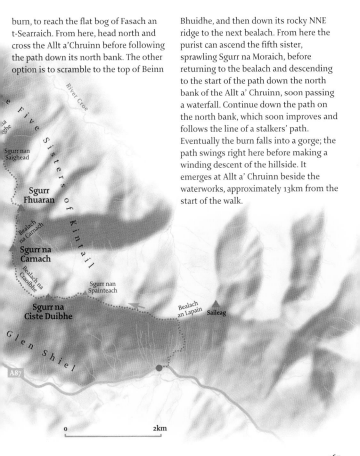

0   2km

Sgurr na Ciste Duibhe and the Cuillin from Aonach Meadhoin

5

The South Glen Shiel Ridge: Creag a'Mhaim Druim Shionnach Aonach air Chrith Maol Chinn-dearg Sgurr an Doire Leathain Sgurr an Lochain Creag nan Damh

Creag a'Mhaim (947m)
rock of the rounded hill
Druim Shionnach (987m) *ridge of the fox*
Aonach air Chrith (1021m)
trembling ridge hill
Maol Chinn-dearg (981m) *bald red head*
Sgurr an Doire Leathain (1010m)
peak of the broad thicket
Sgurr an Lochain (1004m)
peak of the little loch
Creag nan Damh (918m) *rock of the stags*

Distance 26.75km
Ascent 1820m
Time 9 – 11 hours
Start point OS Grid ref: NH079117
Map OS Explorer 414
Public transport Citylink coaches on A87 from Glasgow and Inverness to Skye
Terrain & hazards well-defined ridge with short sections of very simple scrambling

A fantastic high-level ridge walk with the added bonus of adding seven peaks to your Munro tally. The South Glen Shiel Ridge is perhaps even finer than the Five Sisters, with minimal ascent and descent between the summits and superb views throughout.

This linear route ends 12km down the glen from the start, so either arrange to leave a car or arrange your times to coincide with the bus. Start just east of the Cluanie Inn, where the old road from Cluanie to Tomdoun emerges onto the A87. There is limited parking a short distance along this track and more in nearby lay-bys on the main road.

Begin along the track; it is possible to leave it at a bridge after 3.5km to bear due south for a rough and steep ascent of Creag a'Mhaim, but it is more enjoyable to continue for 1km after the bealach and pick up a stalkers' path which zigzags more easily up to the ridge. The summit marks the first staging post on an epic day of list-ticking.

There is only a brief descent to the col before the ridge narrows on the gradual climb to the second Munro, Druim Shionnach. The crest offers simple scrambling, but there is a bypass path on the left. Another 2.5km of undulating ridge leads to Aonach air Chrith, the highest summit on the whole ridge at 1021m.

Beyond this, the ridge narrows to a true rocky arête; negotiating this is easy enough, however, and soon the grassy path returns. There are a couple of very minor bumps along the way before the ascent of Maol Chinn-dearg, where a ridge branching northeast offers an escape route to Glen Shiel. Continuing on the main walk, the path bypasses the upper part of the minor summit of Sgurr Coire na Feinne before ascending the fifth munro, Sgurr an Doire Leathain. Reaching the true summit involves a slight detour along the northeast ridge. This gives an excellent view of the shapely cone of the next peak, Sgurr an Lochain, probably the finest on this walk. The climb to the summit is straightforward enough and there are superb views down into Coire nan Lochain on the right.

Descend to Bealach a'Choire Reidhe. Sgurr Beag, just beyond, doesn't quite make Munro height and so many baggers, keen to avoid any extra ascent, have worn a bypass path on the south side. After a lower, broader bealach there is a tiring ascent to the seventh and final Munro, Creag nan Damh.

From the top continue along the west ridge, negotiating a wee scramble, eventually following a drystone dyke to the Bealach Duibh Leac. From here an old stalkers' path winds down the northern slope, though it can be hard to pick up at first. The path becomes clearer as it heads down the west side of the Allt Mhalagain. Cross a footbridge at NG 970134 and continue down to the A87. Hopefully you have a waiting car here or have timed the walk for the bus, as your starting point is 12km back up the busy road.

Alternatives

The walk can be conveniently split into two shorter excursions by ending the first day at Maol Chinn-dearg and descending the Druim Coire nan Eirecheanach ridge to pick up a stalkers' path leading down to the A87. The second half of the ridge can then be done by starting on another stalkers' path, up the Druim Thollaidh ridge, to rejoin the route at Sgurr Coire na Feinne. Both these ascent and descent routes give excellent going.

The southern side of the range overlooking Glen Loin and Glen Quoich lacks the character of the northern approaches as well as being more difficult to access, so very few make an ascent from this side.

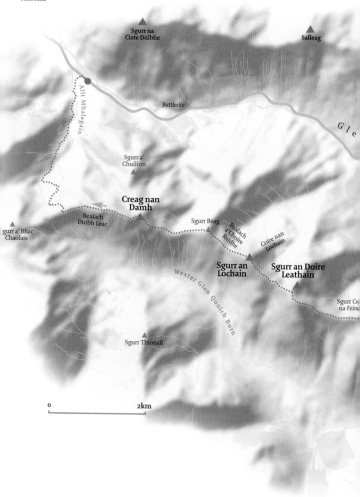

Kintail

Sgurr na Ciste Duibhe

Saileag

Allt Mhalagain

Battlesite

Gle

Sgurr a' Chuilinn

Creag nan Damh

Bealach Duibh Leac

gurr a' Bhac Chaolais

Sgurr Beag

Bealach a' Choire Reidhe

Coire nan Lochain

Sgurr an Lochain

Sgurr an Doire Leathain

Wester Glen Quoich Burn

Sgurr Co na Fein

Sgurr Thionail

0   2km

Sgurr an Lochain

6

The Saddle
Sgurr na Sgine

The Saddle (1010m) *from Gaelic An Diollaid*
Sgurr na Sgine (946m)
peak of the knife

Distance **13km**
Ascent **1350m**
Time **6 – 8 hours**
Start point **OS Grid ref: NG965146**
Map **OS Explorer 414**
Public transport **Citylink coaches on A87 from Glasgow and Inverness to Skye**
Terrain & hazards **the Forcan Ridge is a very exposed scramble (Grade 2), requiring a great head for heights. It can be avoided by those who hate exposure; either way, these are steep and rugged hills**

The finest of all the mountains bordering Glen Shiel, the Saddle offers one of Scotland's most spectacular scrambling routes, the Forcan Ridge. Sgurr na Sgine has nothing to match this, but the descent route via Faochag looks magnificent from higher up the glen.

There is parking at a lay-by on the north side of the A87, 300m east of the track to Achnagart Farm. Walk east along the verge until the start of a stalkers' path which leads up to the col between Biod an Fhithich and Meallan Odhar. The path is well-graded and provides excellent going; from the col, turn left (south). The route climbs towards Meallan Odhar and traverses west of the summit, reaching the ridge once more near the foot of the

Forcan Ridge. For those looking to avoid this airy scramble, the alternative route turns left to contour the slope from the foot of the first steep rise, keeping to the right of a drystone dyke to eventually reach Bealach Coire Mhalagain. Otherwise continue ahead up the ridge.

The scrambling is easy at first, but gradually the exposure increases. There is a well-worn route which keeps to the right of the crest at several points. After the top of Sgurr na Forcan there is an awkward steep descent of about 10m; this can be avoided using a gully to the left. After this, the ridge leads over a minor top to reach the summit of the Saddle – the trig point is slightly further along the ridge.

To descend to Bealach Coire Mhalagain, bear south from the trig point to pick up a path which winds steeply down the upper slopes before reaching the boulderfields further on. Beyond the boulders, a boggy traverse leads eastwards to the bealach. Those who followed the drystone dyke to avoid the Forcan Ridge will head both up and down to the summit via this route.

From the bealach a vague path leads up the steep and rocky slopes to the ridge of Sgurr na Sgine. Bear south along the ridge to gain the northwest top. The final approach to the summit is very rocky, and the cairn is perched above the steep east face.

To head back to Glen Shiel, return over

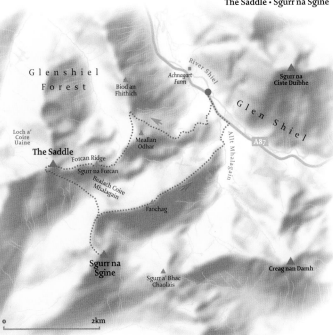

Glenshiel
Forest

River Shiel

Achnagart
Farm

Sgurr na
Ciste Duibhe

Biod an
Fhithich

Glen Shiel

Loch a'
Coire
Uaine

Meallan
Odhar

Allt Mhalagain

A87

The Saddle

Forcan Ridge

Sgurr na Forcan

Bealach Coire
Mhalagain

Faochag

Sgurr na
Sgine

Sgurr a' Bhac
Chaolais

Creag nan Damh

0   2km

the northwest top and continue along the ridge to reach the minor summit of Faochag. This peak has a very dramatic conical outline when seen from higher up Glen Shiel. The descent heads directly down the northeast ridge; despite the help of a path the steep gradient provides a quad-busting finale to the day. It also serves up fabulous views across the glen to the Five Sisters. At the foot of the ridge there is a footbridge over the Allt Mhalagain; cross this and return to the road, around 500m from the start.

Alternatives

The Saddle is a complex mountain of many ridges and, although the Forcan Ridge is the best known of these, there is plenty here to fill further visits. Starting from sea level at Shiel Bridge, the old path to Glenelg provides the key to a strenuous approach via Sgurr a' Gharg Gharaidh, eventually reaching the summit over several tops via the fine west ridge. From the same direction, the Graham of Biod an Fhithich provides a long approach to the Forcan ridge which may appeal to skyline-tracing purists.

The Saddle

7

Beinn Fhada

Beinn Fhada (Ben Attow) (1032m) *long hill*

Distance 18km
Ascent 1110m
Time 6 – 7 hours
Start point OS Grid ref: NG961211
Map OS Explorer 414
Public transport Citylink coaches on A87
from Glasgow and Inverness to Skye;
stop at Allt a' Chruinn 2km from start
Terrain & hazards good stalkers' path
then spacious plateau

The knobbly Sgurr a'Choire Ghairbh ridge
forms an impressive backdrop to
Morvich, but the true character of Beinn
Fhada with its fine northern corries and
spacious plateau are revealed by this
ascent via Gleann Choinneachain.

Start from the National Trust for
Scotland countryside centre at Morvich,
where there is some parking. Begin the
walk by continuing along the minor road,
keeping left at two forks and crossing the
bridge at Inchnacro. Keep ahead on the
track on the far side before looking out for
a path which heads off right after 60m.
The path crosses rough ground but soon
becomes very clear and comes close to the
Abhainn Chonaig. After 2km keep right at
a fork to climb gently up the glen which
becomes increasingly wild and impressive.

Cross the Allt a' Choire Chaoil on
boulders and follow the stalkers' path up
several zigzags. Above these the main path
aims for the Bealach na Sgairne; look out
for a path which branches right at a small
cairn. This contours into the lower reaches
of impressive Coire an Sgairne.

There are great views across to the
jagged Sgurr a'Choire Ghairbh ridge over
to the right. Continue up the stalkers'
path to reach the broad north ridge and
follow it up to the plateau. Continue
beside the northern rim to reach the
summit of Beinn Fhada. By far the easiest
descent option is to retrace your steps.

Alternatives

It is possible for scramblers to make an
alternative descent via the Sgurr a'Choire

Map labels: Sgurr an Airgid; Strath; Morvich Countryside Centre; Loch Duich; Allt a' Chruinn; A87; Kintail Lodge; Sgurr na Moraich; Shiel Bridge; 0 — 2km

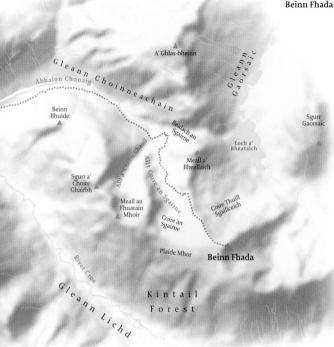

A' Glas-bheinn

Gleann Choinneachain

Abhainn Chonaig

Gleann Gaorsaic

Beinn Bhuide

Sgurr Gaorsaic

Bealach an Sgairne

Loch a' Bheataich

Allt Coire Chaoil

Allt Coire an Sgairne

Meall a' Bheallaich

Sgurr a' Choire Ghairbh

Coire Thuill Sgaillceich

Meall an Fhuarain Mhoir

Coire an Sgairne

Plaide Mhor

Beinn Fhada

River Croe

Gleann Lichd

Kintail Forest

Ghairbh ridge, though this is not recommended in the wet. From the summit head west across the wide plateau of the Plaide Mhor. This slopes downhill before climbing to the Top of Meall an Fhuarain Mhoir. Continue along a fine ridge; there is a steep descent to the Bealach an t-Sealgaire (Hunter's Pass), before the climb up the far side which includes the short slabby scramble to reach Sgurr a'Choire Ghairbh. The undulating ridge leads over a series of knobbly peaks to reach Beinn Bhuide. The

ridge then swings west and featureless slopes lead down to the foot of Gleann Lichd. Turn left along the glen path and then left again at a track to cross the bridge at Inchnacro and follow the road back to Morvich.

Beinn Fhada can also be climbed via its east ridge. Combined with either of the routes given above this would make a grand traverse, but one suited only to wild-campers or those staying at Alltbeithe Hostel or Camban Bothy in the lonely upper reaches of Glen Affric.

481

Sgurr a'Choire Ghairbh on Beinn Fhada

8

A' Ghlas-bheinn

A' Ghlas-bheinn (918m) *the grey-green hill*

Distance 21.5km (includes detour to Falls of Glomach)

Ascent 1195m

Time 7 – 9 hours

Start point OS Grid ref: NG961211

Map OS Explorer 414

Public transport Citylink coaches on A87 from Glasgow and Inverness to Skye; stop at Allt a'Chruin 2km from start

Terrain & hazards clear paths to the Bealach an Sgairne, craggy upper slopes with no real difficulties, good return path from the Falls

Slightly overshadowed by its larger neighbour Beinn Fhada, A'Ghlas-bheinn is perhaps the forgotten mountain amongst the Kintail ranges. The Falls of Glomach – the most spectacular in Scotland – can be added to the route to add greatly to the interest of the day.

Start from the parking area by Morvich Countryside Centre and continue along the road to begin the walk, keeping left at two forks to cross the bridge at Inchnacro. Keep ahead on the track on the far side before looking out for a path which heads off right after 60m. After 2km bear right at a fork as the path heads up Gleann Choinneachan. Near the head of the glen, cross the Allt a' Choire Chaoil on stones; this can be difficult in spate conditions. Beyond it, follow the stalkers' path as it zigzags up and, ignoring the path off to Beinn Fhada, swings left across the

hillside to reach the Bealach an Sgairne.

The bealach is marked by a large cairn and gives great views back down Gleann Choinneachain. Follow the narrow path heading uphill to the north. It keeps left to avoid the crags just above the pass before cutting back up to the ridge. Steep at first, the ridge begins to undulate after passing a small lochan and leads over a series of rocky hummocks during the 2km ascent to the summit. After a number of false summits the small summit cairn of A' Ghlas-bheinn is reached, perched on slabby rocks.

You can retrace your steps for the quickest return, but a good option for a longer walk is to combine the hill with a visit to the Falls of Glomach. Continue north from the summit, dropping steeply down to the bealach below Creag na Saobhie. Continue along the ridge, eventually descending to reach the Bealach na Sroine where you can pick up the wide path to the Falls of Glomach. Turn right along it to begin the descent to the edge of the gorge; almost 200m in height must be lost (and regained on the way back) before you reach the point where you can very carefully peer into the abyss to see the Allt a'Ghlomaich cascading in two great falls. The total height of the cascade is 113m – not the highest in Britain, but with the usually plentiful flow of water and awe-inspiring ravine they are undoubtedly the most impressive.

From the falls walk back up to the

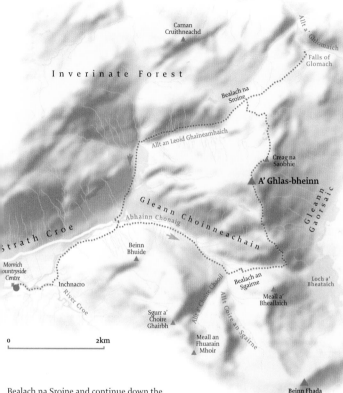

Bealach na Sroine and continue down the far side, heading down the right flank of the glen to reach the top of the forestry plantations. Cross a bridge and follow the track down the east side of the river. At the next fork keep right to cross back over the river. A track joins from the right; keep left at the next fork and then slightly right to reach an open area. As the track nears the river turn left to drop down and cross a footbridge, following the path which climbs to rejoin the outward route. Turn right along the path to return to Morvich.

485

A' Ghlas-bheinn from Sgurr a' Choire Ghairbh

9

Beinn Sgritheall

Beinn Sgritheall (974m) *hill of scree*

Distance **10km**

Ascent **1090m**

Time **5 – 7 hours**

Start point **OS Grid ref: NG843105**

Map **OS Explorer 413**

Terrain & hazards **very steep climb, grass and scree, though much of the latter can be avoided**

After one of the steepest hillwalking ascents in Scotland, Beinn Sgritheall rewards with awe-inspiring views over dramatic Loch Hourn to Knoydart and across to the Cuillin of Skye. Ensure you save this route for a fine day.

Start from Arnisdale, reached along the road from Glenelg. This peaceful and remote village enjoys a stunning setting on the shores of one of Scotland's most beautiful sea lochs. There are a couple of small parking areas, with one 100m east of an old sign which indicates the start of the walk. Climb up behind the village on boggy ground. The path crosses to the other side of the burn before the ascent steepens considerably. Climbing 600m to the Bealach Arnisdail in around 1.5km may seem a punishing start, but what follows is even worse. A truly calf-busting ascent leads directly from the

bealach to point 906m at the east end of the ridge; you may find you are grabbing hold of tufts of grass as the feeling of space falling away behind you grows.

The relief at reaching the top of this section is palpable, and a fine walk now stretches ahead. Cross a wide col and continue along the ridge which narrows on the final climb. The summit is marked by a trig point and on a sunny summer's day there can be few finer places to eat your sarnies. The views are truly breathtaking, with Loch Hourn looking like a Norwegian fjord as Ladhar Bheinn rises magnificently behind it. In the opposite direction the Kintail peaks unfold and, to set the seal on perfection, the Cuillin close the horizon to the west.

The descent leads down the west ridge which is rocky but not too difficult; the steep gradient even has the grace to relent for a couple of short sections. When you reach the small lochan at NG816126 bear left, aiming for the road and picking up a narrow path which winds down the slope and through the Coille Mhialairigh forest. Eventually it emerges on the tarmac 3km from Arnisdale; your knees and ankles may thank you for the only flat walking surface all day.

Beinn a' Chapuill

Creag Bealach na h-Oidhche

Bealach na h-Oidhche

Loch Bealach n h Oidhche

Loch na Lochan

Beinn Sgritheall

Coire Min

Rosdail

Bealach Arnisdale

Coille Mhialairigh

Beinn Bhuidhe

Eilean Rarsaidh

Arnisdale

Eilean Tioram

Amisdale Lodge

Loch Hourn

River Arnisdale

Glen Arnisdale

0   2km

Alternatives

Few walkers explore the north side of
Beinn Sgritheall, but a curving ridge
makes a fine route to the summit from
the Bealach na-Oidhche. The most
enjoyable way of reaching this point is,
after heading up Gleann Beag from
Balvraid, traversing the east ridge of the
Graham, Beinn a' Chapuill. The steep drop
to Bealach Arnasdail can be avoided by
instead heading down into Coire Min
from the bealach on the summit ridge.

Beinn Sgritheall and Loch Hourn

Glen Affric, Mullardoch and Strathfarrar

This area offers some truly challenging epic days in really varied scenery packed full of wildlife. The small village of Cannich is perhaps the most popular centre and makes a good base with a shop, pub, B&B and excellent campsite – what more do you really need? Nearby Tomich is more attractive, a real chocolate box of estate cottages; facilities here consist of a single (walker-friendly) hotel, plus some self-catering accommodation.

Above both villages the lower reaches of Glen Affric, clothed by the most magnificent pinewoods north of the Great Glen, become busy with tourists in the summer, but there is no doubt this is the Highlands at their best.

Solitude soon returns beyond the end of the road as the glen takes on an increasingly stern character and above Loch Affric the upper reaches can appear bleak, though ringed by fine mountains. This is where you will find Alltbeithe, a lonely hostel accessible only by a long trek on foot. This cosy bolthole amidst the wilds has something of a legendary status amongst walkers and really needs to be booked in advance. Nearby Camban Bothy provides a more basic alternative.

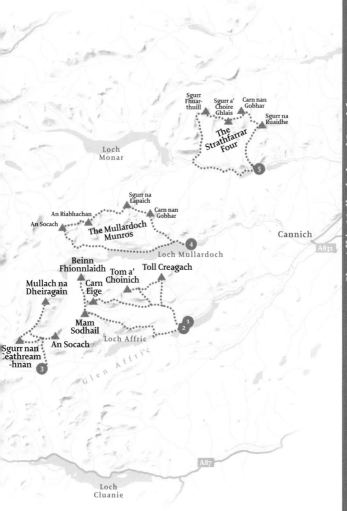

Sgurr Fhuar-thuill

Sgurr a' Choire Ghlais

Carn nan Gobhar

Sgurr na Ruaidhe

The Strathfarrar Four

Loch Monar

5

Sgurr na Lapaich

Carn nan Gobhar

An Riabhachan

An Socach

The Mullardoch Munros

Cannich

A831

Loch Mullardoch

4

Beinn Fhionnlaidh

Tom a' Choinich

Toll Creagach

Mullach na Dheiragain

Carn Eige

Mam Sodhail

1

2

Sgurr nan Ceathream-hnan

3

An Socach

Loch Affric

Glen Affric

A87

Loch Cluanie

Tom a'Choinich
Toll Creagach

Tom a'Choinich (1112m) *hill of the moss*
Toll Creagach (1054m) *rocky hollow*

Distance **17km**
Ascent **1100m**
Time **6 – 8 hours**
Start point **OS Grid ref: NH216242**
Map **OS Explorer 415**
Public transport **Ross Minibuses service from Inverness – summer only**
Terrain & hazards **some pathless sections, steeper ground on Tom a'Choinich**

These two hills give the shortest Munro round in an area known for all-day epics. Toll Creagach is a rather shapeless pudding, but Tom a'Choinich makes up for it with a bolder outline and good views.

Start from the car park (charge) just east of Chisholme Bridge near the head of Loch Beinn a'Mheadhoin. Follow the track off the opposite side of the road, heading up Gleann nam Fiadh. Ignore a track which joins from the right and continue ahead. After a bend to the left the stately Toll Creagach is revealed ahead, with the steep rocky slopes of Beinn Eun, a shoulder of Toll Creagach, on the right. The track narrows to a boggy path and heads up the glen to reach the Allt Toll Easa. Unless it is in spate (in which case continue up the rougher ground on the east side), cross this and take the path that turns off to the right uphill.

A few zigzags bring you into a hanging valley. Here there are two options; it is possible to bear west up Creag na h-Inghinn – steep but without any major difficulties – and continue up the ridge to Tom a'Choinich. An easier route is to follow the burn up and then climb north to the Bealach Toll Easa before turning west up the steep central ridge between two corries to reach the summit. Whichever route is taken, Tom a'Choinich proves to be the best viewpoint of the day.

From the top descend the east ridge steeply to the Bealach Toll Easa. The climb up the far side is much more gentle, levelling off part way before the gradual rise to the summit cairn of Toll Creagach. This is the most easterly summit on the great ridge between Loch Mullardoch and Glen Affric – but also by far the least impressive.

The easiest descent is to bear directly southwards. Keep west of Beinn Eun as the slopes below it are very steep, dropping down towards Gleann nam Fiadh to regain the outward path and follow this back to the start.

Alternatives

Ascents from other directions are rare, but these two summits could be tackled on a mammoth walk, starting with Toll Creagach and continuing along the ridge to take in the summits of the Carn Eige group as well.

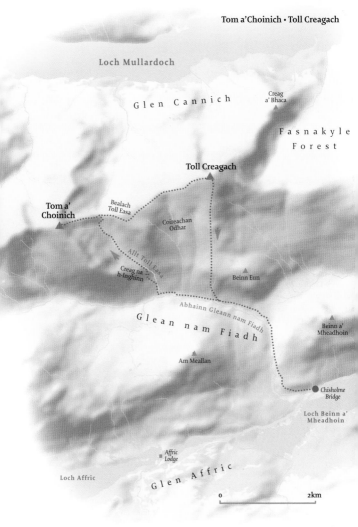

Tom a'Choinich

2

Carn Eige
Mam Sodhail
Beinn Fhionnlaidh

Carn Eige (1183m) *file hill*
Mam Sodhail (1181m) *hill of the barns*
Beinn Fhionnlaidh (1005m) *Finlay's hill*

Distance **28km**
Ascent **1730m**
Time **10 – 13 hours**
Start point **OS Grid ref: NH216242**
Maps **OS Explorer 414 & 415**
Public transport **Ross Minibuses service from Inverness – summer only**
Terrain & hazards **mostly good going on grassy ridges with some rocky sections; boggy on descent**

Carn Eige and Mam Sodhail are the two highest mountains north of the Great Glen. Whilst they lack the spectacle of the summits on the western seaboard, they are great viewpoints and enjoy a wild setting. This long route round a horseshoe of ridges is made into an epic by the inclusion of the very remote outlying Munro of Beinn Fhionnlaidh.

Park in the lay-by on the south side of the Affric road just before Chisholme Bridge, and start along the track opposite which leads up Gleann nam Fiadh. It passes beneath a plantation with views over Loch Beinn a' Mheadhoin before heading into wilder country, with the Munros of Toll Creagach and Tom a'Choinich ahead. The track curves to the left through a scattered pinewood before narrowing to a path, boggy in places. Crossing the Allt Toll Easa is usually straightforward, but can be difficult or impossible in spate. Ignore the path to the right after the crossing and continue up the glen, with the conical peak of Sron Garbh prominent.

After 2km the path forks; take the higher path to the right. Cross the Allt Coire Mhic Fhearchair and aim for the grassy shoulder directly ahead. The path becomes clearer higher up as it zigzags to reach a flat area below the Garbh Bhealach. Easy ground leads up to the bealach between Sron Garbh and An Leth-chreag, where Loch Mullardoch and its own great range of Munros comes into view. At the bealach turn left for the final steep rocky ascent to Sron Garbh. Keep on the crest of the ridge to pick up a remarkably built rock-staircase, the remains of an old stalking path. This leads up to the flatter ground at the Top of Sron Garbh; from here the great ridge walk begins in earnest.

After Stob Coire Dhomhnuill there are a series of jagged, broken pinnacles, bypassed by a path, first on the right and then the left. A short climb leads to Stob a'Choire Dhomhain and then a wide bealach before the final ascent up to Carn

Eige. This summit, marked by a trig point inside a wind-shelter cairn, is 1183m – the highest mountain north of the Great Glen. The views are very extensive, stretching from Skye in the west to the Moray Firth and Ben Rinnes in the east.

At this point a decision must be made whether to include Beinn Fhionnlaidh in the day. Although it involves a hefty loss of height and re-ascent, Beinn Fhionnlaidh is very awkward to reach by any other route, so most Munro-baggers will want to go for it. Descend the northwest ridge on a good path which stays near the crest and avoids a stony section. It traverses left of Stob Coire Lochan before descending to reach the wide Bealach Beag at 832m. From here head up the steep grassy slope towards Beinn Fhionnlaidh, with the reward of a great section of easy ridge walking. This list ticking collector's piece has a wide view along Loch Mullardoch, whilst Carn Eige looms impressively above Coire Lochan.

Brace yourself for the return to Carn Eige. The uppermost section can be bypassed by traversing its western slopes from a flatter shoulder at 1040m; a faint path keeps below the areas of loose stones to emerge back on the ridge at the bealach between Carn Eige and Mam Sodhail. In poor visibility or if unsure of the ground, stick with the ridge over Carn Eige instead.

From the bealach climb southwards, zigzagging near the top to reach the huge cairn on Mam Sodhail. The hollow cairn was built by the Ordnance Survey as the principal triangulation point for northern Scotland. As this suggests, the view is, if anything, even more extensive than from neighbouring Carn Eige.

It is possible to descend the southwest ridge from here which might be a good option in bad weather or to reach lower ground more quickly. Further down you can pick up the zigzag path down the headwall of Coire Leachavie, which is extremely boggy but later reaches a stalkers' path leading to the main Loch Affric path and the long walk out.

However, in good conditions the much more enjoyable option is to continue on the long ESE ridge towards Mullach Cadha Rainich, with the added bonus of including Sgurr na Lapaich. This summit (not to be confused with the Mullardoch Sgurr na Lapaich one hill-range to the north) was a Munro on Sir Hugh's original list. It gives an aerial view down to the lochs and forests of Glen Affric. Head down the steep and rocky southeast ridge; a path avoids any need for scrambling. Once down to the level of the moors bear east to meet a track at a prominent bend. Follow this down to the shores of Loch Affric below Affric Lodge. A left turn along the main track leads eventually to the car park at the end of the road, with another 1.5km of tarmac to get back to Chisholme Bridge and the start.

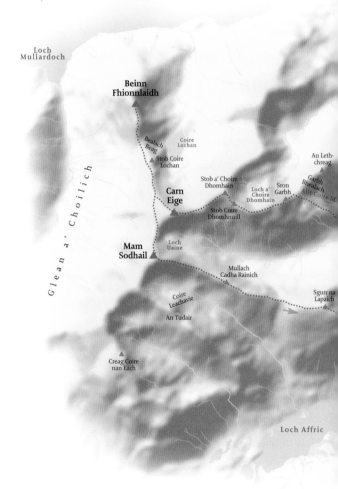

Toll Creagach

Tom a' Choinich

Coireachan
Odhar

Allt Toll Easa

Creag na
h-Inghinn

Beinn Eun

Abhainn Gleann nam Fiadh

G l e a n n   n a m   F i a d h

Beinn a'
Mheadhoin

Am Meallan

Chisholme
Bridge

Loch Beinn a'
Mheadhoin

Affric
Lodge

G l e n   A f f r i c

0   2km

Carn Eige ridge

3

Sgurr nan Ceathreamhnan
Mullach na Dheiragain
An Socach

Sgurr nan Ceathreamhnan (1151m)
hill of the quarters
Mullach na Dheiragain (982m)
summit of the kestrel
An Socach (921m) *the snout*

Distance 20km from hostel (Hostelling Scotland) at Alltbeithe. Alltbeithe walk-in: 10km each way from Cluanie or 14km each way from Glen Affric road end
Ascent 1480m (on circuit from Alltbeithe)
Time 9 – 10 hours
Start point OS Grid ref: NH079202 (no road access to Alltbeithe)
Map OS Explorer 414 (and 415 if using Glen Affric approach)
Terrain & hazards grassy ridges with some rocky sections, paths for most of the route, ascent can be boggy. The short cut via Loch Coire nan Dearcag is steep and pathless with tricky route finding in mist

Sgurr nan Ceathreamhnan is a magnificent peak, the culmination of several fine ridges. Mullach na Dheiragain is prized for its inaccessibility whilst An Socach rewards with great views down Glen Affric. This route assumes an overnight stay at the hostel at Alltbeithe, Camban Bothy, or a wild camp, but it could also be attempted as a very long 40km day by walking in and out from Cluanie.

The Glen Affric hostel – also known as Alltbeithe – is the remotest in Britain, and is inaccessible by road. An overnight stay here is always atmospheric but it gets busy in the summer months. As an alternative there are plenty of wild camp spots nearby, but if you don't fancy battling with the midges, then Camban Bothy offers basic shelter a little further up the glen. The walk described assumes two nights at the hostel with the walk in and out being done on the day either side. The shortest route to Alltbeithe is via the An Caorann Mor from the Cluanie Inn which is extremely boggy. Much more enjoyable are the approaches from the road end in Glen Affric, or alternatively through Gleann Lichd from Morvich in Kintail.

Start by passing the dormitory building behind the main hostel to take a path which bends right to cross the Allt Beithe Min and the Allt na Faing. Beyond this latter burn the well-constructed path passes through a gate in the deer fence and begins to climb, keeping to the east bank. After a second deer fence the path becomes boggier as Coire na Cloiche is reached; continue to the bealach at about 790m. From here, desolate Gleann a'Choilich is revealed ahead.

You could choose to tackle any of the

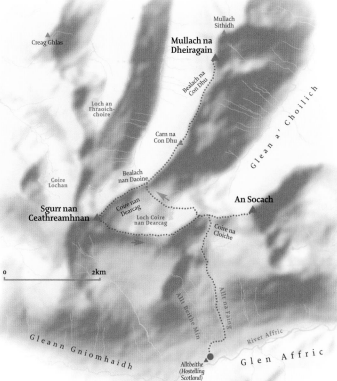

Creag Ghlas

Mullach
Sithidh

**Mullach na
Dheiragain**

Bealach na Con Dhu

Loch an
Fhraoich-
choire

Glean a' Choilich

Carn na
Con Dhu

Coire
Lochan

Bealach
nan Daoine

**Sgurr nan
Ceathreamhnan**

Coire nan
Dearcag

Loch Coire
nan Dearcag

An Socach

Coire na
Cloiche

0   2km

Allt Beithe Min

Allt na Faing

Gleann Gniomhaidh

River Affric

Glen Affric

Alltbeithe
(Hostelling
Scotland)

three Munros first. Beginning with
Mullach na Dheiragain, Sgurr nan
Ceathreamhnan can be bypassed on the
outward route and then climbed on the
way back. Bear west from the bealach
along the ridge for about 200m to reach
what looks like a stream bed heading
northwest off the ridge. This soon leads
to a faint path which descends steeply.

At the 750m contour turn west, aiming
for the outflow at the bottom of the Loch
Coire nan Dearcag lochans. These
lochans have a grand setting in this
remote and craggy corrie. Cross the boggy
area below them and bear northwest up
straightforward slopes to reach the
Bealach nan Daoine.

Turn right along the ridge path to

Sgurr nan Ceathreamhnan from An Socach

climbs to Carn na Con Dhu, the top of which has several bumps which can confuse in poor visibility. Head to the northeast and cross a short boulderfield, continuing along a narrower section of ridge to reach the Bealach na Con Dhu. Tackle the wide and sprawling slopes of Mullach na Dheiragain direct, ignoring the path that takes a dander to the left here. Looking around from the summit cairn it is easy to understand that Mullach na Dheiragain ranks as one of the least accessible of the Munros.

Head back to the Bealach na Con Dhu and over Carn na Con Dhu to return to the Bealach nan Daoine. This time continue along the ridge as it narrows and climbs more steeply to give a direct approach to the summit cairn of Sgurr nan Ceathreamhnan. At 1151m it is the highest peak in the range and with its neighbouring west top it forms the apex of five ridges.

Although the dramatic, narrow west ridge may look tempting, descend the southeast ridge, eventually bearing east to cross several undulations and minor summits before returning to the bealach at the top of the path up from Alltbeithe.

Before descending to Alltbeithe, it is easy enough to include the third Munro, An Socach, in the day's tally. Keep heading east from the bealach, climbing briefly before crossing an area dotted with lochans. The dome of An Socach rears up just beyond and a path leads up to the summit, worthwhile for its view of Glen Affric. Return to the bealach and retrace your steps down to Alltbeithe via the Allt na Faing.

Alternatives

The most logical traverse of these peaks – given the outlying location of Mullach na Dheiragain – is a circuit of the ridges from the north. This becomes more practical with a wild camp and perhaps an approach to Iron Lodge by mountain bike from Killilan, but even then it's a major undertaking with some potentially serious river crossings.

Epic high-level backpackers may include these hills as part of an enormous round of all the mountains encircling Loch Mullardoch.

4

The Mullardoch Munros:
Carn nan Gobhar
Sgurr na Lapaich
An Riabhachan
An Socach

Carn nan Gobhar (992m) *rocky hill of goats*
Sgurr na Lapaich (1150m) *peak of the bog*
An Riabhachan (1129m) *the grey one*
An Socach (1069m) *the snout*

Distance **29km**
Ascent **1825m**
Time **11 – 14 hours**
Start point **OS Grid ref: NH218315**
Map **OS Explorer 430**
Terrain & hazards **exceptionally remote route of epic length; the ridges give good walking with only very mild scrambling; the Allt Taige can be impassable in spate**

The Mullardoch Munros make for a superb ridgewalk in an extremely remote part of the Highlands; from Sgurr na Lapaich onwards these are hills of great character. The return along the shores of the reservoir can be very tiring after such a walk, especially in late summer when the bracken is high and the midges biting.

Start from the end of the minor road to the Loch Mullardoch dam; there is limited parking just beyond the dam and more space on the approach to the right. Follow the track after the gate, passing the

Chisholm Stone – a monument to the traditional clan gathering place of the glen, now submerged by the reservoir. At a fork keep right to cross the bridge over the Allt Mullardoch. Now bear directly northwest towards Mullach na Maoile, soon climbing steeply through heather and bracken. The easiest line is between two tiny stream beds. From the flat top of the Mullach cross a slight dip before heading up the long stony rise to Carn nan Gobhar. The first, finely-built cairn is not the true top, which is just across a depression. From here you'll have a good view across to the lochans, corries and ridges of Sgurr na Lapaich – the next objective.

Descend to the Bealach na Cloiche Duibhe. Sgurr na Lapaich looks intimidating, but the route up is straightforward, grassy at first and rocky higher up. The path keeps just left of the true ridgeline, crossing boulders but avoiding any scrambling to arrive directly at the summit trig point. The view is dramatic, particularly looking back across the cliffs to Loch Tuill Bhearnach, whilst the next objective, the great ridge of An

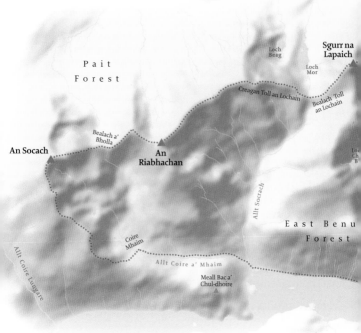

Riabhachan, provides inspiration to get going once more. Descend the fairly grassy ridge southwest to the Bealach Toll an Lochain.

The ascent to An Riabhachan is a fair pull. A path tackles the first broad slope to gain a narrow grassy ridge. This section is a delight, with Sgurr na Lapaich towering impressively above Loch Mor behind, and the ridge itself drawing you onwards. This flattens out and widens at 1120m and an almost level walk leads to the summit cairn of An Riabhachan. Loch

Mullardoch can be glimpsed from the well-built cairn, with the Carn Eige range beyond it, but it is the view north that takes your breath away. Most of Loch Monar can be seen whilst beyond and to the northwest rises a fantastic array of peaks stretching away into Torridon.

Continue along the ridge to the cairned 1080m peak where the main ridge turns sharply left. Follow the path that continues west, soon descending very steeply to a lower ridge. The next section is very narrow but has no difficulties,

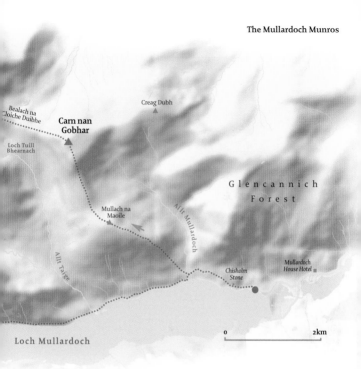

Bealach na
Cloiche Duibhe

Creag Dubh

**Carn nan
Gobhar**

Loch Tuill
Bhearnach

G l e n c a n n i c h
F o r e s t

Mullach na
Maoile

Allt Mullardoch

Allt Taige

Chisholm
Stone

Mullardoch
House Hotel

Loch Mullardoch

0   2km

before a slight ascent to a minor summit
which can be bypassed on the left. Now
bear southwest, following the path which
avoids the slabby rocks to the right.
Another steep descent with some easy
scrambling brings you to the Bealach
a'Bholla. The east top of An Socach rises
as a steep pyramid ahead. Keep following
the ridge path; there is one rocky step
which can be avoided to the right. From
the east top continue to the main summit
cairn and trig point and savour having
reached one of the most remote of the

Munros. On a clear day the west coast and
Skye look surprisingly close whilst there
are fabulous views of the Torridon and
the Monar peaks, as well as across the
dramatic eastern corrie towards Loch
Mullardoch – a reminder of the long
return walk ahead.

Begin the descent by following the
ridge along the edge of the corrie. After
2km it steepens before reaching a flatter
ridge that stretches east to Meall Bac a'
Chul-dhoire. Although a relief from
the steep descent this area is riven by

Sgurr na Lapaich from Creag Dubh

eroded peat hags and it is probably best to bear left across the bogs to reach the nearby Allt Coire a' Mhaim. Cross this and pick up a faint path down the bank, passing several attractive waterfalls before approaching the shores of Loch Mullardoch.

Cross the bridge over the Allt Socrach and walk down almost to the water's edge. From here the walk back along the north shores of the reservoir is long and tiring. There is a narrow path, but care is needed as high bracken can obscure it and there are a number of landslips – a fall onto the rocky tideline of the reservoir would be nasty. For 4km the path hacks along this sloping terrain until it peters out; 1km further on is the Allt Taige. There is no bridge and the easiest crossing is usually near to the loch, but it becomes impassable in spate. On the far side, continue to a small pinewood and pass above this to reach the bridge over the Allt Mullardoch crossed earlier in the day. The track now leads back to the start, any undulations that seemed insignificant at the start of the day looming large after such a long walk.

Alternatives

These mountains can also be climbed from Strathfarrar, although the restricted road access times into the glen mean you would have to move very fast to complete the peaks within a day (see the next route for the Strathfarrar Four). There is parking near the power station at Innis an Locheil and from here the first two Munros can be reached fairly easily, but the return from An Socach at the end of the day is very long and demanding.

The Strathfarrar Four:
Sgurr na Ruaidhe
Carn nan Gobhar
Sgurr a'Choire Ghlais
Sgurr Fhuar-thuill

Sgurr na Ruaidhe (993m) *peak of redness*
Carn nan Gobhar (992m) *rocky hill of goats*
Sgurr a'Choire Ghlais (1083m)
peak of the grey corrie
Sgurr Fhuar-thuill (1049m)
peak of the cold hollow

Distance 25km
Ascent 1565m
Time 7 – 10 hours
Start point OS Grid ref: NH283386
Map OS Explorer 430
Terrain & hazards boggy on the approach
and then good ridges with only a couple
of awkward boulder sections; good
stalkers' path on descent

Strathfarrar is a long and beautiful glen;
it must have been a rival to Glen Affric
itself before the construction of the great
hydro-electric projects of the 1960s. This
round of the four Munros on its northern
side starts off with rounded hills, but
becomes increasingly dramatic as the
day progresses.

The route starts at a flat grassy area
between Loch Beannacharan and Loch a'
Mhuillidh where it is possible to park off
the north side of the road. Follow the
track uphill, passing a small dam. Ignore
the first small path branching left and
continue for a short while on the now
faint track to a clearer path on the left
which follows the Allt Coire Mhuillidh
upstream. Carn nan Gobhar (the second
Munro on the walk) can be seen straight
ahead, and the ascent to the first summit,
Sgurr na Ruaidhe, appears to be a piece of
cake, but the slopes are foreshortened and
it's further than it looks. Cross the first
side stream and climb the easy grassy
slope northeast; there is a path in places.

Just before the top pass a stone shelter;
the summit cairn is just a little further on
at 993m. From here head down to the
Bealach nam Botaichean, the spongy turf
providing an unexpected treat for the
feet. A small steep section leads to the
actual col, followed by a long and
straightforward pull bearing NNW at first
and then west as the gradient eases; it
aims directly for the summit of Carn nan
Gobhar, passing over boulders for the last
few metres. Here you'll find a good view
of the onward route to Sgurr a'Choire
Ghlais. Pick up a pleasant grassy ridge
heading southwards and then southwest

as it descends to Bealach Sneachda at 865m. A path aids the steep climb up the far side to reach the two large cairns and trig point crowning Sgurr a'Choire Ghlais. Glen Orrin and Strathconon are stretched out to the north with the Fannichs visible beyond. From the northern cairn, either descend the rocky ridge or bypass the boulders by bearing west from the trig point and then heading back north to rejoin the ridge, continuing down to eventually reach Bealach Toll Sgaile.

Although the summit of Creag Ghorm a'Bhealaich can be bypassed, the short detour to the top is well worth it for the dramatic views down into the coire. Now there is only a slight descent before the final pull to the summit of Sgurr Fhuar-thuill at 1049m. From the summit continue towards Sgurr na Fearstaig; just beyond the col at 987m a small cairn marks where a stalkers' path leaves the ridge to the southwest, with views of the slabby face of Sgurr na Muice and Loch Toll a' Mhuic below. The clear path descends steeply at first and then traverses below the ridge, finally descending to the eastern side of the Loch. Eventually the path crosses the burn and becomes a track, shadowing the Allt Toll a' Mhuic downhill and passing some impressive waterfalls amongst the birchwoods. When the track emerges on the Glen Strathfarrar road turn left and follow it for over 6km back to the start, passing Braulen Lodge on the way.

The road up Glen Strathfarrar is private and the estate owners restrict vehicular access above the gate at Milton Cottage near Struy. Mountaineering Scotland has negotiated access arrangements which allow a maximum of 25 vehicles to drive beyond this point each day. In the summer months the gate is open from 9am to between 6 and 8pm, depending on the month, and closed all day Tuesday and until 1.30pm on Wednesdays. Access in the winter months has been negotiated for Mountaineering Scotland members only. If you choose to drive in, it is best to check on the Mountaineering Scotland website for current opening times. Up to date details are available online at **mountaineering.scot**

Alternatively there is a car park at Milton Cottage for those planning to cycle up the glen.

The Strathfarrar Four

Carn an Alltain
Riabhaich

Glen Orrin

An Gorm-loch

Meall na Faire

Loch an
Fhuar-thuill
Mhoir

**Sgurr
Fhuar-thuill**

Loch Coire
na Sguile

**Carn nan
Gobhar**

na
staig

Creag Ghorm
a'Bhealaich

Bealach
Toll sgaile

Bealach nam
Botaichean

Loch Toll
a' Mhuic

Bealach
Sneachda

**Sgurr na
Ruaidhe**

Sgurr
na Muice

**Sgurr a'
Choire Ghlais**

Coire Mhuillidh

n an
aimh
nain

Meall a'
Gheur-fheadain

Garbh-charn

Allt Toll a' Mhuic

Allt Uchd Rodha

Allt Coire Mhuillidh

Braulen
Lodge

Meall Dubh

An Carnais

Glen
Strathfarrar
Forest

River Farrar

Loch a'
Mhuillidh

Glen Strathfarrar

0   2km

517

Sgurr a'Choire Ghlais and Glen Orrin

From Slioch looking over Lochan Fada

Achnasheen, Glen Carron and Torridon

Achnasheen

The road leading west from Garve to Achnasheen crosses bleak moors with no hint of the glories of the western seaboard ahead. Achnasheen itself is a tiny settlement, with facilities limited to the railway station (with free toilets) and the Ledgowan Lodge hotel. The latter is a grand pile in the old Highland style, though it is walker-friendly and has a bunkhouse and camping as well as massive four-posters and a vast array of stags' heads.

Glen Carron to Lochcarron

From Achnasheen the roads west split, the A832 bound for Gairloch whilst the A890 heads down into Glen Carron. Soon the glen is clad with Scots pines and contrasting mountains rise on either side – the ridges of Monar to the left and the sandstone monoliths of the Coulin Forest on the right. There are a few scattered facilities; Gerry's Hostel at Achnashellach and the old pub at Strathcarron.

The main centre, however, is at Lochcarron, a long village strung out along the northeastern shore of Loch Carron, a sea loch in the shallows of which the remains of Strome Castle can be seen. It has a couple of well-stocked shops and petrol station, a choice of eating places, pubs and a takeaway. The Wee Campsite sets the standard for cheap and cheerful pitches, and there are several B&Bs, Pathend on Main Street and The Sithean

Loch
Gairloch

on the village outskirts are particularly
walker friendly. There are also plenty of
self-catering cottages and two hotels.
Until 1973 a ferry crossed the narrows
here. It closed when the road opened,
giving rise to the strange road sign for
'Stromeferry (no ferry)', although the ferry
service has been resurrected every so
often to bypass the landslip-prone A890.

Kinlochewe and Torridon

After Kishorn the road curves north to
reach Loch Torridon, passing the picture-
perfect coastal village of Shieldaig. Some
of the most magnificent landscapes on
the entire western seaboard now lead
through Torridon village and along the
glen to Kinlochewe and Loch Maree,
linking once again back to Achnasheen.

Your first trip along Glen Torridon is
unlikely to ever be forgotten. Great walls
of soaring sandstone rear up beside the
road, rising in tiers to reach battlemented
ridges silhouetted against the sky. The
great peaks of Torridon bear little relation
to the grassy mountains of the Southern
Highlands – this is a mecca for all lovers
of the outdoors. Kinlochewe has a decent
shop, B&Bs, a pub and campsite – but
remember to bring midge repellent in
summer as this place can really be
buzzing! Torridon village itself is fairly
small but there is a friendly youth hostel,
well-stocked shop and cafe and a –
sometimes overstretched – informal
campground. Shieldaig offers more in the

Loch
Torridon

Inner Sound

Shieldai

Applecross

K

way of eating facilities, but the Torridon
Inn along the way offers another option
for a pint or meal – activities including
mountain guiding are also offered from
here and if the budget allows you can
always rest your head at the neighbouring
swanky Torridon Hotel.

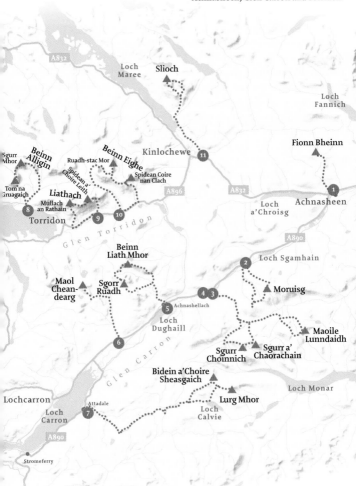

Loch Maree

Slioch

Loch Fannich

A832

Fionn Bheinn

Kinlochewe

11

Sgurr Mhor

Beinn Alligin

Ruadh-stac Mor

Beinn Eighe

Spidean a'Choire Leith

Spidean Coire nan Clach

Achnasheen

1

Tom na Gruagaich

Liathach

Mullach an Rathain

A896

Loch a'Chroisg

A832

8

Torridon

9

10

Glen Torridon

A890

Beinn Liath Mhor

Loch Sgamhain

2

Maol Chean-dearg

Sgorr Ruadh

Moruisg

4

3

5

Achnashellach

Maoile Lunndaidh

6

Loch Dughaill

Sgurr Choinnich

Sgurr a' Chaorachain

Glen Carron

Bidein a'Choire Sheasgaich

Lurg Mhor

Loch Monar

Lochcarron

7

Attadale

Loch Calvie

Loch Carron

A890

Stromeferry

523

Fionn Bheinn

Fionn Bheinn (933m) *white hill*

Distance **7km**
Ascent **815m**
Time **4 – 6 hours**
Start point **OS Grid ref: NG164586**
Map **OS Explorer 435**
Public transport **trains (and buses) from Inverness to Achnasheen**
Terrain & hazards **boggy with only the summit corrie showing some real mountain character**

Fionn Bheinn is very much the Cinderella mountain of the region – saved from complete obscurity only by its Munro status. It makes for a short, straightforward hillwalk, but offers a new perspective on the mighty peaks of Torridon.

Start from the car park near Achnasheen railway station; there are toilets and a café. From here head west back up to the main A832, turn left and cross. Almost immediately take the old road by the telephone box, go over the stone bridge and turn right through the kissing gate (SP Footpath). Follow the track to pass behind a water treatment hut, go through another kissing gate and follow the burn, keeping to the left of a fence. Detour around a fenced area and go through a gate to access the open hill. Aim for the wooded Allt Achadh na Sine coming down the hillside ahead and ascend by the near bank.

After about 2km the slope eases. Leave the burn here to avoid the boggy flat area and bear NNE towards Creagan na Laogh which is steeper going. From the tiny cairn on the flat top continue across a shallow dip before heading up onto the ridge of Fionn Bheinn. Bear left along this, passing round the headwall of Toll Mor, a fine corrie of grassy crags quite unsuspected from the road. The summit is soon reached. Fionn Bheinn is technically an outlier of the Fannichs and looks across Loch Fannich to its higher neighbours, but it is the unfamiliar angle on the Torridon mountains that attracts attention the most. Descend by the same route or by following sections of drystone dyke on Sail an Tuim Bhain to reach a path and then a track down to the A832 east of Achnasheen.

Srath Chrombaill

Lochrosque
Forest

Fionn
Bheinn

Toll Mor

Sail an Tuim Bhain

Meall a'
Chaorainn

Creagan
na Laogh

Allt Achadh na Sine

Achnasheen

A832

Loch a' Chroisg

Ledgowan
Lodge

Achnasheen

River Bran

A890

An Liathanach

Loch Gowan

0   2km

2

Moruisg

Moruisg (928m) *the big water*

Distance 12km
Ascent 1000m
Time 6 – 7 hours
Start point OS Grid ref: NH080520
Map OS Explorer 429
Terrain & hazards boggy ground at first, straightforward open slopes higher up

Moruisg is a rather sprawling and undistinguished mountain. Until recently its more interesting neighbour Sgurr nan Ceannaichean was also a Munro; though it has been resurveyed at below 3000 feet, climbing both together still makes for a much more enjoyable day.

There is parking at a lay-by on the south side of the A890 in Glen Carron, 1km west of the bridge over the Allt Coire Crubaidh. From here follow the path over the bridge and then under the railway. The route then becomes very boggy. Pass through the gate ahead, keeping right at a faint fork. A path continues up the hillside, to a gate in a deer fence. In clear weather you should be able to see the great gullies running down the wide face of the mountain; the path heads just left of the two gullies that run close together near the top.

The going is drier on the steepest section but becomes wetter underfoot again as the slope eases. Continue straight ahead to gain the ridge of Moruisg and reach the summit cairn –

careful navigation may be needed in poor visibility. The best views are over the sandstone peaks of the Coulin Forest and Torridon.

If you are strictly a Munro-bagger then you will retrace your steps from here. However, continuing to the Corbett Sgurr nan Ceannaichean makes for a better walk.

Follow the broad ridge to reach the top of the crags of Coire Toll nam Bian. Bear left, keeping the crags close by, as the ridge curves round and descends slightly, crossing a minor bump before dropping more steeply to the bealach. From here climb straight up the opposite slope to reach the ridge of Sgurr nan Ceannaichean.

Once on the ridge there is a vague path and a final steep climb up to the small summit plateau. Sgurr nan Ceannaichean has kept the makers of hill-lists busy. Originally classed as a Corbett it was re-surveyed in 1981 and found to be 915m and awarded Munro status. However, another survey carried out by the Munro Society in 2009 saw it come in at 913m and it reverted to Corbett status once more. Whatever surveyors say, it is a much better viewpoint than Moruisg.

To descend, head north down the ridge; there is a path slightly on the left side. The descent is mostly grassy with some fairly steep sections; a path leads through the rocky bluff of Creag a' Chait, keeping slightly to the left of the ridgeline once

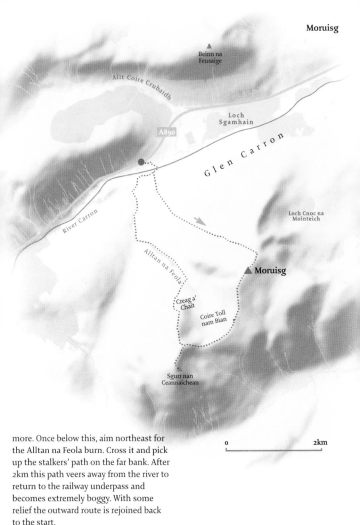

Beinn na
Feusaige

Allt Coire Crubaidh

Loch
Sgamhain

A890

G l e n   C a r r o n

Loch Cnoc na
Mòinteich

River Carron

Alltan na Feola

▲ **Moruisg**

Creag a'
Chàit

Coire Toll
nam Bian

Sgurr nan
Ceannaichean

0   2km

more. Once below this, aim northeast for
the Alltan na Feola burn. Cross it and pick
up the stalkers' path on the far bank. After
2km this path veers away from the river to
return to the railway underpass and
becomes extremely boggy. With some
relief the outward route is rejoined back
to the start.

On Moruisg, with Sgurr a' Chaorachain behind

Sgurr Choinnich
Sgurr a' Chaorachain

Sgurr Choinnich (999m) *the mossy peak*
Sgurr a' Chaorachain (1053m)
the peak of the place of rowanberries

Distance **20km**
Ascent **1230m**
Time **7 – 8 hours**
Start point **OS Grid ref: NH039493**
Map **OS Explorer 429**
Terrain & hazards **good approach tracks then a stalkers' path and finally a rocky ridge; crossing the Allt a' Chonais can be a problem in spate**

The traverse of these two Munros gives an excellent hillwalk in a remote corner, with fine views. The summits are linked by an enjoyable ridge at a high level, but the approach is fairly long.

Start from the Achnashellach Forest car park on the north side of the A890 at Craig. From the car park return to the main road, crossing it and taking the track opposite which leads over a level crossing. This track heads up the glen with good views ahead of former Munro Sgurr nan Ceannaichean; eventually the route crosses a bridge over the River Carron. Fork left after the bridge to begin a long, steady climb above the Sloc Mor gorge. There is good reason to take a breather as a great view of the Coulin peaks gradually opens up behind. First to appear is Fuar Tholl away on the left, later joined by Sgorr Ruadh and Beinn

Liath Mhor. Keep on the main track, ignoring a forestry track to the right and later another track signed 'Allt a' Chonais pinewood'.

Head through a deer fence gate and continue to the top of a pass. Sgurr Choinnich and Sgurr a' Chaorachain are now seen at the far end of the flat, treeless glen which stretches ahead. Carry on along the track which heads downhill, ignoring a track down to the hydro dam on the right. Eventually the route runs alongside the river. Ignore a wire brdge and then a faint path to the right (destined for Sgurr na Feartaig), and continue for another 2km until the track bends left and ascends slightly. Here a cairn marks a stalkers' path to the right – follow this down to the Allt a' Chonais.

The rickety remains of a wire bridge are no longer of use, and the footbridge shown on some maps just downstream has gone, so the river must be forded – bear in mind that this might not be possible in spate conditions. Follow the clear path up the west side of the glen of the Allt Leathad an Tobair, with good views of Sgurr Choinnich. The route keeps high above the burn to reach the wide Bealach Bhearnais.

Keep climbing to gain a second, higher bealach and then begin the ascent of the Streangan nan Aon Pacan-deug ridge. Broad at first, it soon narrows and is

mainly grassy with a couple of rocky steps before the straight and level summit ridge with an excellent view over the void of Pollan Buidhe. The cairn sits right on the edge of the crags at a height of 999m.

From the top continue to the far end of the summit ridge and then descend the rocky ridge to the Bealach Coire Choinnich. Another ascent leads onward to the trig point at the summit of Sgurr a' Chaorachain, the higher of the two Munros. To descend, head north from the summit, down a grassy ridge for around 700m before aiming left down steep slopes. Cross back over the Allt a' Chonais to return to the track back down the glen.

Sgurr Choinnich

4

Maoile Lunndaidh

Maoile Lunndaidh (1007m)
bare hill of the wet place

Distance **26km**
Ascent **1140m**
Time **8 – 10 hours**
Start point **OS Grid ref: NH039493**
Map **OS Explorer 429 and 430**
Terrain & hazards **excellent approach track, then some very rough bogs to cross before the trackless ascent itself**

Maoile Lunndaidh is a remote hill, shyly hidden away from most viewpoints, and ranks amongst the least climbed of all the Munros. Its initially lumpen appearance is enlivened by some fine corries.

Park at Achnashellach Forest car park, which is signed on the north side of the road at Craig. The first part of this route is identical to Sgurr Choinnich and Sgurr a'

Chaorachain given above as far as the bend in the track where the stalkers' path for the Bealach Bhearnais branches off. For Maoile Lunndaidh, remain on the main track for another 3km to a forestry plantation. Leave the track here and bear east over boggy ground, soon crossing a burn. Around 1km of very rough terrain brings you to the Am Crom-allt. Cross this to begin a direct ascent of the steep, heathery slope opposite. The gradient eases at around 800m and soon you come to the rim of the Fuar Tholl Mor corrie. The lochan is visible far below as you bear right and follow the plateau edge up to the top of Carn nam Fiaclan. An easy 0.5km leads to the cairn on the minor summit of Creag Toll a' Choin. This was once regarded as the highest point, but more recent surveys mean you have to head northeast for 700m to reach the summit of the Munro at 1007m. Either return by the same route or head slightly west of north to a minor bealach before descending west beside a burn to the foot of the corries. From here continue west to rejoin the outward route at the Am Crom-allt.

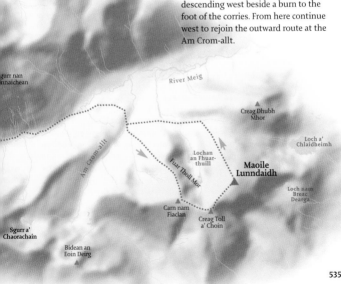

Moruisg

gurr nan nnaichean

River Meig

Creag Dhubh Mhor

Loch a' Chlaidheimh

Am Crom-allt

Lochan an Fhuar-thuill

Fuar Tholl Mor

Maoile Lunndaidh

Loch nam Breac Dearga

Carn nam Fiaclan

Creag Toll a' Choin

Sgurr a' Chaorachain

Bidean an Eoin Deirg

Maoile Lunndaidh

5

Beinn Liath Mhor Sgorr Ruadh

Beinn Liath Mhor (926m) *big grey hill*
Sgorr Ruadh (962m) *red peak*

Distance 16.5km
Ascent 1360m
Time 7 – 9 hours
Start point OS Grid ref: NH004483
Map OS Explorer 429
Public transport train to Achnashellach
Terrain & hazards **good stalkers' paths on the approach; higher up there are steep boulders and heather; much rough ground and crags to avoid on the descent**

These two contrasting but equally rugged hills provide a route of absorbing interest. A steep climb leads up to the long scree-covered ridge of Beinn Liath Mhor. The linking section is complex with intricate route finding to take in Sgorr Ruadh – a beautifully sculpted sandstone peak that shows an impressive face above Coire Lair.

There is space to park at a lay-by on the A890 opposite the telephone box and private road to Achnashellach Station; alternatively let the train take the strain, but remember that it is a request stop. Follow the road up to the railway, turning right after the outbuildings and crossing the line to continue up a track to a crossroads. Turn left here through the forestry; after a gate impressive views open up of the prow of Fuar Tholl ahead.

After a short distance keep a close eye

out for a path on the left indicated by a small cairn – the former sign is no more and a lot of walkers have continued into the woods where the route is eventually blocked by a deer fence. The path goes through a small gate and leads towards the River Lair before climbing up out of the woodland. Once the gradient eases off, turn right at another path junction marked with a cairn. From here both Munros look very impressive, with the sandstone precipices of Sgorr Ruadh on the left and the grey screes of Beinn Liath Mhor's long ridge on the right. Further left the great cliffs of Fuar Tholl – a Corbett – are even more impressive. At a second cairned fork keep right once again to climb almost to the head of the pass, the Drochaid Coire Lair. Just before the highest point, turn left up rough ground to tackle the steep heather and scree-strewn slopes above, eventually gaining the eastern end of the ridge, marked by a large cairn.

From here the going is easier although the quartz rock is slippery when wet. The well-defined ridge heads downhill for about 400m before rising to a central summit. Continue to a second col before the final climb to the third and highest peak. A couple of rocky sections can be bypassed to the right. There are great views across Coire Lair to Sgorr Ruadh, as well as to the Torridon giants of Liathach

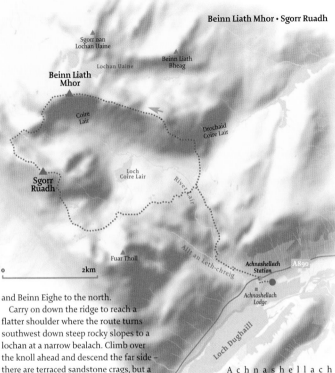

Sgorr nan
Lochan Uaine

Lochan Uaine

Beinn Liath
Bheag

**Beinn Liath
Mhor**

Coire
Lair

Drochaid
Coire Lair

Loch
Coire Lair

River Lair

**Sgorr
Ruadh**

Fuar Tholl

Allt an Leth-chreig

**Achnashellach
Station**

A890

Achnashellach
Lodge

Loch Dughaill

A c h n a s h e l l a c h
F o r e s t

0   2km

and Beinn Eighe to the north.

Carry on down the ridge to reach a flatter shoulder where the route turns southwest down steep rocky slopes to a lochan at a narrow bealach. Climb over the knoll ahead and descend the far side – there are terraced sandstone crags, but a faint path keeps any difficulties down to very simple scrambling, though navigation could be tricky if visibility is poor. The second, lower bealach also has a lochan and is crossed on the stalkers' path up from Coire Lair. Now climb the slope opposite to reach a smaller lochan on the ridge of Sgorr Ruadh. Bear left here, climbing the scree-covered ridge up to reach the summit.

Continue eastwards and then descend down the steep open slope to the bealach between Sgorr Ruadh and Fuar Tholl. From the far side of the bealach pick up the stalkers' path which descends to the River Lair. This can be difficult to cross in spate conditions; at such times it would be better to reverse the route to avoid the chance of being trapped at the end of the day. The path on the far bank soon reaches the outward route. Turn right along this to return to Achnashellach.

An Ruadh-stac and Maol Chean-dearg from Fuar Tholl

Maol Chean-dearg

Maol Chean-dearg (933m) *bald red head*

Distance **14km**
Ascent **930m**
Time **5 – 7 hours**
Start point **OS Grid ref: NG956451**
Map **OS Explorer 429**
Terrain & hazards **good paths up the glen, then an easy to follow stony zigzag path to the bealach; faint path on climb to the summit on steep quartzite scree, then sandstone boulders**

Maol Chean-dearg is well named – 'the bald red head' – as it is a rounded summit of sandstone boulders above steep white quartzite flanks. This shapely Munro starts with a pleasant approach by the Fionn-abhainn, but it is the stunning view of Torridon from the summit that makes this ascent so memorable.

Start from the parking area on the A890 just west of the bridge at Coulags in Strath Carron. Cross the bridge and then go through the gate on the left, signed as a right of way to Glen Torridon. As the track approaches the house in the trees, turn left down steps and continue beside the river. The path soon crosses open moorland as it continues up the glen, eventually crossing the river and heading up the west side to reach the bothy at Coire Fionnaraich. As with other bothies it may be used by the estate during the stalking season; please help the Mountain Bothies Association volunteers by keeping the place tidy and free of litter.

The next landmark is the Clach nan Con-fionn, a large rock resembling a Henry Moore sculpture; it is said to have been used by the giant, Fionn, to tether his hunting dogs. Some 400m further on a small cairn marks a junction of stalkers' paths; bear left (west) here to begin a zigzag climb up to the bealach. Once at Coire Garbh there is an impressive view of the steep rock-slabs of the Corbett An Ruadh-stac ahead. Bear right up a rougher path heading north, then northwest, over quartzite scree at first, the worst of which can be avoided by keeping on the east side of the ridge. A grassy section follows before the final climb up sandstone boulders to the large summit cairn. On the north side Maol Chean-dearg falls abruptly in broken crags, and in good weather it is worth continuing just beyond the cairn to fully appreciate the outlook to Loch an Eion far below, with the Torridon peaks beyond. The quickest return is by the outward route.

Maol Chean-dearg

Loch
an Eion

Bealach na Lice

Loch na
Craoibhe-
caorainn

Coire
Fionnaraich

Sgorr Ruadh

Loch Coire
Fionnaraich

Coire
Garbh

Loch Coire an
Ruadh-staic

Meall nan
Ceapraichean

Clach nan
Con-fionn

An Ruadh-stac

Coire
Fionnaraich

Ruadh Stac Beag

Fionn-abhainn

A890

Coulags
Bridge

Alternatives

The return can be varied by heading back
over Meall nan Ceapraichean from the
bealach before descending steeply to the
bothy. This area has many superb
stalkers' paths and another option for a
longer walk is, after returning to the col,
to take the path round the west side of
the hill and then past the north shore of
Loch an Eoin. Maol Chean-dearg looks its
finest from here, and the route continues
by crossing the Bealach na Lice and then
returning down the glen to complete a
circuit of the hill. Loch an Eoin can also be
reached by another path from Annat in
Torridon for those staying on that side.

0   2km

Beinn Tharsuinn and Sgurr Choinnich from Bidein a'Choire Sheasgaich

7

Lurg Mhor
Bidein a' Choire Sheasgaich

Lurg Mhor (986m) *big shin*
Bidein a'Choire Sheasgaich (945m)
peak of the corrie of milkless cattle

Distance **38km**
Ascent **1645m**
Time **14 – 16 hours total**
Start point **OS Grid ref: NG245871**
Map **OS Explorer 429**
Terrain & hazards **rough and pathless terrain on exceptionally remote hills; excellent track for the approach**

A real Gaelic tongue-twister, Bidein a' Choire Sheasgaich is a graceful pointed summit that would attract great attention were it not hidden in the depths of wildest Monar; its neighbour Lurg Mhor is even more remote. Climbing them from the road and returning in a single day would be an epic walk and an overnight wild camp or night in a bothy is the more usual option. The approach track is possible on a mountain bike, but tough going.

There is a walkers' car park just inside the entrance to the Attadale Estate off the A890. The estate has a very positive approach to walkers and, in addition to the route map it provides an open bothy at Bendronaig which walkers are welcome to use outwith the stalking season.

Begin the walk along the driveway, bearing left to pass alongside the gardens which are well worth a visit on another day. Turn right at the garden entrance to follow the track up the glen, keeping right at a fork and eventually going through a gate onto a rougher track. Ignore two turnings on the right and cross a bridge over the River Attadale to start the long uphill climb. There are excellent views back over Loch Carron with the impressive sandstone hills of Applecross beyond.

After the initial ascent, the gradient eases as the track crosses undulating moorland with forestry on the right. Ignore branches to the right before zigzagging up to a flatter section where Bidein a' Choire Sheasgaich is revealed far in the distance. The track descends into empty Srath Feith a' Mhadaidh and after a brief rise drops down to the Uisage Dhubh (Black Water) where an attractive iron bridge spans a small ravine. Another 1.5km of track brings you to the buildings at Bendronaig. The first is a lodge used for stalking and the second is the very well-maintained open bothy, with flushing toilet, albeit you need to first fill a bucket from the burn. Please help to keep the place tidy by carrying out any rubbish you find here on the way back.

Follow a track east to reach and cross a footbridge over the Allt Coire na Sorna. Keep right at the fork and climb up into Coire na Sorna before crossing a low bealach to reach the lonely shores of Loch Calavie, popular for fishing. The track

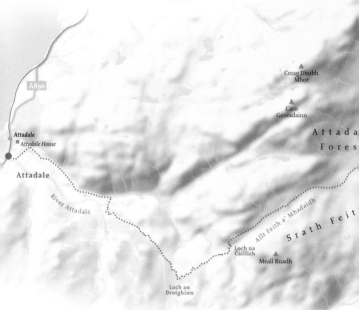

follows the northern shore to where the Allt Coire Calavie flows into the loch. Leave it here and climb up beside the burn; it is wet underfoot lower down; continue the ascent and aim slightly to the right to reach the bealach between Bidein a' Choire Sheasgaich and Lurg Mhor.

Head for Lurg Mhor first. After two fairly steep sections you come to the cairn, a real prize for any bagger as this is undoubtedly one of the remotest Munro summits, with a great setting close to the edge of the northern crags. The fit and

keen may want to extend the route by detouring to Meall Mor from here – this involves a scramble on a narrowing ridge with some exposed slabs requiring care. Otherwise return to the bealach and follow the path up the ridge opposite. The straightforward ascent steepens near the airy summit. Bidein a' Choire Sheasgaich is known as 'cheesecake' by some hill-goers unsure of their Gaelic; its beautiful name actually means the 'peak of the corrie of the milkless cattle'.

To descend, head southwest back along

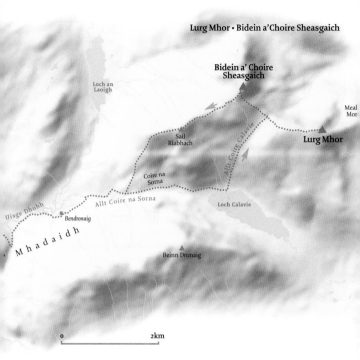

the final section of the summit ridge, but then continue steeply down pathless ground to a small lochan. Continue along the undulating, rocky ridge that leads out to the minor lump of Sail Riabhach, and continue west from here, then pick out a route down the heathery slopes to the path in Coire na Sorna. Bear right to follow the path to Bendronaig and then the long track back to Attadale.

Alternatives

A shorter but tougher approach is from Achnashellach to the north. Follow the route described for Sgurr Choinnich to the Bealach Bhearnais. From here, climb over the intervening Corbett of Beinn Tarsuinn to reach a further bealach at the foot of Bidein a' Choire Sheasgaich's north ridge. This has two steep rocky bands which can be negotiated with care using a bit of path on the left. Continue over the summit to reach Lurg Mhor. The easiest way back is to retrace your steps, with all the re-ascent and descent that this involves.

8

Beinn Alligin: Tom na Gruagaich Sgurr Mhor

Tom na Gruagaich (922m)
the hill of the damsel
Sgurr Mhor (986m) *big peak*

Distance 10km
Ascent 1110m
Time 6 – 7 hours
Start point OS Grid ref: NG868576
Map OS Explorer 433 Torridon
Terrain & hazards steep, rough and rocky path; there is scrambling on the Horns with a significant feeling of exposure – the setting may unnerve some; by tackling the route clockwise, walkers who are over-awed by the Horns can retrace their steps and will still have climbed both Munros

Beinn Alligin well deserves its name, which means the Mountain of Beauty. It is the shortest of the great Torridon ridges, but is in no way inferior. The route is packed with interest, including the Eag Dubh, a dramatic cleft in the ridge as if cut by a giant knife, and the spectacular Horns of Alligin, the highlight of the day for many. Keep this for a good weather day – the close proximity to the sea on one hand and the dramatic rock scenery on the other ensures unforgettable views.

Start from the car park immediately beyond the Abhainn Coire Mhic Nobuil,

3km west of Torridon village, and follow the smaller path which starts on the west side of the burn. Climb a stile over a deer fence and continue up the moor to meet the stream issuing from the deep scoop of Coir nan Laogh.

The path zigzags up the headwall of the corrie to eventually emerge onto the plateau. The summit of Tom na Gruagaich and its trig point is just to the right. Tom na Gruagaich was deservedly promoted to its current Munro status in 1997. It is a fabulous viewpoint, with Skye looking magnificent across the sea on a fine day. More impressive – or daunting, depending on your head for heights – is the view of the ridgewalk that lies ahead.

Head down the narrow north ridge, which is steep and rocky but with an obvious route. From the col, cross a minor top and a level section before the final steep climb towards Sgurr Mhor. Shortly before the summit, the ridge is almost cleaved in two by the Eag Dubh, a deep gully on the southeast flank which is easily passed on the left side, although from many angles it looks to be an impassable obstacle. Sgurr Mhor itself is an even better viewpoint than Tom na Gruagaich and in good weather is a great spot to while away a magical hour. However, the Horns of Alligin beckon the

Beinn Alligin

walker onwards. If the weather is poor or you don't fancy the scramble, it is best to return the same way.

Descend the ridge which dips steeply towards the first of the castellated Horns. Do not be tempted by the tiny bypass path which crosses the very steep grassy slopes on their south side – the path is very narrow and a slip would be fatal. Instead, follow the route which winds up the first Horn, taking in some simple but exposed scrambling. The second Horn is easier, whilst on the final Horn it is necessary to traverse to the right when meeting a steep section before returning to the ridge via a short chimney – again

the scrambling is not difficult, but some find the situation unnerving.

Keep a keen eye out for the path down the southeast ridge. This finds a winding route through sandstone terraces which would otherwise present navigational problems. Eventually you cross the Allt a' Bhealaich to follow the east bank, passing some waterfalls, before crossing the Abhainn Coire Mhic Nobuil on a footbridge. Follow the excellent path that leads down the glen to the start.

Beinn Alligin and Loch Torridon

9

Liathach:
Spidean a' Choire Leith
Mullach an Rathain

Spidean a' Choire Leith (1055m)
peak of the grey corrie
Mullach an Rathain (1023m)
summit of the pulleys

Distance **10km**
Ascent **1220m**
Time **8 – 10 hours**
Start point OS Grid ref: **NG934566**
Map OS Explorer **433**
Terrain & hazards **the Am Fasarinen pinnacles require competent scrambling skills; a good head for heights is needed even for the bypass path, as well as great care; the descent from Mullach an Rathain includes steep scree**

The traverse of Liathach is rated by many mountaineers and hillwalkers as amongst Scotland's finest, but for others the anticipation, exposure and airy scrambling will leave them trembling in their boots. Either way, a trip linking Liathach's two Munros is one which will not be forgotten.

There is a small parking area about 200m east of Glen Cottage; alternatively use the car park near the bridge at NG958568 and walk 2km back down the road. From here Liathach looms overhead looking nigh-on impossible, even though the slopes are foreshortened, but the path following the east bank of the Allt an

Doire Ghairbh suggests otherwise. Start by heading up this relentlessly steep but well-built trod.

At the great cleft in the cliffs above, the path bears right with some short rocky scrambles before reaching the ridge just southwest of Stuc a' Choire Dhuibh Bhig. A detour to this easternmost summit rewards with a fabulous view of Beinn Eighe across the awesome trench of Coire Dubh Mor. Return to the top of the path and continue along the main ridge, following the well-worn route over the two tops of Stob a'Choire Liath Mhor, littered with quartzite scree and boulders. After the second descent the final climb up the impressive summit cone of Spidean a' Choire Leith begins. The summit views are nothing short of awesome – although the ridge now stretching in front of you may be quite intimidating.

Heading down from Spidean a' Choire Leith requires careful navigation in mist; it is all too easy to finish up following the ridge southeast which ends at a precipitous prow projecting out over the glen. Instead, take the initially ill-defined southwest ridge down steep boulders; this eventually levels off as the famous Am Fasarinen pinnacles come into view, giving some hillwalkers palpitations. The

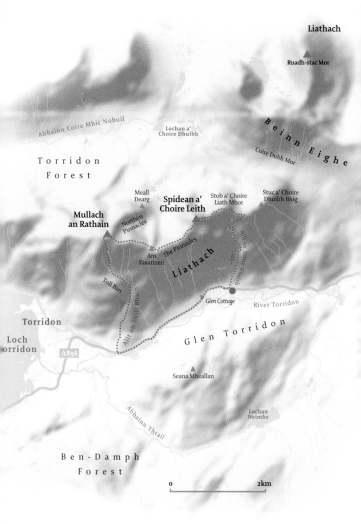

Liathach

Ruadh-stac Mor

Abhainn Coire Mhic Nobuil

Lochan a' Choire Dhuibh

Beinn Eighe

Coire Dubh Mor

Torridon Forest

Meall Dearg

Spidean a' Choire Leith

Stob a' Choire Liath Mhor

Stuca a' Choire Dhuibh Bhig

Mullach an Rathain

Northen Pinnacles

The Pinnacles

Am Fasarinen

Liathach

Allt Coire Ghairbh

Toll Ban

Glen Cottage

River Torridon

Allt an Tuill Bhain

Torridon

Loch orridon

A896

Glen Torridon

Seana Mheallan

Abhainn Thrail

Lochan Neimhe

Ben-Damph Forest

0   2km

553

Liathach rising behind Torridon village

traverse of the pinnacles is a hard and very exposed scramble; there is also a path which traverses along a rocky shelf beneath the pinnacles on the south side to avoid the scrambling, but this is sensationally exposed – if you are able to look down you may see a Tonka Toy version of your car between your feet. Great care is needed where the path has eroded where it crosses the back of a couple of gullies. A good head for heights is needed for the length of the path.

The bypass path rejoins the ridge just beyond the pinnacles – and it is worth detouring easily back up to the top of the final pinnacle for the view. From here on, the ridge changes character completely and leads much more sedately to the second Munro, Mullach an Rathain, where there is a glittering panorama of Loch Torridon backed by Skye and the Outer Hebrides. Others may just be glad to have made it this far – remove your blinkers and try and settle that overworked heart.

Continue west for 200m before curving southwards and descending the very steep scree slopes into Toll Ban. Here you can pick up a rough path down the west bank of the Allt an Tuill Bhain. Further down it bears right away from the burn and weaves and winds around to avoid the many terraces of sandstone cliffs, reaching the Torridon road about 2km west of the start.

Alternatives

You can avoid the most exposed sections of the two Munros by tackling them as separate walks. Spidean a' Choire Leith can be climbed as above before returning the same way, and Mullach an Rathain reached either by the route of descent described above or via its west ridge, gained by taking the Coire Mhic Nobuil path to NG881588 and then aiming for the ridge east of Sgorr a'Chadail.

10

Beinn Eighe: Spidean Coire nan Clach Ruadh-stac Mor

Spidean Coire nan Clach (993m)
peak of the corrie of the stones
Ruadh-stac Mor (1010m) *big red stack*

Distance **18.5km**
Ascent **1185m**
Time **7 – 9 hours**
Start point **OS Grid ref: NG958569**
Map **OS Explorer 433**
Terrain & hazards **steep ascent path, rocky and rough ridges with mild scrambling; descent down eroded scree chute**

Beinn Eighe is the biggest of the Torridon giants, a mammoth range of rocky summits linked by a superb ridge. The complete traverse is a major undertaking, but both Munros are on the western half and can be climbed by this route, descending via one of Scotland's finest corries. For some the revelation of the Triple Buttress towering over the lochan in the corrie is the highlight of the route and makes Beinn Eighe one of the most spectacular of the Munros.

Although many do this route clockwise, the scree climb out of Coire Mhic Fhearchair is very steep and is perhaps better tackled in descent, leaving the stunning rock architecture of the Triple Buttress as a grand finale.

There are two parking options for this route; one is a short way along the track that leaves the A896 at NG977578, but this is very rough so many prefer to head for the car park on the A896 just west of the bridge over the Allt a' Choire Dhuibh Mhoir. If using the latter, walk back along the road to take the Coire an Laoigh track which shortly becomes a path at a cairn. Steady at first, the path steepens as it nears the corrie between the main ridge and the projecting spur of Stuc Coire an Laoigh. The grassy floor of Coire an Laoigh provides a brief respite before the very steep ascent up the headwall to reach the ridge between Stuc Coire an Laoigh and Beinn Eighe itself. A large cairn is a great spot for a breather with Liathach appearing as a great monolith – a stunning backdrop.

Bear right to follow the winding path up the quartzite screes which crown Beinn Eighe and give it its distinctive greyish-white colour in distant views. A trig point marks the main ridge, but the first Munro, Spidean Coire nan Clach, requires a detour along the ridge to the right. A path leads along the narrow crest, bypassing a small rocky outcrop before a very easy scramble brings you to the summit itself. Quartzite requires care when wet as it can be very slippery. The tiny cairn looks out along the ridge towards the eastern summits of Beinn Eighe. Nervous walkers will be relieved that these are not classed as separate Munros as the exposed ridge linking them is tricky in parts.

Instead, return to the trig point and continue west along the ridge, crossing sandstone before a short descent to a bealach and an unexpectedly grassy respite. Climb beyond to reach a cairn at the eastern end of Coinneach Mhor, just a short distance from the edge of the great Triple Buttress. Descend the steep and stony ridge to reach the narrow bealach which separates Ruadh-stac Mor from the main ridge. The climb beyond is rocky at first, but eases before a final pull up scree. Ruadh-stac Mor is the highest of Beinn Eighe's many summits and because it stands slightly apart it is a great vantage point for the whole range.

Return to the bealach and then head northwest down the steep and narrow scree gully. The easiest going is on the right-hand side, but great care is needed. Keep right at the point where the gully narrows and is almost blocked by a large stone. Further down, pick up a path which descends northwest between the scree and the foot of the cliffs, and then pick a route over the boulders down to the flatter ground below. From here, bear left to reach a path close to the base of the buttress; this picks its way down several sandstone terraces on the south side of the corrie, passing a a number of lovely pools and waterfalls before reaching the glassy expanse of Loch Coire Mhic Fhearchair. Keep following the path round the eastern shore to reach the far end; from here the water forms the foreground for the classic view of the Triple Buttress – one of the finest views of its kind in Scotland.

Cross the outflow from the loch to pick up a well-built stalkers' path which curves round the lower slopes of Sail Mhor and gives a great outlook over the wild land beyond the main Torridon peaks. Eventually you reach the large cairn at the junction with a path from Coire Mhic Nobuil. Bear left to follow the main path down Coire Dubh Mor, emerging later at the A896.

Ruadh-stac
Mor

Ruadh-stac
Beag

Loch Coire
Mhic Fhearchair

Sail Mhor

Triple Buttress

Coinneach
Mhor

Spidean Coire
nan Clach

Lochan a'
Choire Dhuibh

B e i n n   E i g h e

Coire an
Laoigh

Coire Dubh Mor

Stuc Coire
an Laoigh

Allt Coire an Laoigh

Spidean a'
Choire Leith

Allt a' Choire Dhuibh Mhoir

Loch
Bharrabch

Liathach

Lochan an
Iasgair

Ling Hut

A896

River Torridon

Glen Torridon

C o u l i n
F o r e s t

Sgurr
Dhubh

0   2km

The Beinn Eighe range from the north

Slioch

Slioch (981m) *spear*

Distance 19km
Ascent 1140m
Time 7 – 9 hours
Start point OS Grid ref: NH038624
Map OS Explorer 435
Public transport Inverness – Gairloch buses call at Kinlochewe
Terrain & hazards a fairly long and tough walk with some boggy terrain and pathless sections

Slioch lords it over Loch Maree, appearing to be an impregnable fortress of rock. However, its formidable appearance relents on its southern side, giving access to this long but moderate walk (by Torridon standards) to a summit which is a superb viewpoint overlooking one of the wildest corners of Scotland.

There is a car park at the end of the minor road in Incheril, just northeast of Kinlochewe. From here climb the steps and go through a gate onto the path past a cemetery. The path joins another coming in from the left, runs by a burn and later joins the Kinlochewe River, flowing through native woodland over its wide shingle bed. After 1km, you reach the shores of Loch Maree, often reckoned to be the most beautiful loch in Scotland.

Cross the bridge over the attractive Abhainn an Fhasaigh, and keep right at a fork to climb towards Gleann Biannasdail. After a few hundred metres take a much rougher path branching left, which climbs steeply beside two small burns aiming for the col to the west of Meall Each. The climb up to the col is often boggy; once reached, however, the continuing ascent up the grassy bowl of Coire na Sleaghaich is much easier.

A number of routes can be taken from here to the summit. The best is along a faint path which makes a rising traverse on the left side of the coire to gain the ridge close to two attractive lochans. Beyond the lochans the climb is steep and rocky before the grassy slopes of the summit plateau are reached. Pass or cross a minor summit en route to the trig point at 980m. Even this is not the true highest point, so continue to the northern peak which is the Munro at 981m. From here the Torridon peaks are spread out to the southwest and Loch Maree stretches magnificently to the sea, but perhaps best of all is the outlook into the great wilderness of the Fisherfield and Letterewe Forests – an area of spectacular hidden peaks to the north.

It is possible to vary the route back by following the path along the east ridge which soon narrows to the fine peak of Sgurr an Tuill Bhain. From here descend into the corrie to rejoin the outward route.

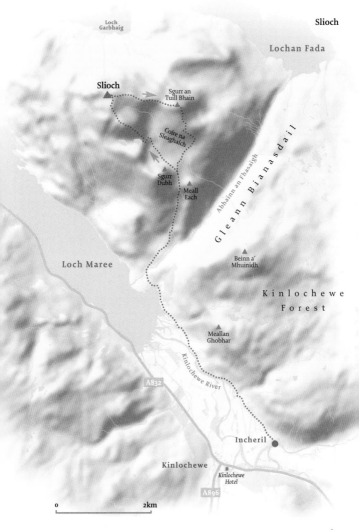

Loch
Garbhaig

Slioch

Lochan Fada

Slioch

Sgurr an
Tuill Bhain

Coire na
Sleaghaich

Sgurr
Dubh

Meall
Each

Abhainn an Fhasaigh

Gleann Bianasdail

Beinn a'
Mhuinidh

Loch Maree

Kinlochewe
Forest

Meallan
Ghobhar

Kinlochewe River

A832

Incheril

Kinlochewe

Kinlochewe
Hotel

A896

0   2km

563

Slioch and Loch Maree

A835

Ullapool

Loch
Broom

Seana
Bhraigh

Dundonnell **8**

Fisherfield
Forest

Bidein a'
Ghlas Thuill

An Teallach

6
7

Eididh nan
Clach Geala
Meall nan
Ceapraichean

Loch na
Sealga

Sgurr
Fiona

Beinn Dearg

Cona'
Mheall

Am
Faochagach

9

A832

Ruadh
Stac Mor

The Fisherfield
Round

A' Mhaighdean

Sgurr Ban

Mullach Coire
Mhic Fhearchair

Beinn
Tarsuinn

Lochan Fada

4 **3**

Meall
a'Chrasgaidh

A835

Beinn Liath
Mhor
Fannaich

2 **5**

Sgurr
Mor

Sgurr nan
Clach Geala

Meall
Gorm

A' Chailleach

Sgurr
Breac

Sgurr
nan Each

An
Coileachan

Letterewe
Forest

Loch
Fannich

Ullapool and the Far North

Ullapool

The only real town in the far northwest, Ullapool was laid out by Thomas Telford and its uniform grid of whitewashed buildings can appear almost to float on the surface of Loch Broom. Nowadays the ferry service to Stornoway dominates the harbour which is also the departure point for cruises to the Summer Isles. For most visitors it makes an excellent place to eat your fish and chips if you can dodge the marauding seagulls – the chippie next to the Seaforth is highly recommended.

A number of good pubs offer traditional fare and somewhere to stay, whilst the

Loch
carnoch

Ben
Wyvis

A835

A832

Ceilidh Place has proved that music, good food, books and beds make a winning combination. At the other end of the scale, Broomfield Holiday Park is a very well-run campsite right on the shores of the loch – great for enjoying some amazing sunsets.

Dundonnell and the Great Wilderness

From Braemore Junction the A832 branches off and passes above the remarkable Corrieshalloch Gorge before beginning the long ascent of a high and desolate pass. The road was built during the Highland potato famine, with crofters forced to work to obtain the oatmeal rations which would save them from starvation; it is still known as Destitution Road.

As the road approaches Dundonnell, however, the bleakness is relieved by the rich woodland of this stunning spot at the head of Little Loch Broom. Towering above is the crazy pinnacled crest of An Teallach – one of Scotland's most impressive sights. Behind An Teallach, however, is a hidden wonderland of remote and rocky peaks, sparkling lochans and secret glens – the Fisherfield and Letterewe Forests, collectively known to walkers as the Great Wilderness. The hotel in Dundonnell or the Sail Mhor Croft Hostel are good bases for walkers.

Sutherland

North of Ullapool the landscape changes completely. The great mountain ranges of the rest of the Highlands are replaced by lochan-spattered moorlands, from which isolated monoliths of great character rise. These mountains may mostly miss out on Munro status, but they concede nothing to their higher counterparts in the south.

Conival and Ben More Assynt are usually climbed together, whilst Ben Hope and Ben Klibreck can be polished off in a single day by the fit. In theory, baggers need never head up to Sutherland again – until, that is, you embark on the Corbetts. However, this is an amazing landscape with many of Scotland's finest hills, such as Suilven, Stac Pollaidh or Foinaven, as well as amazing coastal scenery with stunning beaches.

Lochinver, clustered around a busy harbour, is the main centre for the Assynt region with a good choice of B&Bs, a well-known pottery, and a legendary pie shop. There is a youth hostel at Achmelvich

Ben Hope

11

Altnaharra · · · · · B873 Loch Naver

Ben Klibreck

A836 · · · · · · · · ·

A838

12 · · · · · · · · · ·

Crask

Loch Shin

nearby and a string of campsites by the beaches. Closer to Conival and Ben More Assynt is Inchnadamph; there are few buildings here, but they include a friendly hostel as well as a hotel.

The miles are long and facilities few, with settlements such as Durness, Scourie and Tongue all set by the coast; Durness, in particular, has much to recommend it with some dramatic beaches and the impressive Smoo Cave. Inland the tiny roads run for miles without passing even a building. Near to Ben Klibreck is one of the few oases – the Crask Inn. Complete with four letting rooms and a camping area, this old-style hostelry is set miles from anywhere – a great place to soak up the atmosphere with real honest home-cooking from the friendly hosts.

1

Ben Wyvis

Ben Wyvis (1046m) *hill of terror or gloom*

Distance 14km
Time 5 – 7 hours
Ascent 935m
Start OS Grid NH412673
Map OS Explorer 437
Public transport Inverness to Ullapool bus service passes the car park
Terrain & hazards good path up through the forest and steep ascent up to An Cabar, then a broad featureless ridge to the summit

Ben Wyvis is a familiar sight on the horizon for Inverness folk; in summer the ascent to its spacious summit plateau is a straightforward hillwalk.

There is a dedicated car park for Ben Wyvis just south of the bridge over the Allt a Bhealaich Mhoir on the A835 north of Garve. Follow the footpath which avoids the main road as it heads north and crosses the bridge. The original hillpath is now joined to climb through the trees on the north side of the burn.

After about 1km, the forest thins and the path climbs more steeply. After another 1km and a stile, the trees are finally left behind and the route begins to zigzag uphill towards the top of An Cabar, the prominent peak on the left side of the glen ahead.

The climb leads direct to the 946m top of An Cabar which has a dramatic view down the steep slopes to the south. From here, the gradients are much more gentle although navigation could be an issue in poor conditions as the terrain is featureless. Aim for Cairn a' Chaptein and then across a tiny dip before rising gently towards the summit. Ben Wyvis is a National Nature Reserve, in part because of the rare plants growing on the plateau. Erosion caused by walkers is an ongoing problem in this fragile, high-altitude environment; keeping to the shortest direct route to the summit will help to minimise any damage.

The ridge narrows before you reach the summit trig point at Glas Leathad Mor. On a clear day both coasts can be visible in a panorama that covers vast swathes of northern Scotland, from Torridon to the Black Isle and Easter Ross. Sgurr Mor in the Fannichs is easy to pick out as a sharp cone to the west. It is possible to descend from Tom a' Choinnich, but the quicker and probably more enjoyable option is to retrace the outward walk.

Meallan Donn

Tom a' Choinnich

Loch a' Choire Mhoir

Ben Wyvis

Allt Tom a' Choinnich

A835

Glas Leathad Mor

An t-Socach

Cairn a' Chaiptein

Allt a' Bhealaich Mhoir

An Cabar

Garbat Forest

Tom na Gaillich

Little Wyvis

0   2km

Ben Wyvis

Looking to Sgurr Mor from Sgurr nan Clach Geala

2

Beinn Liath Mhor Fannaich
Sgurr Mor
Meall Gorm
An Coileachan

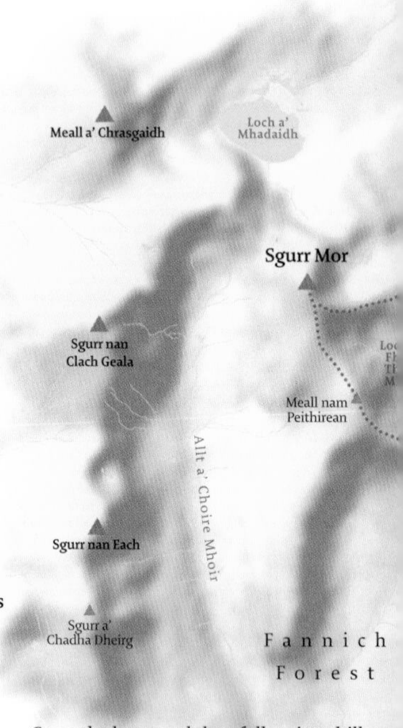

Beinn Liath Mhor Fannaich (954m)
big grey hill of fannaich
Sgurr Mor (110m) *big peak*
Meall Gorm (949m) *blue rounded hill*
An Coileachan (923m) *the little cock*

Distance 24km
Ascent 1280m
Time 8 – 11 hours
Start point OS Grid ref: NH278742
Map OS Explorer 436
Public transport Inverness to Ullapool
bus service passes the car park
Terrain & hazards boggy and pathless
terrain lower down, but excellent
ridgewalking above

Meall a' Chrasgaidh

Loch a'
Mhadaidh

Sgurr Mor

Sgurr nan
Clach Geala

Loc
Fl
Tl

Meall nam
Peithirean

Allt a' Choire Mhoir

Sgurr nan Each

Sgurr a'
Chadha Dheirg

F a n n i c h
F o r e s t

The eastern half of the Fannichs provides
a magnificent ridgewalk, taking in four
Munros. There is a price to pay, however,
in the tough and boggy walk in and
especially the long haul back from An
Coileachan at the end of the day.

There is a small parking area just north
of Torrandhu bridge on the A835. Pass the
Met Office weather station and head west
along the bank of the Abhainn an Torrain
Duibh. An alternative signed start
through the forest joins this route via a
bridge. Continue upstream to the
junction with the Allt an' Loch Sgeirich.

Cross the latter and then follow it uphill
to start the mainly pathless ascent
towards Creag Dhubh Fannaich. Leave the
burn higher up to head over rough,
bouldery ground to the minor summit,
marked by a small cairn.

Cross the wide bealach and climb up the
grass and boulder slope to the summit of
Beinn Liath Mhor Fannaich. The first

An Coileachan

577

Munro of the day sits towards the western end of a small plateau, beside some rocky outcrops. Views open out westwards over Loch a' Mhadaidh, with the prominent dome-shaped summit of Sgurr Mor towering on the left.

In poor weather conditions the next bealach can be difficult to locate. Start by descending steeply for a short distance to join a stalkers' path, then follow this, keeping the cliffs on your right.

The path climbs up the far side of the bealach and passes left of a minor peak before the ridge narrows briefly. When it broadens once more and the stalkers' path contours the slopes to the left, leave the path and climb directly up the steep slopes towards Sgurr Mor. Cross a series of terraces formed during the last Ice Age before reaching the large summit cairn of Sgurr Mor. As the highest mountain for miles around it has a very extensive view, with An Teallach looking superb to the northwest. Sgurr Mor itself is instantly recognisable from most of the other summits in view due to its distinctive outline – often likened to a witch's hat.

Head back down the south ridge, rejoining the stalkers' path and now following it over the minor summit of Meall nam Peithirean across flat outcrops. The ridge gives superb views to the north, looking down into a series of rocky, lochan-filled corries. Continue to a bealach and pass to the right of the lump of Creachan Rairigidh. The path forks at a second bealach beyond; take the branch which climbs up to the summit of Meall Gorm.

From here the ridge leads past a tiny stone shelter built by stalkers. Descend steeper stony ground to reach the broad Bealach Ban, then head up the very wide grass and scree-covered slopes opposite to reach the summit plateau where An Coileachan, the final Munro, is marked by a cairn atop a sandstone outcrop.

Retrace your steps across the plateau before picking your way down steep craggy terrain, aiming for Loch Gorm. Once on flatter ground, aim for the bealach southwest of Meallan Buidhe. From here the route becomes boggy and very rough, crossing deep heather. Traverse the west side of Meallan Buidhe and aim a little east of north to reach the Abhainn a' Ghuibhais Li. Cross this and follow the far bank downstream to rejoin the outward route.

Alternatives

Apart from Beinn Liath Mhor Fannaich, the summits are conveniently positioned for an approach from the south using the private road up to Loch Fannich. The road is closed to vehicular traffic, however, so the route would be a very long one; a bicycle would help.

3

Meall a'Chrasgaidh
Sgurr nan Clach Geala
Sgurr nan Each

Meall a' Chrasgaidh (934m)
rounded hill of the crossing
Sgurr nan Clach Geala (1093m)
peak of the white stones
Sgurr nan Each (923m) *peak of the horses*

Distance **18km**
Ascent **1100m**
Time **7 – 8 hours**
Start point **OS Grid ref: NH163761**
Map **OS Explorer 436**
Terrain & hazards **good approach path
soon replaced by pathless and steep
slopes on the climb and descent**

**Sgurr nan Clach Geala is arguably the
finest of the Fannichs, its impressive
eastern slopes falling precipitously into
Coire Mor. Combined with the
neighbouring Munros of Meall a'
Chrasgaidh and Sgurr nan Each it makes
an excellent ridgewalk.**

Start from the parking area just past the
forestry plantations and the gated, signed
track off the A832 southwest of Braemore
Junction. Head back along the road for 20m
to reach the track leading to Loch a'
Bhraoin, signed for Kinlochewe and Loch
Fannich. Follow the track until a gate, then
turn left onto a new path through the
plantation. This soon leads down to a large
bridge over the outflow of Loch a' Bhraoin.

Follow the stalkers' path on the far side

for 50m before turning left onto a
smaller, boggy trod which soon reaches
a footbridge over the Allt Breabaig
(not marked on the OS map). Cross the
bridge and follow the faint path which
bears right up the valley, staying well
above the burn. It soon joins the clearer
stalkers' route; look out for a good place
to strike off directly up the steep, open
slopes to the east. There is no path
and the ascent is hard going, with
only the views back towards An Teallach
to compensate.

The gradient eases for the final 1km to
the summit of Meall a' Chrasgaidh.
Although the cairn stands at 934m, the
whole peak is somewhat overshadowed
by the greater peaks nearby. From the top
bear south to cross the bealach and then
make a rising traverse to the lochan on
the bealach between Carn na Criche and
Sgurr nan Clach Geala. Known as Am
Biachdaich – meaning 'the place of the
fattening', due to its fine grasses, it is a
good spot for a rest stop. Climb the slope
beyond the col which soon narrows to
form the most enjoyable section of the
day's ridgewalking. Huge sweeping crags
drop to the left as the fine ridge curves
and crosses several undulations before
the trig point at the summit of Sgurr
nan Clach Geala is gained. There is a

579

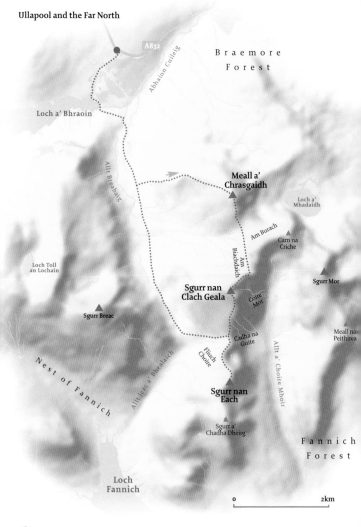

A832

Braemore
Forest

Abhainn Cuileig

Loch a' Bhraoin

Allt Breabaig

**Meall a'
Chrasgaidh**

Loch a'
Mhadaidh

Am Burach

Carn na
Criche

Am
Biachdaidh

Loch Toll
an Lochain

Sgurr Mor

**Sgurr nan
Clach Geala**

Coire
Mor

Sgurr Breac

Cadha na
Guite

Meall na
Peithirea

Allt a' Choire Mhoir

Nest of Fannich

Allt Tarsuinn a' Bhealaich

Fliuch
Choire

**Sgurr nan
Each**

Sgurr a'
Chadha Dheirg

Fannich
Forest

Loch
Fannich

0   2km

magnificent feeling of space all around this airy perch. Continue down the broader south ridge to eventually reach the pass at Cadha na Guite.

Stay on the ridge as it gracefully curves right then left to reach Sgurr nan Each; the highest cairn is at the far end of the summit ridge. Now return to Cadha na Guite and descend the steep western slopes, avoiding the bands of crags before bearing right to reach the col at the head of the Allt Breabaig valley. Take care to avoid descending too far into Fliuch Choire if visibility is poor.

From the boggy col head north, aiming to pick up the stalkers' path just over on the far side of the glen; once gained this makes the going much easier. The path soon crosses back over the burn and rejoins the outward route at the point where the climb to Meall a' Chrasgaidh was tackled earlier in the day. From here retrace the outward route to the start.

Sgurr nan Each and Sgurr nan Clach Geala from Coire Mor

4

Sgurr Breac
A' Chailleach

Sgurr Breac (999m) *speckled peak*
A' Chailleach (997m) *the old woman*

Distance **16km**
Ascent **1130m**
Time **6 – 8 hours**
Start point **OS Grid ref: NH163761**
Map **OS Explorer 435**
Terrain & hazards **steep, often wet path; rocky in places on approach to the easy ridge; return route requires careful navigation in poor visibility and is very boggy near the loch**

This pair of Munros – with a prominent Top on the ridge between them – form a westerly extension to the main Fannichs range.

Start from a rough parking area off the A832 Dundonnell road just beyond Braemore Junction. The parking is just after a forestry plantation and a gated track signed for Kinlochewe and Loch Fannich. Begin by heading back to the track and follow it towards the loch. When a gate is reached take the new path to the left, leading through the plantation and down to the bridge.

On the far side follow the stalkers' path for a short way. At the foot of the ridge heading up to Toman Coinnich turn right onto a faint path aiming straight up the slope of Leitir Fhearna, the nose of the ridge. From here the higher ground looks very rocky but, although wet underfoot,

paths avoid any difficulties. Above the steep section the ridge levels off into a plateau riven with peat gullies. A path along the right-hand edge avoids the wettest ground before a grassier ridge makes for more enjoyable going with views ahead of the two corries that bite into the Munros. The path eventually leads to the col between Toman Coinnich and A' Chailleach; instead leave it to stay on the crest of the ridge straight to the summit of Toman Coinnich, where Loch Fannich is revealed on the far side.

Take the broad southeast ridge down to the col, crossing steps eroded by glacial action. A straightforward climb leads up to Sgurr Breac from the bealach; the summit of the first Munro of the day is about 200m further on from the first cairn across a plateau.

Return to Toman Coinnich and then descend the indistinct ridge to the next bealach before climbing the grassy but well-defined ridge up the far side. There are great views down the cliffs on the right, looking down to Loch Toll an Lochain. The ridge flattens off as it joins with the Sron na Goibhre ridge (with its fenceposts); bear left here on a path up to A' Chailleach.

To descend, retrace your steps briefly before taking the pathless ridge of Sron na Goibhre. Steep at first, it becomes easier, passing some huge rocky blocks.

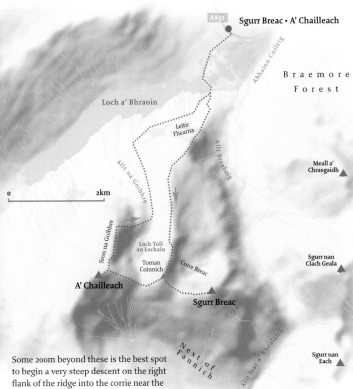

Some 200m beyond these is the best spot to begin a very steep descent on the right flank of the ridge into the corrie near the outflow of Loch Toll an Lochain. Although steep, boggy and dotted with greasy boulders there is no alternative as crags block the northern termination of Sron na Goibhre.

Once in the corrie, bear left beside the burn, crossing it as soon as possible as it later falls into a ravine with a series of waterfalls. Continue heading diagonally downhill towards Loch a' Bhraoin. The loch shore is exceptionally boggy, so aim

to pick up a faint track part way down between the loch and the small crags and trees to the south. Look out for a circular sheep fank just to the left. The track leads to a stile and gate enclosing an area of regenerating oakwood. At the far side go through the gate and aim directly for the bridge at the outflow of the loch. Cross this to return to the A832 by the outward route.

Leitir Fhearna below A' Chailleach

5

Am Faochagach

Am Faochagach (954m) *the heathery place*

Distance 13km
Ascent 720m
Time 5 – 6 hours
Start point OS Grid ref: NH278742
Map OS Explorer 436
Public Transport **Inverness to Ullapool bus service passes the car park**
Terrain & hazards **the start is across a bog followed by a potentially hazardous river crossing; the hill itself is rounded**

Am Faochagach is an undistinguished tongue-twister of a Munro, set amidst vast rolling moorlands north of Loch Glascarnoch. The hill is best left for a dry spell as the start is virtually a swamp, but this ensures it is a quiet hill by Munro standards.

Start from the small parking area just north of Torrandhu bridge on the A835. Cross the road and fence to follow a vague, wet path across the moorland, keeping just left of the flattest part of the glen. Skirt round an area of hummocks to reach the often substantial Abhainn a' Ghrabainn. Take care crossing this river; in spate conditions it can be difficult or even impossible. On the far side follow a faint path round the base of several moraines.

The path becomes clearer as it heads up the east side of Allt na h-Uidhe, becoming drier.

When the upper level of the corrie is reached the going becomes wet once more, diverging from the burn to aim for the bealach north of Sail Liath. From here head north along the gentle ridge, underfoot is grassy with stony patches and provides pleasant walking. There are good views across to Beinn Dearg and Cona' Mheall.

The ridge rises to a broad dome at 844m before a brief dip and then a climb to a shoulder where the ridge coming up from Meall Gorm is joined. It is now only a short ascent to the summit, where Am Faochagach's cairn sits amid a large plateau, robbing the views of any depth, though the distant panorama is extensive. Return by retracing your steps.

Alternatives
The river crossing can be avoided on a longer route by beginning the walk from Strathvaich. Follow the tarmac road towards Strathvaich Lodge before approaching the summit via a very long walk along an undulating, often boggy ridge.

Beinn Dearg

Loch a'
Choire
Ghranda

Carn
Gorm-loch

**Am
Faochagach**

Loch
Coire
Lair

Meall Gorm

S t r a t h v a i c h

Loch a'
Gharbhrain

Allt na h-Uidhe

Sron Liath

F o r e s t

*Abhainn
a' Gharbhrain*

Tom Ban Mor

Loch
Droma

*Torrandhu
Bridge*

Loch
Glascarnoch

A835

0   2km

Creag an Duine from Seana Bhraigh

6

Seana Bhraigh

Seana Bhraigh (926m) *the old height*

Distance **28.5km**
Ascent **1095m**
Time **9 – 10 hours**
Start point **OS Grid ref: NH181852**
Map **OS Explorer 436**
Public transport **Inverness to Ullapool bus service passes the car park**
Terrain & hazards **forestry track and good path for approach, then rough and pathless requiring navigation skills**

Tucked away in the wilds to the north of Beinn Dearg, Seana Bhraigh is a remote summit perched above a spectacular corrie. This long approach is made possible by good paths for much of the distance, but navigation in the later stages could be tricky in poor visibility so the route is best left for a good day.

The walk begins from the same car park as the Beinn Dearg route, and follows the same route as far as Glensguaib. At the fork follow the left track heading steeply uphill and rising in a zigzag. Above a deer fence gate, the route follows a stalkers' path; looking back there are excellent views of majestic An Teallach. After an area of peat hags, drier ground is reached and eventually the route dips to cross the Allt Gleann a' Mhadaidh, potentially impassable in spate conditions.

Loch Broom

Inverlael Farm

Inverlael Forest

Inverlael Bridge

River Lael Glensguaib

Allt Gleann a' Mhadaidh

Gleann na Sguaib

A835

The path now crosses an area of moorland, bleak in poor weather but with extensive views to the Fannichs and even distant Liathach and Beinn Eighe in Torridon on a good day. It climbs low over the northern slopes of Eididh nan Clach Geala before eventually crossing another burn, just below a lochan – a small

cairn on the far side indicates the best crossing spot.

Now head east up a high glen, passing above a series of lovely lochans and some inviting wild camp spots. The path rises gently, but peters out near a small cairn on the flat and featureless watershed beyond. From here, navigation

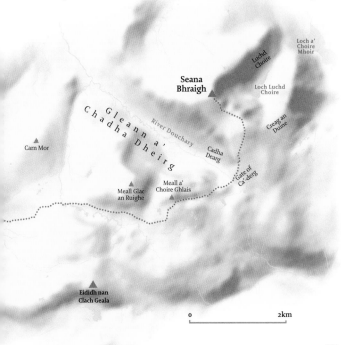

becomes much more challenging.
Aim ENE to descend a rough slope,
keeping to the right of a steep crag.
Once past this, head NE to reach the
headwall above the impressive cliffs of
Cadha Dearg. Follow the rim until you pick
up a path at the Gate of Ca'-derg, where
there is an amazing view back across the
Cadha Dearg.

The path bears north uphill to reach the
Seana Bhraigh plateau. Cross the top to
get superb views down into the dramatic
Luchd Choire, the mountain's finest
feature, then head back from the cliff edge
for the final rise to the summit. Keep an
eye out for the wild goats that graze this
area. The summit itself is marked by a
large wind-shelter cairn – a good place to
stop, take in the view of the isolated peaks
of Assynt and to muster enough energy
for the long walk back by the same route.

Alternatives

The impressive ridge seen enclosing the
opposite side of the Luchd Choire leading
up to Creag an Duine makes a fine but
challenging scramble, approached from
the walkers' car park (outside of stalking
season only) at Corriemulzie Lodge in
Strath Mulzie. For non-scramblers there is
also an easier ascent from the same start
point, reaching the summit from the
north side – scramblers can use this for
their descent.

7

Beinn Dearg
Cona' Mheall
Meall nan Ceapraichean
Eididh nan Clach Geala

Beinn Dearg (1084m) *red hill*
Cona' Mheall (978m) *adjoining hill*
Meall nan Ceapraichean (977m)
rounded hill of stubbly hillocks
Eididh nan Clach Geala (927m)
nest of the white stones

Distance **26km**
Ascent **1590m**
Time **9 – 11 hours**
Start point **OS Grid ref: NH181825**
Map **OS Explorer 436**
Public Transport **Inverness to Ullapool bus service passes the car park**
Terrain & hazards **excellent approach tracks, some boulderfields and scree higher up**

This magnificent walk takes in the four Munros of the Beinn Dearg range, a group of stony, domed peaks in a wild setting with several spectacular hidden corries.

Travelling south from Ullapool you'll find a car park just north of the phonebox and houses on the east side of the road after Inverlael Bridge. Leave the car park to double back through a gate right before turning right onto the private road into Inverlael Forest. Pass a waterworks amongst the trees and ignore tracks leading off on each side, eventually crossing a bridge over the river after about 2km. Keep straight ahead to pass the ruins at Glensguaib; the left branching track is the route to Seana Bhraigh, one of the remotest Munros. Instead continue through the forestry and then follow a stalkers' path up Gleann na Sguaib.

The surroundings become increasingly impressive as you gain height. After 2km the path forks; the left path is used on the return, but for now continue on the main route up the glen. As you reach Coire Mathair Lathail the crags dramatically enclose the south side. Cross the burn on the climb up to Lochan Lathail, a beautiful spot, before continuing up to reach the barren, stony Bealach an Lochain Uaine, littered with tiny lochans.

Three Munros rise above this bealach. To tackle Beinn Dearg first, aim south to join a path which rises up along the west side of a drystone wall, with great views back over Gleann na Sguaib. At a corner bear slightly left to arrive at the huge summit cairn. Standing 1084m high, Beinn Dearg is the tallest Munro north of the A835 and the views are correspondingly extensive, from the Fannichs and An Teallach and up into Assynt.

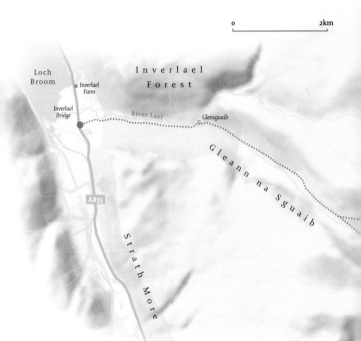

0   2km

Loch
Broom

Inverlael Farm

Inverlael
Bridge

I n v e r l a e l
F o r e s t

River Lael

Glensguaib

G l e a n n   n a   S g u a i b

A835

S t r a t h   M o r e

Return to the bealach, and then bear
slightly east to reach a lower col, with
Coire Ghranda and its fine loch impressive
to the south. From here ascend the scree
slope and then the awkward summit
boulderfield to reach Cona' Mheall. For
many years this was one of the few Munro
summits to remain uncairned, but no
longer. The views remain as wild as ever,
with a superb aspect looking back across
to Beinn Dearg. Return for a third time to
the Bealach an Lochain Uaine, and this

time aim northwest from the lochan
for the easy climb up Meall nan
Ceapraichean. Continue over the minor
bump of Ceann Garbh before descending
towards the lochan-strewn bealach to the
northeast. Care is needed on some steep
rockier sections to avoid bands of crags.

From the bealach the climb up to Eididh
nan Clach Geala leads over grassier slopes.
The summit is worth an extended rest
stop if visibility is clear; the isolated
monoliths of Coigach and Assynt, with

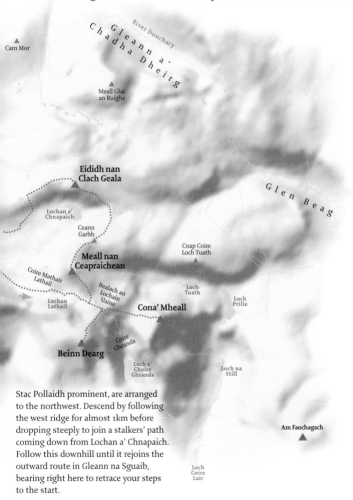

Carn Mor

River Douchary

Gleann a' Chadha Dheirg

Meall Glac an Ruighe

Eididh nan Clach Geala

Glen Beag

Lochan a' Chnapaich

Ceann Garbh

Cnap Coire Loch Tuath

Meall nan Ceapraichean

Coire Mathair Lathail

Bealach an Lochain Uaine

Loch Tuath

Loch Prille

Lochan Lathail

Cona' Mheall

Coire Ghranda

Beinn Dearg

Loch a' Choire Ghranda

Loch na Still

Am Faochagach

Loch Coire Lair

Stac Pollaidh prominent, are arranged to the northwest. Descend by following the west ridge for almost 1km before dropping steeply to join a stalkers' path coming down from Lochan a' Chnapaich. Follow this downhill until it rejoins the outward route in Gleann na Sguaib, bearing right here to retrace your steps to the start.

Beinn Dearg from above Glensguaib

8

An Teallach: Bidein a'Ghlas Thuill Sgurr Fiona

Bidein a' Ghlas Thuill (1062m)
peak of the grey hollow
Sgurr Fiona (1060m) *fair peak*

Distance **19km**
Ascent **1440m**
Time **7 – 11 hours**
Start point **OS Grid ref: NH093879**
Map **OS Explorer 435**
Terrain & hazards **steep and rocky on the upper slopes; the full traverse of the ridge involves hard, exposed scrambling; there are exposed bypass paths, or walkers can return the same way from Sgurr Fiona**

An Teallach is undoubtedly one of the finest mountains in Scotland, giving an unforgettable and dramatic day with unparalleled views. The full traverse involves some challenging scrambling but isn't necessary if the intention is only to climb the two Munros.

There is parking in a large lay-by off the A832 about 250m east of the Dundonnell Hotel. Start by walking a short way along the road (away from the hotel) before turning right onto a path just after a pair of bungalows. The path zigzags up onto the ridge of Meall Garbh. Keep to the old path up this ridge – the newer path round to the Allt a' Mhuilinn is much wetter. After crossing the rocky ridge the path

contours round the smooth slopes at the head of the glen before beginning to climb once more towards Sron a' Choire. On a sunny day the view north over towards the Summer Isles is dazzling.

Continue from Sron a' Choire to reach the bealach at the foot of the north ridge of Bidein a' Ghlas Thuill, almost totally paved with flat sandstone slabs. From here, head south up steep scree and boulders; when the ridge narrows, a short climb to the left leads to the summit, marked by a trig point. The highest of An Teallach's Munros, it has one of the most impressive outlooks amongst all Scottish mountains – Sgurr Fiona and the Corrag Bhuidhe pinnacles make an amazing backdrop to the great gulf of Coire Toll an Lochain.

Head along the rocky ridge, the yawning drop on your left, to descend to a bealach before the steep climb to Sgurr Fiona. Either scramble directly up near the corrie edge or take a scree path across the northern face of Sgurr Fiona to reach its summit up its rocky but easier northwest ridge. The view from here along Corrag Buidhe is impressive, but can't compete with the drama of that first glimpse from Bidein a' Ghlas Thuill.

The traverse of the pinnacles themselves is a tough scramble; there are easier but

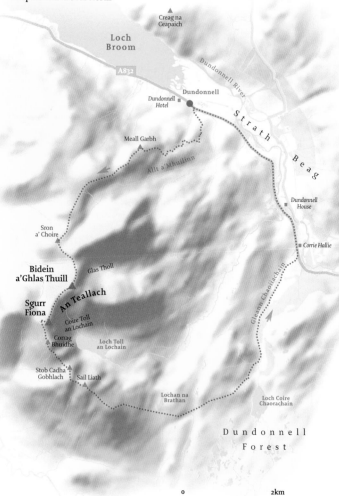

exposed bypass paths on the right flank of the ridge. Fearties may choose to omit the rest of the ridge entirely and retrace their steps to Dundonnell. For those looking to continue using a bypass path, head down the northwest ridge briefly to pick up a clear path leading round to the left; this still has some straightforward scrambling but avoids the pinnacles, rejoining the ridge below Corrag Bhuidhe. If continuing directly along the ridge, the scramble on bare sandstone leads first onto Lord Berkeley's Seat, an awesome pinnacle overhanging Coire Toll an Lochain. Lord Berkeley is supposed to have sat astride this top with his legs dangling over the edge whilst smoking his pipe – not a photo pose we'd recommend. From here the scramble continues over the multiple pinnacles of Corrag Bhuidhe. The final descent off Corrag Bhuidhe is a graded rock climb and has been the scene of several fatal accidents; unless properly equipped and experienced it is necessary to head back a bit to look for a safer way down to the bypass path.

From the Corrag Bhuidhe buttress the scrambling is left behind as the ridge climbs up to Stob Cadha Gobhlach – a good chance to look back on Corrag Bhuidhe. Continue to another bealach before reaching the final peak of Sail Liath. From here a broad ridge descends southeast at first; when it starts to steepen, bear east down the rough slope aiming just south of Lochan na Brathan. Beyond here the stalkers' route reaches a track. Turn left to follow the track all the way back to the A832 at Corrie Hallie. It winds pleasantly downhill, crossing a river with a footbridge and passing through native woodland further down. Unless you have arranged to be picked up, a 3km walk along the road returns to Dundonnell.

An Teallach

9

The Fisherfield Round:
Sgurr Ban
Mullach Coire Mhic Fhearchair
Beinn Tarsuinn
A' Mhaighdean
Ruadh Stac Mor

Sgurr Ban (989m) *white peak*
Mullach Coire Mhic Fhearchair (1019m)
summit of Farquhar's son's corrie
Beinn Tarsuinn (937m) *transverse hill*
A' Mhaighdean (967m) *the maiden*
Ruadh Stac Mor (918m) *big red stack*

Distance 29km circuit from Shenavall;
walk-in to Shenavall 7.5km each way
Ascent 2255m
Time 12 – 18 hours
Start point OS Grid ref: NH065809
(no road access to start)
Map OS Explorer 435
Terrain & hazards steep heathery
hillsides, scree, boulderfields, narrow
ridges, broad grass slopes, some easy
scrambling, potentially dangerous river
crossings – all rounded off with one of the
worst sections of bog you can imagine

The Fisherfield Forest – also known as
the Great Wilderness – contains the
remotest Munros in Scotland. Six great
peaks are arranged around Gleann na
Muice and until recently all were Munros;
Beinn a' Chlaidheimh has been
remeasured at just under 3000 feet.
Whatever their status, climbing all the
hills in a single day is a classic trip with
some of the best views you could
imagine, but in terms of physical effort it
is the crux of any round of the Munros.
It is recommended to stay either at
Shenavall Bothy or a wild camp spot for
two nights, allowing the approach and
exit to be made on the day before and
after – the distances and times given are
for the circular route from Shenavall and
exclude the walk in and out.

This route is described from Shenavall,
a busy open bothy which makes a
convenient base for the round;
alternatively there are a number of wild
camping spots nearby – such as amongst
the trees at NH088788. To reach Shenavall
take the track from Corrie Hallie on the
A832 until you come to a large cairn at the
top of the pass. If heading for a wild camp
you can continue on the track, but for
Shenavall turn right here onto the clear
path which leads over the moor and down
to the bothy. Please remember the bothy

is kept usable only by the efforts of volunteers from the Mountain Bothies Association; it receives lots of visitors so please help by tidying the place up and carrying out any rubbish you find here. As with many others, remember that the bothy is not available during the stag stalking season (15 Sept – 20 Oct).

From here the first peak, Beinn a' Chlaidheimh, rises extremely steeply across Strath na Sealga. Although it is possible to make a direct assault, it is more pleasant to approach it from the east side by first following the path heading ESE from Shenavall. This widens to a track near the half-ruined house at Achneigie, and 1.5km further passes the alder wood that makes the best wild camp spot. Here the track climbs to the left to head back to Corrie Hallie so turn west onto a grassy track to the Abhainn Loch an Nid. This river must be waded; if the water level is too high do not attempt it as there will be similar problems with the two further river crossings at the end of the walk.

On the far bank climb directly up the slopes of Beinn Chlaidheimh. Initial steep and heathery ground gives way to a more gradual ascent until the fierce upper slopes are met at around 500m. Keep left of the crags that guard the prow of the main ridge to reach a flattish shoulder from where there is a short ascent on scree to gain the narrow summit ridge at 900m. From here an airy but grassy ridge leads across a slight dip to reach the cairn

of the summit, with stunning views down the very steep west face and back over the pinnacles of An Teallach.

Head down a scree path to the first of two bealachs at 787m. A broad and bumpy section of ridge leads to a lower bealach at 650m where there are a couple of lochans. Continue south up rough quartzite boulders to reach the broad northeast ridge of Sgurr Ban. The bouldery route up passes a small stone shelter which would be useful in an emergency. Sgurr Ban's summit cairn is in the centre of a small plateau – continue in the same direction to drop down to the bealach at Cab Coire nan Clach. From here the next Munro, Mullach Coire Mhic Fhearchair, looks intimidatingly steep. However, an eroded path leads up scree for the steepest part of the ascent making the going easier than it appears from a distance. Once the gradient lessens a final stony section leads to the summit of the highest mountain on the round.

The descent is time-consuming as it crosses sometimes slippery quartzite boulders. From the next bealach, the steep 851m peak of Meall Garbh looks like a tough climb; however, a narrow bypass path avoids it by cutting across its steep northwestern slopes to reach a second, lower bealach. From here the slopes of Beinn Tarsuinn are broad and grassy; the drama of the far side of this mountain is kept hidden and only revealed as you gain the summit.

From the cairn follow the narrow ridge southwest, soon curving west. At one point the crest of the ridge widens into a rectangular table of relatively flat and grassy ground surrounded by crags – often likened to a tennis court. Following this, the scenery is dramatic with a set of pinnacles ahead, but a clear bypass path runs around the left side. Watch out for a fork in this path and follow the left (west) branch down the steep slope to the wide and very boggy bealach between Beinn Tarsuinn and A' Mhaighdean. This is the lowest point of the entire walk at 525m. Now there is no getting away from the fact that the climb to A' Mhaighdean is a real slog, but the slopes are relatively grassy – and the sudden summit view is a revelation. The cairn sits right on the edge of a vast cliff which plunges 800m down dramatic crags to the Dubh Loch, with Fionn Loch and the sea beyond. This is the remotest of the Munros – many claim it is also the finest viewpoint of them all.

Leave the summit towards the dome-shaped northern top before descending steep but mostly grassy slopes followed by rocky ground to reach the Poll Eadar dha Stac. On the way down try to pick out the line of the route up Ruadh Stac Mor which is easier to see from here. At the bealach a rough stone bivouac could provide some shelter in an emergency. The ascent up the far side looks intimidating from here, barred by a line of crags, but as long as the correct route is

taken there is only very minor scrambling though care is needed as there is much loose rock. A small cairn marks the start up the well-worn scree slope to reach the foot of the cliffs. Now you need to gain an eroded gully above; it is easiest to head right at first, along a ledge from the top of the scree path, and then a big step up leads onto a wide, well-worn stony rake which aims left and then up the gully to emerge amongst the boulderfields above.

From here the going is easier as a vague path winds up over the boulders and through a gap in the summit crags to reach the cairn of Ruadh Stac Mor. If you have the energy to appreciate it, this is another amazing viewpoint, encircled by dramatic rock peaks and glistening lochans. Start the descent by following the WNW ridge for about 250m before aiming directly down to pass between the two lochans to the northeast. From here continue north, following a burn into the hanging valley below. Now cross the burn and aim diagonally up the slope opposite to pick up an excellent stalkers' path above the Clach na Frithealaidh – a prominent rock. It is well worth taking the effort to find the path as the route alongside the water is boggy and rough going.

Bear right along the path towards Loch Beinn Dearg; it soon swings back down into Gleann na Muice Beag, eventually joining a path running along the main Abhainn Ghleann na Muice. Continue downstream until opposite the chalet and cottage in trees at Larachantivore. The river must be waded (a trap for the unwary as it may be impassable after heavy rain), then head directly for Shenavall. There is a path, but the final sting in the tail is that it crosses some of the boggiest ground in all Scotland – care is needed especially in a tired state to avoid a tumble into one of the many deep slime-filled pools. When you meet the Abhainn Srath na Sealga the third and final wade of the day is in order; the bothy is now just a short distance away.

Alternatives

These Munros can also be climbed separately, using a variety of different approaches. Sgurr Ban, Mullach Coire Mhic Fhearchair and Beinn Tarsuinn are sometimes approached from Kinlochewe to the south, first heading to Lochan Fada either by way of Gleann Biannasdail or the Heights of Kinlochewe. The Bealach Odhar is then used to climb the two more southerly of the Munros; including Sgurr Ban involves retracing your steps back over Mullach Coire Mhic Fhearchair.

The best reason for splitting the round is to take in the superb approach to A' Mhaighdean and Ruadh Stac Mor from Poolewe. Stalkers' paths make a memorable approach to the open stable at Carnmore. From here both hills can be reached via a further stalkers' path round the north side of Fuar Loch Mor to Poll Eadar dha Stac. For a more adventurous route leave that for the return and climb A' Mhaighdean via its spectacular pinnacled northwest ridge, requiring some scrambling though the more major obstacles can be bypassed.

Beinn
Dearg Mor

F i s h e r f i e l d   F o r e s t

Loch Beinn
Dearg

Clach na
Frithealaidh

G l e a n n n
M u i c e B e

Lochan Feith
Mhic'-illean

Lochan a'
Bhraghad

Dubh Loch

Fuar Loch
Mor

**Ruadh
Stac Mor**

Poll Eadar
dha Stac

A' Mhaighdean

Gorm Loch
Mor

**Beinn
Tarsuinn**

L e t t e r e w e
F o r e s t

Lochan Fada

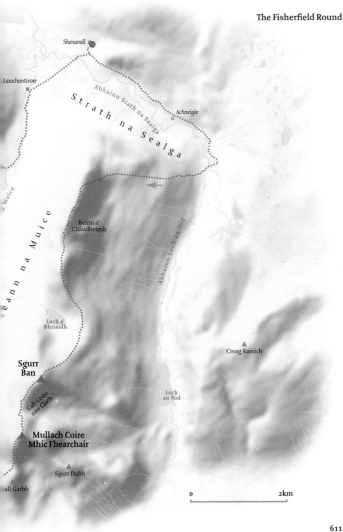

Shenavall

Larachantivore

Abhainn Strath na Sealga

Achneigie

S t r a t h   n a   S e a l g a

Muice

e a n n   n a   M u i c e

Beinn a' Chlaidheimh

Abhainn Loch an Nid

Loch a' Bhrisidh

Creag Rainich

Sgurr Ban

Cab Coire nan Clach

Loch an Nid

Mullach Coire Mhic Fhearchair

Sgurr Dubh

all Garbh

0   2km

Looking north to A' Mhaighdean over Lochan Fada from Slioch

10

Ben More Assynt Conival

Ben More Assynt (998m) *big hill of Assynt*
Conival (987m) *adjoining hill*

Distance **17km**
Ascent **1265m**
Time **7 – 9 hours**
Start point **OS Grid ref: NC251216**
Map **OS Explorer 442**
Public transport **bus to Inchnadamph from Ullapool and Inverness**
Terrain & hazards **the upper slopes are very rugged and littered with quartzite scree**

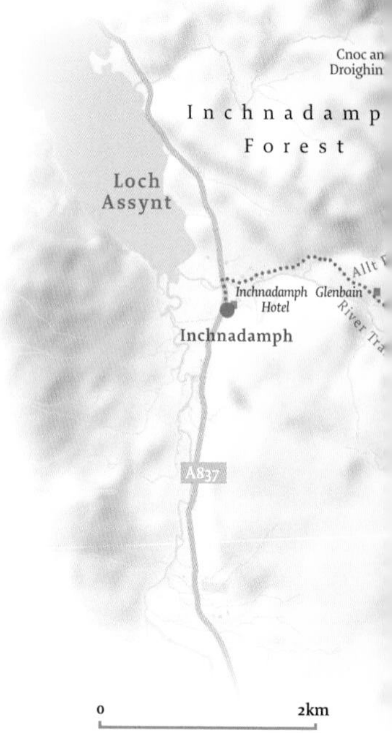

Ben More Assynt and Conival are the only Munros in an area packed with some of Scotland's most remarkable hills. Linked by a fine ridge, they offer a rocky and wild outing with amazing views.

Start from the car park near the Inchnadamph Hotel. Head back to the A837 and follow it briefly north, turning right onto a private road once across the bridge over the River Traligill. This passes Inchnadamph Lodge which now houses a comfortable hostel and field centre. Go through the gate and follow the road, crossing the Allt Poll an Droighinn and later reaching the isolated cottage at Glenbain.

Continue up the glen, keeping left at a fork shortly after a forestry plantation. The right-hand path leads to the Traligill caves, a haunt popular with pot-holers – this is limestone country and the most popular caving area in Scotland. Keep on the north side of Gleann Dubh, which becomes narrower and steeper-sided whilst the going is often wet underfoot.

Take a steeper ascent up the left side of the Allt a' Choinne Mhill to reach a small hanging valley. Aim for the bealach between Conival and Beinn an Fhurain beyond. First cross the burn and bear slightly right to scramble easily up a rocky band en route to the bealach – a few cairns help mark the way. The reward is a

Loch Bealach
a' Mhadaidh

roighinn

G l e a n n   D u b h

Beinn an
Fhurain

Na Tuadhan

Coire a'
Mhadaidh

**Ben More
Assynt**

caves

Allt a' Choinne Mhill

Conival

Loch
Mhaolach-
coire

Dubh Loch
More

Breabag

B e n m o r e   F o r e s t

view down the far side of the bealach into Coire a' Mhadaidh, its lochan overshadowed by the imposing quartzite buttresses of Na Tuadhan.

Now head up the quartzite scree slopes onto a more defined section of ridge. This curves left to reach the summit of Conival at a junction of three ridges. The wind-shelter cairn has grand views, with the east ridge to Ben More Assynt beckoning onwards. Narrow and bouldery, it involves

an easy scramble on the descent to the intervening bealach. The rise beyond crosses more scree to reach the summit of Ben More Assynt. At 998m this Munro is the highest over a vast area of wild mountainous terrain.

Although the south ridge may look tempting it is a challenging scramble and far from the start, so the best bet for the return route is to retrace your steps over Conival and back to Inchnadamph.

Conival from near Inchnadamph

11

Ben Hope

Ben Hope (927m) *hill of the bay*

Distance **7.5km**
Ascent **945m**
Time **4 – 6 hours**
Start point **OS Grid ref: NC462476**
Map **OS Explorer 447**
Terrain & hazards **steep and rocky ascent in places**

The most northerly of the Munros, Ben Hope is a fine isolated peak, often left late in the bagger's Munro schedule. The ascent is short, but provides an excellent introduction to a stunningly beautiful part of Scotland. Although some baggers combine the ascent with Ben Klibreck later in the day, this corner of Sutherland has a great deal more to offer walkers than just its two Munros.

Start from the car park on the minor road up Strathmore, 3km south of the head of Loch Hope. It's hard to miss the path, given the massive signpost; it heads directly uphill from the car park. The path is soon climbing alongside the south bank of the tumbling Allt a' Mhuiseil; confusingly, the OS map shows the path on the opposite side of the burn.

The gradient eases off for a short while as the burn leads you north. Soon the route leaves the water to head east uphill once more. This section is steeper and it is necessary to weave about to avoid the crags, but the views up Strathmore provide an excuse for a breather.

Emerging on the broad south ridge of Ben Hope, which is defined by the steep escarpment on its western side, the sometimes eroded path is followed up the grassy slopes. A steep ascent is followed by an easier section before the final climb to the small summit plateau. Amid the mass of boulders is the summit trig point; this is the highest point for miles around, and the steep drops to the north and west help ensure it is a fantastic viewpoint. The sheer remoteness of the lochan-dotted landscape can be appreciated from here, beckoning any number of backpacking and shorter trips now that the big Munro is in the bag. The plateau ends abruptly, with the extremely steep and airy north ridge plummeting beyond and great walls of crags on each flank. The easiest return route is to head back the same way.

Alternatives

From the summit the route can be extended by continuing along the escarpment of Leitir Mhuiseil to the south and then descending beyond the fine waterfall above Alltnacaillich, eventually following the road back for the final 2km to the start.

Ben Hope from the north appears as a sharp pyramid towering over Loch Hope; usually enough to discourage most hillwalkers from attempting an approach from this direction.

Loch
Hope

Dubh-loch
na Beinne

Loch na
Seilg

Ben Hope

An Garbh-
Choire

Loch a'
Ghobha-
Dhuibh

An Gorm-loch

Allt a' Mhuiseil

Strathmore River

Leitir Mhuiseil

S t r a t h   M o r e

Alltnacaillich

0   2km

Ben Hope

12

Ben Klibreck

Ben Klibreck (961m) *hill of the cliff slope*

Distance **14km**
Ascent **750m**
Time **5 – 7 hours**
Start point **OS Grid ref: NC532271**
Map **OS Explorer 443**
Terrain & hazards **some boggy ground on approach and a final steeper ascent**

Ben Klibreck rises alone above the vast, empty moorlands that characterise central Sutherland. This ascent route is rough and longer than the usual more direct approach, but makes use of a broad ridge to avoid the worst of the extensive bogs.

About 2.5km north of the Crask Inn or 150m south of Vagastie Bridge on the A836 there is a parking lay-by. Start up the rough hillside, with some faint ATV tracks, towards Cnoc Sgriodain, soon passing through a steel gate. Continue climbing east to reach a cairn.

Heading along the ridge, you pass a second cairn and then the ridge dips to a bealach; there are some peat hags to negotiate. Part way up Creag an Lochain it is possible to pick up a path which traverses its western flank to bypass the summit. Once at the next bealach, marked as point 688m on OS maps, the more popular direct route joins from the left. Although shorter, this route has a very steep climb to gain the ridge at this point, as well as unrelenting bogs lower down as it leads past Loch Bad an Loch.

The route along the ridge of A'Chioch is now easy going and soon curves east for the final straightforward pull up to Meall nan Con, the highest point of Ben Klibreck. The top is crowned with both a summit cairn and trig point; the view is one of total desolation. The best return option is to retrace the outward route. It can be varied with a visit to the summit of Creag an Lochain which has good views down to Loch an Fhuarain. The Crask Inn makes an atmospheric place for a pint afterwards or as a base for a fuller exploration of the area.

Crask Inn

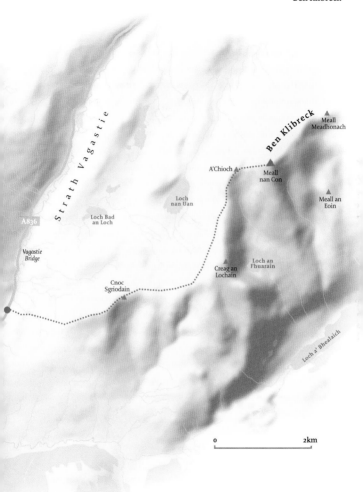

Strath Vagastie

Ben Klibreck

Meall
Meadhonach

A'Chioch
Meall
nan Con

Meall an
Eoin

Loch
nan Uan

A836

Loch Bad
an Loch

Loch an
Fhuarain

Vagastie
Bridge

Creag an
Lochain

Cnoc
Sgriodain

Loch a' Bhealaich

0   2km

The Islands: Skye and Mull

Isle of Skye

The sheer size of Skye can surprise first-time visitors and if Munros are your only objective it is best to base yourself at Sligachan, Carbost, Glenbrittle or Portree to avoid long drives to reach the start of the routes. However, west coast island weather is notoriously fickle so it's best to have a few alternatives; if things get really wet maybe it is better just to soak up the angels' share at Talisker Distillery.

Accommodation options have grown enormously in the last few decades with a good selection of independent hostels, B&Bs, self-catering and even boutique hotels. It is still best to book in the peak season as unlucky visitors have been known to resort to sleeping in their cars.

If you can tough it out with the midges there are good campsites at Sligachan and Glenbrittle, both on the doorstep of the Cuillin. Sligachan has the advantage of the hotel and bar, as well as a nearby bunkhouse, although Glenbrittle boasts a decent beach and is a more attractive spot. Nearby Carbost makes an excellent base, home to Skye's peaty Talisker malt. The Old Inn is recommended for food, beer and music and has an idyllically situated bunkhouse overlooking Loch Harport.

Portree to the north has the most facilities and places to eat, though even here the B&Bs can all be full in the summer. The sloping campsite just outside the village at Torvaig is friendly and very well run, offering unlimited hot showers to revive aching limbs. The Caledonian Café serves traditional, filling fare whilst Café Arriba offers cakes, breakfasts and bistro-style meals in the evening. Inside Out sells a good range of walking and climbing gear. Broadford is the other main centre on the island with useful facilities, including Magpie which sells outdoor gear, and is close to Torrin and Elgol for Bla Bheinn or a boat trip into Loch Coruisk in the heart of the Cuillin. Check out the Waterfront for Skye's best fish and chips or the Claymore for hearty pub food.

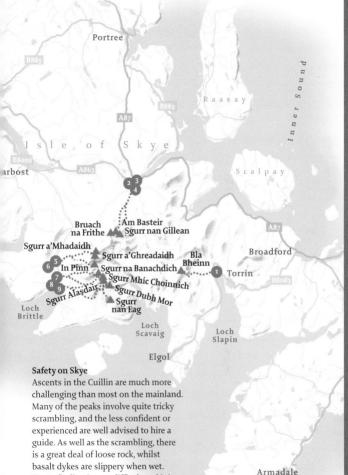

Safety on Skye

Ascents in the Cuillin are much more
challenging than most on the mainland.
Many of the peaks involve quite tricky
scrambling, and the less confident or
experienced are well advised to hire a
guide. As well as the scrambling, there
is a great deal of loose rock, whilst
basalt dykes are slippery when wet.
Route-finding is very difficult and it is
best to wait for clear weather. Note also
that the rocks are magnetic, making
compass readings unreliable.

Sgurr nan Gillean and Bla Bheinn across Loch Scavaig

Mull

Mull can be a barometer of how single-minded a Munro-bagger you are – do you aim to arrive on the island, climb the highest peak, Ben More, and be back on the ferry as soon as possible or do you decide to savour the other hills and superb coastal walking on offer?

There is a choice of ferry routes; the longer and more expensive (considerably so in summer with a car) route from Oban to Craignure or a shorter hop from Lochaline on the Morvern peninsula – a good option if coming from the north or the Fort William area. There is no accommodation directly at the start point for Ben More, but Salen, Craignure and Tobermory all make good bases, Salen being the most central. If time allows, trips to Iona for the abbey and seaweed-munching cows on the pristine white beaches, or cruises to the dramatic columns of Fingal's Cave on Staffa and the puffins on Lunga are well worth taking. Watching white-tailed eagles at the Glen Seilisdeir hide (or anywhere on the island if you're lucky) is also very popular and must be booked in advance.

Lochaline

Sound of Mull

Duart Bay

Craignure

f Mull

A849

Oban

Kerrera

Firth of Lorn

A816

B844

Bla Bheinn

Bla Bheinn (928m) *blue hill*

Distance **8km**
Ascent **990m**
Time **5 – 6 hours**
Start point **OS Grid ref: NG560215**
Map **OS Explorer 411**
Public transport **bus from Broadford**
Terrain & hazards **path for first part of the route; higher up the going is rocky with some loose ground; with careful route finding only a very slight scramble is required**

One of the most magnificent mountains in Britain, Bla Bheinn (or Blaven as it is often called) rises alone, completely separate from the main Cuillin Ridge, though it shares its character. It is a relatively straightforward ascent by Skye Munro standards.

The car park for Bla Bheinn is signed up above the B8083 just south of the bridge over the Allt na Dunaiche. From here, cross back over the bridge to find the start of an excellent path that climbs up the other side of the Allt na Dunaiche. This leads through two gates and passes above the rim of a steep wooded gorge.

After 1.5km the path crosses the burn, and 300m further on crosses a tributary before becoming stony and eroded on the steeper climb up Coire Uaigneich. When you reach the grassy bowl of Fionna-choire, ignore a path continuing ahead and instead turn sharp right to zigzag up the steep slopes once you have passed the edge of the cliffs.

A loose scree gully provides the easiest route for the middle part of the ascent. Further up the gully, climb out on the left side to find a clearer path up the now grassier slopes which rise to the rim of Bla Bheinn's eastern cliffs, where superb views are revealed to the north. The route is more obvious from here, continuing up the slope to the left and passing a dramatic gash in the cliff where the Great Prow, a famed climbers' crag, is revealed.

At a small cairn there is a view across to the shapely peak of Clach Glas – a moderate rock climb even by the easiest route. The way to Bla Bheinn's summit funnels up through a gully with a slight scramble at the top to exit; the cairn is then just a short walk away. Endless sea, mountains and islands can be seen in all directions, but it is only at the last moment that the main Cuillin Ridge is revealed across the immense void of Glen Sligachan. The easiest and quickest return to the start is by the route of ascent.

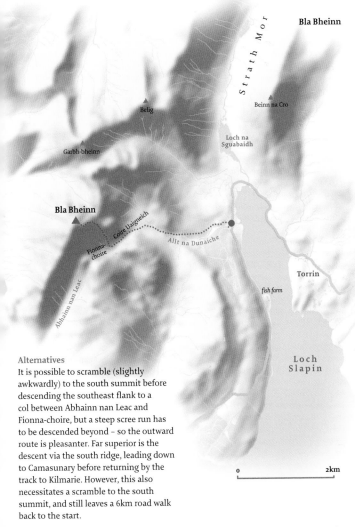

Bla Bheinn

S t r a t h   M o r

Beinn na Cro

Belig

Loch na
Sguabaidh

Garbh-bheinn

Bla Bheinn

Coire Uaigneich

Fionna-
choire

Allt na Dunaiche

Torrin

fish farm

Abhainn nan Leac

Loch
Slapin

Alternatives

It is possible to scramble (slightly
awkwardly) to the south summit before
descending the southeast flank to a
col between Abhainn nan Leac and
Fionna-choire, but a steep scree run has
to be descended beyond – so the outward
route is pleasanter. Far superior is the
descent via the south ridge, leading down
to Camasunary before returning by the
track to Kilmarie. However, this also
necessitates a scramble to the south
summit, and still leaves a 6km road walk
back to the start.

0   2km

Bla Bheinn

Bruach na Frithe

Bruach na Frithe (958m)
slope of the deer forest

Distance **13.5km**
Ascent **940m**
Time **5 – 7 hours**
Start point **OS Grid ref: NG484296**
Map **OS Explorer 411**
Public transport **Sligachan is well served by both local and long-distance buses**
Terrain & hazards **very rocky and rough with scree**

Bruach na Frithe is often the first Cuillin peak to be tackled by Munro-baggers and provides a good introduction to the range. The ascent is easier than most of its neighbours, but it still makes an exceptionally rough walk with difficult navigation in poor conditions.

Take the Dunvegan road from Sligachan to find a parking lay-by on the left, just beyond the start of a track to a cottage. Start by walking along the track towards the white cottage before turning right at a signed path. This follows the Allt Dearg Mor as it rises, soon giving a good view of Pinnacle Ridge on Sgurr nan Gillean. After 3km a cairn marks the place to leave the path and cross the water. Now climb the grassy lower slopes of Fionn Choire. Bruach na Frithe can be seen on the right at the head of this great bowl. Keep climbing and cross the burn after which the route becomes vague for a time before a clearer path ascends the rocky ground and scree on the left (east) side of the corrie, finally heading up steep scree to reach the Bealach na Lice.

This is a confusing place in mist. The rocky sentinel of the Basteir Tooth dominates the scene, whilst to the right is the rock peak of Sgurr a' Fionn Choire. The peak to the north is Sgurr a' Bhasteir; which can be included by a short detour along an airy ridge, rewarded with an amazing view of Sgurr nan Gillean and its Pinnacle Ridge. To get to the summit of Bruach na Frithe, follow the scree path below Sgurr a' Fionn Choire, remaining below the ridgeline until any rocky obstacles are behind you. On the final climb to the summit the easiest route is to keep left of the low crags. Bruach na Frithe has amazing views along the Cuillin Ridge in both directions.

The most straightforward way back is to return the same way, but it is possible to descend the northwest ridge as an alternative. This ridge is normally regarded as a moderate scramble, but in descent the difficulties can be bypassed on a path to the left. This heads along the west side of the northwest ridge and descends well below the crest on scree and rough ground. It is easier to follow in descent and doesn't involve any real scrambling. Further down, the ridge is regained for a narrow traverse reminiscent of Striding Edge in the Lake District. At the end of the ridge the land falls away more steeply. The worst of any scree can be avoided by sticking to the northern

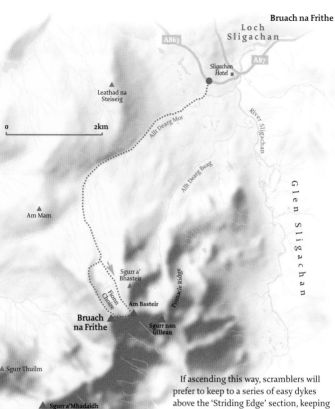

If ascending this way, scramblers will prefer to keep to a series of easy dykes above the 'Striding Edge' section, keeping much closer to the ridge crest. After passing the steepest part of the ridge the path returns to the crest for the final narrow approach to the summit.

Alternatives

It is possible to combine Bruach na Frithe with an ascent of Am Basteir (see following pages).

spur rather than the northwest one to reach a flatter, grassier area. From here it is easy to walk down the grassy slope on the right to rejoin the ascent path near where it crossed the burn at the foot of Fionn Choire.

Am Basteir and Bruach na Frithe

3

Am Basteir

Am Basteir (934m)
the executioner, or *the deep cleft*

Distance **14km**
Ascent **1175m**
Time **5 – 6 hours**
Start point **OS Grid ref: NG484296**
Map **OS Explorer 411**
Public transport **Sligachan is well served by both local and long-distance buses**
Terrain & hazards **the ascent of Am Basteir is a slightly unnerving and difficult scramble with tricky route finding; the remainder of the route is easier, but has steep scree and is still exceptionally rough**

The usual translation of Am Basteir as 'The Executioner' is enough to strike fear into most. This spectacular fin of rock, together with its formidable 'Tooth', makes one of the most instantly-recognisable skylines in Scotland. The ascent is a hard scramble on a narrow ridge with great precipices all around.

Start from Sligachan, using the lay-by on the right on the road to Dunvegan, taking care not to block access to the Mountain Rescue post. Follow the path on the opposite side of the road which soon leads to a bridge. Cross this and continue uphill, coming to another bridge after 2km. Do not cross this time but keep on the west side of the burn. When the path swings round to the left there is a magnificent view of the entrance to the Basteir Gorge, with the Pinnacle Ridge on

Sgurr nan Gillean towering above – surely amongst the most impressive scenes in Britain. The route climbs the steep slopes to the west side of the gorge, keeping to the left edge of a scree slope. Higher up, zigzag to follow small ramps to left and right, with short, easy sections of scrambling. Care is needed to find the route as the path is not clear on the rocky sections.

As the ground levels out, traverse rocky terrain to reach the river once more and then climb over the lip into the bowl of Coire Basteir. This is an atmospheric place, with great walls of rock rising on all sides. Climb out of the corrie using a scree path which starts on the east side of the corrie, just past the foot of a gully coming down from the col between the two highest peaks of Sgurr nan Gillean. This path reaches the foot of the cliffs of Am Basteir. From here continue up the steeper scree slopes to the left, passing an outcrop before slanting left to reach the Bealach Basteir between Sgurr nan Gillean and Am Basteir.

Now head up the ridge to the right towards Am Basteir. Aim left off this ridge onto a faint ledge path after a short distance, just before it starts to steepen. Traverse across to an orange-hued slab seen ahead, climbing it to continue leftwards. After crossing a wall, you bear right up a ramp of purple-hued rock. This returns you to the ridge, which from this point leads more easily to the summit. An

alternative route keeps on the main ridge until just before a vertical drop (the direct descent of which has been made difficult – becoming a rock climb – following rockfalls in recent years). From here it is possible to descend loose rakes on the Harta Corrie side until you can drop down to the ramp below and follow this back up to the ridge at the foot of the difficult section. The very airy summit is then reached without further difficulties.

From the summit return to Bealach Basteir by the same route and then back down below the cliffs. From here you simply follow the outward route to Sligachan. Alternatively, the return can be varied by heading to Bealach na Lice from where it would also be possible to add Bruach na Frithe to the day's Munro tally. To take this route head up the screes, keeping Am Basteir and then the Tooth on your left, to reach the bealach. Now either pass below Sgurr a' Fionn-choire to take in Bruach na Frithe, or descend on the clear path into Fionn Choire. When you reach the grassy floor, follow occasional cairns until you pick up the path again by a large cairn at the burn crossing. Soon you meet the main path up to the Am Mam pass – bear right along this to head back to Sligachan.

Alternatives
None unless you are a competent rock-climber!

Am Basteir and Sgurr nan Gillean

4

Sgurr nan Gillean

Sgurr nan Gillean (964m)
peak of the young men

Distance **12km**
Ascent **985m**
Time **5 – 7 hours**
Start point **OS Grid ref: NG484296**
Map **OS Explorer 411**
Public transport **Sligachan is well served by both local and long-distance buses**
Terrain & hazards **tricky route finding in poor visibility; the final scramble is hard and exposed**

The most celebrated of the Cuillin, the elegant peak of Sgurr nan Gillean is instantly recognisable from afar. The classic view from Sligachan actually hides its most impressive feature, the saw-toothed Pinnacle Ridge. Munro-baggers may find this summit is one of the trickiest to reach, with the southeast ridge being the only route that doesn't involve rock-climbing – and even that is a hard and exposed scramble.

From Sligachan head a short way along the Dunvegan road and use the parking in a lay-by on the right – take care not to block access to the Mountain Rescue post. Start up the path on the far side of the road, soon crossing a new bridge and following a well-made footpath. After 2km fork left across another footbridge and continue uphill.

At a cairn ignore a smaller path that branches right (for Pinnacle Ridge), instead continuing on the main path

which descends slightly into Coire Riabhach. Cross the head of the corrie, keeping well above Loch a' Choire Riabhaich, in the shadow of Marsco and Bla Bheinn on the other side of Glen Sligachan. Zigzag up a slightly loose slope before the path levels out and contours round into a second hanging corrie, ringed by crags. Aim for the obvious wide scree gully on the far side. After some distance up this gully the main scree slope heads up to the right. Leave it and aim up the boulders on the left slope towards a small cairn on the horizon. On reaching the cairn an indistinct route across the boulders climbs uphill to the right. You should soon reach the bottom of a large rock slab, with cairns marking a route along the bottom to the right. Ignore these and keep left of the crag, following a faint path with small cairns. It becomes clearer as it makes its way up the scree slope before eventually breaking left onto the ridge.

Head along the ridge; any difficulties can initially be avoided on the left. Many walkers will appreciate an experienced companion – and perhaps a rope – to complete the final section. There is an awkward step up at the back of a gully and a very steep section which can either be climbed fairly directly up the ridge, or on less steep but more exposed and less reliable sloping rocks out to the left. Above this, the ridge levels off and narrows to a single slab shortly before

Sgurr nan Gillean

Loch Sligachan

A863

A87

Sligachan Hotel

Leathad na Steiseig

Allt Dearg Mor

Allt Dearg Beag

River Sligachan

Am Mam

Glen Sligachan

Sgurr a' Bhasteir

Fionn Choire

Pinnacle Ridge

Am Basteir

Bruach na Frithe

Sgurr nan Gillean

0   2km

Sgurr a'Mhadaidh

Sgurr a'Ghreadaidh

the top – the slab has been well polished by walkers shuffling across on their bums.

The airy summit of Sgurr nan Gillean is just beyond. From here none of the supporting ridges can be seen which gives a feeling of floating in the sky. Unless an experienced rock-climber, the only route down is by reversing the ascent – even trickier in this direction.

Alternatives

Any alternative routes are for competent rock-climbers only.

Sgurr nan Gillean from Marsco

5

Sgurr a'Ghreadaidh Sgurr a'Mhadaidh

Sgurr a' Ghreadaidh (973m)
peak of thrashing
Sgurr a' Mhadaidh (918m) *the peak of fox*

Distance **9.5km**
Ascent **1000m**
Time **6 – 8 hours**
Start point **OS Grid ref: NG409225**
Map **OS Explorer 411**
Terrain & hazards **steep scree to An Dorus; tricky exposed scrambling on the ridges**

Twin-topped Sgurr a'Ghreadaidh is the highest peak on the northern half of the Cuillin Ridge; combined with its neighbour Sgurr a'Mhadaidh it makes a superb day out with some testing scrambling in dramatic positions.

Start from Glenbrittle Youth Hostel (Hostelling Scotland) – there is parking on the verge of the road either side of the bridge. Take the excellent path up the south side of the burn, passing a series of waterfalls. After 2km the route becomes more eroded and then crosses the burn either below or above a massive waterslide before continuing up the far bank. Coire a'Ghreadaidh looks very dramatic from here, with a great gorge issuing from the upper corrie. This route, however, follows the path beside a branch stream heading up to the left, leading towards the more northerly Coire An Dorus.

Sgurr a'Mhadaidh and Sgurr a'Ghreadaidh can be seen directly ahead, with a steep chute between them leading up to An Dorus. Meaning 'The Door' in Gaelic, An Dorus is the lowest point on the ridge between the two peaks. Pass through a dry gorge to pick up the start of a path which zigzags up the steep scree towards An Dorus. Do not be tempted to aim for the higher, even narrower col further south, which is the Eag Dubh or 'Black Cleft'.

The gully narrows part way up and then again near the top, after which the floor is made up of slabby rocks requiring some scrambling. The first part of the route onto Sgurr a'Mhadaidh from the top of An Dorus is a very steep and awkward scramble. It can be avoided by instead leaving the An Dorus gully to the north just before the final narrowing. A faint path slants easily upwards to the left (north) and continues in the same direction for 150m before rounding a corner where the ridge leading from Sgurr Thuilm up to Sgurr a'Mhadaidh comes into view across a wide bowl. Now there is only very simple scrambling to the right to reach a wide and easy scree slope. The cairn visible way over to the right is at the top of the hard section from An Dorus. Continue up the scree on the left to gain the crest of the ridge and continue, with further scrambling, to

Am Mam

Am Basteir

Beinn a'
Bhraghad

Bruach
na Frithe

Sgurr nan
Gillean

Glen Brittle

Sgurr Thuilm

Coire a'
Ghreadaidh

Sgurr a'Mhadaidh

An
Dorus

Allt a' Choire Ghreadaidh

Sgurr a'Ghreadaidh

Sgurr Thormaid

Glenbrittle
Youth Hostel

Sgurr na
Banachdich

Inaccessible
Pinnacle

Loch
Coruisk

Sgurr
Mhic Choinnich

Glenbrittle
Campsite

Sgurr Alasdair

Sgurr
Dubh Mor

Loch
Brittle

0   2km

reach the tiny summit cairn and an amazing view down to Loch Coruisk.

From here the ridge to Sgurr a'Ghreadaidh looks very intimidating. Return to An Dorus (either via the direct tricky scramble or the easier route described above). Climbing out the south side of An Dorus is a very steep scramble initially and a rope may be needed for protection, especially if the rock is wet. Once over this first step, the scrambling is more straightforward. Pass the great gash of the Eag Dubh to the left. The next obstacle is a great boss of rock known as the Wart, but this is avoided to the right over slabby rocks and the summit is not far beyond. The views are superb, especially the sensationally exposed arête which leads to the south peak. The simplest return is to retrace your steps to An Dorus.

Alternatives

From the summit of Sgurr a' Ghreadaidh, keen and experienced scramblers (only) can continue traversing the ridge. This is a committing option as there are no practical descent routes until Sgurr na Banachdich, a whole 1km of scrambling further on. There is nothing on the ridge that is more difficult than the climb out of An Dorus, but the exposure can be breathtaking. This route starts by crossing the airy arête to Sgurr a'Ghreadaidh's south summit – the easiest way is to keep slightly to the right of the true ridgeline, but whatever route is taken will require a great head for heights. The scrambling continues down to a dip in the ridge, before ascending again towards a group of pinnacles known as the Three Teeth – these are avoided to the right. The next peak, Sgurr Thormaid (Norman's Peak, named after Norman Collie, one of the great pioneers of climbing in the Cuillin), looks intimidating. The ascent route is directly up the edge of the slab. Scramble down from the top into Bealach Thormaid, passing right of some small pinnacles, before the final ascent up to Sgurr na Banachdich (see the Sgurr na Banachdich pages for descent routes).

6

Sgurr na Banachdich

Sgurr na Banachdich (965m)
milkmaid's peak

Distance 8km
Ascent 950m
Time 5 – 7 hours
Start point OS Grid ref: NG409225
Map OS Explorer 411
Terrain & hazards **extremely rugged and rocky hillwalk with much steep, rough ground; no hands-on sections**

Sgurr na Banachdich ranks with Bruach na Frithe as one of the easier summits on the Cuillin ridge. No real hands-on scrambling is needed – but the usual unforgiving Cuillin terrain still means a great deal of bare rock and scree, as well as challenging navigation in poor conditions.

Start from the Glenbrittle Youth Hostel (Hostelling Scotland) – there is space to park either side of the bridge. Follow the well-constructed path up the south side of the burn, passing a series of cascading waterfalls. After just over 1km look out for a faint, slightly muddy path forking to the right, passing a large boulder after 200m and continuing across the moor. If you miss this path you can continue to the Allt Coir' an Eich and follow that uphill – though the path is clearer by the burn, underfoot conditions are much rougher.

Cross the water at the foot of Coir an Eich to aim up the steepening grass and then stony slopes that form a ridge leading up to An Diallaid (again, this is much more enjoyable that the steep zigzag scree path at the back of the corrie). When the ridge levels off it becomes grassy again before a final pull up scree to the prominent crag of An Diallaid. The steep section can be avoided by bearing right across the grassy slopes to pick up the path from Coir' an Eich. Now aim for the shallow col between An Diallaid and the main bulk of Sgurr na Banachdich. Twin-summited Sgurr a'Ghreadaidh is revealed across upper Coire a'Ghreadaidh. Continue up the ill-defined ridge towards the summit, keeping the cliffs on your left. The going gets much rockier as you approach the summit but it is only at the last moment as you gain the ridge crest that the stupendous gulf down to Loch Coruisk is revealed. The summit cairn is just a short distance to the right.

This is a wonderful spot on a fine day. To the north the Cuillin Ridge drops over the sharp peak of Sgurr Thormaid and its teeth before sweeping up again to the bulk of Sgurr a'Ghreadaidh, with Sgurr nan Gillean visible beyond. To the east stately Bla Bheinn is seen beyond Coruisk. Looking south the narrow ridge leads the eye to Sgurr Dearg where climbers may be seen tackling the Inaccessible Pinnacle. Beyond it, the jagged teeth of Sgurr Thearlach and Sgurr Alasdair mark the highest summits in the Hebrides. Rum and Canna dot the Hebridean sea. Once you have soaked up the atmosphere the easiest return is by the same outward route.

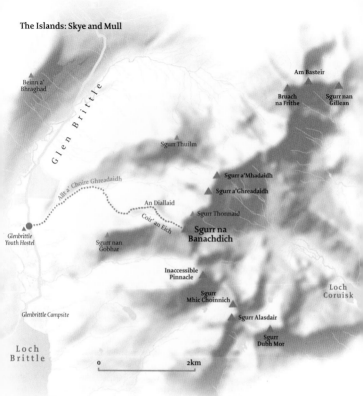

Beinn a'
Bhraghad

Glen Brittle

Allt a' Choire Ghreadaidh

Glenbrittle
Youth Hostel

Sgurr Thuilm

An Diallaid

Coir' an Eich

Sgurr nan
Gobhar

Glenbrittle Campsite

**Loch
Brittle**

Am Basteir

Bruach
na Frithe

Sgurr nan
Gillean

Sgurr a'Mhadaidh

Sgurr a'Ghreadaidh

Sgurr Thormaid

**Sgurr na
Banachdich**

Inaccessible
Pinnacle

Sgurr
Mhic Choinnich

Sgurr Alasdair

Sgurr
Dubh Mor

**Loch
Coruisk**

0   2km

Alternatives

Scramblers may wish to descend the Sgurr nan Gobhar ridge. This involves some fairly straightforward but airy scrambling, followed by a steep scree descent. Most of the scrambling occurs on the steep descent following the first easy section. At the end of the ridge is the summit of Sgurr nan Gobhar (Peak of the Goats), almost encircled by crags. The descent

route is down the steep, extensive screes to the southwest and requires great care.

Sgurr na Banachdich can also be linked to Sgurr a'Ghreadaidh by hard, exposed scrambling. Finally the ridge linking to Sgurr Dearg is also a possibility for scramblers; the hardest sections over the 'Teeth' can be avoided.

Sgurr nan Gobhar ridge

Sgurr Dearg and Sgurr Mhic Choinnich

7

Inaccessible Pinnacle Sgurr Mhic Choinnich

Inaccessible Pinnacle (986m)
Sgurr Mhic Choinnich (948m)
mackenzie's peak

Distance **10km**
Ascent **1150m**
Time **6 – 8 hours**
Start point **OS Grid ref: NG411216**
Map **OS Explorer 411**
Terrain & hazards **rock-climbing skills, experience and equipment needed; the descent of the In Pinn also requires an abseil**

The Inaccessible Pinnacle is, for many walkers, the ultimate obstacle to completing the Munros. Hiring a professional climbing guide is the best option for most, unless you have a friend with rock-climbing skills, experience and equipment. Adjacent is Sgurr Mhic Choinnich, another of the trickier Cuillin Munros – so you might as well make the most of that guide!

Start from a parking area opposite the Glenbrittle Memorial Hut. Follow the road towards the sea for 50m until a large footpath heads off left next to sheep pens. Cross a bridge over the Allt Coire na Banachdich and continue uphill. Higher up the path runs close to the rim of a great bowl where the 24m-high Eas Mor cascades into a tree-filled gorge.

Keep left at a fork and follow the burn for 2km. The going gets rougher and the route passes through a narrow gully, with Window Buttress impressive on the right, before reaching the upper bowl of Coire na Banachdich. The direct route out of the corrie is barred by cliffs avoided by a circuitous route to the right. Cross the burn and then head up its far bank, zigzagging up broken rock and scree as the ground steepens and the route passes high above the gorge of the burn. When you reach a cliff, bear right along its base on a vague path until a wide stony gully – usually marked by cairns – points the way through. Higher up, cross more broken rocks to reach the craggy headwall of the corrie. This time traverse left below the cliffs for quite some distance, ignoring a scree gully heading up the crags. There is a faint path, descending slightly at one point to cross boulders. Beyond this aim right up steep scree and stones to the lowest point on the whole Cuillin Ridge, the Bealach Coire na Banachdich. It is a narrow steep-sided gully with orange-hued soil. It is possible to end up at a second bealach slightly to the north which does not have the distinctive orange soil. If this happens you have gone too far - follow your steps back down the scree before climbing again to reach the Bealach Coire na Banachdich.

Scramble out of the bealach up the right-hand wall which has good footholds, though the rocks can be slippery when

The Inaccessible Pinnacle

wet. The ridge then becomes easier, narrowing briefly with views of the steep north face of Sgurr Dearg before a path zigzags up the broad scree slope. This emerges suddenly at the summit of Sgurr Dearg, with the startling sight of the Inaccessible Pinnacle looming over it – a great spot from which to watch climbers.

The Pinnacle is the most difficult major mountain summit to attain in the British Isles – the only Munro that calls for rock-climbing skills and equipment. If you are not a rock-climber, you can't even think of attempting the In Pinn without help from a mountain guide or a rock-climbing friend, with ropes, harnesses etc. The ascent of this shorter side of the pinnacle is a Very Difficult rock-climb; the east ridge (out of sight from here) is much longer but less steep, being a Moderate rock-climb. The exposure on the easier route is incredible, being a ridge less than a foot wide 'with an overhanging and infinite drop on one side, and steeper and further on the other' as the Victorian climbers had it. The first ascent was made by the Pilkington brothers in 1880 who were two of the leading mountaineers of the time.

To leave Sgurr Dearg, descend the steep slabs beside the In Pinn, then follow a ramp down to the bottom of its east ridge. Take care as there are loose rocks scattered on the rake. Continue down the ramp below An Stac before turning to the left by a cairn (ascending slightly at first)

to reach Bealach Coire Lagan, which has a steep scree descent to Coire Lagan.

Firstly, however, there is Sgurr Mhic Choinnich to climb. Continue along a flatter section of ridge before a short descent leads to the lowest point on the corrie headwall. The scrambling isn't too trying at first, weaving up blocks and grooves. There is a slight flattening two thirds of the way up, with the exit of Hart's Ledge (formerly Collie's Ledge) on the right. Immediately above is the hardest part – a short but very steep rise in the ridge involving a trickier move with great exposure. Beyond, the ridge is exposed but leads without further obstacles to the summit. The views are sensational, though the wild feel is rather spoilt by the memorial plaque. Return to Bealach Coire Lagan and then descend the great curtains of scree to the loch in the corrie far below.

Follow the worn route down from the corrie to reach a cairned junction at about 390m. Here take the right fork to follow the recently-repaired path past Loch an Fhir-bhallaich; this eventually rejoins the outward route near the start.

Alternatives

Another route to Sgurr Dearg (and the In Pinn) is via its west ridge. This involves a very punishing ascent up steep scree above Loch an Fhir-bhallaich. Above this the ridge involves moderate scrambling to reach the summit dome of Sgurr Dearg.

8

Sgurr Alasdair

Sgurr Alasdair (992m) *alastair's peak*

Distance **9.5km**

Ascent **990m**

Time **5 – 6 hours**

Start point **OS Grid ref: NG408206**

Map **OS Explorer 411**

Terrain & hazards **the ascent of the Great Stone Chute is up very steep, loose scree; there follows a fairly straightforward but exposed scramble**

This is the highest peak on Skye – or in Britain outside the mainland. Sgurr Alasdair's tiny, airy summit offers an incredible panorama of mountains, islands and sea, but reaching it requires a punishing slog up a dauntingly steep scree slope.

There is a parking area at Glen Brittle overlooking the beach, just before the campsite. Begin by taking the path to the left of the campsite toilets and follow the newly improved path uphill, keeping left at a fork. As you gain height, expansive views open up of the Isle of Rum and, later, Eigg. After a large cairn the path becomes rougher and to reach Coire Lagan there is an easy scramble.

The corrie is a beautiful spot, the blue water of the lochan surrounded by towering walls of rock and scree. Skirt left around the lochan and start the long slog up the obvious and worn fan of scree leading up between Sgurr Alasdair and Sgurr Thearlaich, the bottom of the infamous Great Stone Chute. The scree is much looser on the lower section; higher up the chute narrows dramatically and is badly eroded. On the higher ground take care not to dislodge rocks onto those following below; wearing a helmet may be a good idea.

The small saddle at the top is reached with great relief, although for some the sight of the ridge leading up to the summit can be intimidating. By Cuillin standards it is fairly straightforward and easier than appearance suggests. The small summit is soon reached and on a clear day has a fantastic view across the bowl of Coire Lagan to the Inaccessible Pinnacle. In the opposite direction is Coir' a' Ghrunnda with its beautiful lochan, backed by a jumble of sea and islands. Sgurr Alasdair is named after Sheriff Alexander Nicolson, a Skyeman who made the first ascent in 1873. For most, the only option is to return down the Chute – though this is at least a little easier than climbing up it!

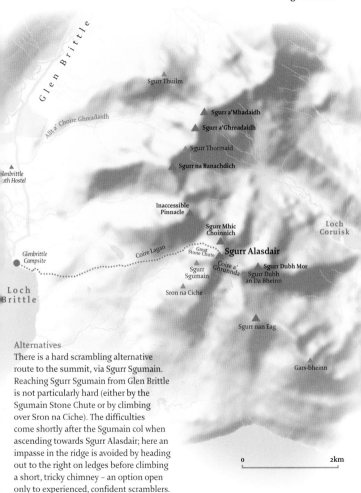

Glen Brittle

Allt a' Choire Ghreadaidh

Glenbrittle
Youth Hostel

Loch
Coruisk

Sgurr Thuilm

▲ Sgurr a'Mhadaidh
▲ Sgurr a'Ghreadaidh

Sgurr Thormaid

Sgurr na Banachdich

**Inaccessible
Pinnacle**

**Sgurr Mhic
Choinnich**

Sgurr Alasdair

Coire Lagan
Great
Stone Chute

Coire a'
Ghrunnda

▲ **Sgurr Dubh Mor**

Sgurr Dubh
an Da Bheinn

Glenbrittle
Campsite

Sgurr
Sgumain

Sron na Ciche

Loch
Brittle

▲ Sgurr nan Eag

Gars-bheinn

0   2km

Alternatives

There is a hard scrambling alternative
route to the summit, via Sgurr Sgumain.
Reaching Sgurr Sgumain from Glen Brittle
is not particularly hard (either by the
Sgumain Stone Chute or by climbing
over Sron na Ciche). The difficulties
come shortly after the Sgumain col when
ascending towards Sgurr Alasdair; here an
impasse in the ridge is avoided by heading
out to the right on ledges before climbing
a short, tricky chimney – an option open
only to experienced, confident scramblers.

Sgurr Alasdair and the Great Stone Chute

9

Sgurr Dubh Mor
Sgurr nan Eag

Sgurr Dubh Mor (944m) *big black peak*
Sgurr nan Eag (924m) *peak of the notches*

Distance 15km
Ascent 1160m
Time 7 – 10 hours
Start point OS Grid ref: NG408206
Map OS Explorer 411
Terrain & hazards **moderate scrambling to reach Coir' a' Ghrunnda and Sgurr nan Eag; hard scrambling and difficult route finding on Sgurr Dubh Mor**

The southernmost part of the Cuillin ridge has sensational sea views. The ascent of these two Munros involves a visit to atmospheric Coir' a' Ghrunnda and gives a long, rough day with plenty of scrambling.

Start from Glen Brittle; there is parking just before the campsite at the beach. Begin along the path to the left of the toilet block and follow the excellent new path uphill. After 500m or so, branch right at a fork onto the path for Coir' a' Ghrunnda. This eventually curves round the base of Sron na Ciche before heading up the left side of lower Coir' a' Ghrunnda. The floor of this part of the corrie is made up of massive slabs of bare, glaciated rock. Keep to the path which stays high on the left side of the corrie before eventually coming close to the burn and a cascading waterfall. Scramble up the rocks close to the waterfall to reach

the upper bowl of Coir' a' Ghrunnda – a breathtaking spot. The surprisingly large loch is ringed by boulder slopes leading up to sharp peaks. Pass to the right of the loch and begin up the boulderfield beyond, aiming to the right of the prominent rock, Caisteal a' Garbh-choire. The boulders here are composed of peridotite, a variant of the main Cuillin rock gabbro. Peridotite is even rougher, with amazing grip – but soon begins wearing through your fingertips!

The reward for reaching the ridge is a sudden gobsmacking view over to Coruisk. Now head right (south) for the ascent to Sgurr nan Eag. There are two options; either a fairly direct route up the ridge involving moderate scrambling, or making use of scree paths slightly lower down on the right which avoids much scrambling but does require careful route finding. The summit has a great view along the ridge towards the Cuillin's final peak, Gars-bheinn – an excellent extension to the walk if you have the time and energy.

Return to where you first reached the ridge beside Caisteal a' Garbh Choire and bypass this along its base to the right. Beyond it, bouldery ground leads up to the peak of Sgurr Dubh an Da Bheinn. From here leave the main ridge to begin the diversion to the Munro of Sgurr Dubh Mor. Head east down to a bealach. From

here both the scrambling and actually finding the route can be tricky. Most people head round to the right a little before finding a way up from ledge to ledge until the summit is reached.

Return to Sgurr Dubh an Da Bheinn and back down to Caisteal a' Garbh Choire. It is possible to descend to Coir' a' Ghrunnda from the near side of this rock by passing through a hole, but it is a little easier to instead return the way you came up.

Loch Coruisk

10

Ben More

Ben More (966m) *big hill*

Distance **14.5km**
Ascent **1255m**
Time **8 – 9 hours**
Start point **OS Grid ref: NM510371**
Map **OS Explorer 375**
Terrain & hazards **rocky mountain ridges with exposed but straightforward scrambling; final ascent is up very steep, loose ground requiring careful route finding; those looking for an easier option can follow the alternative from Dhiseig**

The A' Chioch ridge is the classic approach to Ben More, the only island Munro outside Skye. This airy ridge provides a splendid prelude to climbing up the mountain's most impressive side. Gaining height early by ascending Beinn Fhada makes for a full and satisfying mountain day.

There is a good-sized rough parking area on the north side of the B8035, half way between the bridges over the Abhainn na h-Uamha and the Scarisdale River. Most walkers start up the north bank of the Abhainn na h-Uamha to gain the bealach between A' Chioch and Beinn Fhada, but this is a boggy slog and a disappointing start to such a dramatic day. Instead you can begin with a traverse of Beinn Fhada; walk along the road towards the Scarisdale River bridge, turning right on the near side to ascend the boggy moorland by the burn.

After 1km bear south up the nose of the ridge that leads to Beinn Fhada. Steep in places, there are no obstacles and soon a minor summit at 563m is reached. From here the ridge is rough, rocky and bumpy. After passing a tiny lochan there is a steep section, but this is easier than it looks from a distance. Above this the ridge becomes broader and grassier until the foot of the rocky summit cone. Head up this to reach the cairn – with a great view of the day stretching ahead – but then retrace your steps to the bottom of the cone as the direct descent to the south from here is craggy. Head past a lochan and then down a broad slope towards the bealach with A' Chioch; crags lower down can be easily negotiated to the left.

The ascent of A' Chioch is fairly easy at first, but soon becomes a well-defined ridge with some simple scrambling. When the ridge rises in a rocky tower there is an exposed bypass path – requiring care – on the left side, which regains the crest further on via a grassy rake. Alternatively the ridge can be tackled directly, or via a scramble to the right. After this the ground is loose but without further obstacles and leads up to the summit cairn of A' Chioch.

The view to Ben More from here may take your breath away – and perhaps strike fear into your stomach – but it isn't quite as formidable as it appears. Descend to the bealach – gently at first and then down rocky slopes which are negotiated with the help of a path. From the bealach,

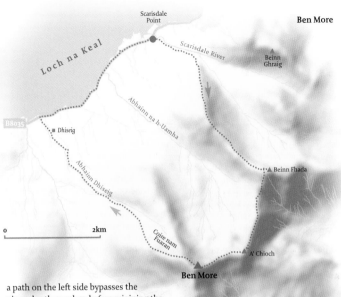

Scarisdale Point

Loch na Keal

Scarisdale River

Beinn Ghraig

Abhainn na h-Uamha

B8035

Dhiseig

Abhainn Dhiseig

Beinn Fhada

0   2km

Coire nam Fuaran

A' Chioch

Ben More

a path on the left side bypasses the pinnacles themselves before rejoining the crest for the long final climb. The loose, rocky and very steep ground requires great care. The easiest line weaves up on the left side where there are many traces of scree paths; remember to continue gaining height and keep within reasonable range of the ridge crest itself. This can be regained above a steep, narrow gully; from here the summit is within reach at last.

As might be expected, the views are superb – a great sweep of mountains and sea, with the sharp peak of A' Chioch providing a dramatic focus. The shelter cairn is often busy with walkers who have come up the easier route from Dhiseig. This provides a straightforward descent; follow the northwest ridge where a stony

path descends the left arm of Coire nam Fuaran. The path later runs beside the Abhainn Dhiseig before crossing to the far bank. Eventually it reaches a gate; pick up the path to the left and then the track at Dhiseig, continuing down to the road. From here it is a 2km walk beside the tarmac to return to the parking area.

Alternatives

A far easier and more popular route to Ben More is to head both up and down using the descent route given above. This route avoids any scrambling and is easier to follow, though there are some fainter, boggy sections. There is parking opposite the entrance to the track at Dhiseig.

The A' Chioch ridge from Ben More

Index